THE HOLOCAUST

The Holocaust: Origins, Implementation, Aftermath presents a critical and important study of the Holocaust. Complete with an introduction that summarises the state of the field, this book contains major reinterpretations by leading Holocaust authors along with key texts on testimony, memory, and justice after the catastrophe.

Many of the pieces challenge conventional interpretations and pre-conceived notions about the Holocaust, whether they have to do with the centrality of anti-Semitism, the importance of economic calculations, or the timing of the decision on the 'Final Solution'. Starting with the background of the Holocaust by focusing on anti-Semitism and scientific racism as being at the root of the 'Final Solution', the book goes on to examine the context of the decision to unleash the genocide of the Jews. Three powerful texts then provide readers with a close look at the psychology of a perpetrator, the attitude of the bystanders, and the fate of the victims. Finally, there is an analysis of survivors' oral testimonies, a deeply revealing discussion on the limits of transmitting the experience of the camps to posterity, and a powerful plea for the prosecution of crimes against humanity.

Omer Bartov is Professor of European History at Rutgers University and has written on the Holocaust, Nazi Germany and modern France. His books include *Mirrors of Destruction: War, Genocide and Modern Identity* (2000); *Murder in Our Midst: The Holocaust, Industrial Killing, and Representation* (1996); and *Hitler's Army: Soldiers, Nazis and War in the Third Reich* (1991).

Series editor **Jack R. Censer** is Professor of History at George Mason University

REWRITING HISTORIES
Series editor: Jack R. Censer

Already published

THE HOLOCAUST

Origins, Implementation, Aftermath

Edited by
Omer Bartov

London and New York

First published 2000
by Routledge
11 New Fetter Lane, London EC4P 4EE

Simultaneously published in the USA and Canada
by Routledge
29 West 35th Street, New York, NY 10001

Routledge is an imprint of the Taylor & Francis Group

Typeset in Palatino by
Keystroke, Jacaranda Lodge, Wolverhampton
Printed and bound in Great Britain by
MPG Books Ltd, Bodmin

British Library Cataloguing in Publication Data
A catalogue record for this book is available from the British Library

Library of Congress Cataloging in Publication Data
Holocaust: origins, implementation, aftermath / [edited by] Omer Bartov.
p.   cm. — (Rewriting histories)
Includes bibliographical references and index.
1. Holocaust, Jewish (1939–1945) 2. Holocaust, Jewish (1939–1945)—Causes.
I. Bartov, Omer II. Re-writing histories.
D804.3.H6478 2000
940.53'18—dc21   99-044232

ISBN 0-415-15035-3 (hbk)
ISBN 0-415-15036-1 (pbk)

CONTENTS

CONTENTS

SERIES EDITOR'S PREFACE

Rewriting history, or revisionism, has always followed closely in the wake of history writing. In their efforts to re-evaluate the past, professional as well as amateur scholars have followed many approaches, most commanly as empiricists, uncovering new information to challenge earlier accounts. Historians have also revised previous versions by adopting new perspectives, usually fortified by new research, which overturn received views.

Even though rewriting is constantly taking place, historians' attitudes towards using new interpretations have been anything but settled. For most, the validity of revisionism lies in providing a stronger, more convincing account that better captures the objective truth of the matter. Although such historians might agree that we never finally arrive at the "truth," they believe it exists and over time may be better approximated. At the other extreme stand scholars who believe that each generation or even each cultural group or subgroup necessarily regards the past differently, each creating for itself a more usable history. Although these latter scholars do not reject the possibility of demonstrating empirically that some contentions are better than others, they focus upon generating new views based upon different life experiences. Different truths exist for different groups. Surely such an understanding, by emphasizing subjectivity, further encourages rewriting history. Between these two groups are those historians who wish to borrow from both sides. This third group, while accepting that every congeries of individuals sees matters differently, still wishes somewhat contradictorily to fashion a broader history that incorporates both of these particular visions. Revisionists who stress empiricism fall into the first of the three camps, while others spread out across the board.

Today the rewriting of history seems to have accelerated to a blinding speed as a consequence of the evolution of revisionism. A variety of approaches has emerged. A major factor in this process has been the enormous increase in the number of researchers. This explosion has reinforced and enabled the retesting of many assertions. Significant ideological shifts have also played a major part in the growth of revisionism. First, the crisis of Marxism, culminating in the events in Eastern Europe in 1989, has given rise to doubts about explicitly Marxist accounts. Such doubts have spilled over into the entire field of social history which has been a dominant subfield of the discipline for several decades. Focusing on society and its class divisions implied that these are the most important elements in historical analysis. Because Marxism was built on the same claim, the whole basis of social history has been questioned, despite the very many studies that directly had little to do with Marxism. Disillusionment with social history, simultaneously opened the door to cultural and linguistic approaches largely developed in anthropology and literature. Multi-culturalism and feminism further generated revisionism. By claiming that scholars had, wittingly or not, operated from a white European/American male point of view, newer researchers argued that other approaches had been neglected or misunderstood. Not surprisingly, these last historians are the most likely to envision each subgroup rewriting its own usable history, while other scholars incline towards revisionism as part of the search for some stable truth.

Rewriting Histories will make these new approaches available to the student population. Often new scholarly debates take place in the scattered issues of journals which are sometimes difficult to find. Furthermore, in these first interactions, historians tend to address one another, leaving out the evidence that would make their arguments more accessible to the uninitiated. This series of books will collect in one place a strong group of the major articles in selected fields, adding notes and introductions conducive to improved understanding. Editors will select articles containing substantial historical data, so that students – at least those who approach the subject as an objective phenomenon – can advance not only their comprehension of debated points but also their grasp of substantive aspects of the subject

As an area of study, the Holocaust has experienced virtually unrivaled controversy and excitement. Our relative proximity to this horrific event, continued incidents of attacks on beleaguered ethnic groups, and the complicated political stakes that still relate to this subject are only a few of the reasons that have attracted so many scholars and created interpretative differences. This edited work contrasts the two most common explanations (anti-Semitism and bureaucratic momentum) and provides several articles that make use of both views. In addition, the editor provides us with valuable studies on the aftermath, a subject that has not received as much attention as it deserves. Here are the complexities of how this event was perceived and understood by perpetrators and victims. These essays, like the others in this collection, show a richness and sophistication of interpretation that only recently have emerged in this field.

ACKNOWLEDGEMENTS

All articles and extracts in this volume (except the Introduction) have already been published. We should like to thank the following copyright holders for permission to reproduce their work.

Introduction   Written for this volume by Omer Bartov

Chapter 1   Reprinted from *The Destruction of the European Jews*, Student Edition (New York and London: Holmes & Meier, 1985), pp. 5–24. Copyright © Raul Hilberg. Reprinted with the permission of the publisher.

Chapter 2   Reprinted from *Ethics and Extermination: Reflections on Nazi Genocide* (Cambridge: Cambridge University Press, 1997), pp. 113–29 (text), 243–7 (notes). Copyright © Michael Burleigh. Reprinted with permission of Cambridge University Press.

Chapter 3   Reprinted from *German Studies Review*, vol. 17 no. 3 (October 1994), pp. 495–507.

Chapter 4   Reprinted from Alvin H. Rosenfeld (ed.), *Thinking about the Holocaust: After Half a Century* (Bloomington and Indianapolis: Indiana University Press, 1997), pp. 3–17.

Chapter 5   Reprinted from Michael Burleigh (ed.), *Confronting the Nazi Past: New Debates on Modern German History* (London: Collins & Brown, 1996), pp. 140–53.

Chapter 6   Reprinted from *The Journal of Modern History*, vol. 70 no. 4 (December 1998), pp. 759–812. Copyright © Christian Gerlach. Translation copyright © Stephen Duffy. Reprinted with the permission of University of Chicago Press.

Chapter 7   Reprinted from *History & Memory*, vol. 9 no. 1/2 (Fall 1997), pp. 162–88. Reprinted with the permission of Indiana University Press.

ACKNOWLEDGEMENTS

Chapter 8   Reprinted from Ernst Klee, Willi Dressen and Volker Riess
                (eds), *"The Good Old Days": The Holocaust as Seen by Its
                Perpetrators and Bystanders*, translated by Deborah
                Burnstone (New York: The Free Press, 1991), pp. 87–106
                (text), 297–8 (note). Copyright © 1988 S. Verlag GmbH.
                Translation copyright © 1991 Deborah Burnstone. Re-
                printed with the permission of The Free Press, a Division of
                Simon & Schuster, Inc.

Chapter 9   Reprinted from Michael Berenbaum and Abraham J. Peck
                (eds), *The Holocaust and History: The Known, the Unknown,
                the Disputed, and the Reexamined*, (Bloomington and
                Indianapolis: Indiana University Press, 1998), pp. 409–20.

Chapter 10   Reprinted from *Under a Cruel Star: A Life in Prague
                1941–1968* (Harmondsworth: Penguin Books, 1986),
                pp. 5–21, by permission from current copyright holder,
                Plunkett Lake Press, Cambridge, MA.

Chapter 11   Reprinted from Peter Hayes (ed.) *Lessons and Legacies:
                The Meaning of the Holocaust in a Changing World* (Evanston,
                IL: Northwestern University Press, 1991, pp. 227–42 (text),
                367–8 (notes). Copyright © Lawrence Langer.

Chapter 12   Reprinted from *The Drowned and the Saved*, translated from
                the Italian by Raymond Rosenthal. (New York: Summit
                Books, 1988), pp. 36–69. English translation copyright
                © 1988 by Simon & Schuster, Inc. Reprinted with the
                permission of Simon & Schuster, Inc.

Chapter 13   Reprinted from *Remembering in Vain: The Klaus Barbie
                Trial and Crimes Against Humanity* (New York: Columbia
                University Press, 1992), pp. 25–37, 51–61 (text); 77–9, 81–2
                (notes). Copyright © 1992 Columbia University Press.
                Reprinted with the permission of the publisher.

INTRODUCTION

Omer Bartov

In the last few years the study of the Holocaust has been profoundly transformed. This development may be seen as the second phase in a trend that dates back to the 1970s, when the Nazi genocide of the Jews began to be perceived by both scholars and the general public as an historical event of major importance. Hence, while the findings and analyses of the 1980s and 1990s will be discussed here, many of the chapters reflect the most updated scholarly work of recent years. To be sure, this scholarship builds on half a century of research and inter-pretation. But the intention of this collection is to provide readers with some knowledge of current developments and debates in an expanding field of inquiry concerned with one of the greatest catastrophes of the twentieth century, whose relevance for, and impact on, our civilization's present condition is becoming increasingly apparent.

During the first few decades following the destruction of the Third Reich, two main hypotheses concerning the nature of Nazism and fascism gained a hegemonic status. One, articulated most coherently by Hannah Arendt, described the Third Reich as the outgrowth of a totalitarian ideology, and claimed close affinities between Nazism and Communism, especially as expressed in Stalinist Russia.[1] The other, defined already by Marxist thinkers in the interwar period, saw Nazism as a brand of European Fascism, which was in turn viewed as the last evil outgrowth of late capitalism in its death throes.[2] Both theories therefore perceived the genocide of the Jews through the lens of a general interpretation of the crisis of European society and politics, and were much less concerned with explaining the Holocaust as such. A third explanatory model, focused more directly on the Holocaust, argued that the "Final Solution" was merely the last and most extreme manifestation of a long European tradition of anti-Jewish sentiments, combined since the second part of the nineteenth century with the emergence of modern political anti-semitism and "scientific" racism.[3] Both the grand models of totalitarianism and Fascism, and the deterministic interpretation of antisemitism, were thoroughly revised during the 1970s and 1980s, making room for the

1

appearance of new, often more subtle and detailed, although no less controversial interpretations of the Holocaust.[4] The fall of the Communist regimes in Eastern Europe and the collapse of the Soviet Union led to the opening up of previously inaccessible archives.[5] Moreover, new approaches to the study of the past have come to influence the historical writing on the Holocaust, introducing a variety of perspectives hitherto neglected by scholars. The increased awareness among historians of the importance of memory and testimony in the reconstruction of the past has made for the study of accounts by those who had personally experienced the event.[6] At the same time, however, the growing chronological distance from the Holocaust has encouraged a tendency either to relativize the event as only one – and perhaps not the most important and relevant – of numerous cases of human barbarism, or indeed to deny its veracity altogether.[7]

One important development in recent writing on the Holocaust has been a renewed interest in the role of antisemitism both as one of the "deep" underlying causes of the eventual Nazi genocide of the Jews and as a specific motivating factor among the perpetrators. While some scholars always asserted the centrality of anti-Jewish sentiments to Nazi policies,[8] until the 1970s the interpretive paradigms of fascism and totalitarianism presented antisemitism as merely a consequence of more profound socio-cultural and political developments. Moreover, with the decline of the fascist and totalitarian schools, the most innovative and influential new interpretations of Nazism similarly relegated anti-semitism to a secondary role, stressing instead structural factors along with such phenomena as economic hardship, charismatic leadership, popular conformity, and bureaucratic modes of operation and rational-ization. Several important studies of popular opinion in Germany argued that anti-Jewish feelings were at most a minor factor in bringing the Nazis to power and in the growing support for Hitler's regime.[9] This consensus began changing in the 1990s, and came under concerted attack with the recent publication of a number of works, the most widely debated of which was doubtlessly Daniel Jonah Goldhagen's controversial study of "ordinary Germans."[10]

The debate over Goldhagen's book has received so much public attention that there is no point in summarizing it here, let alone including contributions to it in this collection.[11] It should be pointed out, however, that the debate assumed – and in some ways also constructed – a dichotomy of views that in point of fact is far less pronounced in the current scholarship. Thus Goldhagen's assertively monocausal explana-tion of the Holocaust as a direct consequence of a unique and deeply rooted German antisemitism was neither new nor – albeit in a far more moderate form – wholly unacceptable to many other scholars of the period. This can be seen in Part I, "Origins," which is devoted to two kinds of "deep," long-term causes of the "Final Solution." In the first chapter, Raul Hilberg, the single most important historian of the Nazi genocide of the Jews, traces the historical precedents of Nazi antisemitic policies to Christian Europe and stresses the extent to which they served Hitler's regime as a model for the exclusion, expulsion, and ultimately mass murder of the Jews. Hilberg is commonly thought of as the first historian to have stressed the bureaucratic aspects of modern genocide, and has consequently been faulted with underestimating the impact of anti-semitism. Yet as this chapter demonstrates, he in fact perceived the long history of Jewish persecution by the Catholic and Protestant churches in medieval and early modern Europe as a crucial, though by no means sufficient precondition for the Holocaust.[12]

The next two chapters focus on another fundamental – and only recently recognized – factor in the legitimization, organization, and implementation of modern state-directed genocide. Michael Burleigh and Henry Friedlander, two of the most prominent scholars of "scientific" racism and "euthanasia," examine the role of the German medical profession in the murder of mentally and physically handicapped people by the Nazi regime.[13] Far from diverting attention from the genocide of the Jews, they argue – from somewhat different perspectives – that the so-called "euthanasia" campaign set the stage, both administratively and techno-logically, ideologically and psychologically, for the far more massive genocide of the Jews, the Roma and Sinti ("Gypsies"), and other categories of racial, social, and political "undesirables." Along with several other important studies on this topic, these chapters also relate the phenomenon of genocide to the very nature of modern society, and hence to our own, post-Auschwitz reality.[14] For while the new interest in the role of science in the Nazi genocide of the Jews, as well as in the "euthanasia" campaign that preceded it, has given us new insights into the nature of the regime, it has also opened the way for viewing the Holocaust as the potential, albeit not inevitable, outcome of "Western" modes of thought and action rather than of a specific German "nature" or historical "peculiarities."[15] Hence all three scholars demonstrate from different perspectives the tension between origins and consequences, long-term causes and specific effects. Hilberg shows the extent to which the Nazis borrowed from past anti-Jewish sentiments and policies, but then devotes the rest of his mammoth work to the modern bureaucratic machinery of genocide. Burleigh and Friedlander recognize the genocidal potential of modern modes of thinking and organization, but simultaneously insist on the specificity of German developments and of the Nazi enterprise of mass murder. In this sense, these chapters provide us not only with different perspectives on the *origins* of the Holocaust, but also with a new under-standing of the relationship between the origins of the event, its actual course, and its implications for future generations.

Part II, "Implementation," introduces readers to new scholarship that goes beyond the two conventional – and radically opposed – interpretations of the Holocaust that reigned supreme during the 1970s and 1980s. It does so both by bringing scholarly analyses that directly confront the earlier assumptions and conclusions of historians belonging to either school, and by providing examples of perspectives and materials that were largely left out of the previous scholarship. The two schools in question, known as the "intentionalist" and the "functionalist" (or "structuralist"), have produced a wide array of scholarship that has – for at least two decades – in large measure defined our understanding of the Holocaust.[16] The "intentionalist" school, which tends to be more closely associated with traditional accounts of the "Final Solution," sees the Holocaust as the outcome of a long-term policy defined especially by Hitler well before it was actually implemented. All Nazi actions preceding the beginning of the "Final Solution" are thus interpreted as leading to that ultimate outcome. This type of analysis stresses the role of Hitler as a crucial figure in the implementation of genocide (and more generally in the Third Reich as a whole) and emphasizes the centrality of Nazi ideology for the formulation of policies by the Reich's leadership.[17]

The "functionalist" school has taken a diametrically opposed stance. While acknowledging Hitler's fanatical antisemitism and the prevalence of anti-Jewish prejudice in Germany – quite an unexceptional phenomenon in interwar Europe[18] – the "functionalists" see the "Final Solution" as the outcome of specific bureaucratic structures, political and military circumstances, and logistical constraints. They argue that while Nazi policies in the 1930s and the first two years of the war do not indicate an intent to carry out genocide, they did create a situation whereby mass murder ultimately seemed the only "rational" solution to self-imposed and otherwise seemingly insoluble logistical conditions, whereby millions of Jews were concentrated in overcrowded ghettos rife with famine and disease. Furthermore, they assert that the "Final Solution" began on the initiative of local, middle-ranking Nazi officials and was only subsequently taken up by the Reich's leadership, which in turn was characterized by a "weak dictator" ruling over a polycratic regime whose predilection for unplanned "cumulative radicalization" was the function of a process of "negative selection" that invariably brought its most violent elements to positions of dominance.[19]

In the last few years the "intentionalists" and "functionalists" have gradually come closer, as further research now seems to indicate that the more extreme new interpretations are just as impossible to sustain as the traditional ones. In Chapter 4, the prominent Holocaust scholar Saul Friedländer points out that there is now much less reason to see these two schools as mutually contradictory; indeed, he argues that we would derive a great deal of explanatory benefit from reconciling them with each

4

other. Friedländer's "moderate intentionalism" is predicated on accepting much of the "functionalist" argument as far as the mechanics of decision-making and organization of the "Final Solution" are concerned, while simultaneously stressing both the centrality of what he calls "redemptive antisemitism" at least for the higher echelons of the Nazi leadership, and acknowledging Hitler's crucial function in legitimizing and providing the essential impetus for the genocide of the Jews.[20] Thus Friedländer's chapter is both a useful survey of previous and current theories and provides a suggestive program to reconcile previously antagonistic positions. One must await the publication of the second volume of his magnum opus, *Nazi Germany and the Jews*, which will cover the years of the Holocaust, to see the effects of Friedländer's hybrid interpretation on the practice of historical reconstruction and explanation.

Coming from the opposite side, the historian Christopher Browning has argued in a series of important articles in favor of what he calls "moderate functionalism."[21] Thus, for instance, Browning's research on the years between the outbreak of the Second World War in 1939 and the beginning of the mass murder of the Jews in 1941 has undermined both the "intentionalist" argument that this was merely a preparatory phase for the "Final Solution," and the "functionalist" assertion that the genocide of the Jews emerged as a local initiative by middle-ranking SS officers. Browning agrees with the "functionalists" that the ghettoization of the Jews in Eastern Europe was initiated by Nazi officials on the ground as an interim solution precisely because they were not given any clear instructions regarding the ultimate fate of the Jewish population. At the same time, however, he demonstrates that contrary to the "functionalist" argument of "cumulative radicalization" on the lower level of the Nazi hierarchy, these officials chose to exploit the labor of the Jews for their own purposes, switching over to mass murder only when instructed to do so "from above," as was always asserted by the "intentionalists." This interpretation therefore complicates the picture of the mechanics and decision-making process of the Holocaust, and while it in no way relativizes the role of local officials in the implementation of brutal policies of exploitation and enslavement, it also implicates the top echelons of the regime as directly responsible for the final decision on mass murder.[22]

Since the publication of Browning's findings, however, even more extensive work on this issue has been undertaken by the German scholar Götz Aly. It should be noted that Aly's earlier work on this topic was the cause of much controversy, not least because of the argument (made with his collaborator Susanne Heim), that the Nazi genocide of the Jews was motivated by apparently rational technocratic arguments as a necessary step in the modernization of Poland's economy.[23] While these assertions have been largely rejected or greatly qualified by most historians,[24] Chapter 5 provides a gist of Aly's more sophisticated and compelling argument, greatly elaborated in his recent book on this topic.[25] Here an attempt is made to contextualize the genocide of the Jews within a general policy of massive population transfers, economic exploitation, and finally outright mass murder. Aly's thorough study leaves little doubt that we can no longer examine the Holocaust in isolation from other Nazi policies geared to a total demographic restructuring of Eastern Europe and Western Russia that would create the basis for a new Germanic *Lebensraum* (living space). To be sure, this thesis does not explain all aspects of the "Final Solution," as Aly would like us to believe. Thus, for instance, Saul Friedländer rightly notes in Chapter 4 that Aly cannot explain why the Nazis transported the Jews of Western Europe to the East and then murdered them there.[26] Yet the abundant documentation on the Nazi plans and actions with a view to a total "ethnic cleansing" of the East and a vast operation of resettlement of ethnic Germans there, both provides a crucial wider context for the Holocaust and contextualizes the entire Nazi enterprise of conquest, enslavement, and genocide, within the wider historical framework of the twentieth century. For while the roots of such policies date back to before the First World War, recent events in South East Europe indicate that "ethnic cleansing" and genocide have unfortunately not disappeared from the European scene, let alone other parts of the world.[27]

Whereas Götz Aly is concerned with the context within which the Holocaust occurred, Chapter 6 offers a major revision of the actual decision on the genocide of the Jews. For a long time it was assumed by most scholars that the Wannsee Conference of January 20, 1942, in which Reinhard Heydrich declared to a group of senior Nazi officials that he was in charge of the "final solution of the Jewish question," was convened several months after the decision itself had already been made and preparations for mass killing were well on their way. Indeed, the conventional assumption was that the Holocaust had already begun at the latest by December 1941. The young German scholar, Christian Gerlach, has now proposed a very different interpretation both of known documentation and of some new documents recently uncovered in formerly Soviet archives, including Heinrich Himmler's appointment book. What is interesting in this chapter is not merely that it attributes a much greater importance to the meeting at Wannsee as the moment at which the top hierarchy of the Reich were informed of the decision to murder up to 11 million Jews (according to Heydrich's and Adolf Eichmann's estimates), but also that this was done only after Hitler reached that decision himself. Hence we have here a fundamental revision of the conventional "functionalist" view of most German scholars, providing a complex yet quite persuasive argument about the centrality of the Führer in transforming the already murderous policy of Germany in the Soviet Union (similarly ordered directly by Hitler but consisting also of local initiatives) into a European-wide, state-organized genocide of the Jews.[28]

One major organization in the Third Reich has, until recently, escaped scrutiny as far the Holocaust was concerned. Although, as Chapter 7 demonstrates, the role of the German army in implementing Nazi policies especially in the Soviet Union has been examined in the 1980s and 1990s, it was generally assumed that the Wehrmacht did not participate directly in the genocide of the Jews.[29] However, in the last few years new studies and documents have indicated that German soldiers on all levels were deeply implicated in the Holocaust, both as a result of orders from above and thanks to the Nazi and antisemitic convictions of many individuals. The realization that the Wehrmacht was anything but a "clean," professional organization has profound implications for our understanding of German society both under the Nazi regime and after 1945, since this was a vast conscript army through whose ranks a major share of the adult male population passed, precisely those men who later built up the two postwar Germanies. Moreover, we now recognize that most cases of genocide and "ethnic cleansing" in the twentieth century were carried out within the context of destructive and bitter wars. Hence the continuing study of military involvement in genocide is of great significance both to our understanding of the Holocaust, to a general revision of our perception of Nazism's impact on the Germans, and to a continuing analysis of the relationship between modern warfare and crimes against humanity.[30]

The last three chapters of Part II introduce a wholly different and, until recently, often neglected dimension of the Holocaust: the experience, self-perception, and actions of the perpetrators, bystanders, and victims as seen from their own contemporary or subsequent perspective. Although we know by now a great deal on the mechanics of the Nazi genocide, and are therefore relatively familiar with the facts and figures of the victims and the administrative and technical apparatus of the killers, we still do not know much about the individuals concerned, especially the "little people" who have always been underrepresented both in history and historiography. The psychology of the perpetrators has interested scholars and laypeople alike ever since the end of the war, if not indeed during the Holocaust itself. Yet it is only recently that substantial documentation on the rank and file of the perpetrators has begun to emerge, thanks to the meticulous research of several German and American scholars. The commonly accepted view of the killers as sadistic, inhuman, faceless individuals, who have very little in common with any of us and can therefore not be understood on the same terms, is now being revised. While Hannah Arendt's well known dictum about the banality of evil in the Holocaust might be seen as a somewhat abstract (and doubtless contentious) definition,[31] the newly examined diaries, letters and postwar statements given to police interrogators and testimonies in court proceedings of run-of-the-mill perpetrators instill this term with new meaning. The best way to approach this issue is first and foremost to let the perpetrators speak for themselves, for their own perception of their actions, both at the time and long after the event, exemplifies the manner in which ordinary people, endowed with ordinary mentalities, passions, needs and aspirations, could become mass killers. To be sure, as we have recently learned from the debate between Daniel Jonah Goldhagen and Christopher Browning about the motivation of the perpetrators, the very same evidence and personal testimonies may be interpreted entirely differently by two different scholars.[32] Nevertheless, readers will learn a great deal from, even if they disagree on the implications of, the chilling excerpt in Chapter 8. It is impossible to understand the nature of the Holocaust without such a document, for it is only in this manner that we can see it not merely as the unprecedented event which it surely was, but also as one which was perceived by its perpetrators as part of their normal routine, a task to be accomplished, a professional duty that must in no way interfere with the normal course of their lives.

Unlike the perpetrators, the bystanders remained by definition outside the process of genocide, or at least subsequently claimed to have had nothing to do with it. In the 1970s and 1980s, the preoccupation with *Alltagsgeschichte*, or the history of everyday life, in the Third Reich, demonstrated the blurred boundaries between complicity, indifference, and opposition to the regime.[33] But this type of historiography paid little attention to the important role played by the communities adjacent to the Nazi "concentrationary universe." This issue is addressed in Chapter 9 by Gordon Horwitz, in an essay which provides the gist of his pathbreaking study on the Austrian town of Mauthausen, whose inhabitants spent long years next to one of the most notorious Nazi concentration camps.[34] The extent to which these civilians were necessary for the daily maintenance of the camp, and the manner in which they rationalized their complicity during the event and repressed it after the war, sheds a horrifying light on the widespread collaboration of large sectors of Europe's population with the Nazis, as well as on the suppression of this episode during the postwar period. This is a crucial and highly neglected component of the Holocaust which is only now beginning to receive appropriate scholarly attention.[35]

During the 1980s and 1990s increasing numbers of memoirs by Holocaust survivors have appeared. This is probably associated with their approaching demise and the consequent urge to record their experiences both for the public at large and especially for their own families, as well as with the passage of time that has made articulating their recollections more bearable than in the past. Moreover, the growing public preoccupation with the Holocaust may have also contributed to the willingness of survivors to speak about their experiences, following a long period during which their reluctance to talk was at least in part also a reflection of the refusal of others to listen. Among such memoirs, some stand out due to their striking literary quality, their keen insights into human psychology, the extraordinary tales they recount, and at times the remarkable personality of the writers. However, until a few years ago, very little attention was given to the often striking differences between the accounts of male and female survivors.[36] While the better known memoirs of the first couple of decades after the war were written mainly by men (especially noteworthy are those by Primo Levi, Elie Wiesel and Jean Améry), more recently many women have finally put pen to paper and recounted their own experiences.[37] One distinct difference between those earlier male accounts and those by women is that in the latter case there is much greater talk of solidarity among female inmates, whereas in many male accounts we read of an individual's struggle to survive in constant conflict with his fellow inmates. To be sure, some women survivors have also claimed that female SS personnel behaved more sadistically toward them than the men; but by and large the impression is that among women inmates of the camps a different dynamic of human relations developed than was the case among the men.[38] Moreover, women's accounts also provide a very different perspective of the circumstances preceding and following the Holocaust, as women often experienced them in radically different ways from men, not least because they tended to be less involved with the "larger" political issues of the day and much more with their disastrous effects on the individual. This more intimate relationship with atrocity included, of course, care for children and elderly people, and a struggle to keep, or rebuild, a sense of home and family.[39] It is indeed no wonder that many of the greatest novels of the twentieth century were written by women, who could perceive the fate of history's victims unencumbered by the distorting lens of ideological commitment, and portrayed the horror of destroying a single, unique human being with much greater personal involvement and sensitivity than even those "great" men with whom some of them were associated. In this context we may think, for instance, of Elsa Morante, whose epic *History: A Novel*, a "view from below" of the destruction of war as seen and experienced (but never understood) by a simple and poor woman and her toddler son, in many ways far surpasses her more famous husband Alberto Moravia's writings;[40] and of Nadezhda Mandelstam, whose memoir is a devastating woman's view of Stalinist terror, and at least the equal of her own husband's (Osip Mandelstam) greatest poems.[41] A third work of exceptional merit is Heda Margolius Kovály's memoir, an excerpt from which is included here. Kovály too married a prominent Czech politician (and Holocaust survivor) after she returned from the camps, and lived to see him murdered in Stalin's last purge. Most of her memoir is devoted to life under Stalinism. And yet the first pages can be counted among the most remarkable (and least known) accounts of a woman's experience in the Holocaust and her ultimate escape from the horror. Written in tight, concise prose, ruthless in its sincerity and yet filled with compassion, it should enable the reader to gain at least a glimpse of the reality of life in what the Nazis called the "anus mundi."[42]

Part III, "Aftermath," addresses some central issues related to post-Holocaust confrontations or coming to terms with the event. In recent years scholars have become increasingly aware of the importance of memory as a phenomenon worthy of historical research and analysis. The Holocaust, one of whose most devastating consequences was a vast erasure of memory, accompanied by widespread trauma and repression, has now come to be seen as an event whose personal ramifications can be understood only by means of a sensitive and subtle analysis of survivors' oral testimonies. The human aspects of the affair, and the long-range effects it has had on future generations, are now being examined by way of interviews with survivors and the application of literary and psychological tools to their analysis in an attempt to uncover their hidden meanings.[43] One of the most perceptive and insightful analyses of such oral testimonies can be found in a recent pathbreaking study by Lawrence Langer.[44] Chapter 11 brings an article by Langer which summarizes some of his arguments and discusses several disturbing aspects of survivors' oral accounts. What we find here is not only that it is impossible for us to imagine the experiences being related by the survivors, but also that even the latter cannot fully reconcile their present selves with their memories of life in the Holocaust. Whereas the interviewers wish to apply current moral and ethical criteria to the memories their questions evoke, the survivors reject the applicability of normal standards of behavior and judgments to a situation of utter and complete abnormality. Hence the very attempt by those who were there to explain their experience to those who were not demonstrates only the yawing abyss between them. Moreover, we realize that the speakers themselves can never integrate the memory of the past into their present reality, but are doomed to a condition of perpetual inner conflict between two irreconcilable identities. This chapter thus provides an example of the crucial importance of this line of inquiry and constitutes a troubling critique of our own inability to come to terms with the realities of past atrocity and its effects on the few who survived it.

While the testimonies given by survivors have by now been acknowledged as fundamental components of our historical reconstruction of the Holocaust and its implications for post-Auschwitz society, some of the more articulate survivors have themselves tried to grapple with the problems and limitations of their own memory, the extent to which they can be seen as representative of the victims who did not survive, and the impact of postwar representations of their experience by the media.[45] No one has been more critical of his own memoirs, as well as of the distortions of the victims' experience in literature and film, than the great Italian writer and Holocaust survivor, Primo Levi. In his last collection of essays, written shortly before his apparent suicide in 1987, Levi tried to confront some of the most difficult and painful issues of death and survival, memory and representation.[46] The chapter included here is an extraordinarily candid, unrelenting, painful, and yet almost serene discussion of what Levi provocatively terms the "gray zone," that ambiguous region where complicity and victimhood, humanity and barbarism overlapped. It is this "dangerous" area that has become so fascinating, especially for postwar filmmakers concerned with the Holocaust.[47] To be sure, Levi expresses outrage in the face of this exploitation of suffering for the purpose of titillating audiences and undermining any faith in human values and decency. At the same time, however, this chapter reveals his own growing pessimism and disenchantment with a world that merely uses the horror of the past for its own instant gratification. Furthermore, while he is deeply concerned with the manner in which the Holocaust has been (mis)represented – and one wonders how he would have reacted to such films as Steven Spielberg's *Schindler's List* (1993) and Roberto Benigni's *La Vita è bella* (*Life Is Beautiful*, 1997)[48] – Levi's discussion of the "gray zone" is about a far more disturbing issue. For while he insists that a clear distinction must be made between the victims and the perpetrators, he nevertheless relentlessly points out both the horribly brutalizing effects of the conditions created by the Nazis on their victims, and the rare moments of humanity that one glimpsed among the most ruthless perpetrators. He cannot judge those inmates who survived at the cost of their comrades' destruction, and will not forgive the perpetrators who revealed a flicker of decency. But for him this "gray zone" is a crucial component of Auschwitz. This is, then, a rumination on the condition of humanity itself, on its capacity for endless evil and its moments of altruism and nobility. No one who reads this chapter with the care that it deserves will ever be able to make facile judgments about the reality and long-term repercussions of the "concentrationary universe."

Primo Levi became increasingly concerned with the degree to which his memoirs about Auschwitz reflected the experience of the vast majority of the inmates, for, while he was among the "saved," the most common fate was that of the "drowned." Tragically, in the last few years we have seen a far more insidious type of skepticism about the accounts of Holocaust survivors and historical reconstructions. This is the phenomenon of what has come to be known as "revisionism," "negationism," or "Holocaust denial," whose main characteristic is either an outright rejection of the very veracity of the Nazi genocide of the Jews, or at least a concerted attempt to minimize both its scale and its importance. Holocaust denial comes from many quarters, at times cloaked in literary or scholarly guises, at others expressed in the most blatant and offensive manner. If it has remained by and large a marginal phenomenon, "negationism" has received and thrives on a great deal of attention by the media, politicians, and scholars. Closely associated with xenophobia, antisemitism, extremism and economic despair – all of which have grown in recent years, especially in some parts of Europe such as southern France and eastern Germany – this is a phenomenon we can ill afford to ignore. And yet, public scholarly and political debates with such extremists pose the threat of merely providing them and their "opinions" with the legitimization and publicity they are constantly seeking. The dilemma, therefore, is how to deny "negationism" any legitimacy but at the same time prevent its dissemination among those who are in no position to realize its implications. Anyone who has taught at a large public institution knows how easily one can instill young, often eager but ignorant and uncritical minds with false ideas and notions which would then be extremely difficult to uproot. It is just as crucial, however, to distinguish between the wholly objectionable politics of denial and the fully legitimate scholarly revision of previously accepted conventional interpretations of any historical event, including the Holocaust. The need to make this distinction is particularly urgent in view of the unfortunate tendency of some scholars to accuse those who revise their interpretations of wholesale denial, even as those who indeed attempt to deny the veracity of the Holocaust argue that theirs is a mere scholarly undertaking.[49]

In 1988 the former Gestapo official, Klaus Barbie, was found guilty of crimes against humanity by a French court in Lyons. This trial, the first to have considered such a charge in France, exemplified many of the problems connected with denial, revisionism, memory, and repression.[50] But as the French philosopher Alain Finkielkraut eloquently argues in the last chapter of this book, the trial in Lyons was about much more than that, since it focused first and foremost on the definition of crimes against humanity and the relevance of the Holocaust for the human experience in the twentieth century.[51] Barbie's defense lawyers argued that while the Holocaust was merely the affair of white European culture, the real genocide to be confronted was that of the West against the Third World. The preoccupation with the genocide of the Jews was thus allegedly intended to repress the fact that the West was still oppressing, exploiting, and exterminating the rest of the world. This attempt by the defense to relegate the Holocaust to a position of irrelevance, an affair of minor importance within the fold of white civilization, claims Finkielkraut, reflects a more general intellectual discourse in the West whose goal is to shed any responsibility for mass murder by diverting attention to the seemingly more urgent issues of the day. Hence it is based on a refusal to come to terms with the real long-term effects of the "Final Solution," namely, that it had shown the very concept of humanity to be in mortal danger, precisely because of a rhetoric which placed ideological goals above the fate of the individual. This is why Finkielkraut insists that every cog in the genocidal apparatus must be held responsible for the act, and argues adamantly against sacrificing the notion of a shared humanity in the name of some higher cause, more immediate need, or more fashionable theory. Finkielkraut's chapter is therefore a concise and forceful plea to recognize the profound implications of the Holocaust and to remain constantly alert in the face of renewed assaults on the very fabric of human civilization.[52] As such, it provides a fitting conclusion to a collection of essays on the origins, implementation, and aftermath of the Holocaust, for it clarifies the centrality of the event for anyone concerned with the predicament of humanity at the turn of the millennium.

NOTES

1 Hannah Arendt, *The Origins of Totalitarianism* (London: André Deutsch, 1986 [orig. pub. 1951]). For an excellent summary, see Abbott Gleason, *Totalitarianism: The Inner History of the Cold War* (New York: Oxford University Press, 1995).

2 For a useful introduction, see Roger Griffin, *The Nature of Fascism* (London: Routledge, 1993). On fascism and Marxist theory see also Stanley G. Payne, *Fascism: Comparison and Definition* (Madison, WI: University of Wisconsin Press, 1980), especially pp. 177–80; Martin Kitchen, *Fascism* (London: Macmillan, 1976), especially pp. 1–11, 60–70.

3 For a good example of this approach, see Robert S. Wistrich, *Antisemitism: The Longest Hatred* (New York: Schocken Books, 1994).

4 Nevertheless, for a recent attempt to resurrect the totalitarian paradigm, see François Furet, *The Passing of an Illusion: The Idea of Communism in the Twentieth Century*, trans. Deborah Furet (Chicago: University of Chicago Press, 1999). For an argument in favor of maintaining the fascist paradigm, see Tim Mason, "Whatever Happened to 'Fascism'?," in Thomas Childers and Jane Caplan (eds), *Reevaluating the Third Reich* (New York: Holmes & Meier, 1993).

5 See, for example, *European Guide of Archival Sources on the Shoah* (Paris: Centre de Documentation Juive Contemporaine, 1999 [multilingual]); Jacques Fredj (ed.), *Les Archives de la Shoah* (Paris: L'Hartmann, 1998 [in French and English]).

6 See, for example, Geoffrey H. Hartman (ed.), *Holocaust Remembrance: The Shapes of Memory* (Oxford: Blackwell, 1994).

7 Deborah E. Lipstadt, *Denying the Holocaust: The Growing Assault on Truth and Memory* (New York: The Free Press, 1993).

8 See, for example, Lucy S. Dawidowicz, *The War Against the Jews, 1933–1945*, 10th edn (New York: Bantam Books, 1986). For a more general argument, see Shmuel Ettinger, *Modern Anti-Semitism: Studies and Essays* (Tel-Aviv, 1978 [in Hebrew]).

9 See, for example, Ian Kershaw, *Popular Opinion and Political Dissent in the Third Reich: Bavaria 1933–1945* (Oxford: Clarendon Press, 1983); Sarah Gordon, *Hitler, Germans and the "Jewish Question"* (Princeton, NJ: Princeton University Press, 1984).

10 Daniel Jonah Goldhagen, *Hitler's Willing Executioners: Ordinary Germans and the Holocaust* (New York: Knopf, 1996). But see also the thorough study by John Weiss, *Ideology of Death: Why the Holocaust Happened in Germany* (Chicago: Ivan R. Dee, 1996), and the far more nuanced work by Saul Friedländer, *Nazi*

Germany and the Jews, Vol. I: *The Years of Persecution* (New York: Harper-Collins, 1997), the main outlines of whose argument on "redemptive anti-semitism" are presented in Chapter 4 in this book.

11 For the main contributions to the debate, see Julius H. Schoeps (ed.), *Ein Volk von Mördern? Die Dokumentation zur Goldhagen-Kontroverse um die Rolle der Deutschen im Holocaust* (Hamburg: Campe, 1996); Robert R. Shandley (ed.), *Unwilling Germans? The Goldhagen Debate* (Minneapolis, MN: University of Minnesota Press, 1998); Norman G. Finkelstein and Ruth Bettina Birn, *A Nation on Trial: The Goldhagen Thesis and Historical Truth* (New York: Owl Books, 1998). My own views were articulated in the review article "Ordinary Monsters," *The New Republic* (April 29, 1996): 32–8. See also Geoff Eley and Cathleen Canning (eds), *History, Memory, Nazism: Hitler's Willing Executioners in European and American Self-Reflection* (Ann Arbor, MI: Michigan University Press, forthcoming).

12 Raul Hilberg's major work is *The Destruction of the European Jews*, rev. edn, 3 vols (New York: Holmes & Meier, 1985). See also Hilberg, *Perpetrators, Victims, Bystanders: The Jewish Catastrophe 1933–1945* (New York: Harper-Collins, 1992). On his perception of his critics, see Hilberg, *The Politics of Memory: The Journey of a Holocaust Historian* (Chicago: Ivan R. Dee, 1996).

13 See especially Michael Burleigh, *Death and Deliverance: "Euthanasia" in Germany 1900–1945* (Cambridge: Cambridge University Press, 1994); H. Friedlander, *The Origins of Nazi Genocide: From Euthanasia to the Final Solution* (Chapel Hill, NC: University of North Carolina Press, 1995).

14 See especially Detlev J. K. Peukert, "The Genesis of the 'Final Solution' from the Spirit of Science," in Childers and Caplan, *Reevaluating the Third Reich*, pp. 234–52; Mario Biagioli, "Science, Modernity, and the 'Final Solution'," in Saul Friedländer (ed.), *Probing the Limits of Representation: Nazism and the "Final Solution"* (Cambridge, MA: Harvard University Press, 1992), pp. 185–205. See further in Robert N. Proctor, *Racial Hygiene: Medicine Under the Nazis* (Cambridge, MA: Harvard University Press, 1988); Paul Weindling, *Health, Race and German Politics between National Unification and Nazism 1870–1945* (Cambridge: Cambridge University Press, 1989); Robert Jay Lifton, *The Nazi Doctors: Medical Killing and the Psychology of Genocide* (New York: Basic Books, 1986); Michael H. Kater, *Doctors Under Hitler* (Chapel Hill, NC: University of North Carolina Press, 1989); Götz Aly, Peter Chroust and Christian Pross, *Cleansing the Fatherland: Nazi Medicine and Racial Hygiene*, trans. Belinda Cooper (Baltimore, MD: Johns Hopkins University Press, 1994).

15 See Zygmunt Bauman, *Modernity and the Holocaust* (Ithaca, NY: Cornell University Press, 1991); David Blackbourn and Geoff Eley, *The Peculiarities of German History: Bourgeois Society and Politics in Nineteenth-Century Germany* (Oxford: Oxford University Press, 1984).

16 The best analysis of the historiography is Ian Kershaw, *The Nazi Dictatorship: Problems and Perspectives of Interpretation*, 3rd edn (London: Edward Arnold, 1993), especially Chapters 4, 5, 9 and 10 for the present context. See also the excellent article (which updates Kershaw), Dieter Pohl, "Die Holocaust-Forschung und Goldhagens Thesen," *Vierteljahrshefte für Zeitgeschichte* 1 (1997): 1–48.

17 For some of the most prominent "intentionalist" studies, see Gerald Fleming, *Hitler and the Final Solution* (Berkeley, CA: University of California Press, 1984); Eberhard Jäckel, *Hitler's World View: A Blueprint for Power*, trans. Herbert Arnold (Cambridge, MA: Harvard University Press, 1981). See also Lucy Dawidowicz, *The Holocaust and the Historians* (Cambridge, MA: Harvard University Press, 1981), for a critique of other interpretations and schools.

18 See, most recently, Vicki Caron, "The Antisemitic Revival in France in the 1930s: The Socioeconomic Dimension Reconsidered," *Journal of Modern History* 70/1 (March 1998): 24–73; William W. Hagen, "Before the 'Final Solution': Toward a Comparative Analysis of Political Anti-Semitism in Interwar Germany and Poland," *Journal of Modern History* 68/2 (June 1996): 351–81.

19 For some of the most influential and forceful "functionalist" interpretations, see Karl A. Schleunes, *The Twisted Road to Auschwitz: Nazi Policy Toward German Jews, 1933–1939*, 2nd edn (Urbana, IL: University of Illinois Press, 1990); Martin Broszat, "Hitler and the Genesis of the 'Final Solution': An Assessment of David Irving's Theses," in H.W. Koch (ed.), *Aspects of the Third Reich* (New York: St. Martin's Press, 1985), pp. 390–429; Hans Mommsen, "The Realization of the Unthinkable: The 'Final Solution of the Jewish Question' in the Third Reich," in Mommsen, *From Weimar to Auschwitz* (Princeton, NJ: Princeton University Press, 1991), pp. 224–53.

20 For another sophisticated interpretation in line with "moderate intentionalism," see Philippe Burrin, *Hitler and the Jews: The Genesis of the Final Solution*, trans. Patsy Southgate (London: Edward Arnold, 1994).

21 For an earlier formulation, see Christopher Browning, "A Reply to Martin Broszat Regarding the Origins of the Final Solution," *Simon Wiesenthal Center Annual* 1 (1984): 113–32; and Browning, "The Decision Concerning the Final Solution," in Browning, *Fateful Months: Essays on the Emergence of the Final Solution* (New York: Holmes & Meier, 1985), pp. 8–38.

22 Christopher R. Browning, "Nazi Ghettoization Policy in Poland, 1939–1941," in Browning, *The Path to Genocide: Essays on Launching the Final Solution* (Cambridge: Cambridge University Press, 1992), pp. 28–56. See also, ibid., Chapter 1 on Nazi resettlement policy and Chapter 5 on the decision for the "Final Solution."

23 Götz Aly and Susanne Heim, *Vordenker der Vernichtung: Auschwitz und die deutsche Pläne für eine neue europäische Ordnung* (Frankfurt am Main: Fischer Taschenbuch Verlag, 1993); Aly and Heim, "The Economics of the Final Solution: A Case Study from the General Government," *Simon Wiesenthal Center Annual* 5 (1988): 3–48.

24 Christopher Browning, "German Technocrats, Jewish Labor, and the Final Solution: A Reply to Götz Aly and Susanne Heim," in Browning, *The Path to Genocide*, pp. 59–76; Ulrich Herbert, "Labour and Extermination: Economic Interest and the Primacy of *Weltanschauung* in National Socialism," *Past and Present* 138 (February 1993): 144–95; Wolfgang Schieder (ed.), *"Vernichtungspolitik": Eine Debatte über den Zusammenhang von Sozialpolitik und Genozid im nationalsozialistischen Deutschland* (Hamburg: Junius Verlag, 1991).

25 Götz Aly, *"Final Solution": Nazi Population Policy and the Murder of the European Jews*, trans. Belinda Cooper and Allison Brown (London: Arnold, 1999).

26 Note also that there was a major difference between Nazi views of the Jews and the "Slavs." See the incisive article by John Connelly, "Nazis and Slavs: From Racial Theory to Racist Practice," *Central European History* 32/1 (1999): 1–33. On the persecution and murder of the Sinti and Roma (Gypsies), see Sybil Milton, "Vorstufe zur Vernichtung: Die Zigeunerlager nach 1933," *Vierteljahrshefte für Zeitgeschichte* 43 (1995): 115–30; Michael Zimmermann, *Rassenutopie und Genozid: Die nationalsozialistische "Lösung der Zigeunerfrage"* (Hamburg: Hans Christians Verlag, 1996); Gilad Margalit, *Postwar Germany and the Gypsies: The Treatment of Sinti and Roma in the Aftermath of the Third Reich* (Jerusalem: Magnes Press, 1998 [in Hebrew]).

27 For a new and complex interpretation of the century that highlights such continuities, see Dan Diner, *Das Jahrhundert verstehen: Eine Universalhistorische Deutung* (Munich: Luchterhand, 1999). Two other analyses on the century which stress its violent features are Mark Mazower, *Dark Continent: Europe's Twentieth Century* (New York: Alfred A. Knopf, 1999); Eric Hobsbawm, *The Age of Extremes: A History of the World, 1914–1991* (New York: Vintage Books, 1996).

28 For a collection of articles that presents some of the cutting-edge scholarship by young German historians on various aspects of the Holocaust, see now Ulrich Herbert (ed.), *National-Socialist Extermination Policies: Contemporary German Perspectives and Controversies* (New York: Berghahn, 1999).

29 On Wehrmacht involvement in Nazi policies and indoctrination of soldiers, see Omer Bartov, *The Eastern Front, 1941–45: German Troops and the Barbarisation of Warfare* (London: Macmillan, 1985); Bartov, *Hitler's Army: Soldiers, Nazis, and War in the Third Reich* (New York: Oxford University Press, 1991).

30 Apart from the works cited in Chapter 7, see now *The German Army and Genocide: Crimes Against War Prisoners, Jews, and other Civilians in the East, 1939–1944*, ed. Hamburg Institute for Social Research, trans. Scott Abbott (New York: The New Press, 1999); Hannes Heer and Klaus Naumann (eds), *War of Extermination: Crimes of the Wehrmacht, 1941–1944* (New York: Berghahn, 1999). For other examples of the links between war and mass killing of civilians, see Robert Jay Lifton and Eric Markusen, *The Genocidal Mentality: Nazi Holocaust and Nuclear Threat* (New York: Basic Books, 1990); Eric Markusen and David Kopf, *The Holocaust and Strategic Bombing: Genocide and Total War in the Twentieth Century* (Boulder, CO: Westview Press, 1995); John W. Dower, *War Without Mercy: Race and Power in the Pacific War* (New York: Pantheon, 1986); Joanna Bourke, *An Intimate History of Killing: Face to Face Killing in Twentieth-Century Warfare* (London: Granta, 1999).

31 Hannah Arendt, *Eichmann in Jerusalem: A Report on the Banality of Evil*, rev. edn (New York: Penguin, 1976).

32 Goldhagen, *Hitler's Willing Executioners*; Christopher R. Browning, *Ordinary Men: Reserve Police Battalion 101 and the Final Solution in Poland* (New York: HarperCollins, 1992).

33 See, for example, Richard Bessel (ed.), *Life in the Third Reich* (Oxford: Oxford University Press, 1987); Martin Broszat and Elke Fröhlich, *Alltag und Widerstand: Bayern im Nationalsozialismus* (Munich: Piper, 1987); Mary Nolan, "The *Historikerstreit* and Social History," in Peter Baldwin (ed.), *Reworking the Past: Hitler, the Holocaust, and the Historians' Debate* (Boston, MA: Beacon Press, 199), pp. 224–48.

34 Gordon J. Horwitz, *In the Shadow of Death: Living Outside the Gates of Mauthausen* (New York: The Free Press, 1990).

35 For the two most comprehensive histories of the Nazi concentration camp system, from two very different perspectives, see Yisrael Gutman and Rachel Manbar (eds), *The Nazi Concentration Camps: Structure and Aims. The Image of the Prisoner. The Jews in the Camps* (Jerusalem: Yad Vashem, 1984 [in Hebrew]); Ulrich Herbert, Karin Orth and Christoph Dieckmann (eds), *Die national-sozialistischen Konzentrationslager: Entwicklung und Struktur*, 2 vols (Göttingen: Wallstein Verlag, 1998).

36 See now Carole Rittner and John K. Roth (eds), *Different Voices: Women and the Holocaust* (New York: Paragon House, 1993); Dalia Ofer and Lenore J. Weitzman (eds), *Women in the Holocaust* (New Haven, CT: Yale University Press, 1998).

37 One French (non-Jewish) survivor, sent to Auschwitz as a political prisoner, wrote some of her memoirs soon after the liberation but published them only decades later. Her extraordinary writings are becoming known in the English-speaking world only in the last few years. See Charlotte Delbo, *Auschwitz and After*, trans. Rosette C. Lamont (New Haven, CT: Yale University Press, 1995); Delbo, *Convoy to Auschwitz: Women of the French Resistance*, trans. Carol Cosman (Boston, MA: Northeastern University Press, 1997).

38 See, for instance, the remarkable study by Felicja Karay, *Rockets and Rhymes: The Hasag-Leipzig Women Labor Camp* (Tel Aviv: Moreshet and Yad Vashem, 1997 [in Hebrew]).

39 This issue is powerfully demonstrated in Marion A. Kaplan, *Between Dignity and Despair: Jewish Life in Nazi Germany* (New York: Oxford University Press, 1998). See also Renate Bridenthal, Atina Grossmann and Marion Kaplan (eds), *When Biology Became Destiny: Women in Weimar and Nazi Germany* (New York: Monthly Review Press, 1984).

40 Elsa Morante, *History: A Novel*, trans. William Weaver (New York: Knopf, 1977). On Alberto Moravia's subsequently denied links with Mussolini's fascist regime (despite his Jewish ancestry), see Ruth Ben-Ghiat, "Fascism, Writing, and Memory: The Realist Aesthetic in Italy, 1930–1950," *Journal of Modern History* 67 (September 1995): 627–65.

41 Nadezhda Mandelstam, *Hope Against Hope: A Memoir*, trans. Max Hayward (New York: Atheneum, 1970); Mandelstam, *Hope Abandoned*, trans. Max Hayward (New York: Atheneum, 1981).

42 Heda Margolius Kovály, *Under a Cruel Star: A Life in Prague 1941–1968*, trans. Franci Epstein and Helen Epstein with the author (New York: Penguin, 1989 [Cambridge, MA: Plunkett Lake Press, 1986]). For two important (albeit male-oriented) recent accounts of life in the camps, one from a harshly sociological perspective, the other striving for a more edifying moral view, see Wolfgang Sofsky, *The Order of Terror: The Concentration Camp*, trans. William Templer (Princeton, NJ: Princeton University Press, 1997); Tzvetan Todorov, *Facing the Extreme: Moral Life in the Concentration Camps*, trans. Arthur Denner and Abigail Pollak (New York: Metropolitan Books, 1996).

43 On the relationship between history, memory, and trauma, see Cathy Caruth (ed.), *Trauma: Explorations in Memory* (Baltimore, MD: Johns Hopkins University Press, 1995); Dominick LaCapra, *History and Memory after Auschwitz* (Ithaca, NY: Cornell University Press, 1998). On trauma and the second generation of survivors, perpetrators, and bystanders, see Rafael Moses (ed.), *Persistent Shadows of the Holocaust: The Meaning to Those Not Directly Affected* (Madison, CT: International Universities Press, 1993).

44 Lawrence L. Langer, *Holocaust Testimonies: The Ruins of Memory* (New Haven, CT: Yale University Press, 1991).

45 Another important example is Jean Améry, *At the Mind's Limits: Contemplations by a Survivor on Auschwitz and Its Realities*, trans. Sidney Rosenfeld and Stella Rosenfeld (New York: Schocken Books, 1986).

46 Primo Levi, *The Drowned and the Saved*, trans. Raymond Rosenthal (New York: Summit Books, 1988). See now also Myriam Anissimov, *Primo Levi: Tragedy of an Optimist*, trans. Steve Cox (Woodstock, NY: Overlook Press, 1998).

47 On this issue see Saul Friedländer, *Reflections of Nazism*, trans. Thomas Weyr (New York: Avon, 1986); Omer Bartov, *Murder in our Midst: The Holocaust, Industrial Killing, and Representation* (New York: Oxford University Press, 1986), chs 6–7.

48 See, for example, Yosefa Loshitzky (ed.), *Spielberg's Holocaust: Critical Perspectives on Schindler's List* (Bloomington, IN: Indiana University Press,

1997); Ruth Ben-Ghiat, review of *Life Is Beautiful* in *The American Historical Review* 104/1 (February 1999): 298–9.

49 See especially Lipstadt, *Denying the Holocaust*; and Pierre Vidal-Naquet, *Assassins of Memory: Essays on the Denial of the Holocaust*, trans. Jeffrey Mehlman (New York: Columbia University Press, 1992).

50 For postwar French historiography, memory, and justice and their relationship to France's role in the Holocaust, see especially Lawrence D. Kritzman (ed.), *Auschwitz and After: Race, Culture, and "the Jewish Question" in France* (New York: Routledge, 1995); Richard J. Golsan (ed.), *Memory, the Holocaust, and French Justice: The Bousquet and Touvier Affairs* (Hanover, NH: University Press of New England, 1996); Erna Paris, *Unhealed Wounds: France and the Klaus Barbie Affair* (New York: Grove Press, 1985); Henry Rousso, *The Vichy Syndrome: History and Memory in France since 1944*, trans. Arthur Goldhammer (Cambridge, MA: Harvard University Press, 1991); Eric Conan and Henry Rousso, *Vichy: An Ever-Present Past*, trans. Nathan Bracher (Hanover, NH: University Press of New England, 1998).

51 The full argument can be found in Alain Finkielkraut, *Remembering in Vain: The Klaus Barbie Trial and Crimes Against Humanity*, trans. Roxanne Lapidus and Sima Godfrey (New York: Columbia University Press, 1992).

52 See now in a similar vein also Berel Lang, *The Future of the Holocaust: Between History and Memory* (Ithaca, NY: Cornell University Press, 1999).

Part I

ORIGINS
Antisemitism and scientific racism

1

THE DESTRUCTION OF THE EUROPEAN JEWS

Precedents

Raul Hilberg

Those who watched Claude Lanzmann's film Shoah *(1985) will recall the imposing figure of Raul Hilberg, the only scholar who features in this reconstruction of Holocaust memory, as he leafs through mounds of Nazi documents and remarks that hardly any of the specific anti-Jewish measures that Hitler's henchmen came up with were, as such, original. To his mind, almost everything had its precedents in centuries of Christian persecution of Jews. The one—crucial —difference was that the Nazis set out to murder each and every Jew they could find, in other words, to commit genocide, whereas the church had first attempted to convert the Jews, then to expel them, but never to organize wholesale murder (despite innumerable massacres and pogroms).*

This chapter, which forms the opening section of Hilberg's magnum opus on the Holocaust, is interesting on several counts. First, it demonstrates that despite Hilberg's almost obsessive focus on bureaucratic measures in the organization of modern genocide throughout the rest of his book, he saw the actual policy (rather than the specific means by which it was implemented) as a direct continuation (although not an inevitable outcome) of a long-term European antisemitism. This is a powerful but contentious argument with which not all historians would agree, since it underlines Judeophobia in the Christian world and pays little attention to the facts of Jewish existence within the fold of European civilization, as well as to the century of optimistic and, until the Nazis, successful emancipation and assimilation that preceded the Holocaust. Second, it sets the basis for Hilberg's highly controversial claim of Jewish passivity, and in many respects complicity, during the Holocaust, which he traces back to modes of behavior that became culturally ingrained among European Jews as a means of withstanding persecution, but became highly self-destructive in the face of the Nazi genocidal onslaught. Here too, many scholars would disagree. Curiously, however, precisely those Zionist historians who objected to Hilberg's study because it allegedly focused only on the perpetrators and neglected the victims, were similarly of the

21

opinion that the "Diaspora mentality" of the Jews made the majority of them "go like sheep to the slaughter."

There are many other possible texts to choose from on the question of antisemitism and the Holocaust. The reason I chose Hilberg is precisely because he is much more often thought of as being committed to a life-long dispassionate, analytical, and meticulous study of the machinery of genocide; it is this that makes his views on the cultural precedents of the Holocaust all the more striking.

* * *

The German destruction of the European Jews was a tour de force; the Jewish collapse under the German assault was a manifestation of failure. Both of these phenomena were the final product of an earlier age.

Anti-Jewish policies and actions did not have their beginning in 1933. For many centuries, and in many countries, the Jews had been victims of destructive action. What was the object of these activities? What were the aims of those who persisted in anti-Jewish deeds? Throughout Western history, three consecutive policies have been applied against Jewry in its dispersion.

The first anti-Jewish policy started in the fourth century after Christ in Rome. Early in the fourth century, during the reign of Constantine, the Christian Church gained power in Rome, and Christianity became the state religion. From this period, the state carried out Church policy. For the next twelve centuries, the Catholic Church prescribed the measures that were to be taken with respect to the Jews. Unlike the pre-Christian Romans, who claimed no monopoly on religion and faith, the Christian Church insisted on acceptance of Christian doctrine.

For an understanding of Christian policy toward Jewry, it is essential to realize that the Church pursued conversion not so much for the sake of aggrandizing its power (the Jews have always been few in number), but because of the conviction that it was the duty of true believers to save unbelievers from the doom of eternal hellfire. Zealousness in the pursuit of conversion was an indication of the depth of faith. The Christian religion was not one of many religions, but the true religion, the only one. Those who were not in its fold were either ignorant or in error. The Jews could not accept Christianity.

In the very early stages of the Christian faith, many Jews regarded Christians as members of a Jewish sect. The first Christians, after all, still observed the Jewish law. They had merely added a few nonessential practices, such as baptism, to their religious life. But their view was changed abruptly when Christ was elevated to Godhood. The Jews have only one God. This God is indivisible. He is a jealous God and admits of no other gods. He is not Christ, and Christ is not He. Christianity and Judaism have since been irreconcilable. An acceptance of Christianity has since signified an abandonment of Judaism.

In antiquity and in the Middle Ages, Jews did not abandon Judaism lightly. With patience and persistence the Church attempted to convert obstinate Jewry, and for twelve hundred years the theological argument was fought without interruption. The Jews were not convinced. Gradually the Church began to back its words with force. The Papacy did not permit pressure to be put on individual Jews; Rome prohibited forceful conversions. However, the clergy did use pressure on the whole. Step by step, but with ever widening effect, the Church adopted "defensive" measures against its passive victims. Christians were "protected" from the "harmful" consequences of intercourse with Jews by rigid laws against intermarriage, by prohibitions of discussions about religious issues, by laws against domicile in common abodes. The Church "protected" its Christians from the "harmful" Jewish teachings by burning the Talmud and by barring Jews from public office.

These measures were precedent-making destructive activities. How little success the Church had in accomplishing its aim is revealed by the treatment of the few Jews who succumbed to the Christian religion. The clergy was not sure of its success—hence the widespread practice, in the Middle Ages, of identifying proselytes as former Jews; hence the inquisition of new Christians suspected of heresy; hence the issuance in Spain of certificates of "purity," signifying purely Christian ancestry, and the specification of "half-new Christians," "quarter-new Christians," "one-eighth-new Christians," and so on.

The failure of conversion had far-reaching consequences. The unsuccessful Church began to look on the Jews as a special group of people, different from Christians, deaf to Christianity, and dangerous to the Christian faith. In 1542 Martin Luther, the founder of Protestantism, wrote the following lines:

> And if there were a spark of common sense and understanding in them, they would truly have to think like this: O my God, it does not stand and go well with us; our misery is too great, too long, too hard; God has forgotten us, etc. I am no Jew, but I do not like to think in earnest about such brutal wrath of God against this people, for I am terrified at the thought that cuts through my body and soul: What is going to happen with the eternal wrath in hell against all false Christians and unbelievers?

In short, if *he* were a Jew, he would have accepted Christianity long ago.

A people cannot suffer for fifteen hundred years and still think of itself as the chosen people. But this people was blind. It had been stricken by the wrath of God. He had struck them "with frenzy, blindness, and raging heart, with the eternal fire, of which the Prophets say: The wrath of God will hurl itself outward like a fire that no one can smother."

The Lutheran manuscript was published at a time of increasing hatred for the Jew. Too much had been invested in twelve hundred years of conversion policy. Too little had been gained. From the thirteenth to the sixteenth century, the Jews of England, France, Germany, Spain, Bohemia, and Italy were presented with ultimatums that gave them no choice but one: conversion or expulsion.

Expulsion is the second anti-Jewish policy in history. In its origin, this policy presented itself only as an alternative—moreover, as an alternative that was left to the Jews. But long after the separation of church and state, long after the state had ceased to carry out church policy, expulsion and exclusion remained the goal of anti-Jewish activity.

The anti-Semites of the nineteenth century, who divorced themselves from religious aims, espoused the emigration of the Jews. The anti-Semites hated the Jews with a feeling of righteousness and reason, as though they had acquired the antagonism of the church like speculators buying the rights of a bankrupt corporation. With this hatred, the post-ecclesiastic enemies of Jewry also took the idea that the Jews could not be changed, that they could not be converted, that they could not be assimilated, that they were a finished product, inflexible in their ways, set in their notions, fixed in their beliefs.

The expulsion and exclusion policy was adopted by the Nazis and remained the goal of all anti-Jewish activity until 1941. That year marks a turning point in anti-Jewish history. In 1941 the Nazis found themselves in the midst of a total war. Several million Jews were incarcerated in ghettos. Emigration was impossible. A last-minute project to ship the Jews to the African island of Madagascar had fallen through. The "Jewish problem" had to be "solved" in some other way. At this crucial time, the idea of a "territorial solution" emerged in Nazi minds. The "territorial solution," or "the final solution of the Jewish question in Europe," as it became known, envisaged the death of European Jewry. The European Jews were to be killed. This was the third anti-Jewish policy in history.

To summarize: Since the fourth century after Christ there have been three anti-Jewish policies: conversion, expulsion, and annihilation. The second appeared as an alternative to the first, and the third emerged as an alternative to the second.

The destruction of the European Jews between 1933 and 1945 appears to us now as an unprecedented event in history. Indeed, in its dimensions and total configuration, nothing like it had ever happened before. As a result of an organized undertaking, five million people were killed in the short space of a few years. The operation was over before anyone could grasp its enormity, let alone its implications for the future.

Yet, if we analyze this singularly massive upheaval, we discover that most of what happened in those twelve years had already happened before. The Nazi destruction process did not come out of a void; it was the culmination of a cyclical trend. We have observed the trend in the three successive goals of anti-Jewish administrators. The missionaries of Christianity had said in effect: You have no right to live among us as Jews. The secular rulers who followed had proclaimed: You have no right to live among us. The Nazis at last decreed: You have no right to live.

These progressively more drastic goals brought in their wake a slow and steady growth of anti-Jewish action and anti-Jewish thinking. The process began with the attempt to drive the Jews into Christianity. The development was continued in order to force the victims into exile. It was finished when the Jews were driven to their deaths. The German Nazis, then, did not discard the past; they built upon it. They did not begin a development; they completed it. In the deep recesses of anti-Jewish history we shall find many of the administrative and psychological tools with which the Nazis implemented their destruction process. In the hollows of the past we shall also discover the roots of the characteristic Jewish response to an outside attack.

The significance of the historical precedents will most easily be understood in the administrative sphere. The destruction of the Jews was an administrative process, and the annihilation of Jewry required the implementation of systematic administrative measures in successive steps. There are not many ways in which a modern society can, in short order, kill a large number of people living in its midst. This is an efficiency problem of the greatest dimensions, one which poses uncounted difficulties and innumerable obstacles. Yet, in reviewing the documentary record of the destruction of the Jews, one is almost immediately impressed with the fact that the German administration knew what it was doing. With an unfailing sense of direction and with an uncanny pathfinding ability, the German bureaucracy found the shortest road to the final goal.

We know, of course, that the very nature of a task determines the form of its fulfillment. Where there is the will, there is also the way, and if the will is only strong enough, the way will be found. But what if there is no time to experiment? What if the task must be solved quickly and efficiently? A rat in a maze that has only one path to the goal learns to choose that path after many trials. Bureaucrats, too, are sometimes caught in a maze, but they cannot afford a trial run. There may be no time for hesitations and stoppages. This is why past performance is so important; this is why past experience is so essential. Necessity is said to be the mother of invention, but if precedents have already been formed, if a guide has already been constructed, invention is no longer a necessity. The German bureaucracy could draw upon such precedents and follow such a guide, for the German bureaucrats could dip into a vast reservoir of administrative experience, a reservoir that church and state had filled in fifteen hundred years of destructive activity.

In the course of its attempt to convert the Jews, the Catholic church had taken many measures against the Jewish population. These measures were designed to "protect" the Christian community from Jewish teachings and, not incidentally, to weaken the Jews in their "obstinacy." It is characteristic that as soon as Christianity became the state religion of Rome, in the fourth century A.D., Jewish equality of citizenship was ended. The Church and the Christian state, concilium decisions and imperial laws, henceforth worked hand in hand to persecute the Jews. Table 1 compares the basic anti-Jewish measures of the Catholic Church and the modern counterparts enacted by the Nazi regime.

No summation of the canonical law can be as revealing as a description of the Rome ghetto, maintained by the Papal State until the occupation of the city by the Royal Italian Army in 1870. A German journalist who visited the ghetto in its closing days published such a description in the *Neue Freie Presse*. The ghetto consisted of a few damp, dark, and dirty streets, into which 4,700 human creatures had been packed tightly.

To rent any house or business establishment outside of the ghetto boundaries, the Jews needed the permission of the Cardinal Vicar. Acquisition of real estate outside the ghetto was prohibited. Trade in industrial products or books was prohibited. Higher schooling was prohibited. The professions of lawyer, druggist, notary, painter, and architect were prohibited. A Jew could be a doctor, provided that he confined his practice to Jewish patients. No Jew could hold office. Jews were required to pay taxes like everyone else and, in addition, the following: (1) a yearly stipend for the upkeep of the Catholic officials who supervised the Ghetto Finance Administration and the Jewish community organization; (2) a yearly sum of 5,250 lire to the Casa Pia for missionary work among Jews; (3) a yearly sum of 5,250 lire to the Cloister of the Converted for the same purpose. In turn, the Papal State expended a yearly sum of 1,500 lire for welfare work. But no state money was paid for education or the care of the sick.

The papal regime in the Rome ghetto gives us an idea of the cumulative effect of the canonical law. *This* was its total result. Moreover, the policy of the Church gave rise not only to ecclesiastical regulations; for more than a thousand years, the will of the Church was also enforced by the state. The decisions of the synods and councils became basic guides for state action. Every medieval state copied the canonical law and elaborated upon it. Thus there arose an "international medieval Jewry law," which continued to develop until the eighteenth century. The governmental refinements and elaborations of the clerical regime may briefly be noted in Table 2, which shows also the Nazi versions.

These are some of the precedents that were handed down to the Nazi bureaucratic machine. To be sure, not all the lessons of the past were still remembered in 1933; much had been obscured by the passage of time. This is particularly true of negative principles, such as the avoidance of riots and pogroms. In 1406 the state sought to make profits from mob violence in the Jewish quarter of Vienna. Christians suffered greater losses in this pogrom than Jews, because the Jewish pawnshops, which went up in smoke during the great ghetto fire, contained the possessions of the very people who were rioting in the streets. This experience was all but forgotten when, in November 1938, Nazi mobs surged once more into Jewish shops. The principal losers now were German insurance

Table 1 Canonical and Nazi Anti-Jewish measures

Canonical law	Nazi measure
Prohibition of intermarriage and of sexual intercourse between Christians and Jews, Synod of Elvira, 306	Law for the Protection of German Blood and Honor, September 15, 1935
Jews and Christians not permitted to eat together, Synod of Elvira, 306	Jews barred from dining cars (Transport Minister to Interior Minister, December 30, 1939)
Jews not allowed to hold public office, Synod of Clermont, 535	Law for the Reestablishment of the Professional Civil Service, April 7, 1933
Jews not allowed to employ Christian servants or possess Christian slaves, 3d Synod of Orléans, 538	Law for the Protection of German Blood and Honor, September 15, 1935
Jews not permitted to show themselves in the streets during Passion Week, 3d Synod of Orléans, 538	Decree authorizing local authorities to bar Jews from the streets on certain days (i.e., Nazi holidays), December 3, 1938
Burning of the Talmud and other books, 12th Synod of Toledo, 681	Book burnings in Nazi Germany
Christians not permitted to patronize Jewish doctors, Trullan Synod, 692	Decree of July 25, 1938
Christians not permitted to live in Jewish homes, Synod of Narbonne, 1050	Directive by Göring providing for concentration of Jews in houses, December 28, 1938 (Bormann to Rosenberg, January 17, 1939)
Jews obliged to pay taxes for support of the Church to the same extent as Christians, Synod of Gerona, 1078	The "Sozialausgleichsabgabe" which provided that Jews pay a special income tax in lieu of donations for Party purposes imposed on Nazis, December 24, 1940
Jews not permitted to be plaintiffs, or witnesses against Christians in the Courts, 3d Lateran Council, 1179, Canon 26	Proposal by the Party Chancellery that Jews not be permitted to institute civil suits, September 9, 1942 (Bormann to Justice Ministry, September 9, 1942)
Jews not permitted to withhold inheritance from descendants who had accepted Christianity, 3d Lateran Council, 1179, Canon 26	Decree empowering the Justice Ministry to void wills offending the "sound judgment of the people," July 31, 1938
The marking of Jewish clothes with a badge, 4th Lateran Council, 1215, Canon 68 (Copied from the legislation by Caliph Omar II [634–644], who had decreed that Christians wear blue belts and Jews, yellow belts)	Decree of September 1, 1941
Construction of new synagogues prohibited, Council of Oxford, 1222	Destruction of synagogues in entire Reich, November 10, 1938 (Heydrich to Göring, November 11, 1938)

Table 1 *continued*

Canonical law	Nazi measure
Christians not permitted to attend Jewish ceremonies, Synod of Vienna, 1267	Friendly relations with Jews prohibited, October 24, 1941 (Gestapo directive)
Jews not permitted to dispute with simple Christian people about the tenets of the Catholic religion, Synod of Vienna, 1267	
Compulsory ghettos, Synod of Breslau, 1267	Order by Heydrich, September 21, 1939
Christians not permitted to sell or rent real estate to Jews, Synod of Ofen, 1279	Decree providing for compulsory sale of Jewish real estate, December 3, 1938
Adoption by a Christian of the Jewish religion or return by a baptized Jew to the Jewish religion defined as a heresy, Synod of Mainz, 1310	Adoption of the Jewish religion by a Christian places him in jeopardy of being treated as a Jew (Decision by Oberlandesgericht Königsberg, 4th Zivilsenat, June 26, 1942)
Jews not permitted to act as agents in the conclusion of contracts, especially marriage contracts, between Christians, Council of Basel, 1434, Sessio XIX	Decree of July 6, 1938, providing for liquidation of Jewish real estate agencies, brokerage agencies, and marriage agencies catering to non-Jews
Jews not permitted to obtain academic degrees, Council of Basel, 1434, Sessio XIX	Law against Overcrowding of German Schools and Universities, April 25, 1933

companies, who had to pay German owners of the damaged buildings for the broken window glass. A historical lesson had to be learned all over again.

If some old discoveries had to be made anew, it must be stressed that many a new discovery had not even been fathomed of old. The administrative precedents created by church and state were in themselves incomplete. The destructive path charted in past centuries was an interrupted path. The anti-Jewish policies of conversion and expulsion could carry destructive operations only up to a point. These policies were not only goals; they were also limits before which the bureaucracy had to stop and beyond which it could not pass. Only the removal of these restraints could bring the development of destructive operations to its fullest potentiality. That is why the Nazi administrators became improvisers and innovators; that is also why the German bureaucracy under Hitler did infinitely more damage in twelve years than the Catholic Church was capable of in twelve centuries.

The administrative precedents, however, are not the only historical determinants with which we are concerned. In a Western society,

Table 2 Pre-Nazi and Nazi anti-Jewish measures

Pre-Nazi development	Nazi measure
The property of Jews slain in a German city considered as public property, "because the Jews with their possessions belong to the Reich chamber," provision in the 14th-century code *Regulae juris "Ad decus"*	13th Ordinance to the Reich Citizenship Law providing that the property of a Jew be confiscated after his death, July 1, 1943
Confiscation of Jewish claims against Christian debtors at the end of the 14th century in Nuremberg	11th Ordinance to the Reich Citizenship Law, November 25, 1941
"Fines": for example, the Regensburg fine for "killing Christian child," 1421	Decree for the "Atonement Payment" by the Jews, November 12, 1938
Marking of documents and personal papers identifying possessor or bearer as a Jew	Decree providing for identification cards, July 23, 1938
Around 1800, the Jewish poet Ludwig Börne had to have his passport marked "Jud von Frankfurt"	Decree providing for marking of passports, October 5, 1938
Marking of houses, special shopping hours, and restrictions of movement, 17th century, Frankfurt	Marking of Jewish apartments, April 17, 1942
	Decree providing for movement restrictions, September 1, 1941
Compulsory Jewish names in 19th-century bureaucratic practice	Decree of January 5, 1937
	Decree of August 17, 1938

destructive activity is not just a technocratic phenomenon. The problems arising in a destruction process are not only administrative but also psychological. A Christian is commanded to choose good and to reject evil. The greater his destructive task, therefore, the more potent are the moral obstacles in his way. These obstacles must be removed; the internal conflict must somehow be resolved. One of the principal means through which the perpetrator attempts to clear his conscience is by clothing his victim in a mantle of evil, by portraying the victim as an object that must be destroyed.

In recorded history we find many such portraits. Invariably they are floating effusively like clouds through the centuries and over the continents. Whatever their origins or destinations, the function of these stereotypes is always the same. They are used as justification for destructive thinking; they are employed as excuses for destructive action.

The Nazis needed such a stereotype. They required just such an image of the Jew. It is therefore of no little significance that when Hitler came to power, the image was already there. The model was already fixed. When Hitler spoke about the Jew, he could speak to the Germans in familiar language. When he reviled his victim, he resurrected a medieval conception.

When he shouted his fierce anti-Jewish attacks, he awakened his Germans as if from slumber to a long-forgotten challenge. How old, precisely, are these charges? Why did they have such an authoritative ring?

The picture of the Jew we encounter in Nazi propaganda and Nazi correspondence had been drawn several hundred years before. Martin Luther had already sketched the main outlines of that portrait, and the Nazis, in their time, had little to add to it. We shall look here at a few excerpts from Luther's book *About the Jews and Their Lies*. In doing so, let it be stressed that Luther's ideas were shared by others in his century, and that the mode of his expression was the style of his times. His work is cited here only because he was a towering figure in the development of German thought, and the writing of such a man is not to be forgotten in the unearthing of so crucial a conceptualization as this. Luther's treatise about the Jews was addressed to the public directly, and, in that pouring recital, sentences descended upon the audience in a veritable cascade. Thus the passage:

> Herewith you can readily see how they understand and obey the fifth commandment of God, namely, that they are thirsty blood-hounds and murderers of all Christendom, with full intent, now for more than fourteen hundred years, and indeed they were often burned to death upon the accusation that they had poisoned water and wells, stolen children, and torn and hacked them apart, in order to cool their temper secretly with Christian blood.

And:

> Now see what a fine, thick, fat lie that is when they complain that they are held captive by us. It is more than fourteen hundred years since Jerusalem was destroyed, and at this time it is almost three hundred years since we Christians have been tortured and persecuted by the Jews all over the world (as pointed out above), so that we might well complain that they had now captured us and killed us—which is the open truth. Moreover, we do not know to this day which devil has brought them here into our country; we did not look for them in Jerusalem.

Even now no one held them here, Luther continued. They might go whenever they wanted to. For they were a heavy burden, "like a plague, pestilence, pure misfortune in our country." They had been driven from France, "an especially fine nest," and the "dear Emperor Charles" drove them from Spain, "the best nest of all." And this year they were expelled from the entire Bohemian crown, including Prague, "also a very fine nest"—likewise from Regensburg, Magdeburg, and other towns.

Is this called captivity, if one is not welcome in land or house? Yes, they hold us Christians captive in our country. They let us work in the sweat of our noses, to earn money and property for them, while they sit behind the oven, lazy, let off gas, bake pears, eat, drink, live softly and well from our wealth. They have captured us and our goods through their accursed usury; mock us and spit on us, because we work and permit them to be lazy squires who own us and our realm; they are therefore our lords, we their servants with our own wealth, sweat, and work. Then they curse our Lord, to reward us and to thank us. Should not the devil laugh and dance, if he can have such paradise among the Christians, that he may devour through the Jews—his holy ones—that which is ours, and stuff our mouths and noses as reward, mocking and cursing God and man for good measure.

They could not have had in Jerusalem under David and Solomon such fine days on their own estate as they have now on ours—which they rob and steal daily. But still they complain that we hold them captive. Yes, we have and hold them in captivity, just as I have captured my calculum, my blood heaviness, and all other maladies.

What have the Christians done, asks Luther, to deserve such a fate?
"We do not call their women whores, do not curse them, do not steal and dismember their children, do not poison their water. We do not thirst after their blood." It was not otherwise than Moses had said. God had struck them with frenzy, blindness, and raging heart.

This is Luther's picture of the Jews. First, they want to rule the world. Second, they are archcriminals, killers of Christ and all Christendom. Third, he refers to them as a "plague, pestilence, and pure misfortune." This Lutheran portrait of Jewish world rule, Jewish criminality, and the Jewish plague has often been repudiated. But, in spite of denial and exposure, the charges have survived. In four hundred years the picture has not changed.

In 1895 the Reichstag was discussing a measure, proposed by the anti-Semitic faction, for the exclusion of foreign Jews. The speaker, Ahlwardt, belonged to that faction. We reproduce here a few excerpts from his speech:

It is quite clear that there is many a Jew among us of whom one cannot say anything bad. If one designates the whole of Jewry as harmful, one does so in the knowledge that the racial qualities of this people are such that in the long run they cannot harmonize with the racial qualities of the Germanic peoples, and that every Jew who at this moment has not done anything bad may nevertheless under the proper conditions do precisely that, because his racial qualities drive him to do it.

Gentlemen, in India there was a certain sect, the Thugs, who elevated the act of assassination to an act of policy. In this sect, no doubt, there were quite a few people who personally never committed a murder, but the English in my opinion have done the right thing when they exterminated this whole sect, without regard to the question whether any particular member of the sect already had committed a murder or not, for in the proper moment every member of the sect would do such a thing.

Ahlwardt pointed out that the anti-Semites were fighting the Jews not because of their religion but because of their race. He then continued:

The Jews accomplished what no other enemy has accomplished: they have driven the people from Frankfurt into the suburbs. And that's the way it is wherever Jews congregate in large numbers. Gentlemen, the Jews are indeed beasts of prey. . . .

Mr. Rickert [another deputy who had opposed the exclusion of the Jews] started by saying that we already had too many laws, and that's why we should not concern ourselves with a new anti-Jewish code. That is really the most interesting reason that has ever been advanced against anti-Semitism. We should leave the Jews alone because we have too many laws?! Well, I think, if we would do away with the Jews, we could do away with half the laws that we have now on the books.

Then, Deputy Rickert said that it is really a shame—whether he actually said that I don't know because I could not take notes— but the sense of it was that it was a shame that a nation of 50 million people should be afraid of a few Jews. [Rickert had cited statistics to prove that the number of Jews in the country was not excessive.] Yes, gentlemen, Deputy Rickert would be right, if it were a matter of fighting with honest weapons against an honest enemy; then it would be a matter of course that the Germans would not fear a handful of such people. But the Jews, who operate like parasites, are a different kind of problem. Mr. Rickert, who is not as tall as I am, is afraid of a single cholera germ—and, gentlemen, the Jews are cholera germs.

(Laughter)

Gentlemen, it is the infectiousness and exploitative power of Jewry that is involved.

Ahlwardt then called upon the deputies to wipe out "these beasts of prey," and continued:

33

If it is now pointed out—and that was undoubtedly the main point of the two previous speakers—that the Jew is human too, then I must reject that totally. The Jew is no German. If you say that the Jew is born in Germany, is raised by German nurses, has obeyed the German laws, has had to become a soldier—and what kind of soldier, we don't want to talk about that—

(Laughter in the right section)

has fulfilled all his duties, has had to pay taxes, too, then all of that is not decisive for nationality, but only the race out of which he was born is decisive. Permit me to use a banal analogy, which I have already brought out in previous speeches: a horse that is born in a cowbarn is still no cow. *(Stormy laughter)* A Jew who is born in Germany, is still no German; he is still a Jew.

Ahlwardt then remarked that this was no laughing matter but deadly serious business.

It is necessary to look at the matter from this angle. We do not even think of going so far as, for instance, the Austrian anti-Semites in the Reichsrath, that we demand an appropriation to reward everybody who shoots a Jew, or that we should decide that whoever kills a Jew, inherits his property. *(Laughter, un-easiness)* That kind of thing we do not intend here; that far we do not want to go. But we do want a quiet and common-sense separation of the Jews from the Germans. And to do that, it is first of all necessary that we close that hatch, so that more of them cannot come in.

It is remarkable that two men, separated by a span of 350 years, can still speak the same language. Ahlwardt's picture of the Jews is in its basic features a replica of the Lutheran portrait. The Jew is still (1) an enemy who has accomplished what no external enemy has accomplished: he has driven the people of Frankfurt into the suburbs; (2) a criminal, a thug, a beast of prey, who commits so many crimes that his elimination would enable the Reichstag to cut the criminal code in half; and (3) a plague or, more precisely, a cholera germ. Under the Nazi regime, these conceptions of the Jew were expounded and repeated in an almost endless flow of speeches, posters, letters, and memoranda. Hitler himself preferred to look upon the Jew as an enemy, a menace, a dangerous cunning foe. This is what he said in a speech delivered in 1940, as he reviewed his "struggle for power":

It was a battle against a satanical power, which had taken possession of our entire people, which had grasped in its hands all key positions of scientific, intellectual, as well as political and economic life, and which kept watch over the entire nation from the vantage of these key positions. It was a battle against a power which, at the same time, had the influence to combat with the law every man who attempted to take up battle against them and every man who was ready to offer resistance to the spread of this power. At that time, all-powerful Jewry declared war on us.

Gauleiter Julius Streicher emphasized the contention that the Jews were criminal. The following is an excerpt from a typical Streicher speech to the Hitler Youth. It was made in 1935.

Boys and girls, look back to a little more than ten years ago. A war—the World War—had whirled over the peoples of the earth and had left in the end a heap of ruins. Only one people remained victorious in this dreadful war, a people of whom Christ said its father is the devil. That people had ruined the German nation in body and soul.

But then Hitler arose and the world took courage in the thought that now

the human race might be free again from this people which has wandered about the world for centuries and millennia, marked with the sign of Cain.

Boys and girls, even if they say that the Jews were once the chosen people, do not believe it, but believe us when we say that the Jews are not a chosen people. Because it cannot be that a chosen people should act among the peoples as the Jews do today.

A chosen people does not go into the world to make others work for them, to suck blood. It does not go among the peoples to chase the peasants from the land. It does not go among the peoples to make your fathers poor and drive them to despair. A chosen people does not slay and torture animals to death. A chosen people does not live by the sweat of others. A chosen people joins the ranks of those who live because they work. Don't you ever forget that.

Boys and girls, for you we went to prison. For you we have always suffered. For you we had to accept mockery and insult, and became fighters among the Jewish people, against that organized body of world criminals, against whom already Christ had fought, the greatest anti-Semite of all times.

A number of Nazis, including the chief of the German SS and Police Himmler, the jurist and Generalgouverneur of Poland Hans Frank, and

Justice Minister Thierack, inclined to the view that the Jews were a lower species of life, a kind of vermin, which upon contact infected the German people with deadly diseases. Himmler once cautioned his SS generals not to tolerate the stealing of property that had belonged to dead Jews. "Just because we exterminated a bacterium," he said, "we do not want, in the end, to be infected by that bacterium and die of it." Frank frequently referred to the Jews as "lice." When the Jews in his Polish domain were killed, he announced that now a sick Europe would become healthy again. Justice Minister Thierack once wrote the following letter to a worried Hitler:

> A full Jewess, after the birth of her child, sold her mother's milk to a woman doctor, and concealed the fact that she was a Jewess. With this milk, infants of German blood were fed in a children's clinic. The accused is charged with fraud. The purchasers of the milk have suffered damage, because the mother's milk of a Jewess cannot be considered food for German children. The impudent conduct of the accused is also an insult. However, there has been no formal indictment in order to spare the parents—who do not know the facts—unnecessary worry. I will discuss the race-hygienic aspects of the case with the Reich Health Chief.

The twentieth-century Nazis, like the nineteenth-century anti-Semites and the sixteenth-century clerics, regarded the Jews as hostile, criminal, and parasitic. Ultimately the very word *Jew* was infused with all these meanings. But there is also a difference between the recent writings and the older scripts that requires explanation. In the Nazi and anti-Semitic speeches we discover references to race. This formulation does not appear in the sixteenth-century books. Conversely, in Luther's work there is repeated mention of God's scorn, thunder and lightning worse than Sodom and Gomorrah, frenzy, blindness, and raging heart. Such language disappeared in the nineteenth century.

There is, however, a close functional relationship between Luther's references to divine blows and Ahlwardt's reliance upon race characteristics, for both Luther and Ahlwardt tried to show that the Jew could not be changed, that a Jew remained a Jew. "What God does not improve with such terrible blows, that we shall not change with words and deeds." There was some evil in the Jew that even the fires of God, burning high and hot, could not extinguish. In Ahlwardt's time these evil qualities, fixed and unchangeable, are traced to a definite cause. The Jew "cannot help himself" because his racial qualities drive him to commit antisocial acts. We can see, therefore, that even the race idea fits into a trend of thought.

Anti-Jewish racism had its beginning in the second half of the seventeenth century, when the "Jewish caricature" first appeared in cartoons.

These caricatures were the first attempt to discover racial characteristics in the Jew. However, racism acquired a "theoretical" basis only in the 1800s. The racists of the nineteenth century stated explicitly that cultural characteristics, good or bad, were the product of physical characteristics. Physical attributes did not change; hence social behavior patterns also had to be immutable. In the eyes of the anti-Semite, the Jews therefore became a "race."

The destruction of European Jewry was fundamentally the work of German perpetrators, and hence it is to them that we must devote our primary attention. What happened to the Jews cannot be understood without insight into decisions made by German officials in Berlin and in the field. Yet every day German exertions and costs were being affected by the behavior of the victims. To the extent that an agency could marshal only limited resources for a particular task, the very progress of the operation and its ultimate success depended on the mode of the Jewish response.

The Jewish posture in the face of destruction was not shaped on the spur of the moment. The Jews of Europe had been confronted by force many times in their history, and during these encounters they had evolved a set of reactions that were to remain remarkably constant over the centuries. This pattern may be portrayed by the following diagram:

Resistance	Alleviation	Evasion	Paralysis	Compliance

Preventive attack, armed resistance, and revenge were almost completely absent in Jewish exilic history. The last, and only, major revolt took place in the Roman Empire at the beginning of the second century, when the Jews were still living in compact settlements in the eastern Mediterranean region and when they were still envisaging an independent Judea. During the Middle Ages the Jewish communities no longer contemplated battle. The medieval Hebrew poets did not celebrate the martial arts. The Jews of Europe were placing themselves under the protection of constituted authority. This reliance was legal, physical, and psychological.

The psychological dependence of European Jews is illustrated by the following incident. In 1096, when the Jewish communities of Germany were warned by letters and emissaries from France that the crusaders were coming to kill them, the Jewish leadership of Mainz replied: "We are greatly concerned with your well-being. As for ourselves, there is no great cause for fear. We have not heard a word of such matters, nor has it been hinted that our lives are threatened by the sword." Soon the crusaders came, "battalion after battalion," and struck at the Jews of Speyer, Worms,

Mainz, and other German cities. More than eight hundred years later, a president of the Jewish council in Holland was to say: "The fact that the Germans had perpetrated atrocities against Polish Jews was no reason for thinking that they behave [sic] in the same way toward Dutch Jews, firstly because the Germans had always held Polish Jews in disrepute, and secondly because in the Netherlands, unlike Poland, they had to sit up and take notice of public opinion." In the Netherlands, as in Poland to the east, Jewry was subjected to annihilation.

For the Diaspora Jews, acts of armed opposition had become isolated and episodic. Force was not to be a Jewish strategy again until Jewish life was reconstituted in a Jewish state. During the catastrophe of 1933–45 the instances of opposition were small and few. Above all, they were, whenever and wherever they occurred, actions of last (never first) resort.[1]

On the other hand, alleviation attempts were typical and instantaneous responses by the Jewish community. Under the heading of alleviation are included petitions, protection payments, ransom arrangements, anticipatory compliance, relief, rescue, salvage, reconstruction—in short, all those activities designed to avert danger or, in the event that force has already been used, to diminish its effects. Let us give a few illustrations.

The ancient city of Alexandria, Egypt, was divided into five districts: α, ß, δ, γ, and ε. The Jews were heavily concentrated in the Delta (waterfront section), but they had residences also in other parts of town. In A.D. 38, Emperor Caligula wanted to be worshipped as a half-god. The Jews refused to pay him the desired respect. Thereupon, riots broke out in Alexandria. The Jews were driven into the Delta, and the mob took over abandoned apartments. Equality of rights was temporarily abolished, the food supply to the Delta was cut off, and all exits were sealed. From time to time, a centurion of Roman cavalry would enter Jewish homes on the pretext of searching for arms. Under these conditions, which have a peculiarly modern flavor, the Jews sent a delegation to Rome to petition Emperor Caligula for relief. The delegation included the famous philosopher Philo, who disputed about the matter in Rome with the anti-Jewish public figure Apion. This is one of the earliest examples of Jewish petition diplomacy. More than nineteen hundred years later, in 1942, a delegation of Bulgarian Jews petitioned for a similar purpose: the Jews were attempting to ward off ejection from their homes.

Sometimes the Jews attempted to buy protection with money. In 1384, when much Jewish blood was flowing in Franken, the Jews sought to ransom themselves. Arrangements for payment were made with speed. The city of Nuremberg collected the enormous sum of 80,000 guilders. King Wenzel got his share of 15,000 guilders from that amount. The representatives of the king, who participated in negotiations with other cities, received 4,000 guilders. Net profit to the city: over 60,000 guilders, or 190,000 thaler. The Jews in Nazi-occupied Europe, from the Netherlands to the Caucasus, made identical attempts to buy safety from death with money and valuables.

One of the most sagacious alleviation reactions in the Jewish arsenal was anticipatory compliance. The victim, sensing danger, combatted it by initiating a conciliatory response *before* being confronted by open threats. He therefore gave in to a demand on his own terms. An example of such a maneuver was the effort of European Jewish communities before 1933 to bring about a significant shift in the Jewish occupational structure from commerce and law to engineering, skilled labor, and agricultural work. This movement, which in Germany was known as occupational redistribution, was prompted by a hope that in their new economic role the Jews were going to be less conspicuous, less vulnerable, and less subject to the criticism of unproductiveness. Another illustration of anticipation is the self-restraint by Jewish firms of pre-1933 Germany in the hiring of Jewish personnel. Jewish enterprises had already become the employers of most Jewish wage earners, but now some companies instituted quotas to avoid an even greater manifestation of such Jewishness. Several years later, in Nazi-dominated Europe, Jewish councils spent many hours trying to anticipate German requirements and orders. The Germans, they reasoned, would not be concerned about the impact of a particular economic measure on those Jews who were least capable of shouldering another burden, whereas the councils might at least try to protect the weakest and neediest Jews from harmful effects. In this vein, the Jewish Council of Warsaw considered confiscating Jewish belongings wanted by the Germans, and for the same reason the council devised a system for drafting Jewish labor, with provisions exempting well-to-do Jews for a fee in order that the money might be used to make payments to families of poorer Jews who were working without wages for German agencies.

The alleviations that followed disaster were developed to a very high degree in the Jewish community. Relief, rescue, and salvage were old Jewish institutions. The relief committees and subcommittees formed by "prominent" Jews, which are so typical of the United Jewish Appeal machinery today, were commonplace in the nineteenth century. Already during the 1860s, collections for Russian Jews were conducted in Germany on a fairly large scale. Reconstruction—that is to say, the rebuilding of Jewish life, whether in new surroundings or, after abatement of persecutions in the old home—has been a matter of automatic adjustment for hundreds of years. Reconstruction is identical with the continuity of Jewish life. The bulk of any general Jewish history book is devoted to the story of the constant shifts, the recurring readjustments, the endless rebuilding of the Jewish community. The years after 1945 were marked by one of the largest of these reconstructive efforts.

Next in our scale is the reaction of evasion, of flight. In the diagram the evasive reaction is not marked as strongly as the alleviation attempts. By this we do not mean the absence of flight, concealment, and hiding in the Jewish response pattern. We mean, rather, that the Jews have placed less hope, less expectation and less reliance on these devices. It is true that the Jews have always wandered from country to country, but they have rarely done so because the restrictions of a regime became too burdensome. Jews have migrated chiefly for two reasons: expulsion and economic depression. Jews have rarely run from a pogrom. They have lived through it. The Jewish tendency has been not to run from but to survive with anti-Jewish regimes. It is a fact, now confirmed by many documents, that the Jews made an attempt to live with Hitler. In many cases they failed to escape while there was still time and, more often still, they failed to step out of the way when the killers were already upon them.

There are moments of impending disaster when almost any conceivable action will only make suffering worse or bring final agonies closer. In such situations the victims may lapse into paralysis. The reaction is barely overt, but in 1941 a German observer noted the symptomatic fidgeting of the Jewish community in Galicia as it awaited death, between shocks of killing operations, in "nervous despair." Among Jews outside the destruction arena, a passive stance manifested itself as well. In 1941 and 1942, just when mass killings began, Jews all over the world looked on helplessly as Jewish populations of cities and entire countries vanished.

The last reaction on the scale is compliance. To the Jews compliance with anti-Jewish laws or orders has always been equivalent to survival. The restrictions were petitioned against and sometimes evaded, but when these attempts were unsuccessful, automatic compliance was the normal course of action. Compliance was carried to the greatest lengths and in the most drastic situations. In Frankfurt, on September 1, 1614, a mob under the leadership of a certain Vincenz Fettmilch attacked the Jewish quarter in order to kill and plunder. Many Jews fled to the cemetery. There they huddled together and prayed, dressed in the ritual shrouds of the dead and waiting for the killers. This example is particularly pertinent, because the voluntary assembly at graves was repeated many times during the Nazi killing operations of 1941.

The Jewish reactions to force have always been alleviation and compliance. We shall note the reemergence of this pattern time and again. However, before we pass on, it should be emphasized again that the term "Jewish reactions" refers only to ghetto Jews. This reaction pattern was born in the ghetto and it will die there. It is part and parcel of ghetto life. It applies to *all* ghetto Jews—assimilationists and Zionists, the capitalists and the socialists, the unorthodox and the religious.

One other point has to be understood. The alleviation-compliance response dates, as we have seen, to pre-Christian times. It has its beginnings with the Jewish philosophers and historians Philo and Josephus, who bargained with the Romans on behalf of Jewry and who cautioned the Jews not to attack, in word or deed, any other people. The Jewish reaction pattern assured the survival of Jewry during the Church's massive conversion drive. The Jewish policy once more assured to the embattled community a foothold and a chance for survival during the periods of expulsion and exclusion.

If, therefore, the Jews have always played along with an attacker, they have done so with deliberation and calculation, in the knowledge that their policy would result in least damage and least injury. The Jews knew that measures of destruction were self-financing or even profitable up to a certain point but that beyond that limit they could be costly. As one historian put it: "One does not kill the cow one wants to milk." In the Middle Ages the Jews carried out vital economic functions. Precisely in the usury so much complained of by Luther and his contemporaries, there was an important catalyst for the development of a more complex economic system. In modern times, too, Jews have pioneered in trade, in the professions, and in the arts. Among some Jews the conviction grew that Jewry was "indispensable."

In the early 1920s Hugo Bettauer wrote a fantasy novel entitled *Die Stadt ohne Juden* (The City without Jews). This highly significant novel, published only eleven years before Hitler came to power, depicts an expulsion of the Jews from Vienna. The author shows how Vienna cannot get along without its Jews. Ultimately, the Jews are recalled. That was the mentality of Jewry, and of Jewish leadership, on the eve of the destruction process. When the Nazis took over in 1933, the old Jewish reaction pattern set in again, but this time the results were catastrophic. The German bureaucracy was not slowed by Jewish pleading; it was not stopped by Jewish indispensability. Without regard to cost, the bureaucratic machine, operating with accelerating speed and ever-widening destructive effect, proceeded to annihilate the European Jews. The Jewish community, unable to switch to resistance, increased its cooperation with the tempo of the German measures, thus hastening its own destruction.

We see, therefore, that both perpetrators and victims drew upon their age-old experience in dealing with each other. The Germans did it with success. The Jews did it with disaster.

NOTE

1   From 1789 Jews had gained military experience in the armies of continental Europe. In 1794 and 1831 they had fought in their own detachments on the side of Polish forces in Warsaw. During 1903–04 Jewish self-defense units, armed with clubs, confronted drunken mobs invading the Jewish quarters of several Russian cities. Yet these experiences, often cited in literature, were limited precedents. The Jewish soldiers of the German or Austrian armies did not wear a Jewish uniform. The Jewish detachments in Warsaw fought as

residents of Poland for a Polish cause. The self-defense units in Russia did not challenge the Russian state. Even so, it is noteworthy that the death camp revolts in Treblinka and Sobibór were planned by Jewish inmates who had been officers, that the principal ghetto rising took place in Warsaw, and that Jewish partisan activity was concentrated in parts of the occupied USSR.

2

PSYCHIATRY, GERMAN SOCIETY AND THE NAZI "EUTHANASIA" PROGRAMME

Michael Burleigh

The history of the German medical profession's complicity in the crimes committed by the Nazi regime has been written from many perspectives. Initially, it was common to speak of such monsters as Dr. Mengele and his horrifying medical "experiments" in Auschwitz. Later on it was discovered that the involvement of physicians in Nazi policies was anything but limited to a few cranks. It thus appeared that the profession as a whole had become polluted by Nazi thinking. Yet thanks to further research we now know that this was not a one-sided relationship. It is not just that German doctors were influenced by Nazi racial thinking, but just as much that Nazi racial thinking was derived from ideas and theories propagated by well-respected scientists. Furthermore, ideas about "racial hygiene" and "scientific racism" were not limited to Germany; indeed, they were also quite popular in such countries as Britain and the United States. The major difference was, however, that with Hitler's "seizure of power" a regime was installed in Germany that was willing, indeed increasingly obsessed with, carrying out the policies implied by such notions to their ultimate conclusion, namely, wholesale destruction of "life unworthy of life," with the willing participation of numerous doctors.

Michael Burleigh's chapter provides one illuminating aspect of this development. As he points out, post-World War I German psychiatry was concerned with finding the appropriate balance between reform of treatment and the economic cost of institutionalization. Under the Nazi regime the argument in favor of cutting costs gained further ground not least because of the mobilization of the nation for war, while eugenic arguments, already current in a more muted form in the Weimar Republic, came to dominate the public and professional discourse in the 1930s. For Burleigh, German psychiatrists both identified the potential victims of the mass sterilization and then "euthanasia" campaigns, and, in part, participated in their implementation. What makes this chapter important is that it demonstrates that murderous policies could grow from what at first sight appear to be highly rational and reasonable arguments and concerns, and that there was a fair amount of continuity between Weimar and Nazi Germany in this respect, as in many others. The psychiatrists (with some exceptions) were neither cranks nor sadists. They initially wanted to reform the system in favor of the patients, both by providing better conditions and by coming up with better methods of treatment. At the same time they felt responsible toward society as a whole, and therefore wanted to save economic resources, and were frustrated as professionals when their methods failed to cure patients. Exposed to the scientific and ideological rhetoric of eugenics and social-Darwinism, and under pressure from the Nazi regime, they reverted to a role of cleansing society from an economic burden and an allegedly racially polluting segment of the population. In the words of another scholar, Robert Jay Lifton, they were transformed from healers to killers. Those in charge of the murder of mentally handicapped people were then transferred directly to organize, administer, and carry out the genocide of the Jews. The experience they gained in the "euthanasia" campaign proved of immeasurable significance in unleashing the Holocaust.

* * *

This chapter is concerned with the complex history of the Nazi 'euthanasia' programme. In order to get this endeavour off the ground, the references are necessarily somewhat attenuated, especially with regard to the perspective of the victims.[1] It begins by establishing the position of psychiatry after the First World War, concentrating upon the interplay between economy measures and limited reform during the Weimar Republic. Each therapeutic advance (such as occupational or somatic therapies) almost immanently involved the definition of irremediable sub-groups within the already socially marginalised psychiatric constituency. Nazi policy towards psychiatric patients during the 1930s involved further economy measures, and the introduction of negative eugenic strategies, similar in kind if not degree, to those pursued in some other countries at that time. The decision to kill the mentally ill and physically disabled was taken by Hitler in order to clear the decks for war, and was justified with the aid of crude utilitarian arguments, as well as with what limited evidence there was regarding popular attitudes on these issues. Many health professionals and psychiatrists accommodated themselves to policies which a few years later became one of the components of the 'Final Solution of the Jewish Question', i.e. Hitler's long-harboured act of vengeance against the Jewish people in circumstances of war he had envisaged much earlier.[2] This approach seems to me to have the merit of setting professionals in a broader political context, not always evident in accounts which stress the contribution of intermediate 'experts' to the solution of a putative 'social question'. One should not give a variegated and murderous 'expertocracy' greater saliency in these things than it actually merits. In the case of psychiatrists, their precise contribution was to define a pool of potential victims and then, in some cases, to participate in the business of selection and murder. The decision to carry out these policies was taken by the Nazi political elite, and was bound up (as indeed was the extermination of the Jews) with their decision to go to war. In other words, these things are not solely explicable through a medico-historical perspective, however interesting that may be in terms of explaining either the inner dynamics of specific areas of policies such as the 'euthanasia' programme or a part of the mind-set responsible for them. This chapter is thus a contribution to the political, as well as the social, history of medicine. It is widely rather than narrowly focused.

In Germany, psychiatry emerged from the First World War with its already poor image as a futile, and scientifically dubious branch of medicine, sullied yet further. Vast numbers of psychiatric patients had died during wartime from a combination of hunger, disease and neglect. Assuming an average annual peacetime mortality rate of 5.5 per cent, recent studies estimate that 71,787, or about 30 per cent of the pre-war asylum population, died between 1914 and 1919 as a result of the extreme privations of war.[3] Exhausted or 'neurotic' soldiers were medically terrorised back into conflict through crude shock therapies.[4] Revolutionaries arrested after the abortive Munich Soviet were liberally diagnosed as 'psychopaths' by forensic psychiatrists.[5] Post-war austerity contributed to a decaying physical fabric in the asylums, while economic cuts affected everything from books, drugs and heating to light-bulbs and soap.

In Wilhelmine Germany, criticism of psychiatry had often come from the Right, for example from the anti-Semitic court chaplain Adolf Stöcker, and was primarily directed against psychiatry's medicalised denial of individual liberty. In the Weimar Republic, a temporarily powerful psychiatric reform movement, including former patients' groups, went on the attack, demanding enhanced patients' rights, checks on committal procedures and an effective inspectorate.[6] Other critics saw the problem rather in terms of profligacy with scarce national resources. In 1920 the lawyer Karl Binding and the psychiatrist Alfred Hoche raised the delicate question of whether a nation faced with a dire emergency could actually afford to sustain what they dubbed 'life unworthy of life', including a putatively growing reserve army of 'mental defectives'. In a controversial tract, which was essentially a search for a post-Christian, utilitarian ethics, Binding and Hoche deliberately conflated the issue of voluntary 'euthanasia' with the non-consensual killing of 'idiots' and the mentally ill; stressed the historical relativity of such notions as the 'sanctity of human life'; highlighted the objective futility of such emotions as 'pity' – 'where there is no suffering, there can also be no pity'; and emphasised the emotional and economic burden allegedly represented by 'entirely unproductive persons'.[7] The altruistic heroism of British Polar explorers, such as Greely or Scott, was invoked to justify chucking overboard 'dead ballast' from the 'Ship of Fools'. Two points about the tract were crucial. Firstly, it was symptomatic of how received Judaeo-Christian or humanitarian values were breaking down, with concern for narrow or wider collectivities, such as the good of a class, the economy, race or nation usurping respect for the rights and value of the individual. Secondly, it argued that in emergency wartime circumstances, where the healthy were making enormous sacrifices, one could justify the 'sacrifice' of 'not merely absolutely valueless but negatively valued existences'.

Faced with such variegated assaults upon their activities, German psychiatrists began to think more kindly of a handful of farsighted reformers in their own midst who had hitherto been cold-shouldered. It was a question of maintaining institutional relevance through anticipatory reformist initiatives, rather than passively awaiting what unsympathetic and cost-conscious governments might do instead. Two rather remarkable men, Gustav Kolb and Hermann Simon, had long been advocating breaching the walls between asylums and the wider society, and between sickness and the world of work.[8] Their liberal recommendations found a ready response from Weimar governments obsessed with cutting costs. Patients were discharged into the arms of a new range of urban out-patient clinics or perambulatory social psychiatrists in rural areas. One can see the economic advantages of this policy: the annual overheads of an out-patient clinic established in Munich in 1924, which by 1930 was seeing over 1,000 clients, were 2,000 RM a year, whereas it cost 1,277 RM to keep one patient for a year in Munich's Eglfing-Haar asylum.[9] However, patients in asylums also were not free from the attentions of the reformers. Depressed by the effects of long-term institutionalisation in environments effectively bereft of therapy, Hermann Simon decided to use occupational therapy to engender self-satisfaction and hence repress the depressed or excitable moods which resulted from enforced idleness. Soon, asylums were humming with patient activity, with both the complexity of the work performed, and hence the degree of freedom and responsibility enjoyed, being the objective indicators of recovery. In many asylums, up to 80 per cent of patients did some form of work, which made the asylums largely self-sufficient or capable of generating modest surpluses. Judging by the flood of articles devoted to community care and occupational therapy published in the professional journals in the 1920s, psychiatry began to be a more optimistic profession.

Inevitably, there was a downside to these developments. Firstly, as psychiatrists followed their discharged patients out into the wider world, they inevitably encountered hitherto unknown ranges of 'abnormality'. What passed before them in the asylums was literally the tip of an iceberg. Being of an increasingly hereditarian cast of mind, they began to construct genealogies of the patients' families.[10] Instead of addressing themselves to questions concerning the socio-economic environment, which in fact they were powerless to affect, they opted for the control function of registering widespread deviance in primitive data banks. The sheer scale of illness they encountered engendered a certain pessimism, and hence enhanced their susceptibility to fashionable and radical eugenicist solutions. Since experience taught that people they deemed degenerate or feckless could not be counselled into voluntary low rates of reproduction, many psychiatrists began to think in terms of compulsory sterilisation. This would enable the person to return to the productive process without risk of reproductive damage ensuing to the collective biological substance of the race or nation, in itself a striking retreat from individual-centred medicine.[11]

Secondly, the widespread introduction of occupational therapy in asylums increasingly meant that patients' recoveries were measured in terms of their economic productivity. Unfortunately, not all patients were capable of rolling cigars, weaving baskets, running errands or answering the telephone. Each asylum therefore had a quantity of 'incurables' languishing in unproductive hebetude, and conditions were often parlous. The adoption of occupational therapy implicitly meant separating the able-bodied and willing from the therapy-resistant chaff. In other words, these reforms were contributing to the creation of a psychiatrically defined sub-class within a group of people already consigned to the margins of society. Long before the National Socialist government appeared on the scene, some psychiatrists advocated, or countenanced, killing this permanent reminder of the limits of their own therapeutic capacities and permanent burden upon the nation's scant resources. This included some of those responsible for running ecclesiastical charitable networks, whose slippery theological justification of such a course of action was that the artificial maintenance of such forms of life represented as much of an interference in God's dominion as the artificial acceleration of death through 'mercy killing'.[12] The Depression, with its renewed conflicts over division of the social product, again raised questions about the utility of provision in the psychiatric sector. Psychiatrists responded to the state's cost-cutting demands by advocating a two-tier system consisting of intensive therapy for acute cases, and minimal provision for the chronic, coupled with sterilisation of discharged patients to lessen the subsequent eugenic damage.[13] Thus 1933 did not mark a decisive break; most of the policies of the Nazi period were more or less apparent in the Janus-faced, and crisis-ridden, health and welfare apparatus of the Weimar Republic.

None the less, the advent of a National Socialist government had dire direct and indirect consequences for the asylum population. Asylums became freak-shows, with thousands of members of Nazi formations being given tours to illustrate the inherent uselessness of the patients. Between 1933 and 1939, 21,000 people trooped through Eglfing-Haar, including 6,000 members of the SS, some of whom came out recommending setting up machine guns at the entrance to mow down the inmates.[14] Reflecting a general brutalisation of thought and feeling, Party newspapers and journals such as the *Völkische Beobachter* or *Schwarze Korps* dilated upon the Goya-esque scenes in the asylums, and advocated killing the mentally ill, often coupling this with heroic instances of 'mercy killing' carried out by individuals.[15] A political movement which fetishised the mindless and narcissistic activism of youth almost axiomatically entailed the neglect of the elderly and frail, let alone the mentally ill or physically disabled. The young were reportedly more crass and vicious in their attitudes towards these groups than older sections of the population.[16]

With the regional health authorities increasingly in the hands of men such as Fritz Bernotat in Wiesbaden or Walter 'Bubi' Schultze in Munich who explicitly advocated killing mental patients, it is hardly surprising that conditions in the asylums soon deteriorated sharply. Specialist facilities were closed, and patients were removed from the private or religious sectors, and crammed into cheaper state institutions to save money and increase control. An asylum like Eichberg in the Rheingau had 793 patients in 1934; 1,236 by 1940. The doctor–patient ratio deteriorated from 1:162 to 1:300 between 1935 and 1938.[17] In some institutions they were as high as 1:500 which made basic care, i.e. hygiene, watering and feeding, let alone any treatment, totally impossible.[18] The meagre sums expended upon patient food were cut, for example, at Haina from 0.69 RM per day in 1932 to 0.54 RM in 1935.[19] This was against a background of general economic recovery. Enthusiastic lower-class National Socialist administrators replaced disinterested boards of upper-class philanthropists in the running of institutions such as the Idstein reformatory, gradually marginalising medical control of what went on in these institutions.[20] With trained doctors no longer necessarily in charge, the economic efficiency of 'the works' became the primary goal. Many of the psychiatrists – and it had always tended to recruit the dross of the medical profession anyway – were SS members, inherently antagonistic towards their patients. Below them, a host of thoroughly unsuitable people, armed with Party cards and Storm Trooper (SA) membership, flooded into nursing in order to escape the dole queues. Independent inspectors, some of whom deplored the fact that patients were sleeping on straw on the floor or going about virtually naked, and who objected to the brutal language used by senior health administrators such as Bernotat, were simply debarred from further visits.[21] In sum, the public presumption that a person was being entrusted to the safe-keeping of an asylum could no longer be taken as self-evident.

Apart from the on-going deterioration of general conditions, psychiatric patients were directly affected by the Law for the Prevention of Hereditarily Diseased Progeny, which sanctioned compulsory sterilisation for a range of putatively hereditary illnesses. Of course, Germany was not unique in adopting these dubious strategies, although it rapidly exceeded competitor eugenic enthusiasts in other nations in terms of numbers affected by these policies. Psychiatrists were among those statutorily responsible for initiating the procedures eventuating in a person's sterilisation, and indeed, often sat on the 220 local Hereditary Health Courts which made the final decisions. Again, this close, 'sweetheart' arrangement between those who initiated sterilisations and those who authorised them was not unique to Germany. At this time, the hereditary character of the illnesses concerned was as much a declaration of faith, as opposed to a matter of scientific certitude, as it is today. As the later 'euthanasia' enthusiast Professor Carl Schneider put it in 1931 during the Protestant Inner Mission's conference on eugenics at Treysa, sterilisation was 'a fashion without clear foundations'.[22] This did not stop the conference from officially adopting these negative eugenic strategies. Leaving aside the fact that one genuinely hereditary illness – haemophilia – was actually omitted from the Law, the prefix 'hereditary' was dropped from schizophrenia in order to sterilise those where the cause was exogenous, while reformed drunks or people with low alcohol tolerance who imbibed relatively small quantities of drink, were sterilised as 'chronic alcoholics', on the grounds that alcoholism reflected some underlying 'asocial or psychopathic disorder', neither of which separate – and equally elastic – conditions were specified in this legislation. Nor did the courts confine themselves to the people who actually passed before them. For example, after he had ordered the sterilisation of a young woman, the Kaufbeuren psychiatrist Hermann Pfannmüller, who was also a judge in the court at Kempten, spent a week isolating twenty-one additional 'degenerates' in her family, recommending the sterilisation of ten of them as being 'highly urgent since the danger of reproduction appeared imminent'.[23] In a thoroughly pernicious development, school teachers were encouraged to set their pupils the task of constructing their own family trees, with a view to helping identify any defective members, while mayors reported single mothers, primarily to curtail the costs involved in looking after their illegitimate children.[24]

Apart from the permanent psychological damage sterilisation caused those affected, it was not uncommon for people to die on the operating table or to commit suicide before or afterwards. This was particularly true of women, in an evolving political climate which set great store upon eugenically fit, prolific, motherhood. The regime's remorseless propaganda campaign to sell these policies inevitably entailed stoking up mass resentment against the 'burden' represented by the asylum population. Propaganda films regularly disputed the human 'personality' of the mentally ill and mentally handicapped through talk of 'beings' and 'creatures'; deliberately and indiscriminately conflated dangerous criminals – notably sex offenders and murderers – with the insane; and advocated a reversion to Social-Darwinian elimination of the weak and the abandonment of a counter-selective, and eugenically deleterious, welfare apparatus. In these films, patients were degraded and stigmatised as an exponential threat to the hereditary health of the racial collective, sometimes with much stress upon the allegedly above-average proportion of Jewish psychiatric cases.[25] Being a totalitarian dictatorship, there was no possibility of alternative views being expressed, as was the case with Hollywood, which produced films actively opposed to the activities of American eugenicists.

From the mid-1930s, what had once more become a very desolate psychiatric landscape, was temporarily and partially illuminated by the arrival of a new range of somatic therapies: insulin coma, cardiazol and electro-convulsive therapy, all of which were enthusiastically adopted during the 1930s.[26] Accounts of their use often included detailed 'before and after' case histories, and the testimonies of people who felt miraculously disburdened from isolating and oppressive illnesses. For example, a young woman treated for persecution mania with a combined course of insulin and cardiazol wrote to her relatives:

> Now I can write to you as the Hilde of old! Imagine, Mummy, Saturday evening in bed, it just dawned following a conversation with the others. Naturally I am eating again, for not eating was just

50

part of the persecution mania. You cannot imagine the feeling of being freed from every fear. One is born again so to speak. Now I look forward to Sunday and to seeing you dear Mummy. It should have clicked together before, then you would have noticed something, but none the less, we should thank our lucky stars. How are you then? I am so very happy.[27]

Notwithstanding the incidences of fractured bones, memory loss or spinal damage, a new optimism was abroad, for with these therapies, psychiatrists could argue that they actually cured people.

But paradoxically, these limited psychiatric successes with acute cases, only served once again to heighten professional embarrassment *vis-à-vis* that proportion of patients for whom they could do nothing. Acute cases could be treated (or exploited) with occupational therapy or these new somatic techniques. Any danger the person might represent to the hereditary health of the collective could be neutralised through compulsory sterilisation, or voluntary sterilisation as a condition of their release. But this still left the problem of the refractory and incurable, upon whom these therapies made no impact. Responding to a report from government auditors in November 1939, Director Hermann Pfannmüller of Eglfing-Haar commented: 'The problem of whether to maintain this patient material under the most primitive conditions or to eradicate it has now become a subject for serious discussion once more.'[28] Selective therapeutic intensity had once again pushed a certain patient constituency to the margins of an already marginal group, but this time, in a political climate where the masters of the state had no moral inhibitions about murder, and wished to clear the decks for the war they were bent on waging. Although it is difficult to reconstruct the thought processes of men who were seriously irrational, Hitler seems to have aired the view in 1935 that he would use the cover of war to kill psychiatric patients. The idea of annihilating the Jews should any war-like venture on his part escalate to the point of global conflict, and hence likely defeat, predated this.

Before turning to the 'euthanasia' programme, one final element needs to be introduced into this discussion, namely the extent to which these policies were consensual. For with this subject, matters are a little more complicated than the conventional triad of victims, bystanders and perpetrators. Most discussions of National Socialist justifications for their policies quite reasonably alight upon the influence of Binding and Hoche's utilitarian tract, without noticing that the Nazis very often refer to an author who was that tract's most passionate critic. In 1925, Ewald Meltzer, the director of the Katherinenhof asylum for backward juveniles at Grosshennersdorf in Saxony, published an extremely powerful critique of Binding and Hoche, which stressed both the joy handicapped people took in life, and the altruistic sentiments caring for them engendered in others, while condemning the inflationary and materialistic character of the arguments used by the two professors.[29]

Meltzer decided to carry out a poll of the views on 'euthanasia' held by the parents of his charges. To his obvious surprise, some 73 per cent of the 162 respondents said that they would approve 'the painless curtailment of the life of [their] child if experts had established that it is suffering from incurable idiocy'. Many of the 'yes' respondents said that they wished to offload the burden represented by an 'idiotic' child, with some of them expressing the wish that this be done surreptitiously, in a manner which anticipated later National Socialist practice. Only twenty of the forty-three 'no' respondents in fact rejected all of Meltzer's four propositions – some of the 'no' group actually consented to their child's death in the event that it was orphaned – it thus being a minority who would not sanction the death of their child under any circumstances.[30] Surveying National Socialist propaganda on these issues, it is thus not surprising that Meltzer should be as frequently cited as Binding and Hoche. The SS Security Service (SD) reports carried out later in connection with the film *Ich klage an* would also reveal that attitudes were far from clear cut on these issues, despite the fact that by that time they were less academic than they were when Meltzer conducted his survey.[31] Meltzer himself was not entirely on the side of the angels, for in 1937 he publicly acknowledged that there could be conditions of national emergency, when because of food shortages or the need for bed-space for military casualties, 'the patient too must pay his dues to the Fatherland' through some form of involuntary 'mercy killing'.[32] These circumstances arose two years later, and notionally involved the issue of 'euthanasia'.

The origins of the Nazi 'euthanasia' programme were indeed partially bound up with requests for 'mercy killing'. The reason Hitler decided to assign the task to the Chancellory of the Führer was not simply that this small prerogative agency could act secretly outside the normative channels of government, but also that the Chancellory of the Führer handled incoming petitions which included requests for 'euthanasia' from the population. These came, *inter alia*, from a woman dying of cancer, from a man blinded and severely injured after falling into a cement mixer, and from the parents of a handicapped infant called Knauer, languishing blind and without a leg and part of an arm in a Leipzig clinic.[33]

Hitler despatched Karl Brandt, the emergency accident surgeon attached to his retinue, to Leipzig to authorise the death of this child. He then commissioned Brandt and Philipp Bouhler, the head of the Chancellory of the Führer, to make similar authorisations in the future.[34] A panel of paediatric specialists – all of whom believed it was time to jettison the Judaeo-Christian ethical heritage based on the doctrine of the sanctity of human life – made the decision, with the children concerned sent 'on hold' to one of several special paediatric clinics. These promised the parents the most up-to-date treatment, with the revealing rider that this might entail serious risks.[35] Parents who had exhausted every avenue, or who were worn down by having to cope with several children, or who simply did not want some sort of eugenic 'taint' on their family pedigree, handed over their children, often in the knowledge that they would not survive the promised treatment.[36] Welfare agencies used coercive powers to compel single parents to relinquish their children.

The latter were killed by a combination of starvation and lethal medication. Some of the nurses involved may have found the work disturbing, but they also thought it right to 'release unfortunate creatures from their suffering', and appreciated the regular bonus payments. The doctors were all volunteers. That one could say 'no' is clearly illustrated by the case of Dr Friedrich Hölzel, who used the opportunity of a vacation spoiled by rain, to write to Pfannmüller declining the job of running the paediatric clinic at Eglfing. Although he approved of these policies, Hölzel felt that it was another matter to carry them out in person, a distinction which reminded him of 'the difference which exists between a judge and executioner'. He thought he was too weak, and too concerned with helping his patients, to be able to 'carry this out as a systematic policy after cold-blooded deliberation'.[37] Pfannmüller never pressed him any further on the matter. In total, as many as 6,000 children were killed in this programme, with the age range being quietly raised to encompass adolescents.

Hitler's wartime authorisation of an adult 'euthanasia' programme was conceived as an economy measure, a means of creating emergency bed-space, and hostels for ethnic German repatriates from Russia and eastern Europe, which anticipates and mirrors the linkages between 'resettlement' and murder later evident in the Holocaust.[38] These were not chimerical, futuristic or metaphorical goals merely designed to remobilise the move-ment's flagging dynamism, but a series of definite aims, coldly determined in advance after a great deal of co-ordination between like-minded indi-viduals. In the eastern areas of the Reich, SS units under Eimann and Lange were sub-contracted to shoot psychiatric patients in a parallel operation. The Chancellory of the Führer established an elaborate covert bureaucracy based at Tiergartenstrasse 4 (hence the code-name 'Aktion T-4'), whose task was to organise the registration, selection, transfer and murder of a previously calculated target group of 70,000 people, including chronic schizophrenics, epileptics and long-stay patients. This apparatus was run by a group of economists, agronomists, lawyers and businessmen, with an expanded pool of academics and psychiatrists, under Werner Heyde and from 1941 Paul Nitsche, whose task was to handle the medical side of mass murder.[39]

Together, this odd assortment of highly educated, morally dulled, humanity set about registering and selecting victims; finding asylums to serve as extermination centres; establishing an effective means; and last but not least, a staff of people willing and able to commit mass murder. Both Herbert Linden, the desk officer responsible for state asylums in the Ministry of the Interior, and his regional equivalents, such as Walter 'Bubi' Schultze in Munich or Ludwig Sprauer in Stuttgart, proved co-operative since they had been advocating such policies for several years anyway. These men either identified suitable asylums, such as Grafeneck, or recommended doctors, orderlies and nurses whose track record and level of objectified ideological commitment singled them out as potential T-4 material.[40] Heyde volunteered the names of former students. The SS, which for various reasons remained at one remove from these policies, provided seasoned hard-men who could cope with the physicality of mass murder. Teams of these people were despatched to six killing centres. The doctors who monopolised killing were given perfunctory briefing sessions in Berlin, and then gradually inducted into murder, progressing from observing the procedures to carrying them out themselves. Most of them were quite young, socially insecure and hugely impressed by major academic names (de Crinis, Heyde, Carl Schneider, etc.) and grand places (the Chancellory of the Führer), that is, the usual accompaniments of petit bourgeois academic ambition. Their narrow professional training added no element of moral inhibition.[41] The nurses and orderlies were products of a professional and societal culture of obedience, and in addition, often had proven records of ideological commitment, or believed in the moral correctness of 'euthanasia' killings, especially on the grounds that monies allegedly squandered on the mentally ill in 'luxury' asylums, could be used to improve public housing.[42]

Registration forms were completed on every patient, and despatched via T-4 to assessors. Many asylum directors, who were unclear concerning the ultimate purpose of the forms, made the fatal mistake of deliberately misrepresenting a patient's capacity to work in order not to lose valuable workers as a consequence of what they took to be a survey of essential labour. Low or merely mechanical productivity, irremediable illness, or the duration of institutionalisation sufficed effectively to sign a person's death warrant. In other words, the pool of victims was drawn from the sub-class created earlier by the psychiatric reformers. The T-4 assessors, such as the ubiquitous Pfannmüller, received batches of 200 to 300 forms at a time, and were remunerated on a piecework basis. This probably accounts for the diagnostic virtuosity of such psychiatric Stakhanovites as Dr Josef Schreck, who completed 15,000 forms single-handedly in a month.[43] On the basis of these forms, groups of patients were taken from the asylums by the Community Patients Transport Service, either directly to their deaths in the gas chambers of one of six killing centres, or to proximate holding asylums, whose purpose was to confuse anxious relatives, and to stagger the burden on the crematoria. An elaborate system of deceit took care of every angle, from faking the cause of death, to lying about when and where it had occurred in order not to arouse suspicions in places where several persons happened to have been in the same asylum.

These killings inevitably meant contacts between T-4 and a host of private, state and religious asylums. Indeed half of the victims of 'Aktion T-4' came from asylums and homes run by the two main ecclesiastical welfare networks, the Protestant Inner Mission and the Roman Catholic Caritas Association. The fact that 1,911 of the 2,137 inhabitants of the Protestant Neuendettelsau asylums in Franconia were taken away and murdered comes as no surprise, given that as early as 1937 the medical director, Dr Rudolph Boeckh, said in a lecture to the local National Socialist German Workers' Party (NSDAP) group, that 'idiots' were 'a travesty of humankind' who deserved to be 'returned to the Creator'.[44] Indeed, some Inner Mission asylums, such as Scheurn in Hesse-Nassau, actually acted as intermediary holding centres for patients en route to Hadamar, while Protestant nursing sisters worked in Bernburg throughout the period when about 20,000 people were murdered there. Some asylums tried to subvert the operation by delaying completion of the forms, once they realised or heard through the grapevine of their malign purpose. The fact that one of those who went to great lengths to rewrite diagnoses in a way less harmful to the patients, Dr Karsten Jaspersen of Bethel Sarepta, was himself a Nazi 'old fighter' suggests that political affiliation was not necessarily a guide to how individuals behaved in these circumstances.[45] A few asylums tried to hide vulnerable individuals or arrange for their families to take them home with them. However, discharge depended upon the willingness of families to take them in, the response sometimes being that there was no more room in the inn.[46] In the absence of co-operation from families, most asylums contented themselves with the fact that they had haggled over the life of this or that patient, for T-4 were clever enough to countenance a degree of plea bargaining. In the case of the network of Bodelschwingh asylums at Bielefeld, the eminence of both the director and some of the patients, including Göring's brother-in-law (according to Heyde he was 'definitely a case for euthanasia'), meant that T-4 sanctioned the use of Bethel's own 'in-house' criteria for selection.[47] The fact that individual churchmen, notably Bishop Galen of Münster, protested against these policies (over a year after he was informed about them by, *inter alios*, Dr Karsten Jaspersen) has received more attention than the fact that T-4 obviously solicited a justificatory memorandum from an academic Roman Catholic theologian before they commenced operations. More damagingly, the Roman Catholic hierarchy entered into negotiations with T-4 to secure an 'opt-out clause' for Catholic asylum staff and the last sacraments for Catholic victims, negotiations which were only broken off when the Church's chief negotiator, Bishop Wienken, went so 'native' in his dealings with T-4 as seriously to embarrass his superiors.[48] One should bear in mind the fact that the Roman Catholic Church's concern with administering the last sacraments was often coupled with its priests' refusal to give Christian burial to the ashes of victims of the 'euthanasia' programme, on the grounds that they had been cremated.

In total, T-4 murdered over 70,000 people, with many of them entering a gas chamber equipped with a towel and a toothbrush. A final report translated the monthly murder rate into graphic form, while precisely enumerating how much money or which commodities, such as butter, bread, coffee or marmalade had been saved through the 'disinfection' of 70,273 persons, figures whose monetary equivalents were then extrapolated down to 1951.[49]

Following a cessation of mass gassings in August 1941, the T-4 medical assessors were turned loose on the inmates of concentration camps, where under 'Aktion 14f13' they proceeded to 'select' persons whom the SS deemed to be 'sick', or people whose race or record they disapproved of.[50] There is no evidence that the doctors involved were even conscious of having stepped across the threshold from the medical into the infernal. That same autumn, Viktor Brack, the economist who ran the T-4 operation, had an interview with Himmler, who had once employed him as a driver. Himmler allegedly said that

> Hitler had some time ago given him the order for the extermination
> of the Jews. He said that preparations had already been made, and
> I think that he used the expression that for reasons of camouflage
> one would have to work as quickly as possible.[51]

The T-4 staff were to become one of the separate groups involved in the various competitive, quasi-experimental pushes designed to solve the 'Jewish Question'. As experts in mass gassing, they were given the lion's share of the operation, apart from Hoess's murder factory at Auschwitz.

Some ninety-two T-4 personnel were made available by Bouhler to the Higher SS and Police Leader in Lublin, the ex-bricklayer, Odilo Globocnik.[52] With the SS 'euthanasia' veteran Herbert Lange installed at Kulmhof, this T-4 team formed the dedicated core responsible for 'Aktion Reinhard'. A motley array of former butchers, cooks, labourers, lorry drivers and policemen, including Erich Bauer, Kurt Franz, Lorenz Hackenholt, Josef Oberhauser, Franz Stangl and Christian Wirth, moved up several social notches to preside over the murder of the Jewish masses of eastern Europe and the Jewish bourgeoisie of western Europe in Belzec, Sobibor and Treblinka. While few of them were convicted psychopaths like Hoess, these men did not become extremely violent, they began like that, indefinitely deferring and evading recognition of their own awfulness through black humour and talk of production targets. Indeed, the final statistical tally, drawn up by Globocnik in December 1943, precisely enumerated the vast sums garnered in the process, as well as nearly 2,000 wagonloads of bedding, clothing and towels, and such quotidian ephemera as sunglasses, opera glasses, powder puffs, and cigarette cases.[53] Following the dismantling of these extermination camps, the T-4 men set off once again, to operate a killing centre on the Dalmatian coast at Trieste called the Risiera, after a former rice warehouse, which they used to torture and murder Jews bottlenecked en route to Auschwitz or putative partisans. About 5,000 people died there.[54]

In the old Reich, 'euthanasia' killings continued on a more decentralised basis in an extended range of asylums. The patients were killed through starvation and lethal medication. Where religious affiliations of the nursing staff made this difficult, as at Kaufbeuren-Irsee, practised T-4 murderers, such as nurse Pauline Kneissler, were sent in with the resulting mortality rates only falling in the weeks when she went away on holiday.[55] Meetings were held in the regional health ministries to sort out the comparabilities of starvation diets, with psychiatrists exchanging 'menus' consisting of nothing more than root vegetables boiled in fluid. There were no food shortages in the asylums, since most of them continued to generate considerable surpluses, surpluses which the administrators sold off at a considerable profit.[56] There is also the well-documented fact of doctors like Friedrich Mennecke of Eichberg, whose letters reveal him gourmandising his way around the country at a time when his patients were literally starving.[57] These are recorded facts about the mentality of those involved, indicative of their unselfconscious tastelessness, if of nothing else. Both this adult programme and the killing of children continued until the last days of the war.

Death was routinely visited upon anyone deemed unproductive or whose behaviour or manner irritated the staff, with patients sometimes being co-opted into killing their fellow inmates. Escape attempts or misdemeanours resulted in lethal injections or handfuls of sedatives being forced down one's throat in the dead of night. Many of the victims were foreign forced labourers, suffering from tuberculosis, as well as from mental illnesses brought about by the inhuman conditions in which they lived or worked. Killing them on the spot was deemed cheaper than repatriation.[58] Since most of them could not communicate in German, there was no attempt to find out what was wrong with them. Indeed, in its later inflationary stages, the 'euthanasia' programme encompassed homes for geriatrics and vagrants or people driven insane by Allied bombing. 'Euthanasia' killings were supplied on demand to create bed-space for civilian casualities. SD reports recently discovered in Russia reveal widespread fear among elderly people regarding geriatric homes, sanatoria , or even a routine visit to the doctor.[59]

Obviously policies, like the ones described above, which were impossible to keep secret, did nothing for the image of either asylums or psychiatry. More importantly, they were like sawing off the branch upon which one was sitting, for depopulated asylums were usually alienated for non-medical purposes. In order to counteract these unwanted tendencies, psychiatrists working for T-4 such as Paul Nitsche or Carl Schneider put forward various proposals for the 'modernisation' of psychiatry, that is using the funds saved through these killings to provide up-to-date therapies for acute cases. The more or less explicit subsidiary agenda was to build up university-based research activities, by integrating this with the neurological 'material' made available to the professors by the 'euthanasia' programme.[60] These plans were thus about reasserting professional psychiatric control over policies which were economically driven, whose effect was to put young recruits off entirely, and whose logic threatened the existence of this entire branch of medicine. They were thus a form of *ex post facto* rationalisation, a means of evading the fact that these men had in fact created conditions in the asylums which a few enlightened doctors described as a 'reversion to the psychiatry of the Middle Ages', with untended and skeletal patients lying naked in their own excrement and urine on straw sacks, and people locked alone in dark vermin-infested bunkers. Doctors bestrode the wards, not as 'modernising' idealists, but as self-styled 'soldiers' for whom the patients, particularly if they were people who spoke not a word of German, had literally become 'the enemy'.[61]

NOTES

1 Bibliographical surveys include the relevant sections of Christopher Beck (ed.), *Sozialdarwinismus, Rassenhygiene, Zwangssterilisation und Vernichtung 'lebensunwerten' Lebens* (Bonn 1992); and in English, Michael Burleigh '"Euthanasia" in the Third Reich: some Recent Literature', *Social History of Medicine*, 4 (1991), pp. 317–28. Also: F. W. Kersting, K. Teppe and B. Walter (eds.), *Nach Hadamar: Zum Verhältnis von Psychiatrie und Gesellschaft im 20. Jahrhundert* (Paderborn 1993). Fuller references to many of the issues explored in this paper may be found in my book *Death and Deliverance. 'Euthanasia' in Germany c. 1900–1945* (Cambridge 1994).
2 For this reading of the genesis of the 'Final Solution' see above all Philippe Burrin, *Hitler and the Jews* (London 1994), especially p. 38.
3 Hans-Ludwig Siemen, *Menschen blieben auf der Strecke* (Gütersloh 1987), p. 29. See also Heinz Faulstich, *Von der Irrenfürsorge zur 'Euthanasie'* (Freiburg im Breisgau 1993), p. 77.
4 Peter Riedesser and Axel Verderber, *Aufrüstung der Seelen* (Freiburg im Breisgau 1985), pp. 11ff.
5 Siegfried Grübitzsch, 'Revolutions- und Rätezeit 1918/19 aus der Sicht Deutscher Psychiater', *Psychologie & Gesellschaftskritik*, 9 (1985), pp. 35–8.
6 For an unsympathetic contemporary account of these various pressure groups see Ernst Rittershaus, *Die Irrengesetzgebung in Deutschland* (Berlin 1927).
7 Karl Binding and Alfred Hoche, *Die Freigabe der Vernichtung lebensunwerten Lebens. Ihr Mass und ihre Form* (Leipzig 1920). The tract has been thoroughly analysed by *inter alios* K. H. Hafner and R. Winau, '"Die Freigabe der Vernichtung lebensunwerten Lebens", Eine Untersuchung zu der Schrift von Karl Binding und Alfred Hoche', *Medizinisches Journal*, 9 (1974), pp. 227–54.

8 For quasi-programmatic statements see Gustav Kolb, 'Reform der Irrenpflege', *Zeitschrift für die gesamte Neurologie und Psychiatrie*, 47 (1919), pp. 137–72, and Hermann Simon, 'Aktivere Kranken-behandlung in der Irrenanstalt', *Allgemeine Zeitschrift für Psychiatrie*, 87 (1927), pp. 97–145 and 90 (1929), pp. 69–121 and 245–309.

9 Bernhard Richarz, *Heilen—Pflegen—Töten. Zur Alltagsgeschichte einer Heil- und Pflegeanstalt bis zum Ende des Nationalsozialismus* (Göttingen 1987), p. 78.

10 See Karl-Heinz Roth, '"Erbbiologische Bestandsaufhahme" – ein Aspekt ausmerzender Erfassung vor der Entfesselung des Zweiten Weltkrieges', in K.-H. Roth (ed.), *Erfassung zur Vernichtung. Von der Sozialhygiene zum 'Gesetz über Sterbehilfe'* (Berlin 1984), pp. 59ff. For an alternative interpretation see P. J. Weindling, *Health, Race and German Politics between National Unification and Nazism* (Cambridge 1989), pp. 383ff.

11 See for example the Tübingen psychiatrist Robert Gaupp's address to the September 1925 meeting of the German Psychiatric Association in Cassel, 'Die Unfruchtbarmachung geistig und sittlich Minderwertiger', *Allgemeine Zeitschrift für Psychiatrie*, 83 (1926), pp. 371–90 for a lengthy version of this line of argument.

12 Sabine Schleiermacher, 'Der Centralausschuss für die Innere Mission und die Eugenik am Vorabend des Dritten Reichs', in T. Strohm and J. Thierfelder (eds.), *Diakonie im 'Dritten Reich'* (Heidelberg 1990), p. 70. I am grateful to the author for a copy of this important article.

13 See especially Hans-Ludwig Siemen, 'Reform und Radikalisierung', in N. Frei (ed.), *Medizin und Gesundheitspolitik in der NS-Zeit* (Munich 1991), pp. 197–8.

14 Gerhard Schmidt, *Selektion in der Heilanstalt 1939–1945* (Frankfurt am Main 1983), p. 26. For an interesting discussion of how psychiatrists responded to Schmidts's work, which was written shortly after the end of the war, and only published in 1965, see Dirk Blasius, 'Das Ende der Humanität', in Walter H. Pehle (ed.), *Der historische Ort des Nationalsozialismus* (Frankfurt am Main 1990), pp. 47–51.

15 For example, 'Ein mütiger Schritt', *Das Schwarze Korps*, 11 (March 1937), p. 18.

16 This worrying aspect of the Nazi youth cult was highlighted in SD reports concerning rumours of a 'euthanasia' programme for the elderly. See Götz Aly, 'SD-Berichte zu Gerüchten über "Euthanasie"-Massnahmen gegen alte Leute', *Beiträge zur nationalsozialistischen Gesundheits- und Sozialpolitik*, 11 (1993), p. 198. I am grateful to Götz Aly for a copy of this article.

17 Horst Dickel, *'Die sind doch alle unheilbar'. Zwangssterilisation und Tötung der 'Minderwertigen' im Rheingau 1934–1945* (Wiesbaden 1988), p. 84.

18 See the extracts from the report by Professor Kleist on Weilmünster reprinted in Imperial War Museum, London CIOS File no. xxviii–50, in Leo Alexander (ed.), *Public Mental Health Practice in Germany*, Appendix 6, p. 169. The accepted ratio of doctors to patients in the 1930s was about 1:180.

19 Manfred Klüppel, *'Euthanasie' und Lebensvernichtung am Beispiel der Landesheilanstalten Haina und Merxhausen* (Kassel 1985), pp. 17–18.

20 Martin Wisskirchen, 'Idiotenanstalt–Heilerziehungsanstalt–Lazarett', in C. Schrapper and D. Sengling (eds.), *Die Idee der Bildbarkeit* (Weinheim and Munich 1988), p. 114ff.

21 This was the fate of Professor Kleist of the psychiatric clinic of the University of Frankfurt. For details of his reports see note 18 above.

22 Schleiermacher, 'Der Centralausschuss', p. 68. Given that Schneider was one of the main actors in the 'euthanasia' programme, his remarks are further illustrations of the dangers of conflating advocacy of sterilisation and 'euthanasia'.

23 Valentin Faltlhauser, 'Jahresbericht des Kreis- und Pflegeanstalt Kaufbeuren-Irsee des Jahres 1934', *Psychiatrisch-Neurologische Wochenschrift*, 37 (1935), p. 372. Pfannmüller became director of Eglfing-Haar in 1937.

24 Ibid., p. 372 for approving comments on this practice.

25 See Karl Ludwig Rost, *Sterilisation und Euthanasie im Film des 'Dritten Reiches'* (Husum 1987) for the details.

26 David Schöne and Dieter Schöne, 'Zur Entwicklung und klinischen Anwendung neuer somatischer Therapiemethoden der Psychiatrie in den 30er Jabren des 20. Jahrhunderts unter besonderer Berücksichtigung der Schocktherapien und deren Nützung in den deutschen Heil- und Pflegeanstalten', Med. Diss., University of Leipzig (1987).

27 Anton von Braunmühl, 'Die kombinierte Schock-Krampfbehandlung', *Zeitschrift für die gesamte Neurologie und Psychiatrie*, 164 (1938), pp. 72–3.

28 Staatsarchiv Munich Staatsanwaltschaften 17460/1, Trial of Hermann Pfannmüller, containing Pfannmüller's memorandum dated 1 November 1939: 'Organisations- und Wirtschaftlichkeitsprüfung bei der Heil- und Pflegeanstalt Eglfing-Haar', p. 9.

29 On Meltzer see the short piece by Jürgen Trögisch, 'Bericht über Euthanasie-Massnahmen im "Katherinenhof" Grosshennersdorf', *Fröhlich Helfen* (Berlin 1986), pp. 40ff.

30 Ewald Meltzer, *Das Problem der Abkürzung 'lebensunwerten' Lebens* (Halle 1925), pp. 87ff. for his poll.

31 Heinz Boberach (ed.), *Meldungen aus dem Reich. Die geheimen Lageberichte des Sicherheitsdienstes der SS 1938–1945* (Herrsching 1984), IX, pp. 3175–8.

32 See Ernst Klee, *'Die SA Jesu Christi'. Die Kirche im Banne Hitlers* (Frankfurt am Main 1989), p. 97.

33 Jeremy Noakes, 'Philipp Bouhler und die Kanzlei des Führers der NSDAP', in D. Rebentisch and Karl Teppe (eds.), *Verwaltung contra Menschenführung im Staat Hitlers* (Göttingen 1986), pp. 209ff.

34 Imperial War Museum, London, US. v. Karl Brandt *et al.* (1947), vol. 6, pp. 2396ff.

35 For examples of this see Klaus Bastlein, 'Die "Kinderfachabteilung" Schleswig 1941 bis 1945', ed. Arbeitskreis zur Erforschung des Nationalsozialismus in Schleswig-Holstein, *Informationen zur SchleswigHolsteinischen Zeitgeschichte*, 20 (1993), p. 39.

36 Schmidt, *Selektion in der Heilanstalt*, p. 129. Henry Friedlander's *The Origins of Nazi Genocide* (Chapel Hill 1995) simply omits evidence that the Nazi 'euthanasia' programme was, in part, a response to requests for 'mercy killing' from distressed individuals or their relatives.

37 Imperial War Museum, London, US. v. Karl Brandt *et al.* (1947), vol. 4, p. 1549 (NO–1313), Friedrich Hölzel to Hermann Pfannmüller dated 20 August 1940.

38 Christopher Browning, 'Nazi Resettlement Policy and the Search for a Solution to the Jewish Question, 1939–1941', in his *Paths to Genocide* (Cambridge 1992), especially pp. 7ff.

39 For the details see Götz Aly (ed.), *Aktion T-4 1939–1945. Die 'Euthanasie'-Zentrale in der Tiergartenstrasse 4*, 2nd edition (Berlin 1989); for a shorter English account see Henry Friedlander, 'Euthanasia and the Final Solution', in David Cesarani (ed.), *The Final Solution* (London 1994), pp. 51ff.

40 Karl Morlok, *Wo bringt ihr uns hin?* (Stuttgart 1990), pp. 7–10 for how T-4 alighted upon Grafeneck; Zentrale Stelle des Landesjustizverwaltungen (Ludwigsburg), hereafter (ZSL), 'Euthanasie', Bra-Bz, interrogation of Viktor Brack dated 21 May 1948, p. 2 for the role of Linden in recommending doctors.

41 For an example of the outlook of these doctors, see Hessische Hauptstaatsarchiv, Wiesbaden (hereafter HHStAW), Abt. 461 Nr. 32061, Hadamar
   Trial, vol. 7, testimony of Bodo Gorgass dated 24 February 1947, pp. 1ff.
42 For example Paul R. (a former Hadamar orderly) in an interview with the
   author in September 1990: author's archive, tape transcript, p. 58.
43 Christina Vanya and Martin Vogt, 'Zu melden sind samtliche Patienten . . .',
   in Vanya (ed.), *Euthanasie in Hadamar* (Kassel 1991), p. 29.
44 Hans Rössler, 'Die "Euthanasie" – Diskussion in Neuendettelsau 1937–1939',
   Zeitschrift für bayerischen Kirchengeschichte, 55 (1986), pp. 204ff.; Ernst Klee, *'Die
   SA Jesu Christi'. Die Kirche im Banne Hitlers* (Frankfurt am Main 1989), no. 40,
   pp. 180–1 for these details.
45 J. Thierfelder, 'Karsten Jaspersens Kampf gegen die NS-Krankenmorde',
   in Strohm and Thierfelder (eds.), *Diakonie im 'Dritten Reich'*, pp. 229ff.
46 Helmut Sorg, '"Euthanasie" in den evangelischen Heilanstalten in
   Württemberg im Dritten Reich', Magisterhausarbeit, FU (Berlin 1987),
   pp. 90–1.
47 Ernst Klee, *'Euthanasie' im NS-Staat* (Frankfurt am Main, 1985), especially
   pp. 320ff.
48 See the letter from Cardinal Faulhaber to Bishop Wienken dated 18 November
   1940 reprinted in Ernst Klee (ed.), *Dokumente zur 'Euthanasie'* (Frankfurt am
   Main 1986), pp. 182–4. On Wienken see especially Martin Höllen, 'Katholische
   Kirche und NS-"Euthanasie"', *Zeitschrift für Kirchengeschichte*, 91 (1980),
   pp. 53ff.
49 National Archives, Washington, T1021 Roll 18, Hartheim Statistics, p. 4.
50 See Walter Grode, *Die 'Sonderbehandlung 14f13' in den Konzentrationslagern des
   Dritten Reiches. Ein Beitrag zur Dynamik faschistischer Vernichtungspolitik*
   (Frankfurt am Main, 1987).
51 Imperial War Museum, London, US. v. Karl Brandt *et al.* (1947), vol. 16,
   p. 7508.
52 ZSL, 'Euthanasie', Na-Oz, interrogation of Josef Oberhauser dated 4 February
   1963, pp. 6–7 for the 'loan' of T-4 personnel to Globocnik.
53 Berlin Document Centre, 0.401 Odilo Globocnik, 'Bericht über die
   Verwaltungsmässige Abwicklung der Aktion Reinhardt' dated December
   1943.
54 Carlo Schiffrer, *La Risiera* (Trieste 1961), for one of the few accounts of this
   Dalmatian coast extermination centre.
55 Staatsarchiv Augsburg, Staatsanwaltschaften IKs/1949, Trial of Valentin
   Faltlhauser *et al.*, file containing graphs illustrating the mortality rate and
   Pauline Kneissler's presence or absence.
56 HHStAW Abt. 461 Nr. 32442, Eichberg Trial, vol. 2, testimony of Friedrich
   Mennecke dated 3 May 1946, p. 30; and Abt. 461, Nr. 31526, Idstein Trial, vol.
   1, report of an inquiry into Wilhelm Grossmann dated 21 January 1945, pp.
   1–6 for examples of the deliberate diversion of asylum produce.
57 For numerous examples see Peter Chroust (ed.), *Friedrich Mennecke.
   Innenansichten eines medizinischen Täters im Nationalsozialismus. Eine Edition
   seiner Briefe 1935–1945* (Hamburg 1988), vol. 1, no. 120, p. 359; no. 131, p. 407,
   etc.
58 Mathias Hamann, 'Die Morde an polnischen und sowjetischen
   Zwangsarbeitern in deutschen Anstalten', *Beiträge zur nationalsozialistischen
   Gesundheits- und Sozialpolitik*, 2nd edition, I (Berlin 1987), pp. 121–87.
59 Götz Aly, 'SD Berichte', pp. 196–8.
60 For a rather literal-minded discussion of these claims see Hans-Walter
   Schmuhl, 'Reformpsychiatrie und Massenmord', in M. Prinz and R.

Zitelmann (eds.), *Nationalsozialismus und Modernisierung* (Darmstadt 1991), pp. 239ff.

61 For a description of actual conditions in the asylums during this period see HHStAW, Abt. 461, Nr. 32442, Eichberg Trial, vol. 1, testimony of Dr Elisabeth V. dated 9 August 1945, pp. 1–15. Dr V. was being rather unfair to the Middle Ages, and indeed probably to most centuries prior to the present one.

3

STEP BY STEP

The expansion of murder, 1939–1941

Henry Friedlander

This chapter presents a rather different point of view on the links between the "euthanasia" campaign and the "Final Solution" than that proposed by Burleigh. Friedlander does not believe that the murder of "life unworthy of life" was primarily or even partly motivated by a desire to "clear the decks" in preparation for war, as argued by Burleigh. For Friedlander, Nazi genocide was geared to the murder of biologically defined groups. While the regime killed political opponents, it set out totally to exterminate only three groups defined by their hereditary qualities as understood by the Nazis: handicapped people, the Jews, and the Gypsies.

As Friedlander forcefully argues, the policies of identifying, isolating, and then murdering such biologically determined groups were based on many years of highly respected scientific research. Hence Friedlander's contention that while anti-semitism played an important role in the persecution of the Jews, it was integrated into an ideology that saw humankind as a whole as being made up of unequal races and polluting genetic agents who had to be exterminated so as to improve the lot of the racially valuable and pure. The Nazi worldview was therefore based on an urgent need to destroy "degenerates" and "alien races."

From this perspective, it is incorrect to speak of the Holocaust as separate from the murder of handicapped people and the Gypsies, since all three "undertakings" were logically derived from the same ideological complex, and constituted practical measures geared toward the realization of the same socio-racial utopia. That handicapped people were murdered first had to do with specific political considerations, just as the official (but not actual) cessation of the "euthanasia" campaign was the result of domestic public pressure, not of any ideological change of heart.

Both Burleigh's and Friedlander's arguments can be criticized. Burleigh can be said to put too much stress on such apparent practical reasoning as "clearing the decks," for, as Friedlander points out, the cost of the killing was greater than the benefits expected, quite apart from the political domestic and international price. Friedlander, for his part, does not sufficiently explain why the Nazis were, after all, more obsessed with killing Jews than with murdering Gypsies or even non-German handicapped persons (as well as homosexuals, habitual criminals, alcoholics, and others). But there is no doubt that both scholars offer us challenging theses that must be taken into account in setting the Holocaust in the appropriate historical context.

* * *

Historians investigating Nazi genocide have long debated who gave the order to commit mass murder, when it was issued, and how it was transmitted. Although the specific mechanism has been a matter of contention between rival groups of historians, who designated themselves either "intentionalists" or "functionalists," there now appears to be general agreement that Hitler had a deciding voice, although no one has ever discovered, or is likely to discover, a smoking gun. Recently historians have focused on the specific dates when the idea to launch the physical annihilation of the European Jews was first advanced and when the decision to do so became irrevocable, and the works of Richard Breitman and Christopher Browning represent competing interpretations.[1] Similarly, Alfred Streim and the late Helmut Krausnick have debated a question with a narrower focus: when and how orders were passed to the *Einsatzgruppen* in the occupied territory of the Soviet Union.[2] My own approach is somewhat different. I am not particularly interested in exact dates. Instead, I want to trace the sequential development of mass murder.

I define Nazi genocide, what is now commonly called the Holocaust, as the mass murder of human beings because they belonged to a biologically defined group. Heredity determined the selection of the victims. Although the regime persecuted and often killed men and women for their politics, nationality, religion, behavior, or activities, the Nazis applied a consistent and inclusive policy of extermination only against three groups of human beings: the handicapped, Jews, and Gypsies.[3]

The attack on these targeted groups drew on more than fifty years of political and scientific arguments hostile to the belief in the equality of man. Since the turn of the century, the German elite, that is the members of the educated professional classes, had increasingly accepted an ideology based on human inequality. Geneticists, anthropologists, and psychiatrists had advanced a theory of human heredity that had merged with the racist doctrine of *völkisch* nationalists to form a political ideology of a nation based on race.[4] The Nazi movement both absorbed and advanced this ideology. After 1933 they created the political framework that made it possible to translate this ideology of inequality into a policy of exclusion, while the German bureaucratic, professional, and scientific elite provided the legitimacy the regime needed for the smooth implementation of this policy.[5]

The usual interpretation assigns the role of racial victim exclusively to the Jews, and sees anti-semitism as the only ideological basis for mass murder. I do not deny that anti-semitism was a major component of Nazi ideology. I agree that the Nazis viewed the Jews as chronic enemies, and that Hitler's preoccupation with the imagined Jewish threat placed the struggle against the Jews high on the list of priorities. But I do argue that anti-semitism was only part of a larger worldview, which divided mankind into worthy and unworthy populations. Both Nazi ideologues and race scientists believed that German blood had been polluted, and that it was the nation's primary task to purge the German gene pool. The enemies were (1) the handicapped, who were considered "degenerate," and (2) "alien races," which in Central Europe meant Jews and Gypsies, since both were considered non-European nations that could not be assimilated.

The handicapped, Jews, and Gypsies had to be excluded. In the language used by both the Nazis and the race scientists, this meant "physical regeneration through eradication" (*Aufartung durch Ausmerzung*). The Nazi regime and its scientists thus wanted to improve the stock of the German *Volk* through the eradication of its inferior members and of the racial aliens dwelling amongst them.

The policy of exclusion required precise definitions of groups and individuals. Only race science could provide such definitions. However arbitrary, the "criteria for selection" had to be scientific, and the cooperation of the scientists was an important prerequisite for the successful implementation of the policy of exclusion. Scientific exactitude provided *Rechtssicherheit*, that is, reassurance for the mass of the population that the law would protect their own security.[6]

Exclusion took a variety of forms during the 1930s, but was always accompanied by an incessant propaganda campaign defaming each excluded group. For the handicapped exclusion meant institutionalization under constantly deteriorating conditions.[7] In addition, it meant compulsory sterilization as a permanent form of exclusion. The Law for the Prevention of Offspring with Hereditary Diseases, issued on 14 July 1933, provided the legal basis under which about 300,000 handicapped persons were sterilized during the 1930s.[8]

Although the people sterilized and later killed were called mental patients (*Geisteskranke*), the group included far more individuals without mental disorders: epileptics, the blind, the deaf, the mute, the retarded, the senile, alcoholics, and those with physical abnormalities. The Germans thus sterilized and killed persons who in the United States today are covered by the Act for Disabled Americans (ADA).

Applied to the Jews, about 0.5 percent of the German population, exclusion meant their removal from participation in public and economic life, as well as the notorious marriage prohibition of the Nuremberg racial laws.[9] During the 1930s, the regime envisioned complete exclusion through expulsion and emigration. Expulsion was used against foreign Jews, especially the so-called *Ostjuden*; emigration, partly voluntary and partly coerced, was used against German and Austrian Jews.[10]

Applied to the Gypsies, about 0.05 percent of the German population, considered in part a "colored" minority, exclusion meant the intensification of older discriminatory legislation as well as total registration, comprehensive police surveillance, and expulsion of foreign Gypsies. In addition, the police prohibited Gypsies from traveling, thus preventing them from engaging in traditional Gypsy itinerant trades (*Wandergewerbe*).[11] Further, race scientists examined all Gypsies to classify their racial characteristics.[12] Finally, the regime also applied the Nuremberg racial laws to Gypsies.[13] But the regime considered incarceration and sterilization as the only complete form of exclusion.[14]

In late 1938, as war was approaching, the Nazi regime decided to implement the most radical form of exclusion—total elimination of the victims through mass murder. First, using the 1938 case of the handicapped infant Knauer as pretext, Hitler authorized the killing of handicapped infants. He commissioned Karl Brandt, his *Begleitarzt*, and Philipp Bouhler, chief of his personal chancellery, to serve as plenipotentiaries for this killing operation. Bouhler handed implementation to Viktor Brack, office chief in the *Kanzlei des Führers* (KdF).[15] In the spring of 1939, Brack and his KdF team, as well as Herbert Linden of the Reich Ministry of Interior (RMdI), developed plans to implement the killing order.[16] They created a front organization, issued RMdI directives to identify victims, recruited physicians, established killing wards in various hospitals, and were ready to act by the end of the year.[17]

In the summer of 1939, Hitler extended his killing order to handicapped adults. For this much larger killing operation he commissioned Leonardo Conti of the RMdI. But afraid of involving a government agency, he soon removed that commission and gave it to Brandt and Bouhler, who again asked Brack to implement the order.[18] As the basic teams had already been assembled, it did not take much time to develop procedures, recruit additional physicians, and get the RMdI to issue the necessary directives, which began to appear in August 1939.[19] To run the killing operation, the managers established a number of front organizations, all eventually housed at number 4 on Tiergarten Strasse, and the entire operation was known thereafter as T4. The euphemism "euthanasia," that is, mercy death (*Gnadentod*), was used to describe these killings, although they were also known as the "destruction of life unworthy of life" (*Vernichtung lebensunwerten Lebens*).[20]

The managers of euthanasia established killing centers, a unique German invention. There human beings were killed in a "process" that took industrial production as its model. Staffs for these killing centers were rapidly assembled, and eventually six such centers operated on German soil: Brandenburg, Grafeneck, Hartheim, Bernburg, Sonnenstein, and Hadamar.[21] Starting with a trial run at Brandenburg in January 1940, the T4 killing centers operated at peak efficiency until August 1941.[22] At that time Hitler ordered them closed, because the killings had become widely known and public opinion had turned hostile.[23] By then at least 70,000 German nationals had been murdered.[24] The killings of the handicapped did, of course, continue in other places and in other ways, and the number of victims killed after August 1941 was at least as large as the number killed before that date.[25]

As the T4 killing centers closed, the murder of the Jews had commenced with the killings by the SS Einsatzgruppen in the East.[26] Killing centers for Jews were also under construction; they opened soon after: Chelmno in December 1941, Belzec in March 1942, Sobibor in May 1942, Treblinka in July 1942.[27] Gypsies were killed alongside Jews. They were deported as Jews were, placed into ghettos already holding Jews, shot by the Einsatzgruppen alongside Jews and the handicapped, and gassed in the killing centers together with Jews.[28]

As the chronology of Nazi mass murder unambiguously shows that the murder of the handicapped preceded that of Jews and Gypsies, we should ask why Hitler and his circle decided to kill the handicapped. Of course, we know that the "destruction" of human beings designated as "life unworthy of life" had long been part of their ideology. Still, one asks whether they were also pursuing some goal that could be considered "rational" from their perspective. At the time, the Nazis, and later, historians and others, pointed to the need to free hospital space as a cause for the killings. But the conservation of resources could not on its own have been a "rational" reason for the killings, although they might have considered this a useful side benefit.[29] The effort expended was totally out of proportion to the economic benefits expected. Moreover, economic benefits could not balance the potential danger to the regime from Allied and German public opinion. Unlike normal economic and military decisions, the decision-making process for killing operations did not include, as far as we can tell, analyses that weighed dangers against benefits. Hitler made his decision because he felt intuitively, not rationally, that he could make it work and get away with it. This may not be surprising, but it was unexpected that the entire party, government, military, and professional elite accepted such a radical decision. Having done so in the case of the handicapped, it should not be surprising that they also accepted the later decision to kill Jews and Gypsies.

The decision-making process also illustrates other connections between the various killing operations. As Lammers testified at Nuremberg, Hitler gave a direct verbal order to start the T4 killing operation, and the KdF readily moved to implement this order. But in the best tradition of CYA (Cover Your Ass), the bureaucrats of the KdF nevertheless needed a written authorization from their Führer for their own protection as well as to obtain the collaboration of physicians and government agencies. The KdF thus prepared the text of a Führer authorization and, backdating it to the day war had started, Hitler signed it in October 1939.[30] Typed on the Führer's private stationery, with the German eagle and swastika as well as the name Adolf Hitler printed at the top left, one copy of this authorization has survived.[31]

I am convinced that the same process of decision making accompanied the implementation of the final solution. Although no testimony has survived to document this, it seems certain that Hitler gave verbal orders that commissioned Himmler and his SS and police to kill the Jews.[32] However, unlike euthanasia, there was no written authorization. The reason for this seems to me self-evident A relatively large circle of persons had read the Führer's euthanasia authorization, and could thus implicate Hitler in the T4 killings. Understandably, he refused to sign another such document. In addition, the loyal SS could hardly attempt CYA by asking their Führer for an authorization. Still, Reinhard Heydrich needed some form of written commission to compel the cooperation of other government agencies. As we know, it was provided by Hermann Göring.[33] Like Hitler with euthanasia, Göring did not initiate but only signed this authorization.[34]

We have no such details about the decision to kill the Gypsies. They were deemed so marginal that their murder produced no intra-agency rivalries and thus required no written authorization. Nevertheless, even here, policy decisions forced Hitler to serve as the final arbiter of their fate. For example, in 1942 Martin Bormann discovered that the Reich Leader SS had exempted certain pure Gypsies so that research on their "valuable Teutonic practices" could be completed. On 3 December, Bormann complained about this arbitrary change in policy in a letter to Heinrich Himmler. On the front of this letter Himmler added a handwritten comment that he must prepare data concerning the Gypsies for Hitler.[35] It is probably no coincidence that thirteen days later Himmler issued his Auschwitz decree on Gypsies.[36]

The status of Gypsies as victims of Nazi genocide has been challenged, and not only by German restitution authorities.[37] The Jerusalem historian Yehuda Bauer has been the leading proponent of an anti-Gypsy interpretation.[38] He has argued that the term "final solution" (*Endlösung*) did not apply to Gypsies. But surviving documents do mention a "complete solution" (*restlose Lösung*) and a "radical solution" (*Radikallösung*) of what was called the "Gypsy problem."[39] He has also argued that there could not have been a policy of extermination, because Himmler exempted pure Gypsies. But as we have seen, Himmler was overruled; and, even if true, Himmler's individual quirk to retain some Gypsies for study as a living museum, next to museums about dead Jews, proves nothing. For example, when Himmler announced that pure Lalleri should not be killed, many of them had already been deported from Berlin-Marzahn to Auschwitz.[40] In any event, survival of some Jews and some Gypsies, and also of some of the handicapped, was always determined by Nazi pragmatism and by chance. Finally, Bauer has argued that even if Nazis killed Gypsies, they did so because they considered them *Asozial*. Of course, they called all Gypsies antisocial and criminal, just as they called Polish Jews "bandits." But even the deputy chief of the Reichskriminalpolizeiamt, Paul Werner, who as a police detective considered Gypsy criminality a "practical" problem, had readily agreed that "the Gypsy problem is primarily a racial problem."[41]

Genocide started with the handicapped in 1939, and there the Nazis discovered that it was possible to murder multitudes. They found that they could easily recruit men and women to do the killings.[42] Why were the chosen killers willing to carry out the assigned task? None did so under duress.[43] All subscribed in some form to Nazi ideology, but only some were particularly rabid Nazis. Most, however, were motivated by careerism. They enjoyed the material benefits, the feeling of power, as well as the promotions and medals. They thought they were participating at the center of events. And they wanted to serve their Führer at a safe distance from enemies who also had guns.

While the killing of the handicapped was in full swing in 1940, German policy makers were still pursuing chimeric solutions: the Madagascar plan and Lublin reservation for their Jewish and Gypsy problems. But having learned what killings could accomplish, and how they could be implemented, Hitler ordered the final solution as soon as conditions seemed favorable. Using older methods, which had been tried in 1939 on a smaller scale with the handicapped in Pomerania, Himmler used SS mobile squads to shoot the victims.[44] But this method proved too public, and the SS soon searched for a better means. They decided to copy the euthanasia killing method. Of course they had learned which mistakes to avoid. They knew it could not be done on German soil, so they established killing centers only in the East. They also realized that public opposition to the murder of the handicapped had been sparked by the relatives of victims, so they were careful to exempt, at least for the moment, Jews related to Germans by blood or marriage.[45]

The euthanasia killings had been carried out by the KdF in collaboration with the RMdI, but the SS and police had also provided limited logistic support.[46] And just as the SS had assisted the KdF in managing euthanasia, the KdF later offered its expertise to the SS in executing the final solution. For example, three chemists associated with T4 went east to help. Albert Widmann, a graduate of the Stuttgart Technical Institute, experimented with explosives and diesel gas engines in Belorussia.[47] August Becker, with a doctorate from Gießen, traveled through the occupied Soviet Union to evaluate the operation of gas vans.[48] Helmut Kallmeyer, who had a brand new doctorate from the Technische Hochschule Berlin, was first dispatched to Riga, where "Brack's remedy" was, however, not required, and then to Lublin, where he advised on gas chambers for the camps of Operation Reinhard.[49] The KdF also posted its master mason Erwin Lambert to Lublin, where he built gas chambers in Treblinka and Sobibor, and later cremation facilities at the *Risiera di San Sabba* in Trieste.[50]

The tangible connections between the T4 killings and the final solution are well known. The Lange Commando that operated Chelmno, using gas van technology, had earlier used gas vans to kill the handicapped in the Wartheland and East Prussia.[51] The staffs that ran the camps of Operation Reinhard had all graduated from the T4 killing centers.[52] The technique they applied and taught in the East involved both the hardware and the software of the killing process. It involved not only gas chambers and crematoria, but also the method developed to lure victims to these chambers, to kill them on the assembly line, and to process their corpses. This technique, which included the extraction of teeth and bridge work containing gold, was developed by T4 and exported to the East.[53]

There is one further connection between euthanasia and the final solution: the fate of handicapped Jews killed as a group in the T4 killing centers. The T4 electrician Herbert Kalisch testified that in June 1940 he observed the murder of handicapped Jewish patients from the hospital complex Berlin-Buch at the Brandenburg killing center. The physician-in charge at Brandenburg, Irmfried Eberl, recorded in his pocket diary (*Taschenkalender*) that on 23 September 1940 he supervised the murder of handicapped Jews from the Hamburg hospital complex Langenhorn and on the 27th of those from Hanover-Wunstorf. There is no reason to doubt that groups of handicapped Jews from other regions, including Eglfing-Haar in Munich and Am Steinhof in Vienna, were also murdered in the T4 killing centers.[54] Although it is never mentioned in histories about the Holocaust, or in exhibits at Holocaust museums, handicapped Jews killed in euthanasia killing centers in 1940 were the first Jewish victims of the final solution.

NOTES

1 For Breitman see his *The Architect of Genocide: Himmler and the Final Solution* (New York, 1991). For Browning, see his *Fateful Months: Essays on the Emergence of the Final Solution* (New York, 1985) and *The Path to Genocide: Essays on the Launching of the Final Solution* (New York, 1992).
2 See Alfred Streim, "The Tasks of the SS Einsatzgruppen," *Simon Wiesenthal Center Annual* 4 (1987): 309–28; "Correspondence (Krausnick and Streim)," ibid. 6 (1989): 311–47.
3 See Benno Müller-Hill, "Selektion: Die Wissenschaft von der biologischen Auslese des Menschen durch Menschen," in *Medizin und Gesundheitspolitik in der NS-Zeit*, ed. Norbert Frei (Munich, 1991), 137–55. Persons persecuted for their politics included communists, socialists, Soviet POWs; for their nationality included Poles, Russians, Ukrainians; for their religion included Jehovah's Witnesses (*Bibelforscher*); for their behavior included homosexuals, criminals; and for their activities included members of the resistance.
4 See *Hundert Jahre deutscher Rassismus: Katalog und Arbeitsbuch* (Cologne, 1988); Robert Proctor, *Racial Hygiene: Medicine under the Nazis* (Cambridge, Mass., 1988); and George L. Mosse, *Toward the Final Solution: A History of European Racism* (paper ed.; New York, 1978).
5 See Benno Müller-Hill, Tödliche Wissenschaft: Die Aussonderung von Juden, Zigeunern und Geisteskranken 1933–1945 (Reinbek bei Hamburg, 1984).
6 Müller-Hill, "Selektion," 146–7.
7 See, for example, *Medizin unterm Hakenkreuz*, ed. Achim Thom and Genadij Ivanovic Caregorodcev (Berlin, 1989), 130–1; and Karl Heinz Roth, "Ein Mustergau gegen die Armen, Leistungsschwachen und 'Gemeinschaftsunfähigen,'" in *Heilen und Vernichten im Mustergau Hamburg: Bevölkerungs- und*

Gesundheitspolitik im Dritten Reich, ed. Angelika Ebbinghaus, Heidrun Kaupen-Haas, and Karl Heinz Roth (Hamburg, 1984), 7–17.

8 "Gesetz zur Verhütung erbkranken Nachwuchses," *Reichsgesetzblatt* 1933, 1:529. On the implementation of the sterilization law, including statistics on numbers sterilized, see Gisela Bock, *Zwangssterilisation im Nationalsozialismus: Studien zur Rassenpolitik und Frauenpolitik* (Opladen, 1986).

9 Reichsbürgergesetz" and "Gesetz zum Schutze des deutschen Blutes und der deutschen Ehre," *Reichsgesetzblatt* 1935, 1:1146. Joseph Walk has compiled an annotated list of all anti-Jewish laws, decrees, and regulations: *Das Sonderrecht für die Juden im NS-Staat: Eine Sammlung der gesetzlichen Massnahmen und Richtlinien Inhalt und Bedeutung* (Heidelberg and Karlsruhe, 1981).

10 On expulsion, see Sybil Milton, "The Expulsion of the Polish Jews from Germany, 1938," *Leo Baeck Institute Yearbook* 29 (1984): 169–99. On emigration, see Herbert A. Strauss, "Jewish Emigration from Germany: Nazi Policies and Jewish Responses," ibid. 25 (1980): 313–61, and ibid. 26 (1981): 343–409.

11 Staatsministerium des Innern, Erlaß, Munich, 28 Mar. 1899, publ. in Ludwig Eiber, *"Ich wußte, es wird schlimm": Die Verfolgung der Sinti und Roma in München, 1933–1945* (Munich, 1993): 14–15; Staatsanwaltschaft (StA) Hamburg, Verfahren Kellermann, 2200 Js 2/84: Preuß. MdI Verfügung (sig. Bethmann-Hollweg), 17 Feb. 1906, "Anweisungen zur Bekämpfung des Zigeunerwesens"; ibid.: Preuß. MdI circular, 3 Nov. 1927, "Fingerabdruckverfahren bei Zigeunern"; ibid.: Reichskriminalpolizeiamt circular (sig. Heydrich), 4 Apr. 1938; and United States Holocaust Memorial Museum, Fojn-Felczer Collection: RFSS circular, 9 Sept. 1939, "Bekämpfung der Zigeunerplage."

12 See Joachim S. Hohmann, *Robert Ritter und die Erben der Kriminalbiologie: "Zigeunerforschung" im Nationalsozialismus und in Westdeutschland im Zeichen des Rassismus*, Studien zur Tsiganologie und Folkloristik, Vol. 4 (Frankfurt, 1991). Part of the records accumulated by the race scientists are now deposited in Bundesarchiv Koblenz (BAK), R/165. See also Susanne Regener, "Ausgegrenzt: Die optische Inventarisierung der Menschen im Polizeiwesen und in der Psychiatrie," *Fotogeschichte* 10, no. 38 (1990): 23–38.

13 Arthur Gütt, Herbert Linden, and Franz Maßfeller, *Blutschutz und Ehegesundheitsgesetz: Gesetz zum Schutze des deutschen Blutes und der deutschen Ehre und Gesetz zum Schutze der Erbgesundheit des deutschen Volkes nebst Durchführungsverordnungen sowie einschlägigen Bestimmungen, dargestellt, medizinisch und juristisch erläutert* (Munich, 2d rev. ed. 1937), 16, 21, 150, and 226; Wilhelm Stuckart and Hans Globke, *Reichsbürgergesetz vom 15. September 1935, Gesetz zum Schutze des deutschen Blutes und der deutschen Ehre vom 15. September 1935, Gesetz zum Schutze der Erbgesundheit des deutschen Volkes (Ehegesundheitsgesetz) vom 18. Oktober 1935 nebst allen Ausführungsvorschriften und den einschlägigen Gesetzen und Verordnungen, erläutert* (Munich and Berlin, 1936), 153.

14 See Sybil Milton, "Nazi Policies toward Roma and Sinti, 1933–1945," *Journal of the Gypsy Lore Society*, ser. 5, vol. 2, no. 1 (1992): 1–18. On sterilization as the preferred method of exclusion, see BAK, R18/5644: RMdI circular (sig. Conti), 24 Jan. 1940.

15 U.S. Military Tribunal, Case 1 Transcript, 2398–99 (testimony Karl Brandt); StA Stuttgart, Verfahren Widmann, Ks 19/62 (19 Js 328/60): interrogation of Werner Catel by StA Hannover (Bd. VI, 2 Js 237/56), 14 May 1962; Generalstaatsanwalt (GStA) Frankfurt, Anklage Heyde, Bohne, und Hefelmann, Ks 2/63 (GStA), Js 17/59 (GStA), 22 May 1962, 53–4 (testimony Hans Hefelmann).

16 The information about planning and early implementation of children's

euthanasia comes from the interrogation of Hans Hefelmann, available at the offices of the Staatsanwaltschaft bei dem Oberlandesgericht Frankfurt. His verbose testimony was obviously selfserving and cannot always be trusted. Crucial portions of Hefelmann's testimony are cited in GStA Frankfurt, Anklage Heyde, Bohne, und Hefelmann, Ks 2/63 (GStA), Js 17/59 (GStA), 22 May 1962.

17 Ibid., 56a–57; StA Hamburg, Sachstandsvermerk, 147 Js 58/67, 25 Feb. 1970, 38; StA Hamburg, Anklage Bayer, Catel, 14 Js 265/48, 7 Feb. 1949, 22–3; U.S. Military Tribunal, Case 1 Transcript, 2494; BAK, R18/5586: RMdI decree (sig. Stuckart), 18 Aug. 1939, "Meldepflicht für mißgestaltete usw. Neugeborene." The front organization was known as the Reich Committee for the Scientific Registration of Severe Hereditary Ailments (Reichsausschuß zur wissenschaftlichen Erfassung von erb- und anlagebedingten schweren Leiden).

18 At Nuremberg, both Brandt and Lammers placed Hitler's appointment of Conti into the early period of the war, September or early October, and the charge to Brandt and Bouhler several weeks later. U.S. Military Tribunal, Case 1 Transcript, 2396, 2400–1 (testimony Karl Brandt); 2668 (testimony Hans Heinrich Lammers). But Brack at Nuremberg, and other witnesses interrogated by German prosecutors years later, placed these events several months earlier. Ibid., 7555–7 (testimony Viktor Brack); GStA Frankfurt, Anklage Heyde, Bohne, und Hefelmann, Ks 2/63 (GStA), Js 17/59 (GStA), 22 May 1962 182–3. Evidence does support the earlier date; thus the KdF called its first planning session for adult euthanasia before the start of the war. U.S. Military Tribunal, Case 1 Transcript, 7565 (testimony Viktor Brack). We can therefore assume that Hitler met with Conti no later than July 1939, and that he gave the final assignment to Brandt and Bouhler no later than August.

19 GStA Frankfurt, Anklage Vorberg und Allers, Js 20/61 (GStA), 15 Feb. 1966, 22–4; GStA Frankfurt, Anklage Heyde, Bohne, und Hefelmann, Ks 2/63 (GStA), Js 17/59 (GStA), 22 May 1962, 188–97; Landgericht (LG) Dresden, Urteil Hermann Paul Nitsche, 1 Ks 58/47, 7 July 1947, 3; StA München I, Verfahren Pfannmüller, 1 Ks 10/49 (1b Js 1791/47): Protokoll der öffentlichen Sitzung des Schwurgerichts beim LG München I, 19 Oct. 1949, 8. For the first directive, see GStA Frankfurt, Sammlung Euthanasie: RMdI decree of 21 Sept. 1939: "Erfassung der Heil- und Pflegeanstalten."

20 See Karl Binding and Alfred Hoche, *Die Freigabe der Vernichtung lebensunwerten Lebens: Ihr Maß und Ihre Form* (Leipzig, 1920).

21 On *Brandenburg*, see GStA Frankfurt, Anklage Ullrich, Bunke, Borm, und Endruweit, Js 15/61 (GStA), 15 Jan. 1965, 175–7. On *Grafeneck*, see Staatsarchiv Sigmaringen, Wü 29/3, Acc. 33/1973, Nr. 1752: StA Tübingen, Anklage Mauthe, 1 Js 85–7/47, 4 Jan. 1949; GStA Frankfurt, Anklage Schumann, Js 18/67 (GStA), 12 Dec. 1969, 78–81. On *Hartheim*, see Archiv Museum Mauthausen, B/15/2: Auszug aus der Gemeindechronik Alkoven; Dokumentationsarchiv des österreichischen Widerstandes (DÖW) file 14900: StA Linz, Anklage Anna Griessenberger, 3 St 466/46, 28 July 1947; DÖW, file E18370/3: Kriminalpolizei Linz, interrogation Vinzenz Nohel, 4 Sept. 1945. On *Bernburg*, see GStA Frankfurt, Anklage Kaufmann, 16/63 (GStA), 27 June 1966, 29; GStA Frankfurt, Anklage Ullrich, Bunke, Borm, und Endruweit, Js 15/61 (GStA), 15 Jan. 1965, 186, 188–9, 205–6. On *Sonnenstein*, see GStA Frankfurt, Anklage Schumann, Js 18/67 (GStA), 12 Dec. 1969, 84–6; GStA Frankfurt, Anklage Ullrich, Bunke, Borm, und Endruweit Js 15/61 (GStA), 15 Jan. 1965, 211. On *Hadamar*, see Hessisches Hauptstaatsarchiv Wiesbaden (HHStA), 461/32061/7: LG Frankfurt, Verfahren Wahlmann Gorgaß, Huber, 4a KLs 7/47 (4a Js 3/46); and

HENRY FRIEDLANDER

Verlegt nach Hadamar: Die Geschichte einer NS-"Euthanasie"-Anstalt, ed. Bettina
Winter and others (Kassel, 1991).

22 For the Brandenburg trial run, see National Archives and Records
Administration (NARA), RG 238: interrogation Karl Brandt, 1 Oct. 1945 p.m.,
13; U.S. Military Tribunal, Case 1 Transcript, 7645 (testimony Viktor Brack);
StA Stuttgart, Verfahren Widmann, Ks 19/62 (19 Js 328/60): interrogation
August Becker, 4 Apr. 1960; LG Dresden, Urteil Nitsche, 1 Ks 58/47, 7 July
1947, 3; GStA Frankfurt, Anklage Heyde, Bohne, und Hefelmann Ks 2/63
(GStA), Js 17/59 (GStA), 22 May 1962, 290–3 (interrogation Werner Heyde),
293–98 (interrogation August Becker); StA Stuttgart, Anklage Widmann und
Becker, (19) 13 Js 328/60, 29 Aug. 1962, 39–41.

23 U.S. Military Tribunal, Case 1 Transcript, 2530–1 (testimony Karl Brandt),
7629 (testimony Viktor Brack).

24 See NARA, Microfilm Publ. T-1021, roll 18, "Hartheim Statistics." Richard
Boylan and this author rediscovered the original volume of the "Hartheim
Statistics" at Suitland in the middle 1980s. The volume (in color) is located in
NARA Suitland, RG 338, USAREUR 1942, War Crimes Branch, Cases Not
Tried, File Lot 600–12–463, but is currently on exhibit at the United States
Holocaust Memorial Museum.

25 See StA Hamburg, Anklage Lensch und Struve, 147 Js 58/67, 24 Apr. 1973.

26 See Helmut Krausnick and Hans-Heinrich Wilhelm, *Die Truppe des Weltanschauungskrieges: Die Einsatzgruppen der Sicherheitspolizei und des SD,
1938–1942* (Stuttgart, 1981).

27 See Adalbert Rückerl, *NS-Vernichtungslager im Spiegel deutscher Strafprozesse*
(Munich, 1977).

28 On deportations, see Sybil Milton, "Gypsies and the Holocaust," *The History
Teacher* 24, no. 4 (Aug. 1991): 375–87. On ghettos, see *The Chronicles of the Lodz
Ghetto, 1941–1944*, ed. Lucjan Dobroszycki (New Haven, 1984), 82, 85, 96, 101,
and 107; and *The Warsaw Diary of Adam Czerniakow: Prelude to Doom*, ed. Raul
Hilberg, Stanislaw Staron, Josef Kermisz (New York, 1979), 346–7, 351, 364–8,
and 375. On Einsatzgruppen, see Ronald Headland, *Messages of Murder: A
Study of the Reports of the Einsatzgruppen of the Security Police and the Security
Service, 1941–1943* (London, Toronto, and Teaneck, N. J., 1992), 53–4, 63–4. 71,
114, 142, 157, 169. On killing centers, see Rückerl, *NS-Vernichtungslager*, 197;
and appropriate entries in Danuta Czech, *Kalendarium der Ereignisse im
Konzentrationslager Auschwitz-Birkenau 1939–1945* (Reinbek bei Hamburg,
1989).

29 But even an economic decision to kill would have been based on ideological
assumptions.

30 U.S. Military Tribunal, Case 1 Transcript, 2369, 2402 (testimony Karl Brandt).
The language of this authorization was prepared for the KdF by a committee
that included leading psychiatrists. GStA Frankfurt, Anklage Heyde, Bohne
und Hefelmann, Ks 2/63 (GStA), Js 17/59 (GStA), 22 May 1962, 201ff.

31 Nuremberg Doc. PS-630. Also available in BAK. R22/4209.

32 See for example, Gerald Fleming, *Hitler und die Endlösung* (Wiesbaden and
Munich, 1982).

33 Nuremberg Doc. PS-710.

34 Raul Hilberg, *The Destruction of the European Jews* (rev. ed., New York, 1985),
401.

35 BAK, NS neu 19/180: Bormann to Himmler, 3 Dec. 1942. The handwritten
notation reads: "Führer. Aufstellung. Wer sind Zigeuner."

36 See StA Hamburg, Verfahren Kellermann, 2200 Js 2/84: RSHA Schnellbrief,
29 Jan. 1943.

74

37 For a detailed refutation of restitution decisions excluding Gypsies as racial victims, see Franz Calvelli-Adorno, "Die rassische Verfolgung der Zigeuner vor dem 1. März 1943," *Rechtssprechung zum Widergutmachungsrecht* 12, no. 12 (Dec. 1961): 529–37.

38 Yehuda Bauer, "Jews, Gypsies, Slays: Policies of the Third Reich," in *UNESCO Yearbook on Peace and Conflict Studies 1985* (Paris, 1987), 73–100; idem, "Gypsies," in *Encyclopedia of the Holocaust*, 4 vols. (New York and London, 1990), 2:634–8; idem, "Holocaust and Genocide: Some Comparisons," in *Lessons and Legacies: The Meaning of the Holocaust in a Changing World*, ed. Peter Hayes (Evanston, 1991), 42. See also exchange of letters between Bauer and Sybil Milton, in "Correspondence," *The History Teacher* 25, no. 4 (Aug. 1992): 515–21.

39 See BAK, R18/6544: Dr. Zindel to Hans Pfundtner, 4 Mar. 1936; ibid.: RMdI circular (sig. Conti), 24 Jan. 1940.

40 BAK, R165/45: Registration list of Lalleri at Berlin-Marzahn, 5 Dec. 1939 to 26 Jan. 1940, as compared with listings in *Memorial Book: The Gypsies in Auschwitz-Birkenau*, ed. State Museum of Auschwitz-Birkenau and Documentary and Cultural Center of German Sinti and Roma, 2 vols. (Munich, 1993).

41 BAK, R73/14005: Paul Werner to Deutsche Forschungsgemeinschaft, 6 Jan. 1940.

42 For a discussion of personnel recruitment, see my "Das nationalsozialistische Euthanasieprogramm," in *Geschichte und Verantwortung*, ed. Aurelius Freytag, Boris Marte, and Thomas Stern (Vienna, 1988), 277–97.

43 See Herbert Jäger, *Verbrechen unter totalitärer Herrschaft: Studien zur national-sozialistischen Gewaltkriminalität*, 2d ed. (Frankfurt, 1982), 94ff.

44 On the Pomeranian killings, see LG Hannover, Urteil Kurt Eimann, 2 Ks 2/67, 20 Dec. 1968; and Nuremberg Doc. NO-2275: Gruppenführer Richard Hildebrandt, "Bericht über Aufstellung, Einsatz und Tätigkeit des SS-Wachsturmbann E."

45 This did not apply to Gypsies, because German officials believed that among Germans "only scum (*Abschaum eines Volkes*) will marry or mate with a Gypsy." BAK, ZSg142/23: report on Marzahn camp by G. Stein, Frankfurt, n.d. (1936).

46 On the support role of Reinhard Heydrich and the RSHA, see BAK, R22/5021: handwritten note by Dr. Günther Joël transmitting to Franz Gürtner comments by Heydrich concerning his relationship to the euthanasia program, 1 Nov. [1940]; and Bundesarchiv-Militärarchiv Freiburg, H20/463 & 465: Viktor Brack to Heinrich Müller, 5 July 1941; Viktor Brack to RSHA, Abteilung IVb2, 9 Apr. 1942.

47 Berlin Document Center (BDC): dossier Albert Widmann; StA Düsseldorf, Anklage Widmann, 8 Js 7212/59, 13 Sept. 1960; LG Düsseldorf, Urteil Widmann, 8 Ks 1/61, 16 May 1961; StA Stuttgart, Anklage Widmann, Becker, (19) 13 Js 328/60, 29 Aug. 1962; StA Düsseldorf, Verfahren Widmann, 8 Ks 1/61 (8 Js 7212/59), interrogation Albert Widmann, 11–12, 15, and 27 Jan. 1960.

48 BDC: Dossier August Becker, StA Stuttgart, Anklage Widmann, Becker, (19) 13 Js 328/60, 29 Aug. 1962; StA Stuttgart, Verfahren Widmann, Ks 19/62 (19 Js 328/60), interrogation August Becker, 4 Apr. 1960, 16 May 1961; Zentrale Stelle der Landesjustizverwaltungen Ludwigsburg (ZStL), interrogation August Becker, 10 and 26 Mar. 1960, 20 June 1961, 8 Oct. 1963.

49 ZStL, interrogation Helmut Kallmeyer, Hanover, 15 Sept. 1961; interrogation Gertrud Kallmeyer, 31 May 1960, 27 Feb. 1961, 5 Sept. 1961, 10 and 15 Feb. 1966; StA Stuttgart, Verfahren Widmann, Ks 19/62 (19 Js 328/60), interrogation

Helmut Kallmeyer, 20 July 1961 (StA Kiel, 2 Js 269/60). On Riga, see Nuremberg Doc. NO-365: Wetzel to Lohse, 25 Oct. 1941.

50 ZStL, interrogations Erwin Lambert, 3 Apr. 1962 and 12 Feb. 1963; StA Stuttgart, Verfahren Widmann, Ks 19/62 (19 Js 328/60), interrogation Erwin Lambert, 26 Apr. 1961, continuation 4 May 1961; StA Düsseldorf, Anklage Kurt Franz, 8 Js 10904/59, 29 Jan. 1963, 50–1; LG Düsseldorf, Urteil Kurt Franz, 8 I Ks 2/64, 3 Sept. 1965, 477ff.; LG Hagen, Urteil Dubois, 11 Ks 1/64, 20 Dec. 1966, 268–75; *San Sabba: Istruttoria e processo per il Lager della Risiera*, ed. Adolfo Scalpelli, 2 vols. (Milan, 1988), 1:15.

51 On Chelmno, see LG Bonn, Urteil, 8 Ks 3/62, 30 Mar. 1963, in *Justiz und NS-Verbrechen: Sammlung deutscher Strafurteile wegen nationalsozialistischer Tötungsverbrechen*, ed. Adelheid L. Rüter-Ehlermann and C. F. Rüter, 22 vols. (Amsterdam, 1968–81), 21, no. 594. On Wartheland and East Prussia, see LG Bonn, Untersuchungsrichter II, Anlage zur Abschluss-Verfügung vom 30. September 1963 in der Voruntersuchung Wilhelm Koppe, 13 UR 1/61, 6/62, 7/62, 10/62, 15–18; StA Bonn, Anklage Koppe, 8 Js 52/60, 10 Sept. 1964, 182–7; and Nuremberg Docs. NO-1073, NO-1074, NO-1076, NO-2908, NO-2909, NO-2911.

52 See Rückerl, *NS-Vernichtungslager*, pp. 47ff.

53 On the collection of gold teeth in the T4 killing centers, see, for example, HHStA, 461/32061/7: LG Frankfurt, Verfahren Wahlmann, Gorgaß, Huber, 4a KLs 7/47 (4a Js 3/46), Protokoll der öffentlichen Sitzung der 4. Strafkammer, 3 Mar. 1947, 32 (testimony Ingeborg Seidel).

54 On Berlin-Buch, see StA Stuttgart, Verfahren Widmann, Ks 19/62 (19 Js 328/60), interrogation Herbert Kalisch, Mannheim, 25 Jan. and 4 Mar. 1960. On Hamburg-Langenhorn and Hanover-Wunstorf, see Eberl's Taschenkalender (Xerox copy in my possession; original at offices of the Staatsanwaltschaft beim Oberlandesgericht Frankfurt). On Eglfing-Haar, see Nuremberg Docs. NO-720, NO-1135, NO-1142, NO-1143, NO-3354. On Am Steinhof, see DÖW, file 8496: Ältestenrat der Juden in Wien (sig. Löwenherz) to Anstalt Ybbs, 2 Feb. 1943. See also Henry Friedlander, "Jüdische Anstaltspatienten im NS-Deutschland," in *Aktion T4, 1939–1945: Die "Euthanasie – Zentrale in der Tiergartenstraße 4*, ed. Götz Aly (Berlin, 1987), 34–44.

Part II

IMPLEMENTATION
Beyond intentionalism and functionalism

4

THE EXTERMINATION OF THE EUROPEAN JEWS IN HISTORIOGRAPHY

Fifty years later

Saul Friedländer

This chapter sets the context for the following debates on the wider background and specific process of the decision on the "Final Solution." While Friedländer concedes that the debates over the history and historiography of the Nazi period and the Holocaust are far from over, he proposes a historiographical synthesis that would settle many of the old disputes, even if it might not resolve newer controversies.

Friedländer argues that the apparent contradiction between a "traditional" interpretation that stresses the role of antisemitism, and a "new" interpretation that asserts the centrality of science, social engineering, and a crisis of modernity for the rise of Nazism and the implementation of genocidal policies, can be resolved by recognizing the ambivalence of Nazi ideology itself and the inner contradictions of Hitler's regime. In other words, he suggests that Nazism was both about anti-semitism and about science, both anti-modernist and informed by modernizing trends. This leads Friedländer to the conclusion that the obvious dichotomy between modernity and myth did not apply in the Nazi image of the Jew, who was perceived both in traditional mythical terms and in modern scientific ones as a representative of evil and pollution. From this perspective, what Friedländer calls "redemptive antisemitism" is composed precisely of these two elements, that of the "Eternal Jew" of medieval Christian lore and that of the "Jewish bacillus" of "scientific" racism. Redemption here is seen either in religious, eschatological terms, or in those of racial utopia and the construction of a racially pure "brave new world."

With this notion of "redemptive antisemitism" in mind, Friedländer critically examines the scholarly literature on the Holocaust and identifies its strengths and weaknesses. He thus accepts certain aspects of the "functionalist" stress on the inherent bureaucratic "logic" of extermination, but insists both on Hitler's ultimate centrality and on a general acceptance of the regime's ideological goals. Similarly, he notes that the "ordinary men" identified by Christopher Browning were apparently not so ordinary after all as far as their antisemitic and pro-Nazi sentiments were concerned. Finally, he views the eugenic thrust of the regime as consistent with the more narrowly defined "redemptive antisemitism" of Hitler and some of those closest to him, since the ultimate eugenic utopia contained a universal vision of redemption for the appropriate races.

Where Friedländer differs from recent theories on the origins of the "Final Solution" is both in relationship to some of the obviously apologetic works that have presented Hitler as modernizer, and as regards Götz Aly's study of Nazi demographic planning (a gist of which follows Friedländer's chapter). He also expresses some anxiety regarding the reappearance of the totalitarian paradigm and arguments about the similarities between the Third Reich and Stalinist Russia. These are of course legitimate concerns, although Aly's recent work seems to warrant more serious consideration. What is important in Friedländer's chapter, however, is that he demonstrates the extent to which two apparently polar modes of explanation can provide a much better understanding of the Holocaust when synthesized into a single explanatory whole, more complex and less neat, perhaps, but better capable of addressing the inner contradictions and ambiguities of the event itself.

* * *

In contrast to the fourteenth anniversary of the end of World War II, no "historians' debate," no *Historikerstreit* marked the semicentennial commemoration of the Allied victory over Nazi Germany in 1995.[1] This may be only a temporary respite. The debates about memory and the Nazi epoch, the Holocaust, and particularly about adequate forms of commemoration of the victims seem to be more intense than ever.[2]

In what follows I will concentrate on some aspects of the present state of the historiography of Nazism, particularly that of the Holocaust. I will attempt to show that notwithstanding the existence of clearly contending interpretations, a historiographical synthesis is possible and that despite all unresolved differences, we presently have at our disposal a body of knowledge and frameworks of interpretation sufficiently interrelated to serve as the basis for further significant historical elaboration. Yet, as I shall indicate at the end of this text, some aspects of the contending interpretations that are muted for now may carry the potential for major new historiographical confrontations.

Contending interpretations

What distinguishes recent approaches which have become part and parcel of present-day historiography of Nazism and of the "Final Solution," from the challenges of some fifteen years ago is the apparent totality of the reinterpretation. We are seemingly faced with a basic reconsideration of the historical categories used in our most general understanding of this aspect of German and European history. In order to describe the contending positions I shall successively refer to a "traditional" and to a "new" interpretation; these terms are used without any value connotation.

Let us consider the historical background of Nazism and of the aspects of it generally linked to the "Final Solution." The traditional position defines this historical background as the conjunction of a secular anti-Semitic tradition, of a crisis of German national identity, and of the growth of a radical *völkisch* ideology as part of this special historical course (*Sonderweg*).[3] The new interpretation—and here I am essentially following Detlev Peukert's work—defines the same historical background in terms of a general crisis of modernity, the rise of racial science (mainly eugenics) and a belief in a social engineering of sorts; all of this is considered to be an offshoot of the social crisis of the turn of the century and later of the German crisis of the 1920s and early 1930s.[4] Both positions describe the 1920s as a period of reinforcement of these trends; but whereas the first (or traditional) position concentrates upon an exacerbation of *völkisch* views, and of anti-Semitism in particular, the new position puts the emphasis on the growth of "negative eugenics" as a result of the increasing disenchantment with the possibility of a positive social therapy and the impact of theories of biological selection fostered by the war.[5]

In terms of the characteristics of the Nazi system, the first position stresses its irrational dimension, its antimodernism, and the special role of Hitler's charismatic impact as a major source of the radicalization of the entire system.[6] The second position focuses on the inherent rationality of the system, its partaking of the most basic aspects of modernity and modernization, as well as on its essentially technocratic features.[7]

Finally, with regard to the "Final Solution" as such, the contrary positions regarding the historical background and the years most immediately preceding the onset of extermination are compounded by a further dichotomy. On the one hand, the traditional view points to anti-Semitism as the direct cause of the exterminations—stressing their counterrational, noninstrumental dimensions—as well as to the irrational aspect of Nazi policies.[8] More recent views, on the other hand, either underline a wider trend—that of an overall policy of extermination of which the "Final Solution" was merely a part—or they accentuate the instrumental rationality of the extermination of the Jews as planned by Nazi technocrats.[9] Obviously, the approach that I define as traditional has always stressed the modernity of the means used by the Nazis to achieve their antimodern and irrational aims. The new position, picking up a thread spun by Max Horkheimer and Theodor W. Adorno in their *Dialectic of Enlightenment*, does not concentrate on the unquestionable modernity of the means but does present the aims of Nazism as the expression of an all-pervasive modern instrumental rationality.[10]

Both approaches, but particularly the latter, have undergone some significant changes in recent years. For example, ongoing historical research again stresses the centrality of Hitler's charismatic impulse within the overall system, a centrality which now emphasizes constant interaction between the Führer and surrounding society.[11] Other recent studies have once more underlined the decisive role of ideology as the central framework for decisions. Most recent historical work in these domains also seems to represent the search for a coherent synthesis between positions which, although divergent in many respects, are not totally exclusive of each other.[12] In my own attempt to present such a synthesis, I will exclude some extreme or marginal interpretations while retaining the two main approaches referred to here as major leitmotifs.

The elements of a synthesis

Modernity and myth

With regard to the general historical background of the Nazi phenomenon and its anti-Jewish impetus, we are apparently faced with the meeting of the logic, the goals, and the instruments of modernity as well as the representations and impulses of myth or, in other terms, with the aims of instrumental rationality *and* the phantasms of irrational thinking. But the two interpretive trends previously mentioned need not be considered as entirely separate positions; they are, in fact, dealing with two *contrary but coexisting aspects* of Nazism.

The dichotomy between modernity and myth does not imply that myth itself cannot be suffused with "scientific" thinking. The Nazi image of the Jew, for example, presented two different aspects of mythic thinking. The first aspect, steeped in *völkisch*-racist theories and imagery, focused on the danger inherent in the biological nature of the Jew, in the racial characteristics carried by Jewish blood. This mythical view partook none-theless of the "modern" and "scientific" discourse of nineteenth-century racial thinking. The presence in the midst of the *Volk* of any group partaking of "racially foreign" (*artfremd*) blood was deemed mortally dangerous. Here, myth and scientific discourse were one. There was, however, another aspect of the myth that did not rely on scientific categories and which was directed solely at the Jews.

According to this second aspect, the Jews were not only dangerous as a result of their innate racial nature, they also represented an active and deadly force in history, one that was bent on world domination and possibly world destruction. This view transformed the struggle against the Jews into one of life or death, the outcome of which would decide the perdition or the salvation of humankind. As mentioned, racial anti-Semitism of the first kind was an integral part of the modern racist discourse; the other face of myth, one that could be defined as "redemptive anti-Semitism," had deeper historical roots.[13] In other words, contrary to Detlev Peukert's formulation, the "Jewish bacillus" *did not replace* the "Eternal Jew" under the impact of modern "scientific" racial thinking.[14] These were two separate aspects of the overall Nazi representation of the Jew.

Redemptive anti-Semitism, nurtured by the deep soil of Christian religious tradition, resurfaced in late nineteenth century Germany as one of several ideologies of salvation brought forth by the forebodings of decline and catastrophe which had seeped into the imagination of the epoch. Paul Rose has linked the new radical wave of anti-Judaism to the revolutionary movements of the nineteenth century.[15] In my view, the structure of these radical views exhibits all the religious, eschatological aspects of the millenarian anti-Judaism of the late Middle Ages so powerfully described by Norman Cohn.[16] In its new form, this representation of evil was not merely religious, not merely racial, not merely political. It was a stage-by-stage aggregation of these successive waves of anti-Jewish hatred, of the successive layers of a tale of Jewish conspiracy against Aryan humanity. The religious-eschatological core of redemptive anti-Semitism was re-inforced at the turn of the century by the racial dimension.[17] Both the religious and the racial visions of redemption through the elimination of the Jew found their final and most extreme justification in the nationalist belief that the Jews had plotted Germany's defeat in the war and that Bolshevism was an instrument of world Jewry. In other words, redemptive anti-Semitism led from Christian millenarianism to the nineteenth-century ideologies of salvation and, by way of the Bayreuth circle and Houston Stewart Chamberlain's reworking of "the role of the Jew in history," to postrevolution and postwar frenzy, to the German adoption of *The Protocols of the Elders of Zion*, to Dietrich Eckart, and finally, in part simultaneously, to Adolf Hitler.[18] Let me restate this first point: with regard to the Nazi myth of the Jew, archaic religious themes and so-called modern scientific theories were interwoven in a multifaceted representation of the archenemy of the Volk.

I shall now indicate, though in a most schematic way, how the historiography of these two trends could converge in an integrated interpretation of the impact of the charismatic impulse on the dual system of party and state, of the internal dynamics of the system itself, of the relation between system and society at large and, finally, of the immediate background to the "Final Solution."

Charisma and bureaucracy

I shall not return here to the historiographical debates about Hitler's centrality and role in the unfolding of Nazism and its policies. Suffice it to recall that the analytic social history of the 1970s played down this centrality for theoretical reasons and also because in the 1950s, the notion of Hitler's centrality had sometimes fulfilled an apologetic function. This being said, Hans Mommsen's projection of a "weak dictator" never took hold within historical thinking, and various conceptual compromises were applied in defining Hitler's role.[19]

In a recent and strange twist, the identification of Nazism and modernity, which usually dwells on the evolution of long-term factors and on social-structural characteristics, has presented Hitler as the ideologist and promoter of the Nazi modernizing drive. This unabashedly apologetic tendency, which systematically downplays Hitler's involvement in the policies of mass extermination, tentatively follows David Irving's trail, and is mainly represented by Rainer Zitelmann and his various coauthors; it now seems to have lost most of its credibility in mainstream historiography.[20] This extreme trend aside, there is nowadays a clear return to the notion of Hitler's decisive role, but in terms of a constant interaction among "Führer," system, and society. There is little doubt that with regard to the anti-Jewish ideology and policies of the movement and the regime, Hitler's impact was decisive, as was well perceived by Eberhard Jäckel and also by Martin Broszat.[21]

The Nazi leader understood how to adapt the fanatical course dictated by total belief to the ad hoc demands of political circumstances. In other words, in relation to the Jews, as in other domains, Hitler radicalized to the utmost the ultimate significance of the myth, but often, during the first years of the regime at least, he pragmatized its immediate corollaries. Hitler embodied the violence and the fanaticism of mythical thinking without losing awareness of the imperatives of modern bureaucratic policies.[22]

The "Führer's" mediation between the ideological-mythical impulse and the dynamics of the system does not by itself explain the inner workings of the system, that consummate expression of the modern bureaucratic state. Here, too, we must consider several different levels: the interaction between various agencies and political fiefdoms within the overall structure; the interaction between the dual system which included party and state and wider reaches of the population; and, finally, the evolution of that overall structure as such. The central question at each level remains that of the nature of the radicalizing process.

As far as the interaction between various agencies is concerned, the *Führerstaat* was indeed "organized chaos," as shown again in the recent work of Dieter Rebentisch.[23] But, in regard to anti-Jewish policies as in other domains, the guidelines expressing the Führer's will led to a constant effort to overcome the chaos by an ongoing alignment of the system. Agencies and individuals were, according to a 1934 formula adopted by Ian Kershaw, "working towards the Führer."[24] Party and state bureaucracies, as well as related economic units or cultural and religious institutions, coordinated their efforts as a consequence of their passive or active acceptance of the main goals of the regime. Coordination, as understood here, did not eliminate bitter infighting; but such infighting was caused by internal power struggles, never by questions as to the legitimacy or validity of the general goals defined by the Führer.

Thus, if "working towards the Führer" is taken as a fundamental impetus of the system, the bureaucratic apparatus involved in the persecution of the Jews was not an autonomous machinery that required only an initial, triggering impetus, as suggested by Hilberg, nor merely a chaotic network of rival agencies whose very rivalry propelled the system to ever more radical measures, as outlined by Mommsen.[25] The apparatus as chaotic as it was, was constantly aligning itself according to *ongoing* orders, notwithstanding delays and internal confrontations. It sometimes antici-pated the concrete steps that could be surmised from the general guidelines; it faithfully ensured the most thorough fulfillment of its tasks in the face of all common obstacles. In other words, the standardized practices of a highly modern industrial bureaucratic state were attuned on an ongoing basis to the ideological goals of the regime as expressed by its leader. When, on an issue of any significance, the order from above was not forthcoming, state and party agencies had to wait.[26]

Such an approach does not reject the inherent "logic" of bureaucratic organizations or the possibility of some sort of cumulative radicalization of the system as the result of the infighting between its constitutive units. Rather, this radicalizing impulse was both controlled and accelerated by Hitler's constant input, and the infighting itself never transgressed the limits of common cooperation within the framework set by Hitler's guidelines for the fulfillment of his goals. In other words, the radicalization process was fed by initiatives taken at various levels of the party hierarchy, but no major decision could be taken without Hitler's assent. More often than not the Führer himself initiated the new and more radical steps, and all agencies aligned themselves accordingly. Finally, initiatives stemming from party agencies often received Hitler's general agreement; their implementation, however, was left to the decisions of the initiators, as was the case, for example, with the genesis and the evolution of the "Final Solution" in the Warthegau.[27]

"Ordinary men" or "ordinary Germans"?

One of the crucial yet unclear aspects of this overall process of radicalization is the role played in it by German society at large. We know of the mobilizing impact of the "myth of the Führer," but we are less certain about the measure of penetration of Nazi ideology into various strata of the population and the support given to the goals of Nazism as a result of the widespread participation of the most diverse groups in the benefits of increased social mobility, economic development, and the general effects of modernization during the years 1933 to approximately 1941. Regarding the more extreme goals, particularly the treatment of the Jews—as long as this hostility remained in the open—Otto Dov Kulka and David Bankier have indicated a growing measure of acceptance and an even wider background of indifference and inertia.[28] These findings have to be qualified to a point, as far as the early phase of the regime is concerned, by a measure of noncooperation of those sectors of society that could derive some advantage from continuing relations with Jews (the peasantry, e.g.).[29] Over the years, this noncooperation was eliminated by the elimination of the Jewish presence as such. In general terms, the growing support for the regime, also as a result of the modernization process, had a numbing effect on any adverse reactions to the massive persecution of the Jews and other groups, even if Nazi ideological tenets did not penetrate the wider reaches of society to any depth.[30]

It is within this context that Christopher Browning's work on those "ordinary men" of "order police" unit 101—who from being ordinary policemen in Hamburg became murderers without being an ideologically committed group and without being coerced by threatening orders—raises a basic issue.[31] Were these policemen merely "ordinary men," or were they "ordinary Germans," the product of a German society totally suffused by centuries old "eliminationist" anti-Semitism, as claimed in Daniel Goldhagen's *Hitler's Willing Executioners*?[32] One could argue, in fact, that

Browning's "ordinary men" were not entirely unideological after all, since as late as the 1960s they still used Nazi terminology in order to explain how they could recognize the Jews whom they chased and killed in the forests of eastern Poland. They were probably not even aware of the ideological tenets that they had internalized during the 1930s. Moreover, serving in the police was not identical to being an ordinary person of the kind one found outside of the network of official agencies and organizations. As for Goldhagen's position, it would be tenable if it were reformulated in a much less extreme form, with the main emphasis on the impact of the political culture produced by the Third Reich and not on an age-old German anti-Semitic tradition. It is unlikely that, in its present uncompromising form, Goldhagen's interpretation will have much impact on current historiography, notwithstanding its extaordinary success with the wider public in a number of countries, particularly Germany.

On the origins of the "Final Solution"

Even with regard to the general background of the "Final Solution," the approach which I defined as traditional and *some* of the new trends may converge. In the debate as it is circumscribed here, the issue is not that of the date of the order of total extermination but rather that of the historiographical interpretation of the genesis of that order, either as a direct result of Hitler's anti-Jewish fury carried to its ultimate pitch by the new circumstances of the Russian campaign, or as the result of a huge extension of the plan for the annihilation of groups "unworthy to live," a view closely linking the onset of the "Final Solution" to the ongoing murder of tens of thousands of German mental patients.[33] In the first instance we would be facing the ultimate consequence of the impact of the deadly myth of the Jewish world enemy, that is, the ultimate consequence of redemptive anti-Semitism; in the second case, one could argue for the convergence of a gruesome instrumental logic with some general tenets of racism.

The point of convergence lies in the fact that both redemptive anti-Semitism and the policies of racial extermination of groups "unworthy of living" were fostered at the same time by Hitler and by party and state agencies as entirely compatible though distinct elements of the overall worldview. There seems to be little doubt that redemptive anti-Semitism was Hitler's dominant obsession and that it inspired the guidelines that determined the fate of the Jews and established the framework for their extermination. But, as we well know, general racial "cleansing" was also on Hitler's agenda and, thus, radical anti-Semites and diverse categories of more "scientifically" oriented race specialists readily cooperated by furthering their own murderous agendas.

At this point, however, brief mention of a seemingly related historiographical interpretation is necessary, namely, that propounded over a number of years by Götz Aly and his different coauthors. In most of his work, until his recent synthesis on the "Final Solution," Aly stressed the central importance in the planning of Nazi exterminations of a group of middle-ranking economists and demographers who, free of anti-Semitic or other racial, ideological motivations, were calculating the cost–benefit effect of the extermination of millions of human beings. In this view, the "Final Solution" was the first result of this program of economic rationality, although it was merely the beginning of a much wider extermination process.[34] I would have presented the extremely cogent arguments formulated by Graml, Browning, Diner, Herbert, and others against these propositions had Götz Aly himself not recently again changed the focus of his interpretation. In his interpretation of the "Final Solution" published in 1995, Aly now perceives the evolution of the increasingly murderous policies directed against the Jews to be the result of the massive transfers of populations that the Nazis started in Eastern Europe after the conquest of Poland.[35] Such explanations leave out too many elements of the overall scene (such as the inclusion of the Jews of Western Europe in the extermination process) to be in any way convincing.

The main issue in the "Historians' Debate" of 1986 was the comparability of Nazi exterminations with those of other totalitarian regimes. Yet the comparison as such was not the main element of the debate but rather its use in order to downplay the nature of Nazi crimes. The Soviet Union became a model of major import and, as Ernst Nolte argued, the Gulag was the original of which Auschwitz was only a copy. Nolte's general thesis about the relation between bolshevism and fascism (Nazism) has recently found the unexpected support of one of the most prestigious historians of the French Revolution, François Furet, though not without some major objections.[36] A new debate on significant historiographical issues may be appearing in regard to the relation between Nazism and bolshevism and the significance of "totalitarianism" as a generalized explanatory framework for Nazi exterminations and the "Final Solution."

NOTES

1 For the major points of contention in the *Historikerstreit*, see Charles S. Maier, *The Unmasterable Past: History, Holocaust, and German National Identity* (Cambridge, MA: Harvard University Press, 1988); Richard Evans, *In Hitler's Shadow: West German Historians and the Attempt to Escape the Nazi Past* (London: I. B. Tauris, 1989); Peter Baldwin, ed., *Reworking the Past: Hitler, the Holocaust, and the Historians' Debate* (Boston: Beacon Press, 1990). See also Saul Friedlander, "West Germany and the Burden of the Past: The Ongoing Debate," *Jerusalem Quarterly* 42 (Spring 1987); Steven E. Aschheim, "History, Politics and National Memory: The German *Historikerstreit*," *Survey of Jewish Affairs* (1988).

2 For a perceptive overview of the German scene (mainly of the Berlin scene), see Jane Kramer, "The Politics of Memory," *New Yorker* 14 August 1995.

3 For the growth and impact of the *völkisch* ideology, see, for example, George L. Mosse, *The Crisis of German Ideology: Intellectual Origins of the Third Reich* (New York: Universal Library, 1964); for the convergence of the various ideological trends in Nazism, see Karl Dietrich Bracher, *The German Dictatorship* (Harmondsworth: Penguin Books, 1973); and for recent surveys of the *Sonderweg* debate, see Jürgen Kocka, "German History before Hitler: The Debate about the German *Sonderweg*," *Journal of Contemporary History* 23 (1988); Steven E. Aschheim, "Nazism, Normalcy, and the German *Sonderweg*," *Studies in Contemporary Jewry* 4 (1988).

4 Detlev J. K. Peukert, "The Genesis of the 'Final Solution' from the Spirit of Science," in Thomas Childers and Jane Caplan, eds., *Reevaluating the Third Reich* (New York: Holmes & Meier, 1993).

5 Peukert, "Genesis of the 'Final Solution'."

6 Eberhard Jäckel, *Hitler in History* (Hanover, NH: University Press of New England, 1984).

7 As far as the most general aspects of this position are concerned, see, for example, from a conservative and apologetic angle, Michael Prinz and Rainer Zitelmann, eds., *Nationalsozialismus und Modernisierung* (Darmstadt: Wissenschaftliche Buchgesellschaft, 1991). For an entirely different approach, see Zygmunt Bauman, *Modernity and the Holocaust* (Ithaca, NY: Cornell University Press, 1989). A leftist-oriented interpretation finds its most systematic presentation in a number of publications by Götz Aly and different coauthors, as indicated below.

8 Each of the elements referred to in this sentence has been dealt with in an immense historiography. For an altogether nuanced and precise illustration of these approaches, see Philippe Burrin, *Hitler and the Jews: The Genesis of the Holocaust* (New York: Routledge, Chapman & Hall, 1994). For an interesting distinction between Nazi irrationalism and Nazi counterrationality see Dan Diner, "Historical Understanding and Counterrationality: The *Judenrat* as Epistemological Vantage," in Saul Friedländer, ed., *Probing the Limits of Representation: Nazism and the Final Solution* (Cambridge, MA: Harvard University Press, 1993).

9 For the first aspect, see mainly Michael Burleigh and Wolfgang Wippermann, *The Racial State: Germany 1933–1945* (Cambridge: Cambridge University Press, 1991); for the second aspect, see Götz Aly and Karl-Heinz Roth, *Die Restlose Erfassung: Volkszählen, Identifizieren, Aussondern im Nationalsozialismus* (Berlin: Rotbuch Verlag, 1984); Götz Aly and Susanne Heim, *Vordenker der Vernichtung: Auschwitz und die deutschen Pläne für eine neue europäische Ordnung* (Frankfurt/M.: S. Fischer Verlag, 1991); Götz Aly, *"Endlösung": Volksverschiebung und der Mord an den europäischen Juden* (Frankfurt/M.: S. Fischer Verlag, 1995).

10 Max Horkheimer and Theodor W. Adorno, *Dialectic of Enlightenment* (New York: Herder & Herder, 1972 [1947]); Bauman, *Modernity and the Holocaust*; Aly and Heim, *Vordenker der Vernichtung*; also Peukert, "The Genesis of the 'Final Solution'."

11 This is to be the guiding theme of Ian Kershaw's Hitler biography.

12 See Ian Kershaw's indications in his *The Nazi Dictatorship: Problems and Perspectives of Interpretation* (London: E. Arnold, 1993); see also the synthesis of these various approaches in Burleigh and Wippermann, *Racial State*.

13 For a discussion of "redemptive anti-Semitism," see my *Nazi Germany and the Jews*, vol. 1, *The Years of Persecution, 1933–1939* (New York: HarperCollins, 1997).

14 Peukert, "Genesis of the 'Final Solution'."
15 Paul Lawrence Rose, *Revolutionary Anti-Semitism in Germany from Kant to Wagner* (Princeton, NJ: Princeton University Press, 1990); Paul Lawrence Rose, *Wagner, Race, and Revolution* (London: Faber, 1992).
16 Norman Cohn, *The Pursuit of the Millennium: Revolutionary Messianism in Medieval and Reformation Europe and Its Bearing on Modern Totalitarian Movements* (New York: Harper, 1961).
17 According to my interpretation it is in Bayreuth and within the "Bayreuth Circle" that these tendencies converged. For an excellent presentation of the ideological positions of the Bayreuth Circle, see Winfried Schüler, *Der Bayreuther Kreis von seiner Entstehung bis zum Ausgang der wilhelminischen Ära* (Münster: Aschendorff, 1971).
18 For each of these stages successively, see Geoffrey G. Field, *Evangelist of Race: The Germanic Vision of Houston Stewart Chamberlain* (New York: Columbia University Press, 1981); Norman Cohn, *Warrant for Genocide: The Myth of the Jewish World Conspiracy and the Protocols of the Elders of Zion* (London: Eyre & Spottiswoode, 1967); Ralph Max Engelman, "Dietrich Eckart and the Genesis of Nazism," Ph.D. diss. (Ann Arbor, MI: University Microfilms, 1971).
19 For one of the most recent and nuanced restatements of Mommsen's position on Hitler's role, see Hans Mommsen, "Reflections on the Position of Hitler and Göring in the Third Reich," in Childers and Caplan, *Reevaluating the Third Reich*; also "Hitler's Position in the Nazi System," in Hans Mommsen, *From Weimar to Auschwitz* (Princeton, NJ: Princeton University Press, 1991).
20 Apart from Prinz and Zitelmann, *Nationalsozialismus und Modernisierung*, see also Rainer Zitelmann's short biography of Hitler, *Eine politische Biographie* (Göttingen: Muster-Schmidt, 1989), as well as Uwe Backes, Eckhard Jesse, and Rainer Zitelmann, eds., *Die Schatten der Vergangenheit: Impulse zur Historisierung des Nationalsozialismus* (Berlin: Propylaen, 1990).
21 Jäckel, *Hitler and History*; Martin Broszat, "Hitler and the Genesis of the 'Final Solution'," *Yad Vashem Studies* 13 (1979).
22 On this dual role, see my *Nazi Germany and the Jews*.
23 Dieter Rebentisch, *Führerstaat und Verwaltung im Zweiten Weltkrieg* (Stuttgart: F. Steiner Verlag Wiesbaden, 1989).
24 Ian Kershaw, "'Working towards the Führer': Reflections on the Nature of Hitler's Dictatorship," *Contemporary European History* 2.2 (1993).
25 Raul Hilberg, *The Destruction of the European Jews* (Chicago: Quadrangle Books, 1961); the same basic position informs the updated German edition, *Die Vernichtung der europäischen Juden*, 3 vols., (Frankfurt/M.: Fischer Taschenbuch Verlag, 1990). As for Hans Mommsen's argument, see especially "The Realization of the Unthinkable: The 'Final Solution of the Jewish Question' in the Third Reich" in Mommsen, *From Weimar to Auschwitz*.
26 For a minor illustration of this general situation, see the description of the paralysis of all German state agencies in regard to the *Haavara* agreement until Hitler's much delayed decision in Avraham Barkai, "German Interests in the Haavara—Transfer Agreement 1933–1939," *Leo Baeck Institute Yearbook* 35 (London: Secker & Warburg, 1990).
27 Ian Kershaw, "Improvised Genocide? The Emergence of the 'Final Solution' in the 'Warthegau,'" *Transactions of the Royal Historical Society*, ser. 6, vol. 2 (1992).
28 Otto Dov Kulka, "Public Opinion in Nazi Germany and the Jewish Question,'" *Jerusalem Quarterly* 25 (Fall 1982); David Bankier, *The Germans and the Final Solution: Public Opinion under Nazism* (Oxford: Basil Blackwell, 1992).

29 On this issue, see my *Nazi Germany and the Jews*.
30 On the nonpenetration of Nazi ideology in the wider strata of the population, see mainly Martin Broszat's studies of everyday life, as well as his theoretical arguments around the notions of ideology, modernization, and *Resistenz* in Martin Broszat, *Nach Hitler: Der schwierige Umgang mit unserer Geschichte* (Munich: Oldenbourg, 1987), and particularly in Martin Broszat, "A Plea for the Historicization of National Socialism," in Baldwin, *Reworking the Past*. For a debate on these issues, see my essay "Some Reflections on the Historicization of National Socialism," in Baldwin, *Reworking the Past*, as well as Martin Broszat and Saul Friedlander, "A Controversy about the Historicization of National Socialism," in Baldwin, *Reworking the Past*.
31 Christopher Browning, *Ordinary Men: Reserve Police Battalion 101 and the 'Final Solution' in Poland* (New York: HarperCollins, 1992).
32 Daniel Jonah Goldhagen, *Hitler's Willing Executioners: Ordinary Germans and the Holocaust* (New York: Alfred A. Knopf, 1996).
33 The traditional presentation of the origins of the "Final Solution" is most cogently presented in Christopher R. Browning's collection of essays, *The Path to Genocide: Essays on Launching the Final Solution* (Cambridge: Cambridge University Press, 1992). For the direct link between euthanasia and the 'Final Solution,' see Peukert, "Genesis of the 'Final Solution'," as well as the series of articles and documents published by Götz Aly and Susanne Heim under the general title *Beiträge zur Nationalsozialistischer Gesundheit- und Sozialpolitik* (Berlin: Rotbuch, 1991). For the most recent statement of this argument, see Henry Friedlander, *The Origins of Nazi Genocide: From Euthanasia to the Final Solution* (Chapel Hill, NC: University of North Carolina Press, 1995).
34 Götz Aly and Susanne Heim, *Vordenker der Vernichtung*. For the criticism directed against Aly and Heim's positions, see mainly the essays published in Wolfgang Schneider, ed., *"Vernichtungspolitik": Eine Debatte über den Zusammenhang von Sozialpolitik und Genozid im nationalsozialistischen Deutschland* (Hamburg: Junius, 1991).
35 Götz Aly, *"Endlösung": Volkerverschiebung und der Mord an den Europäischen Juden* (Frankfurt/M.: S. Fischer Verlag, 1995).
36 François Furet, *Le Passé d'une Illusion: Essai sur l'idée communiste au xxe siècle* (Paris: Robert Laffont; Calmann-Levy, 1995). See in particular pp. 195–6n.

5

THE PLANNING INTELLIGENTSIA AND THE "FINAL SOLUTION"

Götz Aly

One of the most challenging issues confronting historians of the Holocaust is the ideological, political, and economic context within which it happened. The problems are obvious: if we examine the "Final Solution" in isolation from the events that surrounded or preceded it, we are in danger both of gaining only a very partial understanding of the event, and of dehistoricizing the Holocaust to the extent that it would acquire the characteristics of a unique, mythical affair with no links to the rest of the annals of human history. However, if we historicize the Holocaust and view it as inherent to a larger historical context, we may lose sight of its specificity and unprecedented aspects, and end up relativizing and banalizing it as simply one more mass murder in a long history of human massacres and atrocities.

Götz Aly's goal in this chapter is first to demonstrate the extent to which the Nazi regime relied on a group of highly trained experts, mostly with advanced academic degrees, in planning its policies of occupation, enslavement, and genocide. Second, he seeks to show that the Holocaust was not the consequence of an irrational, ideological imperative, but rather of what appeared to the experts and was accepted by the regime as an entirely rational and urgent economic necessity, namely, changing the demographic structure of Eastern Europe and Western Russia so as to both modernize its economy and facilitate the resettlement there of ethnic Germans. The creation of such "living space" (Lebensraum) in the East therefore entailed the mass deportation and death from famine, disease, and exposure of millions of Poles and Russians, as well as the murder of millions of Jews. Yet while this program succeeded only in its first phase—the genocide of the Jews—it was neither haphazard nor limited to "solving the Jewish question." Aly's account can be criticized on several counts. As he concedes, the regime was particularly fanatic about the murder of the Jews, and while it (or some of its middle- or even high-ranking agents) might have seen the "Final Solution" as part of an even grander "General Plan East" (Generalplan Ost), when push came to shove the killing of the Jews gained top priority both in respect to other "racial" or political categories and as far as economic interests were concerned. Indeed, Aly's attempt to distinguish between rational economic policies and irrational ideological imperatives is problematic, since for many Nazi functionaries the necessity to murder the Jews appeared entirely rational and sparing them in favor of economic need for more than a brief period seemed highly irrational, if not suicidal. As noted in the Introduction to this volume, we must also recognize that there was a difference in the Nazi mind between Jews and Slavs, and while the latter were often (but not always) seen as "subhumans" (Untermenschen), they were not necessarily slated for extermination (and in part were treated relatively decently, as for instance the Czechs); the Jews, on the other hand, had to "vanish from the face of the earth," as Himmler put it in one of his speeches. Second, as Saul Friedländer remarks in his chapter, it is unclear how the transportation of hundreds of thousands of Jews from Western, Southern, indeed even South-Eastern Europe to death camps in Poland could have conceivably been part of a demographic plan for the East. Obviously, these deportations constituted an element in another program, that of ridding the world of the Jewish danger. However, it is quite possible that both plans could and for some time did operate simultaneously, and to a certain extent even complemented each other. Such a revision of Aly, which would not subordinate the "Final Solution" to the "General Plan East" but put them side by side (with the former ultimately winning out) would greatly strengthen his thesis. Moreover, his stress on the involvement of academic experts in these brutal demographic plans, among whom were some prominent historians who went on to distinguished careers in postwar Germany and educated several generations of still active scholars, is a major contribution to our understanding of the links between the German elites and the Nazis, and between the past and the present.

* * *

There is a broad consensus among scholars that no rationally conceived motives informed the Nazis' murder of European Jews. The political philosopher Hannah Arendt, for example, emphasised that what made this crime unique was not the number of victims, but rather the absence of any concern for the economic utility of the victims on the part of the perpetrators. When it comes to motives, historians prefer to stress 'irrational racial hatred', 'destruction for destruction's sake', a 'black hole of historical understanding', or the self-propelling radicalising capacities inherent in modern bureaucratic structures.

For many years historians have sought in vain for an order from Hitler to destroy the Jews of Europe. However, from a careful examination of the documents that are assumed to have ordered the murder of German psychiatric patients or the deliberate starvation of 'many millions' of Soviet citizens, it is clear that they 'commission' or 'authorise', which means that recommendations or concrete plans were submitted to Hitler, Himmler or Goering for a decision: to be approved or rejected, redrafted or put on hold. Goering also expressed wishes about how these measures should best be disguised. Regarding the murders perpetrated by SS task-forces in the former Soviet Union, Hitler simply remarked: 'as far as the world at large is concerned our motives must be in accordance with tactical considerations . . . we will carry out all necessary measures—shootings, resettlements etc.—regardless of this.' This raises questions about the authorship of these 'necessary measures', and above all questions regarding aims and motives.

My starting point is that the Nazi regime relied to an exceptional degree upon academically-trained advisers and that it made use of their skills. Their ideas were transmitted upwards to the highest echelons by civil servants, especially by the secretaries of state attached to the various ministries, many of whom belonged to the General Council of the Four Year Plan agency, in which capacity they ranked higher than their own ministers. The Four Year Plan was designed to boost production in strategically vital areas of the economy and it reached the apogee of its power between 1938 and 1942, during which time programmes for the socio-political and economic reorganisation of Europe were developed and converted into both policy and military strategy.

The concept of an 'economy of the Final Solution' was developed by German experts—above all economists, agronomists, demographers, experts in labour deployment, geographers, historians, planners and statisticians. They made up the planning committees of such agencies as the Reich Office for Area Planning, the Reich Commissariat for the Strengthening of Ethnic Germandom and the Four Year Plan authority. They conceived and discussed solutions to the various 'demographic questions', and calculated the possible 'release of pressure' that would be the result of excluding Jews from the economy. They recommended converting the Ukraine into

Europe's breadbasket—taking into their calculations the deliberate starvation of 'many millions' of Soviet citizens. They calculated the losses occasioned by the economies of the ghettos and thus delivered arguments for the mass murder of their inhabitants.

The approach adopted in this study is not that of the conspiracy theory, but to name those who were responsible, and to expose the role of a careerist, academically-trained, intelligentsia in the extermination of millions of people. There were probably a few thousand members of this 'scientific community', who, notwithstanding the usual animosities and petty institutional and personal jealousies, contributed to the formation of the prevailing opinion. It has sometimes been said that these people were not 'real' scholars, but rather half or totally crazy third-rate figures, but arguments such as this fail to explain the involvement of people more usually described as being major intellects, for example the historians Werner Conze and Theodor Schieder, who went on to dominate their profession in the post-war period. The expertise of this 'community' was not a form of *ex post facto* rationalisation of policies upon whose formulation they had exerted no real influence, but rather the basis upon which decisions were made by ministers and state secretaries. The reports produced by the Reich Committee for Economic Affairs concerning the 'conversion' of trade in Vienna or later in the Generalgouvernement in Poland provided the basis for decisions subsequently taken which sought to combine the 'dejudaisation' with the 'rationalisation' of their economies. The Reich Commissar for the Strengthening of Ethnic Germandom had detailed information regarding the optimum distribution of commercial and manufacturing firms in the areas from which Jews and 'Aryan' Poles were dispossessed in the interests of incoming ethnic German repatriates. In other words, both expulsions and compulsory 'germanisation' were carried out according to calculated economic, as opposed to racial-biological criteria. On the basis of these initial practical steps, in whose conception they had played a material part, the economists, demographers and planners could develop yet more elaborate plans. Thus, the Aryanisation of Vienna served as a model for all similar policies, and the expulsion of undesirable ethnic groups to the Generalgouvernement resurfaced later in discussions regarding the economic reconstruction of this territory, in the form of solutions to a self-imposed dilemma. Population pressure urgently demanded 'disburdenment'.

The reason why the links between long-term economic planning and the extermination of people have scarcely been investigated may largely be attributed to the initial connections forged between the uniqueness of the Holocaust and the alleged or assumed absence of any rational, utilitarian calculation. It is also the result of a gross underestimation of the power wielded by professional experts in a regime whose ideological statements were imprecise, vague and open-ended. This can be illustrated by looking at the various 'contributions' to the Nazi 'euthanasia' programme. On 3 April 1940 Viktor Brack, a senior official in the Chancellery of the Führer, speaking at a meeting of senior mayors, outlined recent developments in German psychiatric hospitals. (In what follows, the agencies, individuals or interests responsible for various elements within the 'euthanasia' programme have been included in brackets):

> In many of the asylums in the Reich there are innumerable incurable patients of all descriptions [the doctors and psychiatrists], who are of no use to humanity [Hitler, the doctors]. They only serve to take away resources from other healthy people [military logistics experts, Hitler], and often require intensive nursing [doctors]. The rest of humanity has to be protected from these people [Hitler]. If today one has to make decisions regarding the maintenance of healthy people, then it is all the more essential first to remove these creatures, if only to ensure better care of curable cases in the asylums and hospitals [doctors]. One needs the vacant bedspace for all sorts of important military purposes [army medical corps experts]: sickbays, hospitals, auxiliary hospitals [army medical corps experts]. For the remainder, the action will greatly disburden the local authorities, since each individual case will no longer occasion any future costs for care or maintenance [war finance experts, local authorities].

To this list should be added the bureaucratic ambitions of the officials in the Chancellery of the Führer itself. A close examination of this relatively well-documented decision-making process should disabuse anyone of the idea that 'the bureaucratic machinery functioned automatically', as Hans Mommsen repeatedly states with reference to the murder of European Jews, where there is much less surviving evidence of the decision-making process. Three successive stages can be distinguished in deciding whether there was an 'economy of the Final Solution'.

1. Pogroms and rationalisation

On 12 November 1938, two days after the pogroms of Reich Crystal Night, an important part of the Nazi leadership gathered for a discussion on the Jewish Question. The chair was taken by Hermann Goering, the Plenipotentiary for the Four Year Plan. Among those invited were Goebbels, Reinhard Heydrich and an array of economic experts: the Ministers of Finance and the Economy, a representative of the insurance sector and about one hundred experts, policy advisers and senior civil servants. Goering, the leading light in the economic affairs of the Greater German Reich, introduced himself with the modest disclaimer that he was 'not well versed enough in economic affairs', but then informed the participants that 'since the problem is mainly an economic one, it will have to be tackled from an economic perspective'. The measures necessary to Aryanise the economy would have to be taken 'one after another', with the Jews being excluded from the economy and 'put into the poorhouse'.

It was not a matter of enriching the petty-bourgeois grassroots supporters of the National Socialist German Workers Party (NSDAP), or, indeed, of Aryan competitors expropriating Jewish banks or department stores, but rather that there were too many one-man stores, artisan workshops and small factories in Germany in general. Within a few weeks of the conference state agencies closed two-thirds of all Jewish-owned one-man concerns and small businesses, selling off their stock to Aryan traders and adding the profits to national funds. This was part of what Goering called 'an action to convert non-essential units of production into essential ones', which was also scheduled to take place in the near future. So-called Aryanisation was therefore primarily a matter of economic rationalisation and concentration, what is now known as 'restructuring'.

The decisions taken at this conference were informed by the experiences derived from the annexation of Austria, experiences that were relayed to the participants by the Minister for the Economy and Labour in Austria, Hans Fischbock, who made the trip to the conference from his office in Vienna. According to calculations by the Reich Committee for Economic Affairs, 90 per cent of Jewish concerns in Vienna had been shut down entirely, with only 10 per cent being put up for sale. Fischbock boasted that the closures were based upon studies of each sector of the economy and had been determined in accordance with local needs. This *modus operandi* was adopted a few days later in Berlin and then by the German occupying authorities in Czechoslovakia, Poland and The Netherlands.

Any concerns about adverse socio-political consequences stemming from the Viennese model were allayed by Heydrich who, referring to co-operation between the Ministry of Economics, foreign humanitarian agencies and Adolf Eichmann's SS office for Jewish Affairs, pointed to the 50,000 Jews who had been removed from the economy since the Anschluss by being forced to emigrate. Only some 19,000 Jews had been removed from the Old (pre-expansion) Reich in the same timespan. The Special Pleni-potentiary for Jewish Emigration was the President of the Reichsbank Hjalmar Schacht. Only one person present evinced any scepticism, the conservative nationalist Minister of Finance Schwerin von Krosigk who remarked: 'the crucial point is that we don't end up with the whole proletariat. Dealing with them will always be an appalling burden.' The conference ended with the slogan 'out with what can be got out', by which they meant the Jews. At the same time it was immediately obvious that because of shortages of foreign exchange this would only be partially successful, and that those Jews who remained—the old, sick and unemployed—would 'be a burden on the state'. If before Reich Crystal Night in November 1938 there had been rivalries and clashes of competence between the various agencies occupied with the Jewish Question, this changed dramatically after 12 November 1938. Goering declared: 'Once and for all I prohibit any separate action. The Reich has taken the matter in hand.' Thenceforth, anti-Semitic measures were co-ordinated by the Four Year Plan apparatus; special responsibility devolved upon Erich Neumann, the State Secretary for Exchange Questions and 'special tasks of a general economic nature'. The business of deportations and later extermination was transferred to the Reich Main Security Office of the SS.

2. Developmental policy and demographic questions

The second phase in the economically motivated radicalisation of policy towards the Jews began after September 1939 with the conquest and deliberate territorial fragmentation of Poland. In the eyes of German economic planners, Poland was underdeveloped and its economy both badly organised and starved of capital. Above all, however, too many people derived their livelihood from the land. The economy was charac-terised by subsistence agriculture: the rural population satisfied most of its own demands for foodstuffs and consumer goods, and in the villages barter rather than money was the normal means of exchange, in other words it was 'a system insufficient for rationalisation', basically impervious to the logic of capitalist penetration and exploitation. In the minds of German, and indeed other international economists, Poland's main problem lay in rural overpopulation. A third of the population would be deemed surplus to requirements should modern means of cultivation be adopted. The 'surplus population' was a 'burden on the national economy', or what Theodor Oberländer called, 'a symptom of socio-economic sickness'. Overpopulation had nothing to do with the density of population, but was rather a question of perceived deviation from an allegedly normal or 'optima' population.

The theory of optimum population had been developed at the turn of the century by a number of economists with the aid of Paul Mombert's theory of diminishing returns, or what is known as the Mombert Formula. Mombert (1876–1938) was Professor of Political Economy at Giessen until his compulsory retirement as a 'non-Aryan' in 1933. His formula consists of a simple equation which relates population numbers to economic resources. According to this formula, $F = P \times L$, food-supply (F) equals population numbers (P) times living standard (L). This reductionist abstraction enables the 'explanation' of every misrelationship between resources and living standards to be made in terms of population figures, regardless of such factors as unemployment, lack of capital or raw materials, absence of markets or low productivity and so forth. Every type of economic crisis, including those occasioned by war, could be redefined in terms of the 'population question'.

According to this theory, population becomes an economic variable like any other, which can therefore also be manipulated like any other. Mombert himself seems to have expressly ruled out this possibility, but this was overlooked by his disciples. To German economists, with their sights set upon a vast, dependent, integrated European economy under German hegemony, the size and composition of a population became the factor which, given wartime conditions and the relative scarcity of raw materials, they could adjust most easily. Population policy in the form of 'resettlement' became a way of overcoming capital and foreign currency shortages, of regulating wartime finances and of releasing foodstuffs and raw materials, while at the same time achieving the longer-term goal of a more rational economic structure and enhanced exploitation of labour.

By 1932 Mombert had already calculated the burden upon the national economy of the surplus population created by the Depression. The cost to the state of maintaining the unproductive was of the order of four billion Reichmarks, money which could otherwise have been employed productively by expanding the economic base in the form of domestic investment or export capital. At the time Mombert was thinking in terms of financing colonial projects in Africa, however his model also suggested ways in which capital could be more rapidly accumulated via a 'cessation of population growth'. According to the academics who serviced the occupying authorities in Poland—and who again and again referred to the 'irrefutable Mombert formula'—this was precisely the answer they needed to the underlying problems they discerned in the Polish economy. A reduction of the population would simultaneously break the vicious circle of overpopulation and lead to capital accumulation necessary for the modernisation of the economy. If this did not succeed, then occupied Poland would become a 'burden' upon the entire German-dominated *Grossraum*. The extermination of millions of people would halt population growth in eastern Europe for a few critical years, 'thus' releasing capital resources, which could be used to promote industrialisation and the mechanisation of agriculture, or in other words developments that were in Germany's economic interest. The German academic planners generated quantities of plans and developmental models, which at a stroke rendered entire peoples surplus to requirements and therefore subject to resettlement or deportation as forced labour. 'Negative demographic policy' was the lever of a new type of German developmental economics.

According to German calculations, every second rural Pole was 'nothing more than a dead weight', and overpopulation 'effectively a barrier to capital formation'. Theodor Oberländer, subsequently a minister in Konrad Adenauer's post-war cabinet, reckoned that in many areas of Poland the population was as much as 75 per cent superfluous. Expressed in absolute terms, this meant that some 4.5 to 5.83 million Poles were surplus to requirements. Thinking bigger, the economists calculated that in south-eastern Europe, whose overpopulation would also have to be regulated, there were between twelve and fifteen million workers on the land who would have to be 'set in motion'. If one included their families, then there were about fifty million people who would have to be pushed out of their domestic subsistence lifestyle if the German industrial economy was to benefit. Having occupied large parts of the Soviet Union, the German economic and agrarian experts revised their figures upwards by another thirty million, in other words by precisely the increase of population in Russia that had occurred between 1905 and 1939.

This theory of overpopulation described relatively backward economies. Underactivity and unemployment were the norm, or as economists would say, labour capacity was being only partially used. Disharmony between people and capital resulted in considerable rural and urban poverty; outside intervention designed to rationalise this state of affairs, would necessarily result in the population being divided into those who would have to work more intensively and those who would not be working at all. The state would decide who was deemed to be productive or non-productive. This was precisely the point at which Nazi racial criteria fused with the scientific criteria of population economy.

3. The war against the Soviet Union

The third phase in this demographically conceived programme of mass murder began with the planning for the war against the Soviet Union. The initial aim was to achieve a '180 degree turn' in the direction of the economy of the Ukraine, which should no longer feed Soviet workers, but rather secure the foodstuffs and hence immunity to blockade of Central Europe. The plan of attack incorporated the deliberate starvation of 'many millions' of people in order to secure food for the inhabitants of Western and Central Europe. According to printed guidelines:

> Many tens of millions of people will become superfluous to require-ments in these areas [i.e. the forests and industrial towns of the north] and will die or have to move to Siberia. Attempts to prevent the population there from starving by moving food surpluses from the black earth zone, can only be done at the cost of supplying Europe. This would undermine Germany's capacity to prevail during the war, and would undermine Germany and Europe's capacity to resist blockade.

Underlying these bleak calculations was the knowledge that Germany was only able to provide some 87 per cent of her food requirements, that the only occupied country able to deliver food supplies without starving its own citizens was Denmark and that the rest actually needed to import foodstuffs from Germany. Because of the way in which agriculture tended to become more and more extensive during wartime, involving the cultivation of unsuitable land, the food situation was bound to deteriorate from harvest to harvest. This problem, the only one that might have adversely affected the mood of the German population, was to be resolved by organising the deaths of about thirty million Russians. The plans, which were unparalleled in their clarity, never mentioned the word 'race', but constantly referred to the logic of economic circumstances. 'Negative demographic policy' was the imperative of the hour, with hunger acting as a form of geo-strategic tourniquet. These plans, which were developed some months before the 'Final Solution of the Jewish Question' once again emanated from Goering's Four Year Plan agency. The two million Soviet prisoners of war who died of starvation in German camps before the end of 1941, did not die because of any problems in food supply, but were victims of deliberate murder. In November 1941 Goering remarked that 'this year twenty to thirty million people will starve in Russia. Perhaps that's a good thing, since certain people will have to be decimated'.

These plans connected with the supply of food were accompanied by others—notably the Generalplan Ost—which were concerned with strategies of power and settlement policy. During the preparations for the war against the Soviet Union, the horizons suddenly appeared limitless to German planners. The Institut für Deutsche Ostarbeit in occupied Cracow considered *inter alia* 'the resettlement of the Poles', while a Berlin professor of anthropology who carried out studies of Soviet prisoners of war recommended 'the liquidation of Russiandom'.

The invasion of Russia opened up new ways of solving every social problem, not just in the occupied areas, but also in the Reich itself. As the chief of the Generalplan Ost project noted: 'the victory of our arms and the expansion of our frontiers has destroyed all of the old limitations.' The massive tasks which had 'arisen' for the German nation were not just a matter of 'germanisation' and the reconstruction of conquered territories. Rather, a 'profound reordering of nation and available space' in the old Reich would ensue as a result of the new order created on the new frontiers. It would begin with the reorganisation of the economy and with the cleansing of overfull occupations. Production, markets and prices would be streamlined in accordance with purchasing power. Finally, the whole structure of settlement would have to be reorganised. The Generalplan Ost, which covered the whole area between Leningrad and the Crimea, presupposed the 'evacuation' of thirty-one million people. In the eyes of the authors of these documents, the Solution of the Jewish Question (for some five million Jews lived in the areas covered by the plan), was merely part of their 'great task'.

* * *

In the German Reich, in occupied Poland and, finally, in the entire area subject to German hegemony it was overwhelmingly people designated as being unproductive—the chronically sick, the so-called asocial, and then the Jews—in other words, groups who were already discriminated against and who were hence easy to isolate, who were to be removed from the economic process and denied any form of social security. This meant that in addition to Jews and Gypsies, vast parts of the Slav population were to be victims of extermination. The extermination of the Jews carried out under cover of war was the part of this agenda most fully realised. These plans were founded upon demographic and economic criteria as well as theories of racial hierarchy. Their initial premise was that the population of Europe had to be reduced for medium- and short-term economic and strategic reasons. The dynamics of extermination and the actual course of decision-making can be understood only if the demographic and economic goals which underpinned them are borne in mind.

In destroying the Jews one of the most tangible manifestations of poverty in Eastern Europe would be destroyed, in other words the poorest parts of the cities and towns. Genocide was a means of solving the social question. Because most of the Jews lived in towns, their deportation would set the surplus rural population moving in the direction of the towns, giving them the possibility of social advancement into trade and handicrafts. At the same time, these overcrowded sectors in the towns themselves could be modernised and rationalised, without creating a discontented, declassé, national petty-bourgeoisie which would have been a threat to the German occupiers.

Both in Eastern Europe and, above all, in Germany itself, the expropriation of Jewish property provided an unbureaucratic form of self-help, which provided household goods, housing, new jobs and so forth. In the case of large-scale capital, expropriation enabled German banks and industry to consolidate their holdings. All that remained were unemployed and propertyless people or, in other words, an artificially achieved population surplus. Liquidified assets set free as a result of the deportation of Jews and non-Jewish Poles were taken over by the Main Trustees for the East set up for the purpose and then distributed in the form of development credits in order to strengthen undercapitalised sectors and regions.

Similar calculations informed the cogitations of virtually every German economist, agronomist, demographer and statistician. One example from many is the Berlin economic adviser Alfred Maelicke. Writing in the journal *The German Economy* in 1942, Maelicke remarked:

> Only the total dejudaisation of economic life will facilitate the solution of what is still the main problem in many countries, such as south-eastern Europe and elsewhere, namely overpopulation

and other social questions. The elimination of the Jewish trader mentality and profit-mindedness and the exclusion of the Jews will create space and security (full employment) for many hitherto rootless and impoverished workers and peasants, artisans and others . . . By observing the fundamentals and practices of dejudai-sation as applied in Germany one could effect profound changes in demographic relations, and even wider structural changes, without violently upsetting the nature of any given economy. There will be no need to dismiss workers and no difficulties of supply. One does not even need to worry about a contraction of turnover.

Maelicke had described a racially informed 'cleansing of the population problem'—the structural preconditions for the long-term re-ordering and exploitation of the *Grosswirtschaftsraum* (greater economic space) that once was Europe.

This explains the apparent contradiction between an economic or military interest in exploitation and the mass-extermination of potential sources of labour. In the eyes of German economists, overpopulation confirmed the alleged economic backwardness of economic structures and retarded the implementation of 'optimum labour productivity' within the *Grosswirts-chaftsraum*. In other words, the economic experts presupposed that part of the overpopulation would have to be 'eradicated' if the labour potential of the *Grossraum* was to be effectively exploited by being rendered 'mobile'. The Germans were not prepared to think in terms of capital investment designed to broaden overall resources. The low level of mechanisation to which the Jews were reduced in the ghettos and labour camps following their exclusion from the wider economy was further evidence of 'an effective brake upon capital', because resources were being tied up which, with the better organisation of labour and a more favourable combination of capital and labour, could otherwise have been used to produce greater profits. Himmler and Speer were in full agreement on this issue. The low wages paid to Jews working for German and Polish firms prevented rationalisation because in the short term, a Jewish labour force was a cheaper alternative than new machinery; the advantages that cheap labour obviously had for individual concerns were not mirrored by advantages for the economy as a whole. According to these criteria, it was economically more rational to kill the Jews than to put them to work.

The fact that even Jewish munitions workers were only temporarily reprieved from the gas chambers suggests that these concepts were racially determined. Even the last Jewish craftsman was replaced by an 'Aryan' one. However it is incorrect to talk (as some historians do) of the 'primacy of racially-motivated exterminatory plans above any economic factors'. Rather, especially in the second half of the war, the imperatives of munitions production collided with other economic imperatives, namely the no less acute crisis of food supply, which demanded a reduction of the population numbers and long-term economic restructuring by means of mass murder. Selection in accordance with racial criteria did not contradict economic calculation, rather it was an integral part of it.

Just as contemporary anthropologists, doctors and biologists regarded the marginalisation and extermination of allegedly 'less valuable' elements as a scientific way of improving mankind or 'healing the body of the nation', so economists, agronomists and planners thought their work would result in the 'healing of the structure of society' in underdeveloped regions of Europe. The mere 'co-eaters' would be separated from 'economically really active people'. In so far as the Jews, active in such sectors as trade and handicrafts, which the Germans regarded as overcrowded and superfluous, were not already doomed, socio-political and economic restructuring pushed them yet further into a position where they lost their property and all means of earning a livelihood. In this way racial and economic selection criteria were harmonised, with a consensus replacing alleged conflicts of interest between rational planners and racial fanatics. This consensus and the social sanitising concepts which underlay it gave the systematic and centrally planned murder of millions of people its own gruesome dynamic. Evidence of a technocratically rational agenda does not make these crimes 'comprehensible' let alone 'understandable', in the sense of having empathetic understanding for something. But looked at in this way, the crimes Germans committed in these years assume a rather different character, and require us to undertake the search for causes and continuities afresh and perhaps with yet greater seriousness.

Finally, there is the question of uniqueness. We began by considering Hannah Arendt's statement that no rational motives informed the Final Solution, a view with which most historians concur. In her important work on the origins of totalitarianism, Arendt made the following pertinent observation:

> The imperative 'Thou shalt not kill' fails in the face of a demographic policy which proceeds to exterminate systematically or industrially those races and individuals deemed unfit and less valuable, not once in a unique action, but on a basis obviously intended to be permanent. The death penalty becomes absurd when one is not dealing with murderers who know what murder is, but rather with demographers who organise the murder of millions in such a way that all those who participate subjectively consider themselves free of guilt.

What did the demographic policies of both of the major dictatorships of this century have in common? The Stalinist population policy of the 1930s—the eradication of the kulaks (peasant farmers)—corresponded in many respects to the policies pursued by the Nazis between 1939 and 1944. Discrimination against minorities, the mobilisation of the rural population, forcible colonisation, slave labour, cultural and linguistic homogenisation, and progressive forms of extermination. Both dictatorships pursued strategies of more or less violent modernisation, based upon the degradation of people into 'human contingents', to be administered, dispossessed, resettled, privileged or marginalised at will. At the heart of such policies was the belief that in this way socio-economic structures could be revolutionised more rapidly, indeed almost overnight. Of course this belief was not unique to either Nazi or Soviet thinking. There are echoes of it in the progressive thought of the century as a whole, in the form of the 'agrarian or industrial question', or the 'refugee or overpopulation question'. The most striking example of this can be seen in the 1946 report of the United Nations on the economic reconstruction of Europe: 'In eastern Europe the large-scale elimination of the Jewish population has left the distribution system in a state of virtual disorder. On the other hand the pre-war phenomenon of agricultural overpopulation still prevails.' Only once, in Germany, did such ideas result in Auschwitz. The deed and the crime is unique. However, Auschwitz is part of European as well as German history. Only when one has fully understood this context is it possible to talk meaningfully of the 'limits of understanding'. The Holocaust was not a 'reversion to barbarism', nor a 'break with civilisation', still less an 'Asiatic deed'. But it was also far from being a 'historical black hole', somehow beyond language, poetry and historical understanding, but rather a possibility inherent in European civilisation itself.

REFERENCES

Götz Aly and Susanne Heim, *Vordenker der Vernichtung* (Hamburg, 1991); Aly and Heim, 'The Economics of the Final Solution', *Simon Wiesenthal Center Annual*, vol. 5 (1988), pp. 3–48; Zygmunt Baumann, *Modernity and the Holocaust* (Ithaca, NY, 1989); Michael Burleigh, *Germany Turns Eastwards: A Study of 'Ostforschung' in the Third Reich* (Cambridge, 1990).

6

THE WANNSEE CONFERENCE, THE FATE OF GERMAN JEWS, AND HITLER'S DECISION IN PRINCIPLE TO EXTERMINATE ALL EUROPEAN JEWS

Christian Gerlach

For some students of the Holocaust, questions of timing and decision-making appear disturbingly trivializing and pedantic in view of the horror of the event itself. And yet, as the on-going debate on the origins of the "Final Solution" continues, it becomes all the more apparent that these questions are of crucial importance if we are to understand the manner in which a modern state embarks on a genocidal undertaking of continental dimensions.

Christian Gerlach's chapter is a meticulous, yet consciously and radically revisionist reconstruction of the decision on the "Final Solution." This is certainly a case of finding the Devil in the details. Gerlach's fundamental assumption is both extremely simple and extraordinarily difficult to prove. He argues that at least since his notorious speech on January 30, 1939, Hitler had always warned that he would murder the Jews of Europe if "they" unleashed a world war against Germany. Indeed, Hitler repeatedly referred to this speech in later years, although he tended to postdate it to the outbreak of war in September 1939. And yet, according to Gerlach, in Hitler's mind the war became a world war only after the Soviet counter-offensive before Moscow on December 5, 1941 and the Japanese attack in Pearl Harbor two days later, following which Hitler declared war on the United States. It was at this point, some time between December 7 and 14, that Hitler apparently decided to extend the mass killing of the Jews which was already taking place in the occupied parts of the Soviet Union to a continent-wide, and potentially universal "final solution of the Jewish question."

Gerlach's argument depends on making a clear distinction between the mass shootings by the killing squads (Einsatzgruppen) of the SS and SD which began with the invasion of the USSR on June 22, 1941, and were greatly extended in July and August to encompass all Soviet Jews, and the organization of a genocidal apparatus that included complex logistical planning and the construction of killing facilities. In the first case, Jews were murdered where they were found. In the second, they were brought over thousands of miles to previously built death camps where they were killed with ever greater speed and efficiency. Gerlach also relies on a highly detailed and careful analysis of all available sources, some of which have not been used before. There is obviously an element of speculation here, since we do not have any document signed by Hitler with a direct instruction to unleash the "Final Solution," and there almost certainly never was such a document. Hitler did not want to leave a "paper trail" leading to himself of what he knew would be perceived by much of the world as a vast criminal undertaking. Yet Gerlach makes a powerful argument in favor of Hitler's centrality in the decision-making process, and thereby undermines the old "functionalist" notion of the Holocaust having begun due to initiatives from below. He also provides Hitler with a motivation that explains the timing of the decision (quite apart from Hitler's murderous fantasies and rabid antisemitism), as related to the realization that Germany was now engaged in the kind of life and death struggle he had always both envisioned and feared. At this point, Hitler may well have doubted Germany's ability to win the war; all the more reason, in his mind, to finally and definitively "remove" the Jews, whom he saw as the cause of the nation's misery and misfortune.

Gerlach does not dismiss the "functionalist" argument altogether, since it helps explain events in the months and weeks leading to Hitler's decision (according to Gerlach's dating), such as the killing of Jews who were already deported to the East from Germany in fall 1941. Yet ultimately his is an "intentionalist" argument, both because of Hitler's centrality and because it combines ideological determinants with specific political rather than structural elements. It is therefore of some interest to compare Gerlach's approach with Aly's new type of "functionalism" and Friedländer's "moderate intentionalism" and much larger emphasis on "redemptive antisemitism" even as it was expressed in Hitler's own pronouncements in the months leading to his decision on the final solution (analyzed in an unpublished paper by Friedländer presented in 1998).

* * *

"The most remarkable thing about the meeting at Wannsee (which was not called the 'Wannsee Conference' until after the war) is that we do not know why it took place." So wrote the celebrated German historian Eberhard Jäckel in 1992.[1]

Many historians share this view. They find themselves somewhat puzzled with respect to the meeting at Wannsee.[2] On the one hand, the historical significance of the event is largely uncontested. The minutes prepared by Adolf Eichmann constitute a document of central importance. "No other document from the National Socialist regime," writes Wolfgang Scheffler, "sets out so clearly the complete plan for the extermination of European Jewry."[3] On the other hand, this uniqueness is itself problematic. Since we still know too little about the central planning for the extermination of the Jews, the relative significance of the Wannsee meeting is difficult to gauge. Nevertheless, some recent regional studies of the executions of Jews have shed new light on the protracted and complicated decision-making processes that went on within the German leadership.[4] Other recent research has sought to interpret the course of events from the perspective of the central offices.[5] Most significantly, however, documents connected with the Wannsee Conference itself have been uncovered, documents that provide us with important clues for interpreting previously known and published sources. What emerges is a new perspective on the course of events.

In the following essay I will attempt to show that, despite all the attention paid to it, the significance of the Wannsee Conference of January 20, 1942, has not been fully appreciated. First, it was a precondition not just for the execution of the "eastern Jews" but also for the extermination of German and western European Jews. Second, it was closely connected with Hitler's fundamental decision to proceed with the liquidation of *all* Jews living in Europe. In my opinion, Hitler made this decision in early December 1941.[6] At least that is when he first made it public, with clear and calamitous consequences. It was not a solitary decision. Hitler was reacting to political impulses and initiatives that originated from within the administration and from inside the party apparatus.[7] In order to show this clearly, I will first examine the course of events through the end of 1941. By that time, a liquidation of the Jews had already begun in the German-occupied areas of the Soviet Union and in some other parts of eastern Europe. As of the autumn of 1941, however, when the mass deportations of Jews from the German Reich began,[8] a decision to exterminate them had not yet been made. That becomes evident from the different kinds of treatment the German Jewish deportees received when they arrived at their various destinations.[9]

It was in this context that the Wannsee meeting was originally conceived. At this stage, its purpose—as I will show in the second section of this article—was to resolve existing differences between governmental and party functionaries as to the future treatment of German Jews and, presumably, of Jews from the remainder of western Europe as well. In particular, one of its aims was to work out a viable definition of who was to be treated as a Jew. But the conference had to be postponed, and Hitler's fundamental decision to liquidate all European Jews, which I attempt to document in the third section, altered the context in which the meeting was eventually to take place. The extermination plans of the Reich Security Main Office (*Reichssicherheitshauptamt*, or RSHA), and of other offices, received a strong new impetus. The fourth section deals with the content and results of the Wannsee Conference. During the meeting, no objections were raised by the ministerial bureaucracy to a systematic liquidation of Jews from Germany or from the rest of Europe, though exceptions would continue to be made in the case of "part-Jews" (*Mischlinge*). Thus did systematic planning for the destruction of the Jews throughout Europe begin. In the fifth and final section I examine the consequences of the Wannsee Conference, above all for German Jews. It seems that the coordinated deportation of German Jews to the extermination camps began in early May 1942. But the RSHA's planned liquidation of part-Jews living in western and central Europe never took place, due to objections raised by the Reich interior and justice ministries, and to various other "difficulties."

I The context: the status of extermination efforts in Europe at the end of 1941

In order to evaluate the context of the Wannsee Conference, we need to review briefly the stage that the liquidation of Jews in Europe had reached at the close of 1941.

(a) In the occupied territories of the Soviet Union, immediately following the German invasion of June 22, 1941, a systematic destruction of Jews began with the murder of men of military age. The executions were carried out by special mobile "task forces" (*Einsatzgruppen*) of the Security Police and the Security Service (SD), by police battalions, by brigades of the Armed SS (*Waffen-SS*), and, to a more limited extent, by rear guard units of the army. Beginning in August and September of 1941, women and children were also included. Beginning in September and October, entire Jewish communities were liquidated, initiating the phase of total destruction.[10]

(b) In Serbia, brutal repressive measures implemented by the army were directed primarily at Jews. During the fall of 1941 a majority of Jewish men were murdered.[11]

(c) In the General Government of Poland there were no systematic mass executions of Jews prior to the spring of 1942. The only exceptions occurred in the district of Galicia, which had, however, been a part of the Soviet Union up until June 1941. In Galicia, mass executions of Jews by the Germans began in October 1941.[12] Construction of the extermination camp at Belzec in the district of Lublin was begun in November 1941.[13] It was intended exclusively for the destruction of Jews. Its capacity was relatively limited, however, so that it could not have been designed for a rapid extermination of all Jews living in the General Government.[14]

(d) In the annexed Reich province of the Wartheland, mass murders of Jews began in some areas in late September or early October 1941. At about this same time, construction was begun on an extermination camp in Chelmno, near Lodz. There, beginning on December 8, 1941, an SS-Commando unit used gas vans to exterminate Jews from neighboring districts. On January 16, 1942, the execution of Polish Jews from Lodz itself started.[15]

(e) Sometime between September 14 and September 18, 1941, Hitler approved the inauguration of a program to deport German Jews to the eastern territories. For some time, Himmler, Heydrich, and various regional party leaders (*Gauleiter*) had been pressing him to do so. Starting on October 15, transports filled with Jews departed from cities throughout the Reich (including Austria and the Protectorate of Bohemia and Moravia). They were bound for Lodz, Minsk, Kaunas, and Riga. The German leadership, the SS, and the police viewed these transports as an interim measure. Organizational and technical problems limited the deportations to a small fraction of the Jews living in Germany. It was also in September of 1941 that the deportation of French Jews, limited initially to those being held in detention, was announced.[16]

The point of transition to a policy of exterminating the Jewish people, or the initial preparations for it, can thus be clearly seen in a number of occupied territories and regions beginning in September and October of 1941. Total liquidation began in the occupied Soviet lands. Selective mass executions of those seen as "unfit for labor" began in western Ukraine, in western White Russia, and in the Wartheland. In Serbia, executions of Jewish men served as a prelude to the murders of women and children, groups that were "useless" in the eyes of the occupation authorities. In the context of these developments, most historians have hitherto equated the decision to deport German Jews with the decision to liquidate them. At the most, it is assumed that there were *two* separate decisions. One, involving the execution of Soviet Jews, would have occurred in July or August of 1941.[17] The second, concerning the extermination of Jews from the rest of Europe, is supposed to have been reached in September or October of that year.[18] There are some historians, it must also be noted, who would date these decisions as early as January 1941, or even earlier.[19]

The Wannsee Conference was a meeting between representatives from the RSHA and state secretaries and other officials from the ministerial bureaucracy. Its purpose was to discuss the "Final Solution of the Jewish Question." It took place on January 20, 1942. It had originally been scheduled to occur on December 9, 1941. Initial invitations to participate had gone out on November 29.

These dates are clearly later than the turning point that apparently occurred in the extermination policy in the early fall of 1941. Hence, according to the prevailing view, the purpose of the meeting could not have been a decision about whether to proceed with exterminations. Rather, its purpose must have involved secondary issues such as the division of authority, coordination, and organization. According to the minutes,[20] a variety of topics were discussed, and scholars differ as to which were the most important. Heydrich described the European-wide extermination program to the ministerial representatives in attendance.[21] He furnished them with information and tried to persuade them to accept his ultimate authority in the matter.[22] Heydrich also wanted to clear up any problems or differences of opinion arising from the inclusion of western, northern, and southeast European Jews, German "part-Jews," and Jews working in the armaments industry. His aim was a unified, coordinated effort.[23]

Certainly none of these topics was insignificant. But there was one particular issue that made the meeting seem of utmost urgency in the eyes of the men who were responsible for shaping the extermination policy. This comes as something of a surprise, given the prevailing view that the decision had been made much earlier. Postwar testimony by some of the participants gives us an indication of the importance they attached to the resolution of this issue at the time of the conference. Georg Heuser, then head of the Gestapo offices in Minsk, testified that in the period before the Wannsee Conference "only eastern Jews" were to be executed. "Initially, German Jews were supposed to be resettled in the east. After the Wannsee Conference, we were told that all Jews were to be liquidated."[24] Furthermore, in his initial testimony, Adolf Eichmann also declared that "the Wannsee Conference was indeed the beginning of the real extermination story."[25] Eichmann's interrogator, and after him many historians, countered that the murder to Jews in the Soviet Union had already begun;[26] but of course Eichmann's statement could have referred only to the executions that he himself had to organize.

These statements by Heuser and Eichmann reveal that the authorities evidently still had to face another "problem" at the close of 1941, despite the prevailing notion that a decision on this matter had already been made earlier: should—or, more precisely, could—*German* Jews be executed, too?

II The original theme of the Wannsee Conference: the definition and treatment of German Jews

On the afternoon of November 30, 1941, Himmler held a telephone conversation with Heydrich. After the call, he jotted down the notation: "Jewish transport from Berlin. no liquidation."[27] The call itself came too late. The Berlin Jews, some one thousand of them, whose transport had left Berlin on November 27, had already been shot to death near Riga on the morning of November 30.[28] The radical right-wing British historian David

Irving, relying on this notation made by Himmler, once claimed that Hitler had decided to put a stop to the extermination of the Jews in general. Serious historians have refuted this absurd notion. But the jotted notation has led some historians to surmise that executions of German Jews had aroused quite a stir among German authorities and had caused Himmler to suspend, for a time, any further executions of Jews from Germany.[29] In fact, the executions were carried out on local initiatives, and against Himmler's wishes, as shown by sources recently uncovered by the German historian Christoph Dieckmann. On the following day, December 1, Himmler sent a radio transmission to Friedrich Jeckeln, the Higher SS and Police Leader (*Höherer SS- und Polizeiführer*, or HSSPF) for the Ostland and the person responsible for the Riga executions, stating that "unauthorized actions, or actions contrary to directives issued either by me or by the Reich Security Main Office under my authority" with respect to the "treatment of Jews resettled in the Ostland" would be "punished." Later in the same day, Himmler directed Jeckeln to meet with him on December 4.[30] Whether or not Hitler was involved at this point is not known. What is known is that the dinner conversations that took place in Hitler's presence on the first or second of December dealt with the subjects of Jewish mixed marriages, part-Jews, and, possibly, Jewish frontline fighters as well. Hitler's own remarks on the occasion are ambiguous.[31]

Let us take a closer look at the fate of the deportation trains from Germany for the year 1941. First, some twenty thousand German Jews were transported to Lodz between October 15 and November 4. Many died from starvation, but there were no executions. Protests from the regional administration, under its president, Uebelhör, had succeeded in reducing the number of proposed deportees from sixty thousand to twenty-five thousand.[32] There is no evidence from Lodz to indicate that any consideration was being given to the idea of executing the Jews who arrived from Germany. In the middle of January 1942, when the civil administration and the SS police apparatus began to transport Jews from the Lodz ghetto to the extermination camp at Chelmno, the Jews from Germany were initially *excluded*.[33]

A second destination for the transports was Minsk. Between November 8 and November 28, 1941, some seven thousand Jews from the old Reich, from Vienna and Brünn, were deported there.[34] All the German Jews were herded into the ghetto. Initially, there were no executions. To make room for these arriving German Jews, 6,624 White Russian Jews had been shot to death by the Security Police and the SD between November 7 and November 11. On November 20, another five thousand were executed. The deportation plan had in fact called for some twenty-five thousand Jews to be transported to Minsk, but the transports were canceled due to protests from the Army Group Center (*Heeresgruppe Mitte*), whose rail and supply situation had become critical during the Battle of Moscow.[35]

The situation was different in Kaunas, in Lithuania, the third destination point. Between November 25 and November 29 a total of 4,934 Jews arrived there from Germany and Austria. Einsatzkommando 3 of the Security Police and the SD shot them all.[36] In the absence of documentary source material, it is not clear where the orders for these murders originated. It has sometimes been argued that these transports were diverted to Kaunas unexpectedly and with little advance notice, and that the Jewish deportees were simply executed "to get rid of a problem," as it were. But plans to send the first five trains to Kaunas in the Baltic had been announced three weeks earlier.[37] Just three days before the first massacre, Dr. Peter Kleist, the section chief for the Ostland in the Reich Ministry for the Occupied Territories in the East (*Ostministerium*), met with Karl Jäger, the head of Einsatzkommando 3 in Kaunas, and expressed his satisfaction with the executions of Lithuanian Jews. We are thus justified in concluding that the Ministry for the East, which had been informed about the transports, was in agreement with the plan to execute the German Jews who were expected to arrive in Kaunas.[38] Only the discovery of new documents will be able to shed light on the question of how and by whom this decision was reached, and whether or not any misgivings were voiced by German officials.

It was at the fourth destination point, Riga, that on November 30, 1941, one day after a second mass execution of Jews had occurred in Kaunas, all the deportees on a train from Berlin were murdered. As mentioned above, the executions were carried out by Jeckeln, the Higher SS and Police Leader in the Ostland, using his own units. Later on the same day Jeckeln called in Einsatzkommando 2 to assist at the executions of several thousand Latvian Jews.[39] Hinrich Lohse, the Reich Commissar for the Ostland (*Reichskommissar für das Ostland*), was also present at this massacre.[40] Only two days earlier Lohse had dropped his opposition to the deportation of German Jews into "his" Reich Commissariat, acceding to the wishes of the Ministry for the East.[41] Nevertheless, the execution of the Jews transported from Berlin aroused quite a stir.[42] After this incident, German Jews arriving in Riga were no longer executed immediately. Instead they were held in confinement in temporary camps outside the city. Because living conditions there were atrocious, many died within a short time. Others were shot by the guards, or murdered in the Bikerniki forest. A transport that arrived from Cologne on December 10 was the first whose occupants were permitted to take up residence in the Riga ghetto. Another fourteen transports followed.[43] During December 1941 and January 1942 several thousand Jews apparently died. The toll was especially heavy in the camps. According to some accounts, purportedly by eyewitnesses but difficult to verify, all deportees on several trains that arrived later in December 1941 were executed. Einsatzkommando 2 is reported to have separated out the weak and infirm and executed them. Attempts were made to conceal the murders, so that the reason for the selections would not become known "to local Jews or to Jews in the Reich."[44]

Let us quickly summarize these rather gruesome results. A general order to execute German Jews had not yet been issued. In Lodz and Minsk, German officials and police allowed German Jews arriving in 1941 to survive. In Kaunas, however, all the arriving Jews were murdered. In Riga, finally, Jews on the first transport were openly killed. Those arriving later were initially kept alive, only to be shot later in "smaller" executions or to be killed by the horrendous living conditions, particularly the cold. Direct executions were concealed as much as possible.

Objections were raised almost immediately by the civilian administrations. They did not oppose the executions per se, but rather the deportations of non-Jews or privileged Jews, which could lead to the killing of people who had not been targeted and thus jeopardize political support for the "Final Solution" in general. Both Wilhelm Kube, general commissar in Minsk, and Hinrich Lohse sent to the Ministry for the East lists with the names of individuals who should not have been transported to the east, at least according to the rules then governing the deportations. The lists had been given to them by German Jews in the Minsk and Riga ghettos. On November 29, Kube had visited the separate "German ghetto" in Minsk. He subsequently issued a complaint that among the deportees there were many so-called "part-Jews" (who were not considered Jews under the Nuremberg laws), Jews married to "Aryans," brothers of army servicemen, and decorated veterans of World War I. He lodged an immediate protest at the Ministry for the East. It appears to have been received there by December 8, at the latest.[45] Lohse's reaction a short time later was similar, though less dramatic. Both objections, along with the lists of names, were forwarded to Heydrich by the deputy minister for the East, Alfred Meyer.[46]

This chronological sequence makes it clear, admittedly, that the objections raised by these two officials could not have been a decisive factor in the halting of the executions.[47] But these certainly could not have been the only protests. As early as October 10, Heydrich had declared that "no special consideration should be shown to Jews decorated during the war. On the contrary," they should be "transported in percentages corresponding to their actual numbers."[48] On November 20, Eichmann had circulated a memo outlining deportation directives. Its effect was to reduce the number of victims affected. Apparently Eichmann's actions came because the RSHA had already received some complaints and was expecting more to follow.[49] Heydrich's comments to Goebbels also suggest that this was the case. Heydrich planned to use the new camp at Theresienstadt in the Protectorate of Bohemia and Moravia to intern Jews who were more than sixty years old or who might be regarded as "doubtful cases."[50] But complaints were received anyway, because Eichmann's directives were not followed. In early November, in Berlin, two prominent individuals intervened on behalf of

Dr. Karl Lowenstein, a Jewish attorney who was deported to Minsk in spite of the guidelines.[51] On February 6, 1942, Heinrich Müller, the chief of the Gestapo, wrote that "anonymous letters are constantly arriving, from practically all areas of the Reich" concerning incidents involving mass executions of Jews.[52] As I noted earlier, the numerous protests against including the so-called "part-Jews," decorated war veterans, and Jews married to "Aryans" had obviously contributed to Himmler's November 30, 1941, order halting the executions temporarily.

Before further measures could be taken against the deported German Jews—and there were officials who were pressing for quick executions[53]— there had to be a clear and unambiguous definition of who should be included.[54] In order to formulate this definition, there would have to be a meeting of the government officials involved in the operation. That meeting was the Wannsee Conference. In retrospect, the acting Reich Justice Minister Franz Schlegelberger summed up the situation as follows: "The final solution of the Jewish question presupposed a definitive and final determination of the class of individuals who were to be affected by the proposed measures."[55] This was to be the principal topic of discussion at the conference. Most of the meeting's participants had to deal with the issue directly: Heydrich, Müller, and Eichmann (from the RSHA); Otto Hofmann (SS-Race and Resettlement Office); Wilhelm Kritzinger (Reich chancellery); Wilhelm Stuckart (Reich interior ministry); Gerhard Klopfer (Party chancellery), and Roland Freisler (Reich justice ministry). Others faced it indirectly: Erich Neumann (Four-Year Plan Office), Alfred Meyer, and Georg Leibbrandt (Ministry for the Occupied Territories in the East).[56] The German Jews were to be the primary focus. Many of those invited to attend had no official interest whatever in the fate of Jews from the occupied territories. The representatives from the Reich chancellery, from the Party chancellery, from the interior ministry, and from the justice ministry were concerned solely with Jews in Germany, as can be seen, for example, from a document prepared for Stuckart's use at the Wannsee Conference by the adviser on Jewish affairs in the Reich interior ministry, Bernhard Lösener.[57] In the initial invitations, Heydrich had indicated, with good reason, how important the discussion would be for all officials involved in the "Final Solution," "*particularly because Jews from the Reich territory including the Protectorate of Bohemia and Moravia, have been evacuated to the east in ongoing transports since October 15, 1941.*"[58] What he obviously had in mind was the question of what should be done with them. As it turned out, according to the minutes, the problem of specifying who the Jewish victims were to be occupied a considerable amount of time and led to the only open differences of opinion.[59]

Heydrich had sent out the initial invitations on November 29. That date was shortly before the executions were temporarily halted. Clearly, problems and complaints arising in connection with the deportations had surfaced even before the events in Riga. But after the Riga murders they became more pressing. The issues involved were brought out with extreme clarity in a letter addressed by the Minsk general commissar, Wilhelm Kube, to his superior, Lohse, in Riga on December 16, 1941. In his letter, Kube explained that German Jews, "who come from our own cultural milieu," are "just not the same as the animal hordes from these regions." At the same time, however, Kube wrote to request "an official directive" to execute them. He wanted to avoid issuing such an order "on [his] own authority."[60]

With regard to the issues on the agenda for the Wannsee Conference other than the treatment and definition of the German Jews, the RSHA had already reached complete or nearly complete agreement with the other offices involved even before the conference took place.[61] On October 23, 1941, just prior to the initial deportations, the RSHA and the Economics and Armaments Office of the Armed Forces High Command had reached an accord concerning Jews working in the armaments industry inside the Reich. According to Eichmann's testimony, none of these Jews would be deported without specific approval from those in charge of the relevant armaments. Heydrich had included this provision in the deportation directives, and he forwarded a written copy to the labor ministry in December.[62] When Neumann, state secretary for the Four-Year Plan, requested confirmation of this arrangement during the conference, Heydrich could thus respond that it was already current practice.[63] Additional memoranda from Martin Bormann to party officials[64] and from the Reich Labor Minister to the regional labor offices affirmed the practice in March 1942.[65]

Contrary to Eichmann's expectations,[66] consultations during the Wannsee Conference with State Secretary Josef Bühler from the General Government of Poland also proceeded without conflict. It is possible that Eichmann had not been kept informed about the most recent developments at higher levels. We know that the original invitation list for the conference had not included any representatives from the General Government. Extermination policy in the General Government had not been one of the original topics for the conference, an additional indication that the treatment of German Jews was to be the chief focus. It was only after Heydrich received complaints at the end of November 1941 from Friedrich Wilhelm Krüger, the Higher SS and Police Leader in Krakau, about conflicts with the civilian administration that he directed Eichmann to invite Krüger and the General Governor, Hans Frank.[67] (Opinions differ about whether or not Krüger actually received an invitation.[68] His absence from the meeting may have been due to a broken arm.)[69] In a letter dated January 17, 1942, Krüger mentioned that Josef Bühler—who was to attend the conference in Berlin in Frank's place—had paid him a visit on the previous day, during which he discussed a meeting he had arranged with Himmler on the afternoon of January 13. According to Krüger (on the sixteenth), Bühler still seemed "enthusiastic about the reception he had received in

[Himmler's] special train." Himmler, in turn, earlier in the morning of that same January 13, had received a report from the commander of the security police and the SD in the General Government, Eberhard Schöngarth.[70] In view of the timing of all these meetings as well as the lack of controversy at the Wannsee Conference itself, we may reasonably conclude that a basic understanding between Bühler and the SS leadership about liquidating Jews in the General Government, and the lines of authority for it, had already been reached before the conference began.[71]

There were the usual squabbles between the Ministry for the East and SS and police officials: they argued over the definition of who should be treated as a Jew in the occupied Soviet territories,[72] about authority for Jewish policy,[73] and about the local pace of the liquidations. For the most part, however, they shared the same élan for extermination. The Ministry for the East had already signaled its basic willingness to accept the plan— namely, that a significant portion of the European Jewish population was to be transported into areas under its control and eliminated there, either by liquidation or by exposure to inhumane living conditions.[74] Owing to transport problems, to be sure, the plan could not be implemented immediately.

Support for a European-wide "Final Solution of the Jewish Question" was also obtained from the Foreign Office without a great deal of persuasion or arm-twisting.[75] On the contrary, its representative brought to the conference a lengthy list of demands for additional Jewish deportations and for further antisemitic measures throughout Europe.[76] In November 1941 the foreign ministry had supported the efforts of the RSHA to include in the deportations Romanian, Croatian, and Slovakian Jews living within the Reich.[77] It had also played a leading role in initiating the murders of Serbian Jews in October 1941.[78] Even in sensitive cases, with potential international ramifications, the foreign ministry was not opposed in principle to anti-Jewish measures. It intervened only in those instances in which the measures taken were too blatant. For example, the foreign ministry objected to the continued executions of several hundred Jewish hostages from the Netherlands in the concentration camp at Buchenwald after the deaths had attracted international publicity and the attention of Sweden, the Netherlands's protective power. In the end, Himmler acceded and transferred the surviving hostages to S'Hertogenbosch in the middle of November.[79] But cases involving diplomatic consequences were the exception rather than the rule in the foreign ministry's handling of the "Jewish Question." Certainly the RSHA had to have the foreign ministry's cooperation if the liquidation of the Jews was to be extended to more countries, but this was also possible in bilateral negotiations. In general, however, opposition was not to be expected from the Foreign Office.

There remained the question of who was to be treated as Jewish. Beginning in March 1941 various institutions had sought to broaden the concept of "Jewish" as it was applied within the Reich. The party chancellery, the RSHA, the Racial Policy Office of the National Socialist Party, and the Office of the Four-Year Plan wanted to treat the so-called part-Jews of the first degree—that is, half Jews—the same as Jews.[80] If we can judge by the outcomes of several meetings, the men involved apparently believed by August and September that they were on the verge of having their view implemented throughout Europe.[81] Hermann Göring's commission to Heydrich had been a factor. On July 31, 1941, Göring had assigned Heydrich "to make all the necessary preparations—organizational, technical, and material—for a total solution of the Jewish question throughout the German sphere of influence in Europe."[82] Earlier, on July 28, Göring had declared "that Jews residing in regions under German rule have no further business there."[83] Apparently neither statement envisioned a liquidation of the entire Jewish population. Rather, Jews were to be "expelled" to the occupied Soviet territories after the successful conclusion of the war. It was foreseen, admittedly, and accepted as a matter of course that there would be an enormous loss of life among the deportees.[84] Initially, however, the phrase "Final Solution" did not mean an immediate extermination of the Jewish people. It acquired that meaning only later, especially after the war.

Heydrich proceeded to act on Göring's commission on two fronts. First, he developed plans for deporting Jews from the German Reich to areas in the east while the war was still being fought. Hitler rejected these plans in August.[85] Second, Heydrich's office used the authority conferred by Göring's commission as a basis for justifying "in particular" its efforts to widen the defined meaning of the term "Jew."[86] This effort seemed to meet with some success. The chief of the Reich chancellery, Hans-Heinrich Lammers, supported it, as did the party chancellery, the Führer chancellery, and the Army High Command.[87] They all wanted some new regulation that would reduce the thousands of requests and petitions for exceptions in special cases that had to be processed and forwarded to Hitler.[88] Of all the government ministries, only the interior ministry stood opposed.[89] We can see this in the document prepared by State Secretary Wilhelm Stuckart's adviser on Jewish affairs, Lösener, for Stuckart's use at the Wannsee Conference on its initially scheduled date.[90] But both Hitler and Göring seem to have objected to the proposed changes in the status of the "part-Jews of the first degree."[91] Exactly what Hitler thought about Jews who were married to non-Jewish Germans, in particular on the issue of compulsory divorces, remains unclear.[92] We do know that he wanted to limit the number of exceptions granting preferential treatment to Jews in special cases.[93] But apparently he did not make any official decision, except with regard to the "part-Jews of the second degree" (so-called Quarter-Jews), and for this group he preliminarily refused to approve a reduction in citizenship status.[94] The rather vague reports of his comments on

December 1 or December 2 seem to confirm these leanings.[95] It should be noted that Hitler's misgivings, like those at the interior ministry, were political rather than moral. Part-Jews and Jewish spouses in mixed marriages had too many non-Jewish relatives and friends. Treating them more harshly could cause too much unrest.

The RSHA hoped that the Wannsee Conference would produce a breakthrough. In mid-December, Dr. Walter Labs, counselor in the Reich Ministry for the East, received an oral report from Dr. Werner Feldscher, an adviser in the Reich interior ministry:

> As for the proposed changes in the definition of the term "Jew," Dr. Feldscher gave me the following information. With the approval of the Führer, the Reich Marshall [Göring] commissioned SS-Obergruppenführer Heyderich [sic] to make preparations for carrying out an immediate and unified solution of the Jewish question in Europe *after the conclusion of the war*. In fulfilling this assignment Heyderich scheduled a meeting of the state secretaries from the relevant ministries. Due to the session of the Reichstag, the meeting had to be postponed until January. At the meeting, Heyderich intended to discuss the desire of the RSHA to expand the definition of the term "Jew" in order to include part-Jews of the first degree and to mete out harsher treatment to part-Jews of the second degree. Heyderich planned to use the results of the meeting as a basis for his presentation to the Reich Marshall [Göring] or to the Führer and for his proposal to amend the Nuremberg laws for Germany.[96]

As late as August 1941, the interior ministry had laid claim to "responsibility for the Jewish question" and had received formal acceptance of this from other Reich offices.[97] But on November 24, during a conversation with Stuckart, Himmler disputed this authority, noting "Jew question—belong [sic] to me."[98] The exact content and course of this conversation cannot be clearly determined. In particular, we do not know whether Himmler merely claimed to have authority or whether Stuckart agreed with him. On December 21, Stuckart observed that "more and more, leadership on the Jewish question has slipped away from the interior ministry." He no longer would, or perhaps could, do anything to prevent the mass executions of German Jews, such as the one in Riga.[99]

During the intervening period, something significant must have occurred. It is my belief that the discussions taking place among the central offices of the Reich were overtaken in early December 1941 by Hitler's announcement of his fundamental political decision. This new turn of events meant that the Wannsee Conference would eventually convene in a context quite different from the one that had prevailed when Heydrich had originally planned the meeting.

119

III Hitler's announcement of the decision to exterminate all European Jews

Himmler and Hitler met on the afternoon of December 18, 1941. In regard to the first topic discussed, Himmler recorded, "Jewish question | to be exterminated as partisans."[100] There can be no doubt that what Himmler wrote down after the vertical line represented the results of the conversation. But what did the brief notation mean? Linguistically, the statement is an order. The term "partisans" may at first glance seem to suggest the situation in the Soviet Union, but the execution of Soviet Jews had been decided some time ago and was already under way. Further, at that point there was not yet a significant number of Jewish partisans in the occupied Soviet territories. These considerations suggest that Himmler's notation meant something else—that it referred to potential partisans and to the supposed "Jewish threat." It is significant that Himmler's note lists the topic of conversation not as "Jews in the east" or as "Soviet Jews" but rather as the all-encompassing "Jewish question." By itself, Himmler's notation is difficult to interpret unambiguously, but there is some justification for interpreting Hitler's statement in a global sense.

Himmler's notation may be read in connection with other documents that help shed some light on its meaning. One of these documents is a letter to Himmler written on June 23, 1942, by Viktor Brack, the person responsible for the Euthanasia Program. In the letter, he explained that he had again placed some of his staff at the disposal of Odilo Globocnik[101] for his use at extermination camps connected with "Operation Reinhard"—the code name for the program to liquidate Jews from the General Government in the camps at Belzec, Sobibor, Treblinka, and Majdanek: "Brigade Leader Globocnik took the opportunity to express his opinion that this action against the Jews should be carried out as quickly as possible, so that it not be left unfinished should any difficulties make it necessary to suspend the operation. *At one time, you yourself, Reichsführer, indicated to me [in person] that for reasons of secrecy we ought to complete the work as quickly as possible.*"[102]

Evidence in this same letter suggests that Brack was referring to the decision to execute Jews from throughout Europe, for he remarks that out of "approximately ten million European Jews" it would be better to "preserve" than to liquidate "two or three million of them," in order to use them as a labor supply for the German war economy. The excerpt cited above occurs in the same context. Furthermore, in my opinion, the wording of the last sentence in that excerpt suggests that Brack can only be referring to a personal conversation with Himmler that had taken place some time ago ("at one time"). According to Himmler's appointment schedule for 1941 and 1942 (a rather substantial set of documents), the most recent meeting between Himmler and Brack before this letter occurred on December 14,

1941. Topics of discussion were listed as "[. . .] Course in East Minist[ry]" and "Euthanasia."[103] In light of this chain of evidence, it seems highly likely that Himmler discussed the plans to liquidate all European Jews with Brack at that meeting.

Further, Philipp Bouhler, the head of the Führer chancellery and Brack's superior, was present on December 13, 1941, at a meeting with Hitler attended by Rosenberg and von Ribbentrop. He was also present at a December 14, 1941, meeting with Hitler that Himmler and Rosenberg attended.[104] The frequency of these meetings is striking. According to his letter cited above, Brack, at Bouhler's behest, had provided personnel to Globocnik on at least two occasions for use at the extermination camps. After the war Brack would testify that this had first occurred following a meeting between Himmler and Bouhler.[105] A document written by Bouhler in July 1942 confirms this last point, especially Bouhler's own responsibility: he asserts that "I have placed a large part of my organization at the disposal of Reichsführer Himmler for use in a solution to the Jewish question that will *extend to the ultimate possible consequences.*"[106]

As to exactly when the first large group of personnel from the Führer chancellery arrived in Belzec, there are conflicting opinions as to whether it was in November or December of 1941.[107] Based on all the available evidence, it seems to have been shortly before the Christmas of 1941.[108] It is possible that the exchanges on December 13 and 14 described above led to a shift of personnel on very short notice. But it is also conceivable that, at these meetings, Bouhler, Rosenberg, and Himmler gave Hitler only information about the steps that had already been taken to exterminate the Jews using poison gas—that is, about the murders using gas vans in the Soviet territories and in Chelmno, and about the status of preparations at Belzec. The meetings may also have led to "experts" being sent to the planned extermination sites in order to inspect the liquidation techniques.[109] At the very least, it is difficult to believe that these meetings had no connection at all with the unfolding of the "Final Solution."

What brought about this sudden flurry of meetings? The reason can be seen most clearly in a note made by Rosenberg on December 16, 1941. The entry deals with a meeting Rosenberg had had with Hitler two days earlier. At that meeting, Rosenberg gave Hitler the manuscript copy of a speech for the Führer's approval. Hitler "remarked that the text had been prepared before the Japanese declaration of war, in circumstances that had now altered." Rosenberg's entry continues as follows: "With regard to the Jewish question, I said that my remarks about the New York Jews would perhaps have to be changed now, *after the decision*. My position was that the extermination of the Jews should not be mentioned. The Führer agreed. He said they had brought the war down on us, they had started all the destruction, so it should come as no surprise if they became its first victims."[110]

By "the decision" Rosenberg could not have meant the entry of the United States into the war, for there is no logical connection between that event and the cessation of public threats against the Jews.[111] Hitler's reaction indicates this as well, for he reiterates the justification for his decision to exterminate the Jews. Rosenberg certainly would have been informed immediately about such a decision, so this discussion on December 14 about the need to alter a speech that Rosenberg had written before December 7 indicates that the decision to "exterminate the Jews in Europe" must have been made after December 7 and before December 14, 1941.[112]

It is well known that Hitler, in an infamous speech to the Reichstag on January 30, 1939, had spoken as follows: "If the world of international financial Jewry, both in and outside of Europe, should succeed in plunging the nations into another *world war*, the result will not be the Bolshevization of the world and thus a victory for Judaism. The result will be the extermination of the Jewish race in Europe."[113] Hitler announced his declaration of war against the United States in the Reichstag on December 11, 1941. For Germany, that made the war a world war.[114] Thus the situation Hitler had envisioned in 1939 had come about. With complete logical consistency— consistent within the framework of his antisemitic worldview—Hitler then proclaimed his decision to exterminate all Jews in Europe. He did not, to be sure, include this announcement in his Reichstag speech of December 11, a speech broadcast on radio. In that speech he claimed only that Jewish war agitators were behind Roosevelt.[115] But on the following afternoon, December 12, 1941, Hitler addressed a meeting of the most important sectional leaders of the National Socialist Party (the *Reichsleiter*) and of regional party leaders (the *Gauleiter*).[116] According to Goebbels's notes on this meeting of the *Reichsleiter* and *Gauleiter*, Hitler spoke as follows:

> Regarding the Jewish question, the Führer is determined to clear the table. He warned the Jews that if they were to cause another world war, it would lead to their own destruction. Those were not empty words. Now the world war has come. The destruction of the Jews must be its necessary consequence. We cannot be sentimental about it. It is not for us to feel sympathy for the Jews. We should have sympathy rather with our own German people. If the German people have to sacrifice 160,000 victims in yet another campaign in the east, then those responsible for this bloody conflict will have to pay for it with their lives.[117]

There were other occasions, too, both before and after December 1941, when Hitler made reference to his infamous "prophecy." But he never before did so as clearly, as unambiguously, or in such a matter-of-fact way as recorded here by Goebbels.[118] What Hitler said was not intended metaphorically or as propaganda—that is the meaning of Goebbels's phrase, "Those were not empty words." Above all, Hitler had now spoken of the beginning of total annihilation. He had made his remarks before a group of listeners outside his most inner circle of confidants. It was the leadership of the party that was assembled together. Because attendance at such meetings was mandatory, we can be virtually certain about which individuals were present: Himmler, Martin Bormann, Rosenberg, Hans Frank; Arthur Greiser, Fritz Bracht, and Fritz Sauckel (the *Gauleiter* in Warthegau, in Upper Silesia, and in Thuringia, respectively); Hinrich Lohse and Erich Koch (the Reich commissars for the Ostland and for the Ukraine, respectively); Alfred Meyer, Goebbels, and Philipp Bouhler.[119] These were the decisive political figures involved in the destruction of the Jews in Europe. They were also the administrative heads of all the regions containing the centers where, both then and subsequently, Jews were exterminated. Hermann Göring was not present. He held no party office that would have required his attendance at the meeting. It is probable, too, that Reinhard Heydrich was not in attendance.[120]

Several tightly woven elements contributed to the reasoning behind Hitler's decision and the timing of its announcement. The first was retribution for the supposed anti-German activities of "World Jewry" and the alleged responsibility of the Jews for the war, recalling his 1939 "prophecy." In the intervening years he had repeated his threat on numerous occasions, some of them public, thus emphasizing its importance. In Hitler's nationalistic perspective, all German claims to preeminence were justified. At the same time, his antisemitism caused him to view any opposition to these claims as stemming from a Jewish conspiracy. Thus his "prophecy" was of necessity a self-fulfilling one. Second, the entry of the United States into the war gave him a welcome pretext to announce a decision that he and others presumably had been contemplating in any case. A third consideration could have been that the European Jews had lost, for the Nazi leadership, their role as hostages who might deter the United States from an open entry into the war.[121] The war situation entered into Hitler's rationalization in yet another way, for it created, in the fourth place, a kind of European fortress mentality among the Germans. The new prospect of a second front, combined with the military defeat in the Battle of Moscow, had created a rather serious situation for the German leaders.[122] Within this more threatening context, Hitler viewed the Jews as opponents, revolutionaries, saboteurs, spies, "partisans" in his own backyard—an area that now, in light of the expected United States attack, included all of Europe. That was what Hitler had meant by his remark, recorded by Himmler on December 18, 1941, "to be exterminated as partisans."[123] Heydrich's perspective on the geopolitical situation was very similar. This can be seen clearly in a speech he delivered on December 17 in which he observed that Hitler's speech to the Reichstag and Japan's attack on the United States had created "a perfectly clear situation in the world. The forces of Judaism, of Bolshevism, of unscrupulous profit, and of egoism are ranged together in opposition to a united Europe."[124] Alfred Rosenberg, too, viewed the Jews as troublemakers.[125] Toward the end of 1943, Himmler employed the same "argument" when he noted that the aerial bombardments, the attacks by partisans, and the retreats at the front lines might have led to a collapse of German resistance if the Jews had still been present as an "element of uncertainty"—in other words, if the Germans had not already destroyed them.[126] By "removing" the Jews, Hitler himself was to assert in a secret address on May 26, 1944, he had "prevented the formation of any possible revolutionary kernels or cells." The matter could not "have been handled more humanely" since Germany was "in a fight to the death."[127]

The context in which Hitler announced his decision is itself revealing. The announcement was made not in the innermost circle, not informally in a confidential conversation with Himmler, and not within the narrow confines of his close circle of advisers, Göring, Heydrich, and Bormann.[128] Nor was it a meeting of government officials, though some of the men present did hold such posts. Rather, the announcement was made before an official body that included his oldest and closest political comrades; some fifty people were present. His message was this: the destruction of the Jews was first and foremost a party matter. Subsequent events would confirm the party's special role, in particular with regard to the extermination of German Jews.[129] Some of those present at the announcement had already urged Hitler to take harsher steps against the Jews. These included such men as Joseph Goebbels; Karl Kaufmann; Baldur v. Schirach, who had been involved in the decision to deport the German Jews;[130] and Martin Mutschmann, who had even urged, possibly in that very fall of 1941, that Jews be executed.[131] Gauleiter Carl Röver personally signed the deportation order for each and every Jewish citizen transported from Bremen.[132] Lohse had himself been present at an execution two weeks earlier, as noted above. So there was no one in this audience who needed to be converted. Formally, Hitler was not giving an order; he was simply announcing a decision. One thing more about the meeting should be noted. Meetings of the *Reichsleiter* and the *Gauleiter* were normally held in the conference rooms of the New Chancellery or in one of the party buildings. For this meeting, however, despite the official occasion, the setting was a private one, in Hitler's residence.[133]

In such a circle of listeners, the quoted passage from Hitler's address had the effect of a directive. Other documents in addition to the Rosenberg passage cited earlier are indicative of this. On December 18, 1941, Dr. Otto Bräutigam, the section chief for general politics in the Ministry for the East, wrote to Lohse concerning the issue of whether exceptions should be made for workers when Jews were to be executed:

As for the Jewish question, *oral discussions* that have taken place in the meantime have brought about clarification. As a general rule, economic factors should not be considered in deciding the matter. In the future, any questions that may arise should be settled directly with the Upper SS and Police Leader.[134]

Bräutigam was thus aware from various conversations that were now taking place that a new situation had arisen following Hitler's speech on December 12. Most probably, however, he had not been informed of the exact course of events at the higher levels, an indication of the fact that the proceedings at the meeting of the *Reichsleiter* and *Gauleiter* were being treated as strictly confidential.[135] Lohse himself later said that Hitler's address to the *Reichsleiter* and *Gauleiter* was confidential and as a general policy the participants at such meetings were not to discuss them.[136] Further, the ministry guidelines communicated by Bräutigam did not signify that all Jews were to be executed immediately. The ministry guideline provided merely the general line.[137] This is important to remember in understanding Hitler's initiative of December 1941. His was not a concrete directive to begin immediately with an all-encompassing liquidation of the Jews. Rather, it was a decision in principle. The practical implementation, organization, and tempo of the extermination remained matters for the relevant local bodies to determine.

On December 16, at a meeting of the officials of the General Government, Hans Frank delivered an infamous address. In several of its passages he alluded unmistakably to Hitler's announcement of his decision on December 12:

> As for the Jews, well, I can tell you quite frankly that one way or another we have to put an end to them. The Führer once put it this way: if the combined forces of Judaism should again succeed in unleashing a world war, that would mean the end of the Jews in Europe.... I urge you: Stand together with me ... on this idea at least: Save your sympathy for the German people alone. Don't waste it on anyone else in the world, ... As a veteran National Socialist I also have to say this: if the Jews in Europe should survive this war, ... then the war would be only a partial success. As far as the Jews are concerned, I would therefore be guided by the basic expectation that they are going to disappear. They have to be gotten rid of. At present I am involved in discussions aimed at having them moved away to the east. In January there is going to be an important meeting in Berlin to discuss this question. I am going to send State Secretary Dr. Bühler to this meeting. It is scheduled to take place in the offices of the RSHA in the presence of Obergruppenführer Heydrich. Whatever its outcome, a great Jewish emigration will commence.
>
> But what is going to happen to these Jews? Do you imagine there

will be settlement villages for them in the Ostland? In Berlin we were told: Why are you making all this trouble for us? There is nothing we can do with them here in the Ostland or in the Reich Commissariat. Liquidate them yourselves! . . . For us too the Jews are incredibly destructive eaters. . . . Here are 3.5 million Jews that we can't shoot, we can't poison. But there are some things we can do, and one way or another these measures will successfully lead to a liquidation. They are related to the measures under discussion with the Reich. . . . Where and how this will all take place will be a matter for offices that we will have to establish and operate here. I will report to you on their operation at the appropriate time.[138]

Frank was referring here to Hitler's speech of December 12, and above all to his words on "sympathy." His manner of expression clearly suggests, however, that he could not reveal precisely what had happened at the meeting of the *Reichsleiter* and *Gauleiter*. He went on to mention the discussions with the Ministry for the East and a centralized plan, still in its formative stages, for exterminating the Jews. Within the context of that plan, a liquidation organization would be created in the General Government.[139] According to him, a scheduled meeting with Heydrich would clarify the issues. That meeting was the Wannsee Conference.

On June 9, 1942, the day of a memorial service for Heydrich, who had been assassinated, Himmler delivered an infamous programmatic speech before an audience of high-ranking SS- and police officers. There he too employed a formula Hitler had used in his December 12, 1941, address: he announced a plan to exterminate all European Jews within a year, noting that "the table must be cleared."[140] Hitler recalled his own words when he declared on February 14, 1942, that there was "no place for sentimental feelings" in connection with the destruction of the Jews.[141] Upper SS leaders such as Himmler-intimate and SS-Gruppenführer Gottlob Berger began to speak quite openly after December 1941 about killing all the Jews.[142] Further, new guidelines on the subject may have been issued in the Wartheland on January 2, 1942.[143]

It is possible, hypothetically, that Hitler had already announced his decision before a smaller circle at some point between December 7 and December 12.[144] Statements made by Eichmann after the war, however, make this seem relatively improbable. On several occasions Eichmann stated that Heydrich had called him in one day and told him that Hitler had ordered the extermination of the Jews.[145] Two details of his account are significant. First, according to Eichmann, Heydrich had clearly gotten the information from Himmler. If a meeting had been held between December 7 and December 11 to allow Hitler to announce his decision to exterminate all European Jews before a smaller circle of advisers, it is difficult to imagine that Heydrich would not have been present and would have had to learn about the decision from Himmler instead. After all, Heydrich was in town until December 11, so he was available to attend such a meeting, and it was Heydrich who had been given the commission to prepare the "total European solution of the Jewish question."[146]

Second, Eichmann stated that he was sent immediately after his conversation with Heydrich to meet with Globocnik at the concentration camp in Belzec.[147] Eichmann's descriptions of the status of construction at Belzec make it clear that his visit could not have occurred before December 1941.[148] Most experts have declared this to be impossible since, according to their theories, such a date would be "too late."[149] Eichmann's more general recollection of being sent to Belzec immediately after an important decision had been announced would, however, be consistent with Hitler's having made his decision in December 1941.

Hitler announced his decision to liquidate European Jewry to the party leadership on December 12.[150] Just five days later the leaders of the seven regional evangelical churches announced the exclusion from the church of all individuals bearing the Jewish star. They demanded that Jews be deported from Germany as "born enemies of the Reich and of the world," employing a formulation similar to Hitler's. Finally, they demanded that "the most severe measures" be taken against the Jews. Logically this could mean only one thing: their destruction.[151] Such a proclamation, offensive as it is by itself, seems even more incriminating in view of its proximity to the meeting of party officials and regional leaders. Church leaders were usually well-informed politically. Further research will be needed to show whether some connection actually existed.

IV The Wannsee Conference and its new context: contents and results

On December 8, 1941, one day before it was originally scheduled to take place, the Wannsee Conference was postponed indefinitely.[152] Various explanations for the postponement have been proposed. In the second set of invitations, sent out on January 8, 1942, Heydrich wrote that he had to cancel the original meeting "because of events that were announced suddenly, requiring the attention of some of the invited participants."[153] Some historians believe that Heydrich was referring to the Japanese attack on Pearl Harbor on December 7. Others believe he meant the Soviet counteroffensive in the Battle of Moscow, which began on December 5.[154] At the originally scheduled time for the conference, at noon on December 9, there was something "requiring the attention" of Heydrich himself: he had to present a report to Himmler.[155] According to the account cited earlier by Labs, the meeting had to be postponed "because of the session of the Reichstag."[156] That is a possibility. The session did not actually take place until December 11, but it had been postponed more than once. Why the conference had to be postponed for six weeks is unclear. Perhaps Hitler's speech on December 12 had so altered the context for the meeting that new preparation was needed.[157] Hitler's fundamental decision had, as a matter of fact, created a new and rather horrible "framework for planning" for the RSHA. Perhaps Heydrich's meeting with Göring on January 12, 1942, furnished another opportunity to discuss the new situation in antisemitic policy.[158]

We have already reviewed the participants at the conference. Present were five representatives from the Security Police and the SD, eight politicians and functionaries from the civil administration, and two representatives from the party, one from the party chancellery and one from the Race and Resettlement Office of the SS. Some of those invited sent representatives. Two were absent: Leopold Gutterer, the state secretary from the propaganda ministry, and Ulrich Greifelt, the director of the Staff Office of the Reich Commissar for the Strengthening of Germandom. (Greifelt may have been at a conference in Italy.)[159] Since policy issues rather than technical matters were under discussion, representatives from the Reich finance ministry and from the Reich transportation ministry had not been invited.[160] Of all the offices affected by the problem of how to define "Jewish," only the Führer chancellery and the Armed Forces High Command were not present.[161]

Heydrich opened the meeting with a long presentation. He reviewed Göring's commission to "prepare a Final Solution for the Jewish Question in Europe." He emphasized that overall responsibility and authority were his. He expressed his desire that all their efforts should proceed, after appropriate consultation, in parallel. Finally, he summarized the progress of antisemitic policies, emphasizing developments since 1939: the stage of forced individual emigration and, "with appropriate prior approval by the Führer," the stage of collective "evacuation of the Jews to the east."[162]

He then went on to outline his plan for a "Final Solution," involving the mass murder of Jews from all the countries of Europe, including allied, neutral, and hostile nations. Some of the Jews would first be employed for forced labor.[163] A brief discussion involving Heydrich, Martin Luther (from the Reich foreign ministry), and Otto Hofmann (from the SS Race and Resettlement Office) touched on potential difficulties and possible diplomatic initiatives that could be involved in implementing the plan in occupied and allied countries. Few problems were foreseen, though Heydrich did note that the deportations would be dependent on military developments on the eastern front.[164]

Next, Heydrich presented his ideas for expanding the definition of "Jewish." Basically his ideas reflected the proposals that had been agreed to several months earlier by a commission drawn from RSHA, party chancellery, and Four-Year Plan officials.[165] "Part-Jews of the first degree" were to be treated, with few exceptions, "like Jews." Further, the same treatment was to be meted out to some "part-Jews of the second degree" and to Jews married to non-Jewish spouses.[166] Hofmann objected, proposing voluntary sterilization as an alternative to deportation. Wilhelm Stuckart objected as well, though he favored involuntary sterilizations of "part-Jews of the first degree." Stuckart also suggested passage of a law requiring the dissolution of such "mixed marriages," to be followed by the deportation and execution of the Jewish spouse. But he made no use of the arguments prepared by his subordinate, Lösener, to object to further measures against these two groups.[167]

Finally, State Secretary Josef Bühler (from the General Government) acknowledged the authority of the Security Police and the SD for conducting anti-Jewish activities. Bühler and Alfred Meyer, the representative from the Ministry for the East, pressed for a beginning of the "Final Solution" in their territories.[168] It should be noted that Meyer, the Gauleiter for North Westphalia, was the only participant at the Wannsee Conference who had also been present at Hitler's address to the *Reichsleiter* and *Gauleiter* on December 12, 1941.

Heydrich was quite pleased with the results of the conference.[169] One may well wonder why. He had expected opposition from Bühler and especially from Stuckart.[170] Bühler, after the discussions preceding the conference, had raised no objections—quite the contrary! But Stuckart had been ready to compromise only on the issue of mixed marriages. As for the issue of the "part-Jews," no agreement had been possible, nor was one ever reached later.[171] On January 29, the party chancellery released a report that this issue was still undecided. Indeed the adviser on racial affairs in the Ministry for the East, relying on Bernhard Lösener, noted that the party chancellery was now opposed to the harsher treatment of "part-Jews."[172] One certainly cannot say that the issue was decided in Heydrich's favor at the Wannsee Conference.[173] On the contrary, on the one apparently undecided subject Heydrich's proposal had failed.

Nonetheless, Heydrich's ultimate authority had been recognized, explicitly so by Bühler, implicitly by the others. That should hardly be surprising. If the term "Final Solution" was now to be equated with "murder," who would have been in a position to dispute his responsibility? Who would have wanted to? In fact, some officials were quite pleased to be able to act as if they could wash their hands of the matter. One adviser from the Ministry for the East, present at a follow-up meeting to the Wannsee Conference, was struck by the fact that the meeting chairman, the section leader Dr. Otto Bräutigam, from his own office, appeared so eager to submit and to make concessions to the SS. When asked why, Bräutigam said, "that as far as the Jewish question was concerned he was quite happy to emphasize the responsibility of the SS and the police."[174] His statement is all the more worthy of note in that Bräutigam had already stated publicly, at the time, that Germany could no longer achieve a military victory in the war.[175] Apparently his thoughts had already begun to turn toward his own personal future.[176]

In my opinion, Heydrich's satisfaction with the outcome of the Wannsee Conference arose for another reason. No one had voiced opposition to the extermination of the Jews, including those in the German Reich and in western Europe.[177] In official terminology: no reservations were expressed. The minutes support this conclusion indirectly. They record no objections, though differences and disagreements on other topics are noted. It certainly would have been conceivable for governmental or administrative officials to voice reservations, practical or political if not moral ones, in the face of Hitler's decision on December 12.[178] They did not do so. Luther and Bühler voiced agreement, Kritzinger and Freisler remained silent, and Stuckart confined his objections to the issue of "part-Jews." It was not without some reason, therefore, that Heydrich could write, on February 26, that Wannsee, "happily, has settled the basic outlines for the *practical implementation* of the final solution of the Jewish question." He admitted that not all the details had yet been settled.[179] For Heydrich, January 20, 1942, was a day to celebrate, a day when he had also signed a list of nominees for the War Service Cross Second Class. At the top of the list was Paul Blobel, up until now the head of the Sonderkommando 4a and the man responsible for the slaughter of Jews at Babi Yar. Third on the list was Dr. Albert Widmann, who had carried out extermination experiments using poison gas in Mogilev in White Russia. Also on the list were Widmann's assistant, Schmidt, three other RSHA officials from Referat II D 3 a, the office responsible for the development of the gassing vans, and various members of the Einsatzkommandos.[180]

Yet the plan Heydrich presented on January 20, 1942, was not completely clear. Heydrich died on June 4, 1942, and it is very likely that he never succeeded in presenting to Göring a "Complete Proposal" for the "Final Solution of the Jewish Question," as his commission of July 31, 1941, had put it.[181] Just five days before Heydrich's assassination, Lammers had sent him a letter from the Reich interior minister concerning the issue of "part-Jews of the first degree" in order for Heydrich "to review it for your report to Reich Marshall Göring."[182] Presumably Heydrich had been hoping for Hitler's fundamental decision for some time. When it was announced on December 12, 1941, however, Heydrich had no ready-made plan for extermination that he could simply pull off the shelf. And if Heydrich did not have a complete plan in December 1941 indicating how the murder of all European Jews was supposed to be carried out, the conclusion has to be that such a plan could not have existed before the beginning of 1942. What Heydrich proposed at the Wannsee Conference had a provisional, in some places utopian, character. This much is reflected in the central passages of the minutes about the future treatment of the Jews:

In the course of the final solution, the Jews should be brought in an appropriate manner and under appropriate direction to work in the east. In large detachments, with the sexes separated, the Jews who are able to work will construct roads in these regions. It is to be expected that a sizable number will disappear due to natural causes.

The Jews who survive, however many there may be, will no doubt be the hardiest. They will have to be treated accordingly. Otherwise these select few, should they escape, could form the basis for a new Jewish line of descent. (See the experience of history.)

Gerald Reitlinger has observed that "unless the words of the German language had lost their meaning," what Heydrich meant was execution.[183] And if that was true for the surviving Jews who were capable of working, it must have been truer still for those unable to work, especially for the women and children. Bühler pointed this out explicitly. Despite the deliberate use of misleading terms, it is clear that large programs of forced labor continued to play a significant role in the RSHA's plans. Road construction in the Soviet Union was one project. Another involved vaguely discernible plans for labor and penal colonies in northern Russia, near the Arctic Ocean.[184] Not much was to come of these plans. In a meeting with Himmler on February 17, 1942, Hitler himself rejected the Arctic Ocean schemes, which he had learned about from a memorandum that presumably had been worked out by the RSHA. He reaffirmed his position in early April, noting that he had a more pressing need for this labor power in the German war economy.[185]

Two other parts of Heydrich's plan differed from what was later to take shape. In Heydrich's scheme, Europe was to be "combed from west to east." Jews were to be deported first from the Reich, then from the Protectorate of Bohemia and Moravia, then from western Europe, and finally from eastern Europe. Hitler expressed similar ideas in May 1942.[186] But this approach conflicted with the plan of the foreign office, according to which the deportations were to begin in southeast Europe.[187] A considerable difference of opinion on this issue surfaced at the Wannsee Conference. As a matter of fact, the systematic and complete extermination of the Jews began in the occupied territories of the Soviet Union and in the General Government, just as Bühler and Meyer had insisted. Bühler had argued that a majority of Jews in the General Government were not capable of work, endangered the economy through their black-market activities, and ought to disappear.[188] As noted earlier, Hans Frank had already characterized the Jews in his liquidation speech on December 16, 1941, as "extraordinarily destructive eaters."[189]

Finally, the schedule underlying the discussions in Wannsee seems not to agree with the later tempo of extermination. The huge forced labor projects were not realized. The destruction of the Jews was accelerated in April of 1942, and then again during the summer of that year. This much is indicated by the pace of construction at the extermination camps. It is also confirmed in later statements made by one of the conference participants, Otto Hofmann. In late September 1942 he revealed his ideas on future generations to a meeting of SS Officers, noting that "They will no longer recognize any Jewish danger. *In twenty years there may not be a single Jew left.* In the European part of Russia there are a total of some 11 million Jews [!]. So there is still plenty of work to do. *I cannot believe that we have exterminated more than one million of them thus far.* It will take some time until we have freed Europe from this pestilence."[190]

Hofmann was clearly referring to his recollection, even then somewhat dim, of the Wannsee Conference. The pace of liquidation had actually been faster than he thought. For he had not been kept informed about current developments and had just met with Himmler for the first time since February 1942.[191]

V The results of the Wannsee Conference

News about the outcome of the meeting in Wannsee spread quickly. Heydrich gave Himmler a telephone report on the following day. Alfred Meyer reported to Rosenberg. Globocnik traveled to Berlin, probably on January 23. Hitler, too, seems to have been informed without delay.[192] It is possible that reports reached Slovakia as early as the end of January.[193] By July 1942 German officials in the General Commissariat in Latvia were fully informed.[194]

On the issue of "part-Jews" and "mixed marriages" the discussions soon deadlocked. The new deportation directives issued by Eichmann on January 31, 1942, continued to follow the Nuremberg Laws. Jews married to non-Jews, Jewish foreigners, Jewish workers in armaments plants and in agriculture, and the elderly continued to be exempted.[195] On March 6 the first official follow-up conference at the expert level was held. The suggestions Stuckart had made at Wannsee were examined. Sterilization was rejected as an organizational impossibility, but more detailed plans for compulsory legal divorce were formulated.[196] On March 16 Stuckart continued to insist that the class of individuals labeled as part-Jews of the first degree should not receive harsher treatment than before. At this point he adopted the arguments that had been drafted for his use at the Wannsee meeting by Lösener. The acting Reich justice minister, Franz Schlegelberger, wrote two letters in support of Stuckart's position. Subsequently, on April 10, Lammers met with Schlegelberger to discuss the "Complete Solution of the Jewish Question."[197] By September 1942 Stuckart seems to have succeeded in convincing Himmler. Consequently, the second follow-up meeting to the Wannsee Conference, held on October 27, produced no new results.[198] At about this same time the new Reich justice minister, Otto Thierack, and Goebbels expressed their opinion that "the issue of part-Jews should not be resolved during the war." Even the notorious RSHA chief of Section III B (Foreign Nationalities), Hans Ehlich, declared that the "lineage investigations" of the Reich Genealogy Office were dispensable "because in the course of nine years the percentage of cases discovered involving foreign blood was relatively small" and could be ignored.[199] Further, despite an apparent breakthrough in March 1943 when Reich Interior Minister Wilhelm Frick obtained Hitler's approval, the plans developed by various offices for compulsory legal divorces in cases of "mixed marriages" came to nothing.[200] The majority of "half Jews," "quarter Jews," and Jewish partners in "mixed marriages" were thus able to survive the war despite these repeated efforts at persecution.

In the immediate aftermath of the Wannsee Conference, however, the RSHA believed that the time was ripe to hunt down "part-Jews" throughout Europe and to execute them. In early February 1942, the adviser on Jewish affairs in the SD office in Paris, Theodor Dannecker, urgently requested that a genealogical researcher be hired to begin an immediate examination of the lineages of "Jews and part-Jews."[201] It was an opinion from Mayer, the chief of the Reich Genealogy Office, in March that first put a damper on the enthusiasm. He concluded that there simply were not enough documents available to carry out an investigation for Jewish ancestors in the family lineages of some seventy thousand cases. The project was canceled.[202] In the Netherlands, too, where the SS had compiled a national "registry of Jews and part-Jews," a systematic deportation of part-Jews seems never to have been undertaken.[203]

For the German Jews in Riga and Minsk, however, the results of the Wannsee Conference were soon to prove calamitous. In early February 1942, in Riga, selections began to be made openly: Jews deemed "incapable of work" were shot by the Security Police or murdered in gassing vans.[204] After being informed in Riga of the outcome of the Wannsee Conference, the Commander of the Security Police and of the SD (KdS) in Minsk, Walter Hofmann, announced on January 29, 1942, that he wanted to initiate a "vigorous schedule of executions" in the spring. Hofmann cynically remarked that one had to cultivate the belief prevailing among the deported German Jews that they would be allowed to return to their homes after the war in order to get them to work harder. On February 6, General Commissar Wilhelm Kube indicated that he would order the executions of Jewish deportees arriving on subsequent transports from the Reich because there was not enough food or shelter for them.[205] Members of the German Jewish Council were arrested by the Security Police in early February. One month later they were executed. According to one witness, on March 31, German

Jews in the Minsk ghetto were executed for the first time in the course of a "small" massacre.[206]

The new wave of deportations to the east from within the German Reich and from central and western Europe began slowly. The crisis in rail transport in the occupied Soviet territories had had significant effects on the situation in the Reich. On January 26, Albert Speer informed Rosenberg that additional Jewish transports would have to be postponed until April. Even the deportations of 150,000 Jews from the German Reich to concentration camps announced by Himmler on the same day had to be delayed for a time owing to the rail crisis.[207] In late March the deportation of French and Slovakian Jews to the Lublin district and to Auschwitz began. At first, they were still viewed as laborers, but many of them died quickly. German Jews were brought to the Lublin district. Initially they were housed in the ghettos once inhabited by the Polish Jews who had been executed. In April 1942 the Reich Railway could again supply thirty-seven special trains for Jewish deportations.[208]

At the beginning of May 1942 a coordinated action began involving the transport of German Jews directly to various extermination sites. Between May 4 and 15, 1942, the first 10, 161 German Jews were transported from the Lodz ghetto and exterminated in gas chambers in Chelmno.[209] On May 6, the first fatal transports left the Reich from Vienna, bound for Minsk. On May 11, 1942, these deportees were shot or gassed in the camp at Trostinez.[210] On May 2, Undersecretary of State Martin Luther from the foreign office issued assurances to the Slovakian government that Jews deported from Slovakia would never return.[211]

On April 17 Himmler visited Kolo (Warthbrücken), the transfer point for Jews being deported from Lodz. It is possible that he visited the nearby extermination camp Chelmno as well. On June 18, 1942, Reich Interior Minister Frick also visited Kolo. According to a witness, local residents complained to Frick about episodes of brutality during the "reloading." Frick saw to it that subsequent trainloads of Jews were transported to their final destination on the narrow gauge railway.[212] Frick's visit occurred shortly after the systematic extermination of the German Jews in Chelmno had begun. Up until the end, the Reich interior ministry sought to assert its authority.

The National Socialist Party played a significant role in this newly accelerated genocide of European Jews and of German Jews. In the face of the countless, often desperate requests submitted by Jewish citizens and their non-Jewish advocates, Bormann issued two directives to the *Gauleiter* and *Kreisleiter* at the end of June and the beginning of July 1942. He instructed them to subject any requests for exceptions to the "most meticulous scrutiny." Lammers followed suit in a directive to government offices.[213] Bormann went one step further on October 9, 1942. In a confidential memorandum he offered a justification for the extermination of the

Jews and issued gag orders to party functionaries. He seems to have wanted to counter rumors circulating about "extremely harsh measures" being taken against the Jews while at the same time apparently justifying them. Bormann's text was a short and simple paraphrase of the presentation Heydrich gave according to the minutes of the Wannsee Conference.[214]

The question may well be raised, in conclusion, as to the value of the evidence presented in this essay. Does the thesis that Hitler made a decision in principle in early December 1941 to exterminate all European Jews contradict any supposedly secure results of previous research? If not, what significance does it possess?

A comprehensive directive by Hitler authorizing the extermination of European Jews has never been discovered. Nor is there any evidence to suggest that such a directive ever existed. But the same could be said about any supposed personal *decision* by Hitler. Theoretically such a decision might have occurred long before any directive was ever issued. Clearly, an inner decision is much more difficult to substantiate than a directive.[215] All the various theories about when Hitler decided to exterminate the Jews employ the same method: they try to juxtapose some supposed development of plans or preparations for executions with statements made by Hitler that seem to indicate that he had made such a decision. But the latter are generally unclear or ambiguous.

The decision to execute Soviet Jews must be distinguished from the decision to destroy the remaining European Jews. Most historians now make this distinction.[216] The former decision was made much earlier than the latter, by August 1941 at the latest. In my view it had already been made in the first months of that year.[217]

The notion that the decision to deport the German Jews was equivalent to the decision to exterminate them has no evidence to support it. It is contradicted by events at Lodz, Minsk, and Riga. One of the purposes of the Wannsee Conference was to discuss the unresolved issue of what to do with the German Jews. It is also entirely possible that Hitler first announced his decision after the conference had been initially scheduled.[218] The issue was ripe, so to speak. Himmler, Heydrich, Rosenberg, and Lohse all apparently urged that at least some of the deported Jews be executed. Nonetheless, a decision by Hitler on the subject has not previously been documented. Nor do we have evidence of any decision by him with regard to plans for the deportation of Jews from France in the fall of 1941. In the French case, however, it was a matter first of all of deporting, and possibly executing, just a limited number of Jews who were already in custody, or who were being held as hostages. The permission to do so did not yet apply to all French Jews.[219]

There is no disputing the fact that on several occasions Hitler merely *approved* the antisemitic measures and partial extermination programs that had been developed by others and that he did not often devise or promote plans of his own. At the Wannsee Conference, Heydrich himself remarked that the deportation of German Jews had begun in September 1941 after "prior approval from the Führer."[220] He surely would not have dared, nor would he have wanted, to use the term "approval" if in fact it had been at Hitler's order. In similar fashion Hitler approved the execution of Jews in the newly occupied area of France on December 10, 1942, and the extermination of the remaining Polish and Soviet Jews on June 19, 1943.[221]

If one can believe the testimony of Eichmann, who claimed to have acted as the messenger, on two or three occasions during the early stages of extermination efforts in the General Government, Odilo Globocnik received permission from Heydrich to execute a limited number of Jews—in each case groups of 150,000 to 250,000 individuals.[222] Here, too, it was a regional initiative that was approved, though admittedly one that was closely tied to the whole European-wide extermination program. The extermination camp at Belzec, whose construction had begun as early as November 1941, was initially designed to experiment with methods for mass extermination of Jews by poison gas in stationary gas chambers and then to carry out the first efforts.[223] The scheme may have been preceded by permission from Hitler or by a decision from him, but up until now none has been documented. Exactly what future expectations were associated with the erection of the Belzec camp remains unknown.

Evidence recently uncovered indicates the probable existence of a plan to deport some Jews from the rest of Europe to Mogilev, in White Russia. The same evidence indicates the construction of a crematorium at the close of 1941 and a possible plan for construction of a gas chamber.[224] But none of this provides unconditional proof that there existed a comprehensive plan for the extermination of the Jews. Exactly when a gas chamber was planned there remains uncertain. The intention could well have been to transport a large number of Jews there, to employ them at forced labor, and to let them perish from inhuman living conditions.[225] Rosenberg's remark on November 18, 1941, three days after a meeting with Himmler, that the occupied Soviet territories were to serve as the location for a "biological extermination of the whole of European Jewry," could also have been intended to refer to a slow process of annihilation, but he considered this to be possible only in the distant future. Rosenberg and Himmler had met with Hitler on November 16, following their own conversation the previous day. Then, on November 17, Himmler had a telephone conversation with Heydrich on the subject of the "removal of the Jews," but this may have been with reference to the topic they discussed previously, "the situation in the General Government," or to difficulties concerning the deportation of Jews from the German Reich to the East. Heydrich discussed the last subject with Goebbels on the same day.[226] As of October 13 Rosenberg had continued to declare that a deportation of Jews living in the General Government to the occupied territories of the Soviet Union was impossible.

All he could give were vague promises for the future. These were of dubious value. In any case Rosenberg withdrew them in the middle of December.[227] An article written by Goebbels for the weekly *Das Reich* on November 16, 1941, which has sometimes been interpreted as proof of the existence of a comprehensive plan for extermination, is in fact ambiguous. In that article Goebbels defended the deportation of Jews from Germany because there had been some indications of solidarity with them by segments of the non-Jewish population. Goebbels wrote that "Jewry" was "facing a gradual process of destruction."[228] All this evidence indicates that the events that occurred in the fall of 1941 will have to be examined further before a final judgment can be made.[229]

In the final analysis, what really matters is that the suggestion that there never was a central decision made by Hitler regarding the extermination of the European Jews cannot be sustained.[230] Equally unsupportable is the thesis that the final decision was not made until May or June of 1942.[231] The fundamental decision announced in December of 1941 is a crucial missing piece of the decision-making process leading up to the liquidation of the Jews. Hitler's decision put the planning for these crimes on a new basis. But it relieved no one of responsibility. Its result was that the various existing ideas, proposals, and initiatives for extermination projects at the regional levels received support and legitimation. They received new impetus and became systematized. Significantly, only four days before the Führer's decision, and independent of it, the first extermination camp at Chelmno had begun its grisly work.[232] Arthur Greiser had literally received special permission from Himmler and Heydrich to execute one hundred thousand Jews. It is unlikely that Hitler was involved. If Greiser had received permission from Hitler he would not have had to express his gratitude to Himmler, yet he did so.[233]

Let me make the following points clear. The purpose of my essay has not been to reject the results of more than twenty years of basic research, particularly by the so-called functionalist school. The extermination of the Jews was by no means based either simply on this one decision by Hitler or even on the entirety of his decisions, directives, or initiatives. What we are concerned with is one significant point within a whole process that led to the liquidation of the European Jews. Among other things, the analysis of this impulse can contribute to a more precise view of Hitler's actual role. It certainly is difficult to understand how Hitler could have made a fundamental decision in principle to exterminate all the Jews in Europe only after nearly one million Jews had already fallen victim to organized mass murder in a number of countries. It is difficult to comprehend that this decision was not made all at once but rather step by step in one area after another. But this is precisely what the case of Chelmno indicates. The prevailing view that the fundamental decision had already been made between the spring and the fall of 1941 is based on the belief that some kind of prior approval by the government leadership must have preceded the transition to mass murder of the Jews. For the National Socialists, however, the various decisions to proceed with the exterminations were political and not moral decisions. They could thus be made and applied in limited fashion to specific territories or to particular groups of individuals—those "incapable of work," for example.

How are the contents and results of Hitler's fundamental decision to be evaluated? His remarks on December 12 were contained in a relatively brief passage within a long speech. At the time, the attention of the German leadership was far more intently focused on political problems that were seen as much more urgent than the persecution of the Jews. This small part of the address was clear and unambiguous, but it still was not specific. We have to remind ourselves that Hitler's various meetings with Himmler, Bouhler, Frank, Rosenberg, and others would have been much more detailed and concrete. As far as the events of December 1941 are concerned, it is not a matter of whether or not the historical agents used a more or less radical language (since they did that at other times as well). Rather it is a matter of ascertainable consequences. To summarize, Hitler's December 12 speech and the other meetings had three crucial results: (1) new, fundamental directives regarding the execution of all Jews by the General Government and by the Ministry for the East, the administrative units with control over the majority of Jews living in areas under German rule; (2) an intensification of planning and of preparations for exterminating the Jews in various regions using poison gas; and (3) a determination of policy regarding German Jews. In announcing his decision to exterminate *all* European Jews, Hitler had also decided the fate of the deported German Jews. The last point is confirmed, for example, by Hans Frank's remark in Kraków on December 16, 1941, concerning the executions of the Jews in the General Government: "Whatever happens in the Reich will at the very least have to happen here as well."[234]

For the officials involved, Hitler's decision was a *necessary* one as far as it concerned the execution of German Jews. It was also necessary as a basis for the centralized planning of the mass exterminations. Despite their use of language aimed at cloaking the realities, the indications in Frank's speech in Kraków on December 16 and in Heydrich's address as recorded in the minutes of the Wannsee Conference must be taken seriously. We witness there the initial sketches of a comprehensive plan for total liquidation. Prior to this there had not existed such a comprehensive plan for systematic extermination to be carried out within a brief span of time. With regard to the savage treatment already being meted out to Jews in the occupied territories of the Soviet Union, the new directives of December 1941 hardly meant much. They may have had a slightly greater effect in the General Government, though there, too, regional impulses from the police and from elements in the civil administration in favor of large-scale exterminations had already become so powerful that sooner or later a catastrophe was inevitable.

What this evidence shows is that Hitler by no means decided everything, even in what may have been his most significant intervention in the processes leading to the mass exterminations. Nor did he need to decide everything. The results of his intervention were clear, but in a certain sense they were also limited. Earlier findings by various researchers as to the grave responsibility shared by other official bodies, particularly by the authorities directly in charge in the occupied territories, are confirmed by our analysis.

In order to understand the decision-making process that led to the destruction of the European Jews it may be useful to refer to the concept of the utopian. The National Socialists, with Hitler foremost among them, certainly entertained ideas about eliminating the Jews and indicated a willingness to put these ideas into practice well before 1941. But there is a difference between having ideas or intentions to exterminate a people and the actual implementation of those ideas and intentions. The initial schemes for a "Final Solution" involved various plans for a forced migration. They were markedly destructive in character, with features such as slow annihilation through brutal living conditions and limits on reproduction. In a way, however, these plans were also utopian, principally because none of them, however seriously pursued, had any practical chance of being realized. This was as true of the Madagascar plan as it was of the 1939–40 plan to deport Jews to the Lublin district. Destructive elements grew more pronounced in the plan to deport European Jews to conquered regions of the Soviet Union following a successful conclusion of the war there. Exactly how to go about exterminating the Jews became imaginable only little by little, even though a widespread readiness to do so had long existed. What was decisive for the actual realization of mass murder plans were the intermediate steps between the utopian emigration and extermination schemes, on the one hand, and liquidation programs that could be practically implemented, on the other. The scheme proposed at the outset of 1941 to reduce some thirty million individuals in the Soviet Union to starvation in order to guarantee food supplies to the European areas controlled by Germany proved to be impractical. It was replaced in the fall of 1941 by programs for eliminating groups of specific individuals, like the millions of Soviet war prisoners who were "incapable of work." For the antisemitic efforts, the steps undertaken in December 1941 marked an ominous turn toward the practical implementation of concrete measures for racial genocide.

Although these monstrous developments could certainly not be called normal politics, and although Hitler intervened directly, in one sense this life or death decision regarding the fate of the Jews living in Europe came to pass in a manner very much like any other "normal" political decision.

The Führer did not make the decision alone; he made it only after some
time had passed; and, in a specific situation and for a specific set of reasons,
he gave his approval to initiatives that had arisen from the administrative
and party apparatus. As with many evolving policies, the demands for the
extermination of the European Jews came from many sources. Before they
could all be acted upon in some systematic manner, however, the National
Socialist system required a leadership decision by Hitler.

NOTES

Translated for the *Journal of Modern History* by Stephen Duffy, Simpson College.
An earlier version was published as "Die Wannsee-Konferenz, das Schicksal der
deutschen Juden und Hitlers politische Grundsatzentscheidung, alle Juden Europas
zu ermorden," *WerkstattGeschichte* 18 (October 1997). I am very grateful to Martina
Voigt, Michael Wildt, Armin Nolzen, and Christoph Dieckmann for their advice
and support during the preparation of this article. Independently of me, and at the
same time, Peter Witte has come to similar conclusions about the dating of Hitler's
decision to December 1941, a topic discussed in the third section.

1 Eberhard Jäckel, "Die Konferenz am Wannsee," *Die Zeit* (January 17, 1992),
   p. 33.
2 Wolfgang Scheffler also noted that "the question has often been raised as to
   Heydrich's reasons for convening the conference at all." See Scheffler, "Die
   Wannsee-Konferenz und ihre historische Bedeutung," in *Erinnern für die
   Zukunft* (Berlin, 1993), p. 17.
3 Ibid. The authenticity of the document is not in question. See also n. 197
   below. Eichmann himself identified it with no reservations. Of the works
   cited here, see esp. Scheffler; Johannes Tuchel, *Am Grossen Wannsee 56–58:
   Von der Villa Minoux zum Haus der Wannsee-Konferenz* (Berlin, 1992); Peter
   Klein, *Die Wannsee-Konferenz vom 20. Januar 1942* (Berlin, n.d.), pp. 5–14.
4 For the General Government of Poland, see, e.g., Dieter Pohl, *Von der "Judenpolitik" zum Judenmord: Der Distrikt Lublin des Generalgouvernements 1939–
   1944* (Frankfurt am Main, 1993), and *Nationalsozialistische Judenverfolgung in
   Ostgalizien, 1941–1944* (Munich, 1996); Thomas Sandkühler, *Die "Endlösung"
   in Galizien* (Bonn, 1996). For Serbia, see Christopher Browning, *Fateful Months*
   (New York and London, 1985), pp. 39–56, 68–85; Walter Manoschek, *Serbien
   ist judenfrei* (Munich, 1993). See also Yitzhak Arad, "The Holocaust of Soviet
   Jewry in the Occupied Territories of the USSR," *Yad Vashem Studies* 21 (1991):
   1–47; Andrew Ezergailis, *The Holocaust in Latvia, 1941–1944* (Washington and
   Riga, 1996). Additional studies of Lithuania by Christoph Dieckmann, of
   Einsatzgruppe D by Andrej Angrick, and of the Reich province Wartheland
   by Peter Klein and Michael Alberti are in preparation.
5 For completely new approaches, see Götz Aly and Susanne Heim, *Vordenker
   der Vernichtung* (Hamburg, 1991); Götz Aly, *"Endlösung": Völkerverschiebung
   und der Mord an den europäischen Juden* (Frankfurt am Main, 1995). In addi-
   tion, see Richard Breitman, *The Architect of Genocide: Himmler and the Final
   Solution* (London, 1992); Christopher Browning, *The Path to Genocide*
   (Cambridge, Mass., 1992); Hans Safrian, *Die Eichmann-Männer* (Vienna and
   Zürich, 1993); Philippe Burrin, *Hitler und die Juden: Die Entscheidung für den
   Völkermord* (Frankfurt am Main, 1993).

6 Up until now, the Dutch historian L. J. Hartog (in *Der Befehl zum Judenmord: Hitler, Amerika und die Juden* [Bodenheim, 1997], Dutch ed., 1994) is the only scholar to have provided documentary evidence in support of this view. I examine his position in detail below.

7 This fundamental political decision has to be distinguished from Hitler's personal, inward decision to destroy the Jews of Europe. The latter would be extremely difficult to date (and this essay does not attempt to do so).

8 During 1940 and in the spring of 1941 several thousand Jews had already been deported from Stettin and Vienna to the Lublin district or from Baden to the south of France.

9 *Nationalsozialistische Vernichtungspolitik, 1939 bis 1945: Neue Forschungen und Kontroversen*, ed. Ulrich Herbert (Frankfurt am Main, 1998).

10 In occupied Lithuania the transition to total extermination had already occurred by the middle of August. Only in three larger cities did German authorities permit some thirty thousand Jewish workers and their families to survive. See Helmut Krausnick and Hans-Heinrich Wilhelm, *Die Truppe des Weltanschauungskrieges: Die Einsatzgruppen der Sicherheitspolizei und des SD, 1938–1942* (Stuttgart, 1981); Arad, "The Holocaust of Soviet Jewry," pp. 1–22; Ralf Ogorreck, *Die Einsatzgruppen und die "Genesis der Endlösung"* (Berlin, 1996); Christian Gerlach, "Wirtschaftsinteressen, Besatzungspolitik und Judenvernichtung in Weissrussland, 1941–1943," in Herbert, ed., pp. 263–91.

11 Browning, *Fateful Months*, pp. 39 ff.; Manoschek, pp. 69 ff.

12 In the former Polish areas that had been annexed by the Soviet Union in 1939, German units began a systematic execution of Jews in early October 1941 in order to reduce their numbers and thus be rid of "useless eaters." As a rule, however, they did not destroy entire Jewish communities until later. In those areas during 1941 approximately 15–25 percent of the Jewish inhabitants were killed. In the territories that had originally been part of the Soviet Union, and in the Baltic countries, virtually all Jews were executed. See Gerlach; Arad, "The Holocaust of Soviet Jewry," esp. pp. 18–22; Shmuel Spector, *The Holocaust of Volhynian Jews, 1941–1944* (Jerusalem, 1990); for Galicia, see Pohl, *Judenverfolgung*, pp. 139 ff.

13 Compare Adalbert Rückerl, *Nationalsozialistische Vernichtungslager im Spiegel deutscher Strafprozesse* (Munich, 1977), pp. 106 f. and 132 f.; Yitzhak Arad, *Belzec, Sobibor, Treblinka: The Operation Reinhard Death Camps* (Bloomington, Ind., 1987), pp. 23–29; Ino Arndt and Wolfgang Scheffler, "Organisierter Massenmord an Juden in nationalsozialistischen Vernichtungslagern," *Vierteljahrshefte für Zeitgeschichte* (hereafter cited as *VfZ*) 24 (1976): 105–35, esp. pp. 117–19. It is thought by some that the extermination camp at Sobibor was also under construction at this time. For a summary see Pohl, *Von der "Judenpolitik,"* p. 106.

14 Pohl, in *Von der "Judenpolitik,"* p. 101, presents convincing arguments on this point.

15 Arndt and Scheffler, pp. 116 ff.; Rückerl, pp. 259–68; Aly, p. 355; Florian Freund, Bertrand Perz, and Karl Stuhlpfarrer, "Das Getto in Litzmannstadt (Lodz)," in *"Unser einziger Weg ist Arbeit." Das Getto Lodz, 1940–1944* (Frankfurt am Main, 1990), pp. 17–31.

16 The best summary, along with new evidence, can be found in Peter Witte, "Two Decisions concerning the 'Final Solution to the Jewish Question': Deportations to Lodz and Mass Murder in Chelmno," *Holocaust and Genocide Studies* 9, no. 3 (1995): 318–45.

17 Browning, *The Path to Genocide* (n. 5 above), (July); Ogorreck; and Burrin (n. 5 above), (August). Earlier works date the decision to execute Soviet Jews to

the spring of 1941. See Gerald Reitlinger, *Die Endlösung: Hitlers Versuch der Ausrottung der Juden Europas*, 5th ed. (West Berlin, 1979), pp. 89 ff.; Helmut Krausnick, "Die Einsatzgruppen vom Anschluß Österreichs bis zum Feldzug gegen die Sowjetunion," in Krausnick and Wilhelm, pp. 107 ff. and 150 ff.; Raul Hilberg, *Die Vernichtung der europäischen Juden*, rev. and expanded ed. (Frankfurt am Main, 1990), pp. 288 ff. (sometime before June 22, 1941).

18 Burrin, pp. 133 ff. (September); Browning, *The Path to Genocide* (October); Uwe Dietrich Adam, *Judenpolitik im Dritten Reich* (Düsseldorf, 1979), p. 312 (between September and November); Raul Hilberg, "Die Aktion Reinhard," in *Der Mord an den Juden im Zweiten Weltkrieg*, ed. Eberhard Jäckel and Jürgen Rohwer (Frankfurt am Main, 1987), pp. 125–36, esp. p. 126 (during the summer).

19 As in Breitman (n. 5 above), pp. 145 ff.; for a more cautious view, see Leni Yahil, *The Holocaust: The Fate of European Jewry, 1932–1945* (New York and Oxford, 1990): esp. pp. 253 and 320.

20 A facsimile of the original has been published in John Mendelsohn, ed., *The Holocaust: Selected Documents in Eighteen Volumes*, vol. 11 (New York and London, 1982); and in Tuchel, pp. 121–36 (along with Heydrich's letter of February 26, 1942, to the Foreign Office). Hereafter I cite Tuchel.

21 Reitlinger, pp. 105 ff.

22 Scheffler (n. 2 above), pp. 24 f. and p. 30. The second point is emphasized especially by Jäckel (n. I above).

23 Hilberg, *Vernichtung*, p. 421. The first two aspects are emphasized by Adam, p. 314, because they were the only issues that had not been resolved beforehand. For a combination of the various elements as more or less equally important, see Aly and Heim, p. 455; Kurt Pätzold and Erika Schwarz, *Tagesordnung: Judenmord. Die Wannsee-Konferenz am 20. Januar 1942*, 2d ed. (Berlin, 1992), pp. 33 ff.; Klein; Wolf Kaiser, "Die Wannsee Konferenz' in *Täter-Opfer-Folgen: Der Holocaust in Geschichte und Gegenwart*, ed. Heiner Lichtenstein and Otto R. Romberg (Bonn, 1995), pp. 24–37, esp. pp. 28 ff.

24 Interrogation of Georg Heuser, March 18, 1969, Staatsanwaltschaft (StA) Mainz 3 Ks 1/67, Protokolle B, vol. 1 (Hauptverhandlung), fol. 177. It should be emphasized that this statement was made during legal proceedings. There had been no prior preparations in which this formulation could have been suggested to Heuser. Furthermore, this particular issue had nothing to do with the subject of the proceedings, which concerned Jewish executions in Lida.

25 Interrogation of Adolf Eichmann, June 6, 1960, cited in State of Israel, Ministry of Justice, *The Trial of Adolf Eichmann: Records of the Proceedings in the District Court of Jerusalem*, vol. 7 (Jerusalem, 1995) (cited hereafter as *Trial of Adolf Eichmann*) (Ton-) Band 5, fol. 5 (p. 169).

26 Ibid.; and Jäckel, p. 34.

27 Himmler, notes on telephone conversations, November 30, 1941, Bundesarchiv (BA) NS 19/1438.

28 Gerald Fleming, *Hitler und die Endlösung: "Es ist des Führers Wunsch . . ."* (Wiesbaden and Munich, 1982), pp. 88 ff.

29 See Martin Broszat, "Hitler und die Genesis der 'Endlösung': Aus Anlass der Thesen von David Irving," *VfZ* 25 (1977): 739–75, esp. pp. 760 ff.; Scheffler, p. 20; Aly and Heim (n. 5 above), p. 465; David Irving, *Hitler's War* (London, 1977), pp. 330–32. It remains uncertain who called whom and whether the suggestion not to execute the deported German Jews originated with Himmler or with Heydrich.

30 Two radio messages from Himmler to Jeckeln, December 1, 1941, Public Record Office, HW 16/32, GPD 471 Nr. 2 (for December 4, 1941). I am very grateful to Christoph Dieckmann for this reference. See also Himmler, appointment calendar, December 4, 1941, OSOBYi archives Moscow 1372-5-23, fol. 350. Himmler noted three topics for the meeting: "Jewish question | SS Brigade. Business enterprises."
31 Werner Jochmann, ed., *Adolf Hitler: Monologe im Führerhauptquartier: Die Aufzeichnungen Heinrich Heims* (Munich, 1982), pp. 147–49 (dated December 1–2, 1941).
32 See Hilberg, *Vernichtung* (n. 17 above), pp. 222–24. Among them were 5,000 gypsies from the Burgenland.
33 See n. 209.
34 Urteil LG Koblenz 9 Ks 2/62, May 21, 1963, in Adelheid L. Rüter-Ehlermann et al., eds., *Justiz und NS-Verbrechen*, vol. 19 (Amsterdam, 1979), p. 190; undated report of Einsatzgruppe A and of the Commander of the Security Police and the SD in Minsk (January 1942), Institut für Zeitgeschichte (IfZ) Fb 101/34 and Fb 104/2.
35 On November 11 the first transport from Hamburg arrived in Minsk. On November 14, the chief of the general staff of the Army Group Center, Major General Hans von Greiffenberg, issued a communication by telephone to General Walter Braemer, the commander of the armed forces in the Ostland, in Riga, to lodge a protest with the Head of Transportation in the Army's High Command. Braemer did so by November 20 at the latest. His protest led to an immediate cancellation of other scheduled transports, with the exception of one train that left Cologne on November 28. See war diary of Army Group Center, November 11 and November 14, 1941, Bundesarchiv-Militärarchiv (BA-MA) RH 19 11/387, fols. 55, 63; Safrian (n. 5 above), p. 150; Chef Sipo/SD, Incident Report Nr. 140, December 1, 1941, BA-MA SF-01/28934.
36 Einsatzkommando 3, Report, December 1, 1941, Zentrale Stelle der Landesjustizverwaltungen Ludwigsburg (ZStL), UdSSR, vol. 401, fol. 91, published in facsimile in Heinz Artzt, *Mörder in Uniform* (Munich, 1979), esp. p. 189.
37 Einsatzgruppe A to the Reich Commissar for the Ostland, November 8, 1941, BA R 90/146. According to a handwritten notation, shortly thereafter the Reich Commissariat for the Ostland (RKO) sent a copy to the General Commissar for Lithuania in Kaunas, who was thus notified in advance as well.
38 Kleist, personal notebook, entry for November 22, 1941, Staatsanwaltschaft Hamburg 147 Js 29/67, vol. 65, fol. 12460. Before handing over his notes to the authorities, Kleist had made one of these lines illegible (as he did in several other sensitive passages). But he overlooked the following passage: "Very good impression by Staf. Jäger. He agrees completely with Lith.[uanian] cooperation. If the local administration can be involved in this sensitive area, then there will be no excuse for other areas." It is known that Jäger made widespread use of Lithuanian commandos in the executions of Jews. On November 21, Kleist made the following notation on his stay in Kaunas: "Afternoon in the ghetto, chicken in the pot, isolation hospital, covered graves next to it."
39 Safrian (n. 5 above), p. 153. See also the interrogation of Friedrich Jeckeln, December 14, 1945, Bundesarchiv-Zwischenarchiv Dahlwitz-Hoppegarten (BA D-H) ZM 1683, vol. l, fols. 12f.
40 This was reported the next day to Kleist by officials of the Reich

Commissariat Ostland in Riga: "Told about shootings of 10, 000s of German and Latvian Jews by SS. Reich Commissar was witness." Kleist, personal notebook, entry for December 1, 1941, StA Hamburg 147 Js 29/67, vol. 65, fol. 12460. Kleist received the news of the massacre of the German Jews with no visible reaction. This, too, suggests agreement by the Ministry for the East. After the war, Lohse voluntarily admitted that he had witnessed a mass execution in Riga in Jeckeln's presence. He put its date at the beginning of December 1941. See interrogation of Hinrich Lohse, April 19, 1950, Staatsanwaltschaft Hannover 2 Js 499/61, Sonderheft 4, fols. 82 ff.

41 Safrian, p. 149.

42 Frank Flechtmann, "November 1944: 'Und nun erst recht!' Ein Homberger lässt schiessen" (*Die Ortenau* [1996]: 471–91, esp. p. 482). It is asserted, with no source cited, that reports of the event had been broadcast that same evening by British and Soviet radio. The assertion is based on eyewitness accounts from some of the perpetrators at their trial after the war. I am grateful to Dieter Pohl for calling my attention to this publication. On December 19, a report of the incident reached the Reich interior ministry; see Bernhard Lösener, "Als Rassereferent im Reichsministerium des Innern," *VfZ* 9 (1961): 264–313, esp. p. 310.

43 See Ezergailis (n. 4 above), pp. 352–59; Hans-Heinrich Wilhelm, *Die Einsatzgruppe A der Sicherheitspolizei und des SD, 1941/42* (Frankfurt am Main, 1996), pp. 124–31; excerpt from an undated report of Einsatzgruppe A, in Pätzold and Schwarz, eds. (n. 23 above), pp. 99 f.

44 Undated report of Einsatzkommando 2, cited in Wilhelm, p. 130. See also Bernhard Press, *Judenmord in Lettland, 1941–1945* (Berlin, 1992), pp. 117–19; Reitlinger (n. 17 above), p. 103.

45 See Kleist, personal notebook, entry for December 8, 1941: "Jew-Kube-shot? Schmitz," StA Hamburg 147 Js 29/67, vol. 65, p. 12460. Schmitz was the relevant official in Section I (Politics) of the Ministry for the East. See also official report of the commander of the Security Service in Minsk, November 29, 1941; and Heydrich's reply to Kube, March 21, 1942, in report of Strauch, Abwehroffizier of the Head of the Anti-partisan Units of the Reichsführer-SS, to his Supervisor, Bach-Zelewski, July 25, 1943, BA NS 19/1770, fols. 15–27 (published in Helmut Heiber, "Aus den Akten des Gauleiters Kube," *VfZ* 4 [1956]: 67–92, esp. pp. 83–85 and p. 90 [notation dated December 2, 1941]); report of Burkhart, adviser on Jewish Affairs for the Commander of the Security Service in Minsk, January 1942, IfZ Fb 104/2. Kube took notice of the matter relatively late because he had been in the Reich between November 10 and November 20. See Kleist, personal notebook, entry of November 17, 1941; interrogation of H. v. R., May 18, 1966, Staatsanwaltschaft Hamburg 147 Js 29/67, fols. 7149 f., and the indictment for the same case, *Anklageschrift*, ibid., pp. 446 ff.; Kube to Rosenberg, November 4; Marquardt to DAF-Oberführer Zillig, November 18, 1941, BA R6/27, fols. 23, 26.

46 As mentioned by Eichmann on March 6 at a conference to discuss the new deportation directives, according to notes made by a police inspector from the State Police Office in Düsseldorf, March 9, 1942. See H. G. Adler, *Der verwaltete Mensch: Studien zur Deportation der Juden aus Deutschland* (Tübingen, 1974), pp. 194 ff.

47 One must concur with Safrian (p. 167, n. 96), who finds it unlikely that Kube's protest following his visit to the ghetto on November 29 would have reached Himmler just twenty-four hours later.

48 Note dated November 10, 1941, in re the "Solution of Jewish Questions,"

Eichmann Trial Document Nr. 1193, BA F 5493. In Heydrich's opinion, only "a few special Jews under the protection of higher Reich offices" should be spared, "in order to avoid too great a volume of requests for the sake of such Jews."

49 It seems that the RSHA did make exceptions for, among others, decorated war veterans. In a teletype dated April 17, 1942, Eichmann referred to the directive of November 20, 1941, and stated that Jews with decorations for wounds received during the war "are *also* exempt from deportation to the east" (quoted in Fleming [n. 28 above], p. 129, n. 258 [emphasis added]). In fact the deportation directives had been issued prior to November 20, 1941. See Adam (n. 18 above), p. 316.

50 See entry in Goebbels of November 18, 1941, quoted in Broszat (n. 29 above), p. 752.

51 The individuals were (Hellmuth James) Graf v. Moltke and Lieutenant-Commander Albrecht. See undated memoir by Karl Loewenstein, before June 1, 1956, copy in the Bibliothek des Zentrums für Antisemitismus-forschung, Berlin. For violations of the deportation guidelines in the case of the Riga transports see also Fleming, pp. 88 f., n. 188.

52 Quoted in Andreas Seeger, *"Gestapo Müller": Die Karriere eines Schreib-tischtäters* (Berlin, 1996), p. 121.

53 Dr. Wetzel, the racial adviser in the Ministry for the East, wrote to Lohse on October 25, 1941 (draft, Nuremberg Document NO-365). What he wrote can be interpreted to mean that Lohse, too, wanted to eliminate *German* Jews incapable of work using "Brack's method," i.e., poison gas, and that the Ministry for the East expressed "no reservations." But the meaning is not absolutely clear. I am grateful to Christoph Dieckmann for calling my attention to this reference. The authenticity of the document was confirmed by Erhard Wetzel during his interrogation, September 20, 1961, Staatsanwalt-schaft Hannover 2 Js 499/61, vol. 2, fols. 18 ff.

54 Aly and Heim (n. 5 above), pp. 468 ff., have emphasized this issue. See also John A. S. Grenville, "Die 'Endlösung' und die 'Judenmischlinge' im Dritten Reich," in *Das Unrechtsregime*, vol. 2: *Verfolgung, Exil, Belasteter Neubeginn*, ed. Ursula Büttner (Hamburg, 1986), pp. 91–121, esp. p. 108; see also Adam, pp. 314 ff.; with regard to the deportations, see Hilberg, *Vernichtung* (n. 17 above), p. 421.

55 Franz Schlegelberger to Hans-Heinrich Lammers, April 5, 1942, in "Re: The Final Solution of the Jewish Question," published in Mendelsohn, ed. (n. 20 above), vol. 18, p. 201.

56 The Ministry for the East was involved in the issue of the definition of German Jews because the individuals deported to Riga and Minsk had been stripped of their citizenship according to the eleventh ordinance to the Reich Citizenship Law of November 25, 1941, and were thus subject to the guidelines in effect there. For the same reason, the problem of the definition of Jews in the occupied Soviet territories, which had not yet been resolved, was connected with this question. Cf. BA R 6/74. See Ordinance 11 with addendum, December 3, 1941, and its history in BA R 43 II/136a. For the Four-Year Plan Office, see Document 1 with Bernhard Lösener's (Reich interior ministry) notation, December 4, 1941, BA R 18/5519, fols. 483–85. The other participants at the meeting were Undersecretary of State Martin Luther (Reich foreign ministry) and two "practitioners" of mass execution from the occupied territories, Schöngarth and Lange, the heads of the Security Police and the SD in the Government General and in Latvia. See the biographies in Pätzold and Schwarz, eds. (n. 22 above), pp. 201–45.

57 See Bernhard Lösener's notation. December 4, 1941, with two attached documents, BA R 18/5519, fols. 477, and 483–95.
58 Heydrich to Undersecretary of State Luther, November 29, 1941, reproduced in facsimile in Tuchel (n. 3 above), pp. 112 ff.; emphasis added.
59 Undated minutes, fols. 8 f., 10–14 (Tuchel, pp. 129–35).
60 Kube's letter is sometimes interpreted in just the opposite sense; see above all Hilberg, *Vernichtung*, pp. 371 f. Kube wrote: "I personally request from you an official directive regarding the treatment by the civil administration of Jews being deported from Germany to White Russia. Among these Jews are men who fought at the frontline, . . . individuals who are half-Aryan, and even some who are three-fourths Aryan. . . . These Jews will probably freeze or starve to death in the next few weeks. For us they pose a huge risk of contagion. . . . On my own authority I will not give the SD any order for the treatment of these people [this is referring to the Nazi expression "special treatment," that is, killing] although certain units of the army and of the police have now shown a keen interest in the possessions of these Jews from the Reich. . . . I can be hard, and I stand ready to help solve the Jewish question. But individuals who come from our own cultural milieu are just not the same as the animal hordes from these regions. Do you really want me to have Lithuanians and Latvians slaughter these people? I could not do it. I therefore request, keeping in mind the reputation of the Reich and of our party here, that you issue clear directives indicating the most humane way of accomplishing what is necessary." Kube to Lohse, December 16, 1941, reproduced in facsimile in Max Weinrich, *Hitler's Professors* (New York, 1946), pp. 153 f.
61 So too in Aly (n. 5 above), pp. 362–67.
62 Compare Hilberg, *Vernichtung*, p. 460; memorandum from the Reich Labor Minister to the Regional Labor Offices, December 19, 1941, quoted in *Verfolgung, Vertreibung, Vernichtung. Dokumente des faschistischen Antisemitismus, 1933–1942*, ed. Kurt Pätzold (Frankfurt am Main, 1984), pp. 326 f.
63 Minutes, fol. 14 (Tuchel, p. 135).
64 Bormann emphasized that these exceptions were temporary. See memorandum from the head of the NSDAP Party Chancellery 35/42 Re: Employment of Jews in Armaments Plants, March 14, 1942, BA NS 6/337, fols. 68 f.
65 It appears that the labor ministry "made inquiry" and was informed by the Four-Year Plan Office about the discussion of this issue at the Wannsee Conference. Compare the reference to the "directives currently in force and discussions that recently took place," in Reich Labor Minister Va 5431/1936/42g Circular Re: Workforce, March 27, 1942, To: Regional Labor Offices, Heydrich, and General Georg Thomas (WiRüAmt) (copy), Nuremberg Document L-6 1.
66 Interrogation of Adolf Eichmann by his defense counsel, June 26, 1961, in *Trial of Adolf Eichmann* (n. 25 above), vol. 4, p. 1423.
67 Notation by Adolf Eichmann, December 1, 1941, reproduced in Pätzold and Schwarz, eds. (n. 23 above), p. 90, facsimile reproduction in Yehoshua Büchler, "A Preparatory Document for the Wannsee 'Conference,' " *Holocaust and Genocide Studies* 10, no. 1 (1995): 121–27, esp. p. 122. This document had been previously published during the proceedings against Eichmann in Jerusalem, where it appeared as Document No. T/ 182. See Eichmann's remarks on the incident in his interrogation, June 23, 1961, in *Trial of Adolf Eichmann*, vol. 4, pp. 1421 f.
68 In Adolf Eichmann's letter to Krüger dated December 1, 1941, the invitation formula is absent (Büchler, pp. 123 f.). For an interpretation, see Büchler, p. 126; and Klein (n. 3 above), pp. 13 f.

69 In a letter to Himmler on January 17, 1942 (BA NS 19/2653, fol. 50), just three days before the date of the conference, Krüger mentioned that his upper arm was in a splint and that he had to spend "hours at forced rest." However, just shortly before this, approximately on January 13, Krüger apparently traveled to Lublin to meet Odilo Globocnik. See letter from SS-Hauptsturm-führer Max Schuster to SS-Gruppenführer Gottlob Berger, January 27, 1942, BA D-H ZM 1454, A. 1, fol. 263.

70 Krüger to Himmler, January 17, 1942, BA NS 19/2653, fol. 50. Cf. Grothmann, appointment calendar (Grothmann was Himmler's personal adjutant) for January 13, 1942, BA NS 19/3959, with Bühler's request, Himmler, notes of telephone conversations, January 2, 1942, BA NS 19/1439.

71 After the war, Bühler also mentioned a meeting with Heydrich just prior to the Wannsee Conference. With regard to the content of the meeting, he made patently false statements in an effort to exculpate himself. See report by Josef Bühler, February 19, and interrogation, April 23, 1946, in Pätzold and Schwarz, eds., pp. 131 ff., 135 ff.

72 The relevant documents can be found in BA R 6/74.

73 Rosenberg to Lammers, January 8, 1942, and March 25, 1942, with accompanying documents, BA R 43 II/684a, fols. 110–13, 136–47.

74 Speech by Rosenberg, November 18, 1941, BA NS 8/71, esp. fols. 10, 18.

75 The basic study on this subject is Christopher Browning, *The Final Solution and the German Foreign Office* (New York and London, 1978); see also Hans-Jürgen Döscher, *SS und Auswärtiges Amt im Dritten Reich: Diplomatie im Schatten der "Endlösung"* (Frankfurt am Main and Berlin, 1991).

76 Notes prepared by Referat D III for Undersecretary of State Luther, in "Re: Suggestions and Ideas from the Foreign Office Regarding the Impending Total Solution of the Jewish Question in Europe," December 8, 1941, reproduced in facsimile in Döscher, *SS und Auswärtiges Amt*, pp. 222 f. See also the talking paper prepared by Luther for State Secretary Ernst von Weizsäcker (D III 660g, December 4, 1941) with its suggestion to seek a European-wide solution to the Jewish question (Nuremberg Document NG-4667).

77 The respective governments had already signaled their lack of interest in the fate of their Jewish citizens. See the retrospective note for Joachim von Ribbentrop, April 20, 1943, BA F 72891; Browning, *Final Solution*, pp. 67 f.

78 Browning, *Final Solution*, pp. 55–67.

79 Reich Führer-SS and Chief of German Police IV D 4 to Lammers, September 30, October 30, and December 5, 1941, BA R 43 II/675a, fols. 107, 114, 117; Browning, *Final Solution*, p. 69; Seeger (n. 51 above), p. 127. These people had been taken as hostages by the SS after the non-Jewish workers' strike in Amsterdam supporting the Jews in early 1941. The Reich foreign ministry had recommended that a relatively high number of hostage deaths not be reported on any one day. They also recommended that the hostages be returned to the Netherlands since Sweden's role as protective power did not apply to affairs inside the home country. They emphasized that, "In principle the position of the Foreign Office is the same as that of the RSHA and for its part the Office recommends repressive measures against the Jews as instigators [in the sense that they were intellectual instigators of conspiracies]" (D III 588g to Heinrich Müller [RSHA], November 5, 1941, Nürnberg Document NG-3700).

80 On the subject of "part Jews," the basic study is Jeremy Noakes, "The Development of Nazi Policy towards the German 'Mischlinge,' 1933–1945," *Leo Baeck Institute Yearbook* 34 (1989): 291–354. See also Grenville (n. 54

above); Hilberg, *Vernichtung* (n. 17 above), pp. 436–49; Adam (n. 18 above), pp. 316–33.

81 Noakes, pp. 338–41; Adam, pp. 319 f.; Burrin (n. 5 above), pp. 136 f.

82 Göring's commission to Heydrich, July 31, 1941, contemporary photocopy (with accompanying letter to State Secretary Karl-Hermann Frank, Prague, January 25, 1942), BA D-H M 501, A.3, fols. 4, 7, reproduced in Pätzold and Schwarz, eds. (n. 23 above), p. 79.

83 Communications Office of Armed Forces High Command, Economics and Armaments Office at the Reich Marshall, to General Georg Thomas, July 29, 1941, BA-MA (BArchP) F 44544, fol. 104.

84 See, e.g., Aly, pp. 306 f.

85 Compare Witte (n. 16 above), pp. 318 ff.; Broszat (n. 29 above), p. 750. On August 7, the RSHA completed its first estimate of the number of Jews living in Europe. Number of Jews, Absolutely and as a Percentage of Population, in the Countries and Regions of Europe, August 7, 1941, Archiwum Glownej Komisji Gadania Zbrodni przeciwko Narodowi Polskiemu, Warschau, CA 362/218, fols. 5–10. The exhibit was presumably prepared by Eichmann.

86 Notation by an official in the Reich Commissariat of the Netherlands, September 19, 1941, regarding a conversation with Bernhard Lösener on September 16, 1941, IfZ, Eichmann Trial Document 1355.

87 Noakes, pp. 341 f.; Adam, pp. 320 f.; notations by Erhard Wetzel and Walter Labs (both of the Ministry for the East), October 27, 1941, and January 16, 1942, BA R 6/74, fols. 24 f. and 54R. For a positive (and thus, in my view, unsupported) evaluation of the positions taken by Lammers and the Reich chancellery in regard to Jewish policy, see Dieter Rebentisch, *Führerstaat und Verwaltung im Zweiten Weltkrieg* (Stuttgart, 1989), pp. 434–41.

88 According to the First Ordinance of the Reich Citizenship Law, November 14, 1935, Hitler had the power to grant exceptions to the provisions regulating the definition of Jews and part-Jews. See Adler (n. 46 above), p. 280. On the large number of special requests, see Adam, pp. 301 f.; and the file BA 62 Ka 1, Nr. 63.

89 See, in particular, Lösener, "Rassereferent" (n. 42 above), esp. pp. 296 ff. Although this postwar memoir contains elements of self-justification, it agrees for the most part with the files of 1941/42, insofar as these have survived. See also Noakes, pp. 353 f. There must remain some doubt, however, as regards the genuineness of documents cited by Lösener that no longer exist.

90 Notation by Bernhard Lösener, December 4, 1941, with two accompanying documents, BA R 18/5519, fols. 477, 483–95.

91 Noakes (n. 80 above), pp. 353 f.; notation by an official of the Reich Commissariat of the Netherlands, September 19, 1941, concerning a discussion with Lösener on September 16, IfZ, Eichmann Trial Document 1355; notation by Lösener, August 18, 1941, concerning a report by Kritzinger (Reich chancellery) and outline by Lösener of a Stuckart memo, August 21, 1941 (accompanied by the notation that Heydrich had purportedly communicated Hitler's contrary opinion to Rosenberg), in Lösener, "Rassereferent," pp. 304, 306. The claim made by Adam, p. 321 (cf. p. 330) that at the Wannsee Conference Heydrich put forward a position that had been approved by Hitler is speculation. With regard to the eleventh ordinance, Hitler had rejected the more far-reaching first drafts. Initially, the Reich interior ministry and the Reich justice ministry had sought to deprive German Jews generally of their German citizenship. See R 18/5519 and R 43 II/136a, esp. a notation by Lammers, May

29, and Lammers's note to Wilhelm Frick, Schlegelberger, and Bormann, June 7, 1941, fols. 122–124R.

92 According to an unsigned note, outcome of a meeting in the main office of the Security Police, in "Re the Solution of the Jewish Question in Europe" (undated; presumably the author was Dr. Werner Feldscher), Hitler rejected the idea. See BA R 18/5519, fol. 485; see also Lammers to Finanzminister Lutz Graf Schwerin von Krosigk, June 19, 1941, BA 7.01, Nr. 4112, fol. 270.

93 Lammers to Schwerin v. Krosigk, February 17, 1942, regarding a statement made by Hitler in July 1941, BA 7.01, Nr. 4112, fol. 284.

94 Agitated, Hitler had insisted that any ultimate decision on this issue would be made by him. See Lammers to R. Walther Darré, April 10, 1941, BA R 43 II/598, fol. 60/R; Noakes, p. 340 (September 1941).

95 As far as can be ascertained, he expressed himself in relatively positive terms about individuals in so-called mixed marriages and about "second and third generation part-Jews." He spoke positively about the existing racial laws but opposed the granting of exceptions. See Jochmann, ed. (n. 31 above), pp. 147–49.

96 Recorded in a confidential note by Walter Labs, hand-dated, January 16, 1942, BA R 6/74, fol. 54; emphasis added. Labs was section chief for general administration in the Ministry for the East. Aly and Heim (n. 5 above), p. 469, brought this document to the attention of scholars.

97 Note by Lösener, August 17, with note by Acting State Secretary Pfundtner, August 20, 1941, and the notation, "The Minister has approved this note," in BA R 18/3746a, published in Lösener, "Rassereferent," p. 303; notation by Lösener about a meeting in the Propaganda Ministry, August 15, 1941, in "Rassereferent," p. 301 (statements by the Four-Year Plan Office and by the propaganda ministry).

98 Himmler, meeting notes, November 24, 1941, Sonderarchiv Moskau 1372-5-23, fol. 360.

99 Lösener, "Rassereferent" (n. 42 above), p. 311.

100 Meeting notes, "Meeting with the Führer at Wolfsschanze, December 18, 1941, 4 PM, Führer," Himmler, appointment calendar (n. 30 above), fol. 334. A published version of this source, with commentary, is in preparation. To the knowledgeable discussions of its editorial group I owe a deeper insight into the structures of the decision-making process that led to the extermination of European Jews.

101 Odilo Globocnik was SS- and Police Leader in the Lublin district of the Government, General from 1939 to 1943.

102 "Bei dieser Gelegenheit vertrat Brigadeführer Globocnik die Auffassung, die ganze Judenaktion so schnell wie nur irgend möglich durchzuführen, damit man nicht eines Tages mitten drin steckenbliebe, wenn irgendwelche Schwierigkeiten ein Abstoppen der Aktion notwendig machen. Sie selbst, Reichsführer, haben mir gegenüber seinerzeit schon die Meinung geäußert, daß man schon aus Grunden der Tarnung so schnell wie möglich arbeiten müsse." Viktor Brack to Himmler, June 23, 1942, BA NS 19/1583, fol. 34; emphasis added.

103 Compare Sonderarchiv Moskau 1372-5-23, esp. fol. 341 (the first short or incomplete word is indecipherable); Grothmann (n. 70 above). The surviving correspondence between Himmler and Brack mentions no other meeting between them during this period.

104 Jochmann, ed., pp. 150, 152.

105 Brack to Himmler; "Sworn Statement of Viktor Brack," October 12, 1946, Nuremberg Document NO-426.

106 "Anders wäre ja nicht zu verstehen, wenn ich einen großen Teil der mir unterstehenden Organisationen dem Reichsführer zu einer bis in die letzte Konsequenz gehenden Endlösung der Judenfrage zur Verfügung gestellt habe." Philipp Bouhler to Bormann, July 10, 1942, BA 62 Ka 1, Nr. 83, fol. 109; emphasis added.

107 According to Arad, *Belzec, Sobibor, Treblinka* (n. 13 above), p. 17, it was in 1941, between the end of October and the end of December. It was somewhat later according to Michael Tregenza, "Belzec Death Camp," *Wiener Library Bulletin* 30 (1977): 8–25, esp. pp. 14–16. According to the account by Eugen Kogon et al. in *Nationalsozialistische Massentötungen durch Giftgas* (Frankfurt am Main, 1983), pp. 153 f., Christian Wirth, a member of the Führer chancellery, became commandant of Belzec in the latter half of December. When he arrived there was already snow on the ground. Pohl, *Lublin* (n. 4 above), p. 105 (cf. p. 101) claims that personnel from the Führer chancellery arrived in November 1941, but he makes erroneous use of statements by Tregenza and Kogon et al. Only Josef Oberhauser and two other individuals were sent as early as September 1941, but that seems to have been for other purposes.

108 See interrogation of Josef Oberhauser, December 14, 1962, in Ernst Klee, Willi Dressen, and Volker Riess, eds., *"Schöne Zeiten": Judenmord aus Sicht der Täter und Gaffer*, 2d ed. (Frankfurt am Main, 1988), p. 208. The Polish laborers were discharged on December 22, 1941, when the barracks construction was complete. See interrogation of Stanislaw Kozak, in Kogon et al., pp. 152 f.

109 It is possible that Heydrich sent Eichmann to Belzec at this time (see n. 146). One of the "experts" who may have been sent was August Becker, a technician in charge of the gas vans. He said that he was transferred from the Führer chancellery to the RSHA following a conversation between Himmler and Brack, and then sent on to Riga. Becker stated later that he was involved in an accident in Deutsch-Eylau (East Prussia) on his way to an inspection in Riga on December 14, 1941, but his recollection may be mistaken by several days; he said he came out of the hospital before Christmas. See interrogation of August Becker, March 26, 1960, in Klee, Dreessen, and Riess, eds., p. 71. The exact date of Becker's accident is apparently no longer documented, and it was never checked by any historian or juridical institution at the Wehrmachtauskunftsstelle Berlin, which is in charge of this matter. Information from the Wehrmachtauskunftsstelle Berlin, December 1997. If this general interpretation is correct, it is a further indication that the RSHA first had to gather information about the status of regional planning for extermination efforts.

110 Notes on a discussion with the Führer, December 14, 1941, prepared by Rosenberg on December 16, 1941, BDC, SL 47F (copy), published as Nuremberg Document PS-1517 in IMT, vol. 27, p. 270; emphasis added. Hartog (n. 6 above), p. 71, also draws attention to this passage, connecting its essential elements with Hans Frank's speech in Kraków on December 16, 1941 (see below), and with Hitler's January 30, 1939, prophecy that another world war would lead to the extermination of the Jews in Europe.

111 This is what Rosenberg maintained during his interrogation, April 17, 1946, IMT, vol. II, pp. 606–8, though he could not explain why that meant that further threats against the Jews should not be made in public. The words "now, after the decision" (*jetzt nach der Entscheidung*) were not investigated further by the court, since the court believed that any such decision would have been made considerably earlier.

112 The manuscript of the speech still exists, apparently in a version prepared after the discussion with Hitler. (The first version was prepared before the Japanese

attack on Pearl Harbor, and this version includes a reference to that attack.) In it, Rosenberg threatened the "New York Jews" in response to their supposed "world-wide agitation against Germany and associated policy of military encirclement" with "corresponding German measures against the Jews living in the east." "For in the eastern territories currently under the control of German armed forces, there are more than 6 million Jewish inhabitants. For more than a hundred years, eastern Jewry has been the source and spring of Jewish power throughout the world." Rosenberg talked about "destroying the springs from which the New York Jews had drawn their powers," about "a negative elimination of these parasitic elements." See "The Great Moment of the East. Speech by Reichsleiter Rosenberg in the Sports Palace," December 18, 1941, BA R 6/37, fols. 31 ff., esp. fols. 47–49.

113 See Hitler's speech for the session of January 30, 1939, in *Verhandlung des Reichstages*, 4th Wahlperiode, 1939, vol. 460. Stenographic Reports, 1939–1942. Photocopy Bad Feilnbach 1986, p. 16; emphasis added.

114 Similarly Hermann Göring, Reichstag Session, December 11. 1941, ibid., p. 106.

115 Ibid., pp. 93–106. The speech was supposed to be broadcast live outside Germany as well. See Elke Fröhlich, ed., *Die Tagebücher von Joseph Goebbels*, pt. II, vol. 2 (Munich, 1996), p. 476 (for December 11, 1941).

116 On the invitations dated December 9, 1941, the meeting was scheduled for December 10. Later on December 9, the meeting was rescheduled for December 11 and then obviously postponed once again. See two teletype messages from the Party chancellery of the NSDAP, December 9, 1941 (Martin Bormann, 10:45 A.M.; Friedrichs, 3:45 P.M.), BA NS 8/186. I am indebted to Armin Nolzen for this reference.

117 Goebbels, *Tagebücher*, pt. 2, vol. 2, pp. 498 f. (see entry for December 13, 1941).

118 Breitman (n. 5 above), p. 155 (January 30, 1941); Broszat (n. 29 above), pp. 749 f. (August 18, 1941, based on Goebbels's record); Jochmann, ed., p. 106 (October 25, 1941); Adam (n. 18 above), p. 316 (January 30, 1942); quite clearly in his speech on February 24, 1942 (excerpts published in Pätzold, ed., pp. 345 ff.).

119 Rosenberg and Frank were *Reichsleiter*; Lohse was *Gauleiter* in Schleswig-Holstein; Koch was *Gauleiter* in East Prussia; Goebbels was *Gauleiter* in Berlin; Meyer was *Gauleiter* in Westphalia. It has been documented that Greiser, Frank, and Lohse were in the Reich, or in Berlin. We have already discussed Himmler, Rosenberg, and Bouhler; see also Himmler, appointment calendar, fol. 343. See also Schlegelberger to Greiser, December 15, 1941, BA R 22/850, fols. 215R–216 (on December 10, Franz Schlegelberger called Greiser in Berlin). For Lohse, see Göring, appointment calendar, December 8, 1941, IfZ ED 180/5 (I am indebted to Christoph Dieckmann for this reference). Werner Präg and Wolfgang Jacobmeyer, eds., *Das Diensttagebuch des deutschen Generalgouverneurs in Polen 1939–1945* (Stuttgart, 1975), p. 449. Wilhelm Kube still held the formal title of *Gauleiter* but was no longer active as one, and thus he was not invited to the meeting of the *Reichsleiter* and *Gauleiter*. I am grateful to Armin Nolzen for this information. This explains why Kube had to write for information in his letter of December 16, 1941, cited above in n. 59.

120 At the same hour Göring was scheduled to meet with Keitel and with General Osterkamp, the head of the army administrative office, at his Carinhall estate. See Göring, appointment calendar, December 12, 1941, IfZ

ED 180/5. On December 9, however, Göring had spoken at length with Hitler (ibid.). For Heydrich, see his report to Bormann, 'December 30, 1941, which suggests that he was in Prague on December 12, 1941; see Miroslav Kárny et al., eds., *Deutsche Politik im "Protektorat Böhmen und Mähren" unter Reinhard Heydrich 1941–1942* (Berlin, 1997), p. 205.

121 This consideration is emphasized by Hartog (n. 6 above), esp. pp. 11 ff., 75 ff.

122 In view of the dates, and of the whole fabric of rationalizations, it cannot be maintained that Hitler decided to exterminate the Jews in the euphoria of victory or because he thought he was invincible. This position has been put forward by Christopher Browning in "The Euphoria of Victory and the Final Solution: Summer–Fall 1941," *German Studies Review* 17, no. 3 (1994): 473–81. See also Andreas Hillgruber, *Hitlers Strategie: Politik und Kriegführung 1940–1941* (Frankfurt am Main, 1965), pp. 524 f.

123 See n. 100. Apparently Himmler made the notation because he considered this the most important result of the discussion. Hitler repeated the phrase often in his justifications. See in addition his conversation with Goebbels the previous day (Goebbels, *Tagebücher*, pp. 533 ff., for December 18, 1941). In fact, the meeting with Himmler probably concerned some concrete arrangement, unknown to us, for implementing the Jewish extermination.

124 Reinhard Heydrich, "Die Wirtschaft als massgeblicher Faktor der staatlichen und politischen Neuordnung Böhmens und Mährens im Reich," in *Tagung der Südosteuropa-Gesellschaft und der Deutschen Gesellschaft der Wirtschaft in Böhmen und Mähren* (Berlin, Prague, Vienna, 1942), p. 11 (BA R 63/279). On the question of the dating, see Heydrich's report to Bormann, December 30, 1941, and see Kárny et al., eds., p. 205.

125 On the same day, Rosenberg sent Hitler a letter suggesting that Jewish leaders being held in France as hostages should be shot, because worldwide Jewry was responsible for the assassination attempts and the agitation actions of the French communists. (See Rosenberg to Hitler, December 18, 1941, in Pätzold and Schwarz, eds., pp. 96 f.) Hitler's reaction to the letter was positive, at least in part. See Lammers to Rosenberg, December 31, 1941, BA R43 II/1444, fol. 56.

126 Himmler, speech at the meeting of SS-Group Leaders, October 4, 1943, IMT, vol. 29, pp. 145 f.; for additional examples, see Bradley F. Smith and Agnes F. Peterson, eds., *Heinrich Himmler: Geheimreden, 1933–1945* (Frankfurt am Main, 1974), pp. 169, 200–5.

127 Hitler, speech to generals and officers at Platterhof, May 26, 1944, IfZ, MA 316, fol. 5022, cited in Broszat, p. 759, who makes the connection between this address and the crisis in the winter of 1941–42.

128 This suspicion was expressed by Hartog, p. 65. One cannot rule out the possibility that there may have been one or more meetings on the subject. It would be very difficult to prove that there were not (see n. 144). But if it truly is the case that Heydrich first learned about the announcement of the decision from Himmler, then the occurrence of any such meetings is less likely.

129 See Sec. V. The important role of the Führer chancellery in "Operation Reinhard" should also be kept in mind. Further, the Lublin SS- and Police Leader, Odilo Globocnik, who became the leader of "Operation Reinhard," had himself at one time been a *Gauleiter*.

130 See Witte (n. 16 above), pp. 318 ff.; Frank Bajohr, "Gauleiter in Hamburg. Zur Person und Tätigkeit Karl Kaufmanns," *VfZ* 43 (1995): 267–95, esp. pp. 291 f.

131 From the Reichsstatthalter in Saxony (Martin Mutschmann) to Himmler, July 25, 1944, BA NS 19/1872, fols. 1 f. According to Mutschmann, he had already brought up the "argument" mentioned earlier, namely, that Jews

would turn into partisans and create disorder behind the frontlines. This suggests that he had raised the idea between June and December of 1941. Prior to June 1941 there would have been no reason for such a position. After December 12, 1941, the suggestion would have become superfluous. In February 1940 Mutschmann had demanded the wearing of the Jewish star; see Lösener (n. 42 above), p. 302.

132 Günther Rodenburg, "Die letzten 26 Tage in Bremen," in *Es geht tatsächlich nach Minsk*, ed. Rodenburg and Andreas Röpcke (Bremen, 1992), pp. 7–20, esp. p. 9.

133 See Himmler, *Appointment Calendar* (n. 30 above). These were Hitler's private rooms in the Old Reich chancellery, rooms that normally were not used for official meetings such as this. Hitler thus announced his decision just twelve days before he put a final stop, at least according to David Irving, to the extermination of the Jews.

134 Bräutigam to Lohse, December 18, 1941, facsimile reproduction in Weinreich, p. 156; emphasis added.

135 According to his interrogation, November 19, 1948, Staatsanwaltschaft Nürnberg-Fürth 72 Ks 3/50a–b, vol. 1, fol. 53R (in the Bayerisches Staatsarchiv in Nuremberg) Otto Bräutigam was referring to a discussion between Rosenberg or Alfred Meyer and Lohse. Bräutigam's superior, Georg Leibbrandt (interrogation of October 7, 1948, fol. 42R), referred to a meeting between Rosenberg and Lohse that was supposed to have occurred following a conversation between Rosenberg and Hitler. If they had been acquainted with the exact course of events, both of these men would surely have tried to mitigate their guilt at this crucial point in the proceedings by referring to the events of the *Reichsleiter*'s and *Gauleiter*'s meeting and by claiming that they had been obliged to act as they did because of a direct command from Hitler.

136 In his letter to Rosenberg, February 5, 1942 (BA-MA FPF-01/7865, fol. 790), Lohse mentioned a "confidential address to the *Reichsleiter* and *Gauleiter*" that Hitler had delivered not long before. The details of his description agree with Goebbels's notes. For the general order to keep silence cf. Rebentisch (n. 87 above), p. 290.

137 Otherwise additional discussions between the civilian authorities in the occupied territories and the Higher SS- and Police Leaders on the subject would have been pointless. The executions of the Jews in the Reich Commissariat Ostland were suspended for several months beginning December 1941. They were not resumed on a large scale in the Baltic until 1943.

138 Speech by Hans Frank, December 16, 1941, in Präg and Jacobmeyer, eds. (n. 119 above), pp. 457 ff.

139 Frank had also conferred with Hitler at some point between December 10 and December 13. See Pohl, *Lublin* (n. 4 above), p. 103, n. 71.

140 Speech to the 55-district leaders and Main Office heads, June 9, 1942, in Smith and Peterson, eds., p. 159.

141 Goebbels's record, cited by Broszat, p. 758. See also Goebbels, *Tagebücher* pt. 2, vol. 2, pp. 533 ff. (December 18, 1941).

142 "Jews are second-class or third-order individuals. Whether or not one is justified in eliminating them is beyond debate. One way or another they must vanish from the face of the earth." Gottlob Berger to Oskar Dirlewanger, January 22, 1942, BA D-H ZM 1454, A. 1, fols. 245 f.

143 Artur Eisenbach, "Operation Reinhard: Mass Extermination of the Jewish Population in Poland," *Polish Western Affairs* 3 (1962): 80–124, esp. p. 83.

Eisenbach mentions an enactment by Greiser, dated January 2, 1942, "regarding liquidation of the Jews (*Entjudung*) in the Wartheland." The enactment is mentioned in another document, but a record of it does not appear to have been preserved.

144 On December 9, 1941, Hitler had a lengthy conversation with Göring (see n. 120). On the evening of December 7, and probably on December 10, he met with Himmler. Himmler himself met with Heydrich on December 9 and on December 11 (Himmler, appointment calendar, December 7–11, 1941, fols. 344–47).

145 During his interrogation (May 31, 1960, in *Trial of Adolf Eichmann* [n. 25 above], p. 169), Eichmann maintained that this had occurred two months after the June 1941 invasion of the Soviet Union. In a handwritten correction he later added, "It might also have been three months afterwards." But abstract dates and temporal sequences of events related by Eichmann must be treated with caution and verified through other sources: his accounts are notoriously inconsistent and cannot in themselves be used to prove or disprove any thesis. Eichmann's statements can, however, be evaluated in the context of other evidence to determine which of these are most likely to be correct.

146 This is another reason making it less likely that Hitler could have issued his order in the Reichstag, perhaps in a closed session following the official meeting on December 11, 1941, for Heydrich was a member of the Reichstag. Rosenberg's assertion during his interrogation on April 17, 1946 (IMT, vol. 11, pp. 607 f.), could be interpreted to mean that Hitler did issue such a statement as part of his December 11, 1941, Reichstag address. But Rosenberg's assertion is ambiguous. For Göring's commission to Heydrich of July 31, 1941, see Pätzold and Schwarz, eds., p. 79.

147 Ibid. For Himmler's information to Heydrich, see Rudolf Aschenauer, ed., *Ich, Adolf Eichmann: Ein historischer Zeugenbericht* (Leoni, 1980), pp. 177 ff. On another occasion, in his interrogation of July 5, 1960, Eichmann asserted that the visit to Globocnik occurred some two months after the Wannsee Conference (*Trial of Adolf Eichmann*, vol. 17, fol. 56 [p. 845]).

148 So, too, in Safrian (n. 5 above), p. 171.

149 Hilberg, *Vernichtung* (n. 17 above), p. 421; Burrin (n. 5 above), pp. 146 ff., maintains that Eichmann is confusing two different things.

150 In a handwritten statement on June 22, 1945, Dr. Rudolf Mildner, the last commander of the Security Police in Vienna, also drew a connection between the United States's entry into the war and the execution of Hitler's threat that the Jews in Europe would "be exterminated for it" (Nuremberg Document PS-2376).

151 Cited in Daniel Jonah Goldhagen, *Hitlers willige Vollstrecker* (Berlin, 1996), pp. 142 ff., with whose conclusions I concur at this point. For an earlier reference see Raul Hilberg, *Täter, Opfer, Zuschauer: Die Vernichtung der Juden, 1933–1945* (Frankfurt am Main, 1992), p. 285.

152 Tuchel (n. 3 above), p. 114.

153 Heydrich to Undersecretary of State Martin Luther, January 8, 1942, facsimile reproduction in Tuchel, p. 115.

154 See Safrian, p. 169.

155 Himmler, appointment calendar, December 9, 1941, 12:40 P.M., fol. 346.

156 For documentation, see n. 96.

157 One should also recall in this connection the meeting between Himmler and Bühler on January 13, which had been arranged on January 2, 1942 (for documentation, see n. 69). Jäckel (n. 1 above), p. 33, suspects that Heydrich was

in no hurry because the meeting was to deal primarily with the issues of representation and the establishment of his authority.

158 The contents of the conversation are unknown. The original purpose of Heydrich's visit to Göring had simply been to convey his birthday greetings. But Heydrich "remained with the Reich Marshall for official purposes," and Heydrich's next appointment had to be postponed for an hour. See note by Franz Bentevegni (Armed Forces High Command, Office for Foreign Defense), January 13, 1942 (unsigned), BA-MA RW 5/v.690, fol. 21. The incident is also mentioned in Heydrich to Canaris, February 5, 1942, BA NS 19/3514, fols. 141–45.

159 Aly (n. 5 above), p. 364, where the general role in Jewish policy played by the Reich Commission for the Strengthening of the German People is also discussed. For more information about the participants, see Sec. II.

160 Scheffler (n. 2 above), p. 25.

161 For more information about the role of the Armed Forces High Command, see Bryan Mark Rigg, "Jüdische Mischlinge in der Wehrmacht" (in press). On the issue generally, see Noakes, pp. 328–36.

162 Undated minutes, fols. 2–5 (Tuchel, pp. 123–26).

163 Minutes, fols. 5–8 (Tuchel, pp. 126–29).

164 Minutes, fols. 9 f. (Tuchel, pp. 130 f.).

165 Notation by Lösener for Stuckart, December 4, 1941, enclosure 1, BA R 18/5519, fols. 483–85.

166 Minutes, fols. 8 f., 10–13 (Tuchel [n. 3 above], pp. 130 f., 132–34).

167 Minutes, B1 13 f. (Tuchel, pp. 134 f.). On this point the accuracy of the minutes is confirmed by Stuckart's letter to some of the conference participants, March 16, 1942, in Pätzold and Schwarz, eds., pp. 121 f. Lösener's Notation for Stuckart, December 4, 1941, BA R 18/5519, fols. 477, 483–95.

168 Minutes, fols. 14 f. (Tuchel, p. 135 f.).

169 In this regard, at least, Eichmann's postwar testimony (e.g., interrogation, June 26, 1961, in *Trial of Adolf Eichmann*, vol. 4 [Jerusalem, 1993], p. 1423) is confirmed by Heydrich's cover letter accompanying the minutes, February 26, 1942 (reproduced in facsimile in Tuchel, p. 121).

170 Eichmann Document, March 7, 1961, in Pätzold and Schwarz, eds., p. 184; interrogations of Eichmann, June 26 and July 17, 1961, in *Trial of Adolf Eichmann*, vol. 4, pp. 1423, 1711 ff.

171 Wilhelm Stuckart's role is a matter of dispute. A definitive answer does not seem to me to be possible. He later contended that he made his proposal to substitute compulsory sterilization for deportation knowing that the former was technically impossible to implement, and his assertion is difficult to dispute. Furthermore, with regard to the issue of compulsory divorce, he proposed a legal measure that could be delayed in a great variety of ways, and this is just what did happen later.

172 "The future treatment of this class of individuals [the so-called part-Jews of the first degree] remains undecided," memo of the party chancellery, January 29, 1942, cited in a circular letter from the Main Office for National Prosperity (*Hauptamt für Volkswohlfahrt*), April 13, 1942, in Herwart Vorländer, *Die NSV* (Boppard, 1988), p. 427; Aly and Heim (n. 5 above), p. 470; see also their source document, undated note by Dr. Wetzel, BA R6/74, fol. 79.

173 Adler (n. 46 above), p. 304. On this issue, see also record of Franz Rademacher, March 7, and note from the Reich Foreign Ministry D III, June 11, 1942, in Klein (n. 3 above), pp. 57–60.

174 Note by Lindemann (Main Office II, Administration, Ministry of the East), February 11, 1942, BA R 6/74, fol. 78.

175 See Himmler's indignant notation in his meeting notes from his meeting with Hitler, Rosenberg, Lammers, and Wilhelm Keitel on February 15, 1942: "Remark by Bräutigam: [']The war in the east can no longer be won militarily, [']" BA NS 19/1448, fol. 12.

176 As a matter of fact Bräutigam was to escape punishment after the war. In the opinion of the Landgericht of Nürnberg-Fürth, Bräutigam's personal responsibility for the murder of Soviet Jews had not been proven. See the Proceedings Staatsanwaltschaft Nürnberg-Fürth 72 Ks 3/50a–b in the Staatsarchiv Nürnberg. In 1955 Bräutigam became director of the Section for Eastern Affairs (Ostabteilung) in the foreign ministry of the Federal Republic. Public pressure later forced him to retire.

177 In itself that is nothing new. See, e.g., Wolfgang Scheffler, *Judenverfolgung im Dritten Reich* (West Berlin, 1964), p. 38; Ludolf Herbst, *Das nationalsozialistische Deutschland, 1933–1945* (Frankfurt am Main, 1996), p. 387. It must be stressed, however, that this was the most important outcome of the meeting.

178 As a parallel, one might point out Hitler's repeated prohibition against using the inhabitants of the occupied Soviet territories as armed collaborators (e.g., document note by Bormann on the Leadership Conference, July 16, 1941, IMT, vol. 38, p. 88). This was a significant ideological issue in terms of the creation of a German empire in the east. Hitler never succeeded in compelling either the armed forces or the SS to observe his prohibition.

179 Quoted from the facsimile reproduction in Tuchel, p. 121; emphasis added.

180 BA D-H ZR 759, A. 14.

181 Göring's commission of July 31, 1941, is in Pätzold and Schwarz, eds. (n. 23 above), p. 79. The minutes of the Wannsee Conference were not the desired "comprehensive plan" as Pätzold and Schwarz assert (p. 47). This is clear from the fact that on February 26 Heydrich sent out invitations for a follow-up conference to be held on March 6 "in order to prepare the necessary document for the Reich Marshall" (facsimile reproduction in Tuchel, p. 121). Hence the "comprehensive plan" could not have been completed in February, and it cannot be identical with the RSHA discussion document that Goebbels read on March 7 (for the opposite view, see Aly and Heim, p. 460). Similarly, the suggestion that Göring appointed Heydrich "Commissar for Jewish Affairs in Europe" (Aly and Heim, p. 460) appears to be not correct (see Scheffler, "Wannsee-Konferenz," p. 33, n. 9).

182 Lammers to Heydrich, May 22, 1942 (copy), BA R 18/5519, fol. 481. A report by Heydrich to Göring was planned but probably never delivered because Göring was able to discuss the issues important to him with Himmler on July 2, 1942. See document from Ministerial Counsellor Dr. Ing. Fritz Görnnert (Göring's personal adviser) "with request for documents for scheduled meeting with Obergruppenführer Heydrich," May 24, 1942, and documents from Görnnert, July 1, 1942, for the meeting with Himmler, BA 34.01 FC Nr. 376, fols. 7569, 7984 f., 7897; Himmler, appointment calendar, July 2, 1942, fol. 182. Strictly speaking, Heydrich could not possibly have presented a "comprehensive plan" to Göring because he had not yet obtained approval from all relevant offices. Because of a clerical error, the RSHA had neglected to send a copy of the minutes from the follow-up meeting held on March 6, 1942, to the foreign office. It only did so on July 3, 1942, some time after Heydrich's death. The reply from the foreign office is dated October 2, 1942. See RSHA IV B 4 (Friedrich Suhr) to the Foreign Office (Franz Rademacher), July 3, 1942, and the reminder, August 12; and Foreign Office D III 67 gRs to RSHA, October 2 and December 7, 1942, BA F 10531.

183 Reitlinger (n. 17 above), p. 108. See also Pätzold and Schwarz, eds., p. 51; interrogation of Adolf Eichmann, July 5, 1960, in *Trial of Adolf Eichmann*, vol. 7, Band 17, fols. 56 ff. (p. 845 ff.). Eichmann admitted that the "possible solutions" mentioned in the minutes meant methods of execution. Interrogation, July 21, 1961, in *Trial of Adolf Eichmann*, vol. 4, p. 1810. The "certain preparatory measures" mentioned by Bühler and Alfred Meyer, which were "to be implemented in the relevant territories themselves, in a manner that would not create unrest among the inhabitants" (minutes, fol. 15, in Tuchel, p. 136) were nothing more, in my opinion, than code words for "mass shootings."

184 See Hermann Kaienburg, "Jüdische Arbeitslager an der 'Strasse der SS,'" *1999*, no. 1 (1996): 13–39, esp. pp. 13 f.; Sandkühler (n. 4 above), pp. 137 ff. Heydrich is said to have mentioned an "Arctic Ocean camp" in preliminary discussions with Bühler, interrogation of Josef Bühler, April 23, 1946, in Pätzold and Schwarz, eds., p. 135. On the subject generally, see Karl Heinz Roth, "'Generalplan Ost'-'Gesamtplan Ost.' Forschungsstand, Quellenprobleme, neue Ergebnisse," in *Der "Generalplan Ost,"* ed. Mechtild Rössler and Sabine Schleiermacher (Berlin, 1993), pp. 25–117, esp. pp. 40 ff., 62 f.; Burrin, p. 151 (conversation between Heydrich and Goebbels, September 25, 1941); speech by Heydrich, February 4, 1942, in Kárny et al., eds., p. 229; Himmler to Heydrich and to Wilhelm Rediess, the Higher SS- and Police Leader in Norway, February 16, 1942, BA NS 19/2375, fols. 1 f.

185 See Himmler, report notes, February 17, 1942, BA NS 19/1447, fols. 55 f.; Henry Picker, *Hitlers Tischgespräche im Führerhauptquartier*, 3d ed. (Stuttgart, 1977), p. 192.

186 Minutes, fol. 8 (Tuchel, p. 129); Goebbels, *Tagebücher*, pp. 533 f. (December 18, 1941); Hitler, May 29, 1942, in Picker, p. 340.

187 On this subject, see Browning, *Final Solution* (n. 75 above), p. 79.

188 Minutes, fols. 14 f. (Tuchel, pp. 135 f.).

189 Präg and Jacobmeyer, eds., p. 459.

190 See final comments by SS-Gruppenführer and General Lieutenant of the Waffen-SS, Hofmann, at a Conference of SS-Leaders from the Race and Resettlement Office, September 29–30, 1942, BA 17.03, Nr. 2, fol. 58; emphasis added. At the Wannsee Conference it had been asserted that in Europe there were 11 million Jews, in the European part of the Soviet Union 5 million. The mistake may have been made by the individual who prepared the minutes of the speech.

191 See Himmler, appointment calendar; Grothmann, appointment calendar.

192 Himmler, notes on telephone conversations, January 21, 1942 ("Jewish question. Meeting in Berlin"), BA NS 19/1439; Rosenberg, appointment calendar, January 21, 1942, BA NS 8/133, fol. 8; Globocnik report in Dirlewanger to Friedrich (SS Main Office), January 22, 1942, BA D-H ZM 1454, A. 1, fol. 231; Hitler's antisemitic outbursts in the presence of Himmler and Lammers on January 25, 1942 are documented in Jochmann, ed., pp. 228 f.; on the flow of information in the foreign office, see Browning, *Final Solution*, pp. 76 ff.

193 An official in the Slovakian Office for Jewish Affairs is said to have remarked in late January of 1942 that Slovakian Jews would soon be deported and executed. See Walter Lacquer, *Was niemand wissen wollte: Die Unterdrückung von Nachrichten über Hitlers Endlösung* (Frankfurt am Main, 1981), pp. 175 ff.

194 General Commissar for Latvia, IIa-Sch/Hue to the Reich Commissar for the Ostland, July 11, 1942: "In the Reich, the direction of current efforts is not to equate part-Jews of the first degree with Jews; the former are to be sterilized (see the meeting of the state secretaries on January 20, 1942)" (Lettisches

Staatsarchiv Riga 69-1a-6, fol. 53). I am indebted to Christoph Dieckmann for calling my attention to this document.

195 RSHA IV B 4, express letter, in re: Evacuation of the Jews, January 31, 1942, in Kurt Pätzold and Erika Schwarz, *"Auschwitz war für mich nur ein Bahnhof": Franz Novak, der Transportoffizier Adolf Eichmanns* (Berlin, 1994), pp. 119–22.

196 Undated and unsigned report, reproduced in facsimile in Mendelsohn, ed. (n. 20 above), pp. 86–94; undated report by Franz Rademacher, in Mendelsohn, ed., pp. 208 f.

197 For these two prominent participants in the Wannsee meeting, see Wilhelm Stuckart, March 16, and Franz Schlegelberger, April 5, 1942, in Mendelsohn, ed., pp. 201–7; Schlegelberger to Lammers, March 12, 1942, Nuremberg Document NG-839; Noakes, pp. 345 f.; Adam, pp. 324 ff.; Hilberg, *Vernichtung*, pp. 441 f. In addition, see note by Lösener, December 4, 1941, Anlage 2, BA R 18/5519, fols. 487–95; meeting notes of Lammers, April 10, 1942 (the actual record is missing), BA R 43 II/4023, fol. 2/ R. Stuckart and Schlegelberger referred directly to points in the minutes of the Wannsee Conference. So they were familiar with this document, as was Martin Bormann (see n. 214). Distribution of the minutes was announced on January 21, at the latest; see Rademacher's note, dated January 21, on Heydrich's invitation to the foreign office of January 8, 1942, "Minutes of the meeting are announced to arrive later" (reproduced in facsimile in Tuchel, p. 115). Hence suspicions that have been expressed (see Klein [n. 3 above], pp. 16 f.) that the distribution of the minutes was narrowly limited are unfounded.

198 Stuckart to Himmler, September 1942, in Lösener, "Rassereferent," pp. 298–301; Adam, pp. 327 f., but see also p. 329, n. 132; Grenville (n. 54 above), pp. 111 f.

199 Note by Otto Thierack, October 26, 1942, BA R 22/4062, fols. 14 f.; Note, in re: Reich Genealogy Office by Hans Ehlich, January 25, 1943, BA RW 42/4, Heft 2. (There were some 24, 000 "cases" requiring 140,000 investigations.)

200 See Hilberg, *Vernichtung*, pp. 446–49; Adler, p. 299; Adam, p. 329; Noakes, p. 348; for the course of events, see BA R 22/460, particularly Wilhelm Frick to Otto Thierack, March 20, 1943, fol. 334; BA R 18/5519, fols. 509 ff.

201 SS Race and Resettlement Main Office, Ancestry Section, to Kurt Steudtner, February 12, 1942. See the additional correspondence between the same parties in February and March, 1942, and the reaction of the applicant, Kurt Steudtner, in a letter to Otto Hofmann, March 2, 1942: "In the midst of my antiquarian historical researches came your job offer, holding out the promise of new struggles in the country beyond the Rhine. . . . The realization of this project is still subject of official discussion. . . . I can assure you that from the very first moment of my arrival at the Paris battle station, I will be ready to apply all my powers and abilities without rest in the struggle against the world's number one enemy!" BA NS 2/1002. In addition, see report by Theodor Dannecker, February 22, 1942, in Pätzold. ed., pp. 343–45.

202 Teletype by Dannecker to Wilhelm Osiander, March 21, and letter, March 31, 1942, BA NS 2/1002; note, in re: Mechanisms for Identifying Concealed Jewish Identities in France, March 24, 1942, BA R 39/762; see notes, November 8 and November 11, 1941 (BA R 39/762).

203 Hanns-Albin Rauter (Higher SS- and Police Leader, Northwest) to Otto Hofmann, December 20, 1941, BA NS 2/83, fol. 81/R; SS-Leader in the Race and Resettlement Office to Rauter, July 14, 1942, BA NS 2/81, fol. 122.

204 Safrian, pp. 180 f.; Press, p. 120; Ezergailis, p. 359.

205 Interrogation of Georg Heuser, February 14, 1966, Staatsanwaltschaft

Hamburg 147 Js 29/67, Bd. 35, fol. 6803; Wilhelm Kube to Hinrich Lohse, February 6, 1942, StA Hamburg 147 Js 29/67, Sonderband E, fols. 66 f.; Minutes of the Proceedings of the Office and Section Leaders Meeting, January 29, 1942, Zentrales Staatsarchiv Minsk 370-1-53, fols. 164 f. (a document first uncovered by Jürgen Matthäus). In a report by the adviser on Jewish affairs for the Commander of the Security Police, Kurt Burkhart, dated January 1942, it is also hinted that the German Jews are to die (IfZ Fb 104/2). For the period prior to January 20, 1942 there is no sure evidence for any executions of German Jews in Minsk.

206 See Karl Loewenstein, *Minsk. Im Lager der deutschen Juden* (Bonn, 1956); Heinz Rosenberg, *Jahre des Schreckens* (Göttingen, 1992); for the date of March 31, see Anna Krasnoperka, *Briefe meiner Erinnerung* (Haus Villigst, 1991), pp. 56 f.

207 Adler, p. 193; Teletype from Himmler to Richard Glücks, Inspector of the Concentration Camps, January 25, 1942, NS 19/1920, fol. 1; Klaus A. Friedrich Schüler, *Logistik im Russlandfeldzug* (Frankfurt am Main, 1987), pp. 518 ff.

208 Office of the Deputy for the Four-Year Plan, Traffic Office, Activity Report for April, May 18, 1942, BA R 26 IV/vorl. 47; Arad, *Belzec, Sobibor, Treblinka*, pp. 140, 147; Pohl, *Lublin*, pp. 107 ff.

209 Proclamation of the Jewish Council, May 1, 1942; Situation Report of the Office of State Police in Litzmannstadt, June 9, 1942; Director of the Office for Railroads and Traffic to Gestapo Office Litzmannstadt, May 19, 1942, all in Adolf Diamant, *Getto Litzmannstadt* (Frankfurt am Main, 1986), pp. 107, 120, 125; Lucjan Dobroszycki, ed., *The Chronicle of the Lodz Ghetto, 1941–1944* (New York and New Haven, Conn., 1984), pp. 156–72 (for April 29–May 14, 1942); Freund, Perz, and Stuhlpfarrer, eds., esp. p. 29.

210 Transport Lists of the Vienna Transports, Staatsanwaltschaft Koblenz 9 Ks 2/62, Dok. vol. 5; interrogation of Survivor J.S., April 11, 1948, StA Koblenz 9 Ks 2/62, vol. 71, fol. 10546; Minsk Railway Control Office, Rail Service Telegram, May 7, 1942, ZStA Minsk 378-1-784, fol. 64; Activity Report of the Second Wing of the Waffen-SS Battalion for Special Projects, May 17, 1942, in *Unsere Ehre heisst Treue* (Vienna, 1984), p. 246.

211 Christopher Browning, "A Final Hitler Decision for the 'Final Solution'? The Riegner Telegram Reconsidered," *Holocaust and Genocide Studies* 11, no. 1 (1996): 3–10, esp. p. 4; Aly, p. 408.

212 It is not certain whether this incident actually occurred. For Himmler, see Witte, p. 335. For Frick's visit to the Landrat's Office in Kolo (Warthbrücken), see Rückerl, p. 277 (for the eyewitness account); aide to the Reich minister of the interior, travel plan, June 15–27, 1942; newspaper article [probably from the *Ostdeutschen Beobachter*] "Besuch im Osten des Warthelands," BA R 18/5231, fols. 99 ff., 115. According to the schedule and to the report, a visit by Wilhelm Frick to Chelmno itself, as asserted in the witness account, is unlikely. With regard to complaints lodged following the murders in Chelmno in February, see Seeger, p. 121.

213 NSDAP, Party Chancellery, "Reichsverfügungsblatt," Ausgabe A, July 1 and July 4, 1942, with Regulations 34/42 and 37/42, in re: Treatment of Part-Jews in the Armed Forces, June 23, and in re: Recommendations for Part-Jews from the Party, July 3, 1942, BA 62 Ka 1, Nr. 83, fols. 128 f.; see also Adler, p. 298.

214 Circular letter from the Party Chancellery, in re: Preliminary Measures for the Final Solution of the Jewish Question in Europe. Rumors concerning the Situation of Jews in the East, October 9, 1942, in Pätzold, ed., pp. 351–53.

215 It is certain, however, that Hitler was well informed about the progress of efforts to exterminate the Jews and never rejected the idea. See Fleming; Burrin; Broszat.

216 See nn. 16 and 17. This is made especially clear in Burrin, pp. 106 ff.; Browning, "Euphoria," p. 476.

217 And it was made after Hitler had approved related plans by military and civilian offices for an unparalleled program of mass murder to be carried out against large segments of the Soviet population for economic and military purposes. For more on this subject, see Gerlach, "Wirtschaftsinteressen" (n. 10 above).

218 Hitler's leadership decision would then have had significant consequences for the Wannsee Conference by putting it, and Heydrich's planning for it, on a new basis and giving it added impulse. This may have contributed to the lengthy delay in rescheduling the conference.

219 For a different interpretation, see Burrin, p. 145. But even Heydrich's letter of November 6, 1941, cited in Burrin, in which he reports that "at the highest level, and with utmost severity, the Jews have been branded as the real incendiary force in Europe," does not provide proof. In addition, see Witte, pp. 327–29; German ambassador in Paris, Carltheo Zeitschel, to the chief of the Security Police for Belgium and France, October 8, 1941, in Pätzold, ed., pp. 309 f.; teletype from Himmler to Heydrich, January 27, 1942, BA NS 19/1920, fol. 2 in regard to the limited number of individuals.

220 Minutes, fol. 5 (Tuchel, p. 126).

221 See Broszat, pp. 766 ff.

222 On one occasion, however, this is said to have occurred *after* the fact; see Pohl, *Lublin*, p. 125.

223 See ibid., esp. pp. 101, 115; Aly, p. 398.

224 Aly, pp. 339–47; Christian Gerlach, "Failure of Plans for an SS Extermination Camp in Mogilev, Belorussia," *Holocaust and Genocide Studies* 12, no. 1(1997): 60–78.

225 A recently discovered document regarding a significant increase in the area included in the town's ghetto could provide some indirect evidence of this. Nearly all of the ghetto's original residents were shot in October. See Jürgen Matthäus, "Perspektiven der NS-Forschung," *Zeitschrift für Geschichtswissenschaft* 44 (1996): 991–1005, esp. p. 1002.

226 For Rosenberg's speech, see n. 73. Cf. Jochmann (n. 30 above), p. 140; and Himmler's notes on telephone conversations, November 17, 1941 (n. 27 above). For an interpretation of the latter as a comprehensive agreement with Hitler concerning the liquidation of the Jews, see Breitman, pp. 218 f. (also for the other mentioned contacts). See also Goebbels, *Tagebücher*, pt. 2, vol. 2, p. 309. I am indebted to Christoph Dieckmann, who referred me to that document.

227 Präg and Jacobmeyer, eds., October 14 and December 16, 1941, pp. 413, 457.

228 "Das Reich" No. 46 of November 16, l941, p. 1 f. A similar report on some of Hitler's remarks by Goebbels on August 18, 1941 (Broszat, pp. 749 f.) referred only to events "in the east." See in addition an article in the *Völkischen Beobachter*, Munich ed. (November 12, 1941), referring to Hitler's speech on November 9 (BA NS 22/567, fol. 1).

229 The same is true of the background to Hitler's remarks on November 28, 1941 to the Grand Mufti of Jerusalem, Haj Amin El Husseini, when Hitler asserted that, in the event of a German advance into the Middle East, the German objective would be the "destruction" of "Judaism" in Palestine. Hitler could have had tactical reasons because El Husseini had asked him for

such a statement during the meeting. Note of Gesandter Schütt about the discussion between Hitler and El Husseini of November 28, 1941, in *Akten zur deutschen auswärtigen Politik*, Ser. D, vol. 13, 2 (Göttingen, 1970), pp. 718–21.

230 See Hans Mommsen, "Die Realisierung des Utopischen: Die 'Endlösung der Judenfrage' im 'Dritten Reich,' " in *Der Nationalsozialismus und die deutsche Gesellschaft*, ed. Mommsen (Reinbek, 1991, 1st ed., 1983), pp. 184–232, esp. p. 214.

231 Compare Jean-Claude Pressac, *Die Krematorien von Auschwitz* (Munich and Zurich, 1993), esp. pp. 51–55; in regard to Broszat, see Aly (n. 5), p. 398, for comments typical of the opinions of some scholars who nowadays favor this view.

232 Conversely, Hartog, pp. 65–69, sees a direct connection between the entry of the United States into the war and a decision he believes Hitler made immediately on December 7, 1941. Based on some mistaken dates he concludes that Hitler needed only to "nod his head," since "Himmler and Heydrich had already known for months that Hitler intended to liquidate the Jews throughout Europe" (p. 65). Nonetheless, at a meeting in the Reich labor ministry on November 28, 1941, the representative from the Wartheland noted that "some 300,000 Jews were still living" in his district. He continued that "by the end of March 1942, they should all have been evacuated, with the exception of those able to work." That could only have meant their extermination at Chelmno. If one follows Hartog, the administrative offices in the Wartheland could only have developed this schedule if they had known in advance about the impending Japanese attack on Pearl Harbor, which they surely did not. See report on the department meeting in RAM (undated [November 28, 1941]), BA R 22/2057, fol. 208. For the date, see fols. 206 f.

233 Greiser to Himmler, May 1, 1942, BA NS 19/1585, fols. 1 f. For the fall of 1942 it has been documented that Arthur Greiser asked Hitler what measures should be taken in his district against the Jews and that Hitler told him to proceed "as he thought appropriate," Greiser to Himmler, November 21, 1942, BA NS 19/1585, fols. 17 f. Aly mistakenly refers to this as the fall of 1941.

234 Hans Frank's speech at the government session in Kraków on December 16, 1941, BA R 52 II/241, fol. 77.

161

7

GERMAN SOLDIERS AND THE HOLOCAUST

Historiography, research and implications

Omer Bartov

For many years after 1945 the history of World War II was written with the Holocaust left out. There were many reasons for this omission, some of which are outlined in this chapter. But the result was that the genocide of the Jews, along with the mass killing of other real or imaginary opponents of the Nazi regime, even when they gradually entered the mainstream of the war's historiography, were rarely associated with the military context in which they occurred, or were linked to it in distorted and apologetic ways. What is important to recognize is that apart from the obvious reasons many Germans had to avoid associating the Wehrmacht with the crimes of the Third Reich, many other nations were reluctant to view the Holocaust as a central event in and of the war. It was one thing to indict top officials of the Nazi regime with crimes against humanity, quite another to identify the Wehrmacht as a criminal organization employed in mass murder. To do so would have made the postwar Germanies into unacceptable allies for both superpowers; it would have also greatly diminished the aura of having fought an honorable and "clean" war from the victor nations' perspective, and would have raised questions regarding their failure to prevent genocide and their lack of enthusiasm in recognizing its postwar effects. In other words, identifying the Wehrmacht as a Nazi tool of genocide was tantamount to leveling an accusation of collective guilt at Germany at a moment when both its successor states were needed as allies in the Cold War, and would have highlighted the old Allies' anything but altruistic conduct in Word War II.

This chapter provides a critical overview of the development of research on the Wehrmacht's complicity in the crimes of the Nazi regime. It argues that since the late 1960s there has been a progressive realization of the military's close links, on the level of both ideology and policy, with Nazism. This trend followed the general development of research on the Third Reich, but always remained several steps behind. The obvious defensiveness of older German scholars, who had themselves served in the Wehrmacht, about the army's involvement in war crimes, gave way to a lack of interest in military matters among younger historians, or a narrow focus on tactics and operations among military specialists. That a direct focus on the army was a potential time-bomb as far as our understanding of German society under Nazism was concerned, was occasionally recognized. But despite some major works on this issue, it was only with the reunification of Germany, the fall of Communism, and the emergence of a third generation of scholars more detached from the events and more open-minded methodologically and ideologically, that research on the criminal activities of the army and its links to civilian society became a major public issue. And yet, even now, work on the involvement of the Wehrmacht specifically in the genocide of the Jews is still in its early phases. As this chapter notes, not only will further research in this area greatly expand our understanding of the Holocaust and the dynamics of German society as represented by the conscripts, but also it will teach us a great deal on the brutalizing effects of modern war and its links to genocide.

* * *

Recent research on the involvement of the German army in the Holocaust has begun to transform our understanding of the scope, course and context of the Nazi attempted genocide of the Jews. It also has some important implications for the study of the Third Reich, its historiography and the lacunae that can still be identified in the scholarship on the period.

In what follows I begin by briefly sketching out some of the distinguishing characteristics of the literature on the Wehrmacht in the early decades of the postwar period. I then discuss the important advances in the scholarship on this issue made between the late 1960s and the reunification of Germany and proceed to examine the most recent research on and interpretations of the Wehrmacht's role in the Holocaust. Finally, I point out what is still missing from this growing body of scholarly work and suggest some ways of addressing these lacunae and enhancing our understanding.

1 Professional soldiers

Until the late 1960s the German army was generally presented in Germany and in much of the rest of the world as a professional organization that had fought a host of enemies with remarkable tenacity and skill and had little in common with the ideological world view and criminal policies of the Nazi regime. This view was disseminated by Wehrmacht veterans in postwar publications such as military formation chronicles and former generals' memoirs, just as much as in popular fiction and film; it was also the official line of the West German government.[1] German scholars rarely challenged the notion of the Wehrmacht's "purity of arms" even as they gradually shifted toward a positive evaluation of the military-conservative opposition that had attempted to overthrow Hitler, allegedly due to the threat he posed to the army's "shield of honor," and more obviously because of the looming defeat by the Allies whose anticipated catastrophic consequences might have been somewhat diminished by doing away with the Nazi leadership.[2] Western scholars generally accepted this view, not least because their perspective of the war was based on the manner in which it was fought in the West, where, with the possible exception of the very last months of the fighting, both sides adhered to some conventions of warfare that had long disappeared under torrents of blood and material devastation in the East.[3]

The German soldier's presentation as a professional fighter, untouched by or uninvolved in the crimes of the regime, was of course directly related to the context of domestic and international political circumstances immediately following the end of the war. Domestically, it seemed impossible to rebuild West German society without as narrow as possible a definition of the so-called Nazis and their accomplices.[4] The idea that the Wehrmacht as such might have been a criminal organization was not only anathema to German public opinion, but would have implicated such vast portions of German society in Nazi criminality that one would have had either to declare a general amnesty (thereby legitimizing the notion of unpunished crimes) or to give up altogether the possibility of resurrecting some form of a German national entity. Considering that as many as twenty million Germans had passed through the ranks of the Wehrmacht at one point or another, neither of these options was realistic, especially in the face of a perceived Soviet threat and the rapid deterioration of international relations that swiftly led to the Cold War. Not only was it unthinkable to eliminate Germany as a nation, it also very quickly transpired that the hopes and expectations of some Nazi leaders and Wehrmacht generals in the last phases of the war, namely that Germany would be a crucial factor in a Western anti-Communist alliance, were to be realized within a few years after the collapse of the Third Reich.[5]

The Nuremberg Trials and the attempted denazification of postwar Germany eventually served precisely this end, since in both cases the criminality of the regime and the extent of participation in crimes of war and genocide were defined in a manner that made possible the quick re-emergence of the German state and society as somehow purged of the misdeeds of the past.[6] If the initial purpose had been to punish and purge, the ultimate result was to acquit and cover up. One should point out that this was not merely a consequence of either the inability to imagine the horror of genocide and find the appropriate legal discourse for it or of cold political calculations; it also manifested the sheer meaninglessness of indicting a whole nation and therefore served to demonstrate humanity's incapacity to confront the crime of modern genocide in a manner compatible with its scale and enormity and the range of agencies, professions and individuals that must perforce be complicit in it. Since 1945 we have witnessed many more cases of genocide whose makers were eventually welcomed back into the community of nations, not least because the evil they committed could never find appropriate retribution.[7]

It should also be noted that the state of knowledge regarding the army's involvement in Nazi crimes was not a function of any substantial lack in archival sources. Large quantities of German documents were taken to Britain and the United States after the war and later returned to Germany; much of the material eventually used by scholars had been available long 1before it was examined. What was lacking in those first two decades was scholarly interest, not evidence, as well as the more obvious limitations imposed on research by the vast amounts of material and the laborious process of its organization and categorization. At least as crucial, however, was the impact of certain interpretive concepts of Nazism specifically and methodological conventions about historical research more generally. This meant that during the reign of the paradigms of totalitarianism and fascism, scholars were often more interested in theory than in fact, and that with the emergence of social history, historians devoted little attention to the military.[8] Consequently, the only scholars to examine army records were so-called "pure" military historians, whose interests lay more in tactics and strategy, command and logistics, than in ideology and criminality. Mainstream historians therefore tended to rely mainly on the memoirs of German generals and veterans' accounts for the reconstruction of the soldiers' experience in the war. And precisely because former soldiers understandably stressed their professionalism and denied any ideological or organizational links with the regime, they were viewed as objective and reliable sources. It took a generation of scholars more skeptical about the explanatory power of the old paradigms, less trustful of former soldiers and, not least, willing to undermine the myths on which West German society was founded, to finally venture into the archives and begin to write the history of the Wehrmacht's relationship with the Nazi regime.

2 Ideological soldiers

German scholars such as Gerhard Ritter and Friedrich Meinecke, former Wehrmacht generals such as Heinz Guderian and Erich von Manstein, as well as Western military historians and former officers such as B. H. Liddell Hart and J. F. C. Fuller, and scholars such as Gordon Craig and John Wheeler-Bennett all stressed the vast distance between the "old" officer corps and the upstart Nazis and found it unthinkable that such respectable and "correct," if perhaps conservative and even reactionary, officers and gentlemen could have condoned, let alone organized, a criminal war and unprecedented genocide.[9] There were, to be sure, some rotten apples, who were justly condemned at Nuremberg; but by and large, it was argued, they were unrepresentative of the whole. Soviet claims that the Wehrmacht had engaged in genocidal war in the East were—with some reason—dismissed as communist propaganda. Western generals by and large preferred to think of the war they had fought as chivalrous, and of the enemy as worthy of the fight. And military historians, as indeed much of the public, were more interested in the heroic exploits encapsulated in such popular novels and films as *The Longest Day* or *A Bridge Too Far* than in the horrors of genocidal war.

All this began to change thanks in large part to the efforts of a few outstanding and courageous German scholars, some of whom belonged to an important German research institute closely linked to the West German Ministry of the Interior and the Bundeswehr, which eventually produced a massive study, as yet still uncompleted, of the Wehrmacht in World War II.[10] Complemented by works written outside of Germany, this important body of literature is thus the outcome of a joint, and often contentious and controversial, effort by historians of several nations working over a span of some three decades who have, by the early 1990s, succeeded in drastically changing our understanding of the Wehrmacht's role in the Third Reich.

The publication in 1965 of the two-volume work *Anatomie des SS-Staates*, which included an important analysis by Hans-Adolf Jacobsen of the so-called Commissar Order (the instruction to kill on the spot all political officers attached to Red Army units captured by the Wehrmacht), heralded the beginning of scholarly writings on the criminal activities of the Wehrmacht during its campaign in the Soviet Union.[11] This was followed in 1969 by a comprehensive study of the policies of ideological indoctrination in the Wehrmacht written by Manfred Messerschmidt, a path-breaking work on the maltreatment and murder of Soviet prisoners of war by Christian Streit, published in 1978, and a thorough investigation of the collaboration between the *Einsatzgruppen*, the death squads of the SS and SD, and the Wehrmacht by Helmut Krausnick and Hans-Heinrich Wilhelm, which appeared in 1981.[12] Along with several other studies such as Volker Berghahn's comprehensive article on "educational officers" and Klaus-Jürgen Müller's analysis of the army's relationship with the Nazi state, these works established a new standard for the examination of the role of the Wehrmacht in the planning and execution of Hitler's policies in the East.[13] Moreover, since 1979 the *Militärgeschichtliches Forschungsamt* (Institute for Military History) in Freiburg (recently moved to Potsdam) has been publishing a massive series of volumes on the Third Reich and World War II. These tomes, and especially Volume 4 published in 1983, written by such leading German scholars in the field as Jürgen Förster, Bernhard Kroener, Rolf-Dieter Müller, Wilhelm Deist and Gerd Ueberschär, have vastly expanded our knowledge of the Wehrmacht and its links with the regime's policies.[14] Put together, this literature has had a major and lasting effect on the scholarship on the Third Reich and has become a *sine qua non* for any future research on the period, superseding older works by non-German scholars such as Alexander Dallin and Robert O'Neill.[15] The enormous archival ground work on which these studies were based swept aside many of the conventional assumptions on the Wehrmacht. Among them, and most important to the present context, was the idea of the army's professionalism and ideological detachment.

What the works cited here demonstrated was that, contrary to previous assertions, the Wehrmacht had come under the influence of the regime from very early on and remained a major tool in the implementation of Nazi policies until the very end of the war. This was expressed in the Wehrmacht command's willingness, if not eagerness, to subject the troops to substantial ideological training; in its participation in the planning and brutal execution of conquest and occupation on a vast scale; and in its central role in doing away with conventional rules and regulations of warfare, all of which deeply implicated it in the war of destruction and subjugation conducted by Germany in Eastern Europe and the Soviet Union. Such revelations, though anchored in a mass of documentation, were not immediately or easily accepted in Germany. Indeed, one characteristic of these publications was that they were repeatedly greeted in the media and by the public with expressions of astonishment and disbelief, horror and rage. As even some of the most recent debates on the Wehrmacht, to be discussed below, have indicated, the views expressed by these historians are still encountering a great deal of public resistance, although by now most scholars tend to accept them. The political impact of these works is of course immense, since they not only call for a profound reevaluation of the meaning and implications of the Nazi regime for German society during and after the war, they also discredit some of the most dearly held assumptions on the ability of postwar Germany to "come to terms" with its past.

Nevertheless, this body of scholarship suffers from several serious limitations. Employing a rather traditional methodology, these historians have mainly focused on the upper echelons of the military and the regime, have emphasized matters of higher policy and decision making and have shown a distinct reluctance to identify the links between the penetration of Nazi ideology into the Wehrmacht, its criminal conduct vis-à-vis the local population and enemy soldiers especially in the East, and the planning and implementation of the Holocaust. As will be noted in the next section, the connections between the Wehrmacht and the genocide of the Jews have only recently begun to receive appropriate scrutiny by historians. For the moment, however, let me first discuss a few more studies, mainly by non-German scholars, which have complemented and enriched the existing scholarship by concentrating on a "view from below" of the Wehrmacht, that is, on the manner in which the rank and file of the army behaved during the war, were influenced by the ideology of the regime and the views of their immediate superiors, and ultimately perceived their own actions at the front.

Studies of soldiers, rather than generals, were motivated both by developments in historical research and by the increasingly obvious limits of earlier work on the Wehrmacht. The new trend among historians in the 1970s and 1980s to "lower their gaze" and examine the everyday lives of "ordinary" people, rather than focus on either high politics or anonymous structures and mechanisms, was reflected in attempts to write an "Alltagsgeschichte" of the Wehrmacht somewhat akin to works being written at the time on German civilian society.[16] Similarly, the spate of "local histories" that strove to gain more insight into social and political changes by focusing in depth on a limited community was reflected in studies of discrete military units.[17] At the same time these studies tried to test the assertions of scholars writing about the top echelons, according to which the efforts to indoctrinate the troops were largely unsuccessful and the criminal orders issued by the high command rarely reached the units on the ground. Ironically, therefore, the very same historians who had documented the involvement of the Wehrmacht in Nazi policies were unwilling to go so far as to concede that the soldiers were actually influenced by their generals' decision to implement the policies of conquest and genocide dictated by the regime and to legitimize them by employing Nazi ideological arguments. Instead, they assumed that the troops were far more preoccupied with their own survival and accepted at face value the apologetic postwar argument by field commanders that they had refused to hand down to the soldiers such orders as the *Kommissarbefehl* of which they claimed to have strongly disapproved.[18] Thus the new studies that focused on the lower echelons were consciously aimed at investigating the extent to which the troops were both influenced by ideological arguments and received and carried out the criminal orders of the regime and the army high command.

Works in this vein began appearing in the mid-1980s, but more than ten years later one can say that there is still a great deal of research to be done in this area. Earlier works by Theo Schulte and myself have more recently been followed by Stephen Fritz's and Thomas Kühne's studies.[19] Despite the rather meager scholarship on the everyday life of the troops, these scholars both tend to debate each other's conclusions and have met with a fair amount of criticism from other quarters. Nevertheless, some of the more fundamental findings of these studies seem to have gained acceptance within the larger academic community. Among those most relevant to the present context is, first, that the soldiers were indeed exposed to a massive indoctrinational effort by the military authorities. Second, that especially as regards ideological teachings that had already been disseminated among German youth prior to their conscription in school, the Hitler Youth and the Labor Service, and which corresponded to preexisting prejudices in German society, the concerted propaganda aimed at the troops was largely successful in molding the men's views on the supreme quality of their political leadership, the inhuman character of the enemy, the ruthless manner in which fighting should be conducted, and the catastrophic consequences of defeat. Third, that under the combined influence of a dehumanizing ideology and a brutal war the troops of the Wehrmacht were involved in widespread crimes against enemy soldiers and the civilian population, acting both on orders by their superiors and in many instances also on their own initiative, even when such actions were explicitly forbidden by their commanders. All these factors put together led to what I have called the "barbarization of warfare" on the Eastern Front which resulted in the devastation of vast tracts of land, especially in the occupied parts of the Soviet Union, and caused the deaths of millions of civilians and POWs whether by outright murder or from starvation, epidemics, exposure to the elements and economic exploitation. In other words, both from the perspective of the generals and from that of the troops on the ground, the campaign in the East was conducted as a war of annihilation.

Taken as a whole, the scholarly study of the Wehrmacht and its relationship with the Third Reich, Nazi ideology and the policies of conquest, subjugation and annihilation pursued by the regime has made major strides in the past thirty years. However, one crucial area has been sorely neglected until very recently, namely, the role of the army in the genocide of the Jews. This was partly caused by disciplinary compartmentalization, whereby military historians studied issues deemed relevant to war and occupation, to which genocide did not seem to belong, while historians of the Holocaust refrained from studying the Wehrmacht and focused either on the agencies directly involved in organizing genocide or on the victims. Partly, this was a result of ideological and national biases, which in the German case meant that one found it exceedingly difficult to associate the Wehrmacht—for a long time after the war seen as the organization least contaminated by the Nazis and most representative of the common folk—with the Holocaust—recognized as the very worst of the many crimes committed by the Third Reich. Still another reason for this neglect was the realization of the implications that the potential findings of such research would have for the understanding of postwar German society, let alone for the many veterans and their relatives whose numbers have begun dwindling only in recent years. If the argument that the Wehrmacht's soldiers were involved in war crimes was already explosive and has indeed met with a great deal of resistance in Germany, associating the army with the Holocaust is far more disturbing. After all, the argument could have, and indeed has, been made that there was nothing unique about the involvement of German troops in wanton destruction, looting, exploitation and murder; war is hell, and nothing better could be expected of soldiers fighting in such terrible conditions as on the Eastern Front. The fact is that even those who rejected this position, such as myself, have written on the barbarization of warfare *from the perspective of the troops* and within the context of a horrendous war, which somehow made the narrative more palatable by making for a certain empathy with the soldiers themselves. The Holocaust, however, has commonly been presented as separate from the war (even if genocide on this scale could only have been practiced within its context), and its perpetrators were seen as separate from the soldiers. Associating the two therefore threatens to undermine the last defensive barrier of the Wehrmacht's remarkably solid postwar fortifications. Precisely because in Germany the Holocaust was seen as the epitome of evil, it had to be ascribed to perpetrators kept rigidly apart from the rest of the population; linking it with the Wehrmacht therefore opens the floodgates and erases all distinctions, for the army included (virtually) everyone, and the survivors of the war became the founders of the two postwar Germanys. No wonder that this has always been perceived as a most threatening exercise.

3 Genocidal soldiers

In the mid-1980s, just a few years before reunification, the German academic community and much of the more respectable media were shaken by a controversy over the uniqueness of the Holocaust and the manner in which the history of the Nazi regime should be contextualized in the creation of a new German national identity.[20] The *Historikerstreit*, as it came to be called, is relevant to the present discussion for two main reasons. First, because it concerned the effort by some German scholars to "normalize" the single most horrible undertaking of the Third Reich, the Holocaust, by linking it to other cases of genocide carried out by other states at other times in history. Second, because it included an attempt to present the German army's war in the East as a desperate struggle against an invading Bolshevik-Asiatic enemy who threatened to destroy not only Germany but the rest of Western civilization.[21] Hence the "revisionists" of the *Historikerstreit* were interested neither in denying the Holocaust nor in refuting claims about the barbarous manner in which the war in the East was conducted by the Wehrmacht, but rather in relativizing them both as "unoriginal" and as "necessary" because genocide had been originated by the very same regime whose alleged genocidal intentions had made fighting a barbarous war necessary, namely, the Bolsheviks.

As several critics of the historians' controversy noted at the time, the *Historikerstreit* introduced no new evidence, nor any original interpretations, but was a political and ideological debate over the sense and meaning of the past and the manner in which it should (be allowed to) influence the present.[22] In one sense, it was a rearguard action by conservative historians at a time when a growing number of scholarly works indicated that the Nazi period could neither be confined to a so-called criminal clique nor traced back to foreign origins, nor indeed be presented as a reaction to even greater dangers. And yet, although the "revisionists" themselves have been largely discredited, the sensibilities they reflected have not gone away, indeed, have surfaced repeatedly since then in reaction to a new wave of works on the Nazi era and in the context of a newly unified Germany.

One such case has been a controversial and unique exhibition that has been circulating in Germany and Austria for the last couple of years, provoking a flood of media reports, political pronouncements and academic responses. The exhibition, entitled *Vernichtungskrieg: Verbrechen der Wehrmacht 1941 bis 1944* (War of Annihilation: Crimes of the Wehrmacht, 1941–1944), is the first public display of documents and photographs collected in German archives, and especially in the archives of the former Soviet Union and other East European states formerly under communist domination, concerning the criminal conduct of German soldiers in the East during World War II. What has been most shocking to many German visitors and commentators has been the clear evidence that the Wehrmacht was deeply involved not "only" in killing POWs and partisans or in carrying out large-scale operations of collective punishment against civilians, but also, in a direct and massive manner, in the implementation of the Final Solution. The exhibition, organized by Hannes Heer and Klaus Naumann of the Hamburg *Institut für Sozialforschung* and accompanied by an important collection of essays edited by the organizers and written by leading scholars in the field, unleashed a public debate over the extent to which the Wehrmacht could indeed be called a criminal organization, a designation that had previously been eschewed by most scholars ever since the Nuremberg Trials, where only the SS was seen as worthy of that title.[23]

Among the many reactions to the exhibition (which some cities in Germany refused to host and which met with especially strong opposition in Bavaria and Austria) was a series of articles in the influential weekly *Die Zeit*, subsequently published in a special issue under the title *Gerhorsam bis zum Mord? Der verschwiegene Krieg der deutschen Wehrmacht* (Obedience to Murder? The Hidden War of the German Wehrmacht).[24] Clearly, the argument of the exhibition touched a raw nerve, for here one could no longer speak of excesses by individuals or a few criminal generals, nor about SS atrocities or crimes committed "behind the back of the fighting troops," since the evidence was there for all to see: photographs taken by the soldiers themselves of massacres, hangings and torture, documents directing military units to murder Jewish communities, clear indications of the close collaboration between the SS and the regular army. Moreover, an important article by one of the organizers, Hannes Heer, presented previously unknown documents taken from newly opened archives, showing the process whereby Wehrmacht units had become directly involved in genocide.[25] Heer's findings were obviously only the tip of the iceberg and indicated that further research in formerly inaccessible archives would possibly lead to far more information on this dark episode in the Wehrmacht's history. Once more, the conventions of scholarship on the army's involvement in Nazi policies were shaken, and many old assumptions had to be revised.

Indeed, even before the storm over the exhibition had receded, Germany found itself embroiled in an even bigger and more disturbing controversy. The book that caused the row, Daniel Jonah Goldhagen's *Hitler's Willing Executioners: Ordinary Germans and the Holocaust*, is only marginally relevant to this article.[26] But the debate in Germany is highly revealing and tells us a great deal about the difficulties Germans still face in relating the Holocaust to actual flesh-and-blood killers rather than to anonymous forces or evil leaders.[27] For whatever the faults of the book in question (and they are many), it shows in no uncertain terms the involvement of middle-aged German men, not distinguished by either ideological fervor or political affiliation, in the brutal torture and murder of thousands of Jews in face-to-face situations which, at least initially, they could have in fact chosen to avoid. If the book is written with a great deal of passion and rage (which does not add to its argument but has increased its appeal to readers), reactions in Germany were also passionate and often ill-considered. Although the killers with whom Goldhagen is concerned were not soldiers, they in many ways resembled the type of reservists one would have encountered in any number of regular army units. That they apparently not only willingly killed Jews but also enjoyed their "work" was highly unsettling to a public grown used to far more detached interpretations of that past and to explanatory models which kept the horror and gore at bay.

The storm over Goldhagen's book is thus related to the general reluctance to accept the involvement of regular army soldiers in the Holocaust. Since the men of the reserve police battalions greatly resembled the so-called "sober" army reservists who were said to have been mainly concerned with their own survival,[28] one could assume that the latter might just as readily have taken part in, and derived pleasure from, the mass murder of men, women and children. This would in turn mean that millions of Germans who came back from the war in 1945 could have well been, at one time or another in their military career, "willing executioners." To be sure, this vision of a postwar Germany inhabited by innumerable killers contradicts Goldhagen's more comforting assertion that the Germans had miraculously been transformed after 1945 or 1949 and no longer harbored the anti-Semitic sentiments he believes were the main motivation for the Holocaust. But this is only one of the many contradictions in a work whose main importance and interest lies in its reception rather than in its inherent value as a scholarly study.[29]

Just as the storm over Goldhagen's book seems to be ebbing (though it has now begun in France and Italy with the recent publication of the book in those countries),[30] another revelation promises to fuel the debate over the Wehrmacht and further clarify the links between the case of the police battalions and the criminal activities of the regular soldiers. Recent reports inform us that some 1.3 million pages of cables sent by German murder squads in summer 1941, which were intercepted and decoded by British signals intelligence but have only now been declassified by the United States National Security Agency, clearly show that not only SS and police units but also regular army formations were involved in mass killings of Jews from the very first days of "Barbarossa," the German invasion of the Soviet Union launched on 22 June 1941. Although much of this has been known before, these documents provide more details on the beginning of the Holocaust and the apparently universal participation of German agencies on the ground in its implementation. Quite apart from raising questions about Allied reactions to mass killings, since contrary to their subsequent assertions of ignorance they now appear to have had the information right at their fingertips, these cables are certain to ignite another debate over the participation of the fighting troops—the professional soldiers—in genocide. Moreover, it has also been reported that the Russian government has handed some 15,000 documents of its own to the United States Holocaust Memorial Museum, which include information collected by Russian agents behind the lines, translations of German documents, and eyewitness accounts compiled by the Soviet War Crimes Commission at the end of the war.[31] All of this, along with an unknown number of documents still being unearthed in Russian and East European archives, is certain to significantly enhance our knowledge on this period and seems to point in the direction of far more killers and accomplices, and higher numbers of victims, than had been previously estimated, not least due to the direct involvement of the Wehrmacht in the killing. There may of course still be room to debate the question of whether the Wehrmacht as such was a criminal, indeed a genocidal, organization; but its participation in genocide on a grand scale seems no longer in doubt.

4 The soldiers' victims

For all the progress made in the scholarship of the Wehrmacht, its historiography still suffers from one major lacuna, which in turn reflects a more general problem in the historiography of the Holocaust, namely, the interaction between perpetrators and victims. As we have seen, the first step toward contending with this hiatus, that of recognizing the role of the army in genocide, has been made, although the scholarship on this issue is still in its infancy. Thus, for instance, the mammoth ongoing publication *Das Deutsche Reich und der Zweite Weltkrieg*, despite its immense contribution to our knowledge of the Third Reich during World War II, has refrained from devoting even a single chapter to the involvement of the Wehrmacht in the murder of the Jews. Indeed, since the institute charged with its production, the *Militärgeschichtliches Forschungsamt*, was moved from Freiburg to Potsdam in the wake of German reunification, it seems to have been undergoing a quiet conservative transformation, with the result that the vision of its former academic director, Manfred Messerschmidt, to produce a social history of the military, may well be eroded, and future publications be devoted to traditional, "pure" military history reminiscent of such works written in the pre-1914 and interwar periods.[32] Nevertheless, as more and more evidence becomes available, it will be impossible in the long run to avoid writing on the Wehrmacht's role in genocide. The problem that remains to be resolved, therefore, is not one of documentation, but rather, just as was the case in the early postwar decades, a problem of perception, methodology and political, ideological or national bias. For the all too rigid separation between works on the perpetrators and works on the victims, which afflicts much of the scholarship on the Holocaust, reflects the limitations of the historians writing on the event much more than the limits of sources, understanding and representation. It is to this issue that I turn in this final section.

If the perpetrators made no distinctions between their victims, but rather wished to see them as a gray, faceless mass of (sub)humanity, most of the victims were not in a position to distinguish between the various affiliations of their persecutors. The killers deprived their victims of any specific identity by designating them all as "Jews," a term which meant that they were targeted for extinction. The victims spoke of their persecutors as "Germans," whether they were regular soldiers or SS men, Gestapo agents or civilian administrators, a term which meant that they were all potential murderers. But it is the task of the historian to do away with these generalizing categories which, as the case of the Holocaust so clearly demonstrates, begin by erasing individual identity and thereby create the preconditions for annihilating vast, anonymous masses of human beings. German historians, among them historians of the Wehrmacht, have done a great deal to make finer distinctions between the various categories of Germans involved or not involved in the genocide of the Jews.[33] But they have done very little to investigate the victims; rather, they refer to them as the perpetrators did, namely, as "Jews," a term seen as synonymous with "victims." And yet, when writing the history of any historical event, including genocide, as well as the specific case of the German army's involvement in the Holocaust, it is just as important to include the perspective of the victims. On the face of it, a history of the genocide based on the documents of the perpetrators may appear to be more reliable than one using accounts and memoirs by survivors; for while the former cites official documentation found in respectable archives, the latter employs "subjective" evidence that lacks any official sanction.[34] But such a history perforce creates a false picture of the event and thereby distorts our understanding. If we see the victims only through the killers' eyes, we become necessarily complicit in their dehumanization; not only do we learn very little about the victims' experience (which was of little concern to the perpetrators), we also gain only limited knowledge of the perpetrators' own conduct, since we must take their word for it rather than view it also from the perspective of those on the "receiving end." Indeed, it is precisely because the victims' perspective has generally been eschewed by German historians of the Holocaust, just as much as by historians of the Wehrmacht, that an array of misunderstandings and misperceptions has come into being. For as long as we view the soldiers' actions only through their own eyes, we are bound to perceive their victims merely as the products of the "process" we wish to explain rather than as protagonists of equal importance and relevance to the historical event we claim to be reconstructing.[35]

The Wehrmacht used an array of euphemisms to describe its victims.[36] This, of course, reveals a certain sense of embarrassment, or at least worry, on the part of superiors about their soldiers' reactions to the killing of innocent men, women and children. At the same time, however, it appears that soldiers accepted and employed these euphemisms as they went about their "work" of widespread killing. But one would like to know much more about actual encounters between soldiers and those they killed, and that makes it necessary to investigate the other side as well. Who were these so-called Bolsheviks and enemy agents, partisans and guerrillas, Asiatics and *Untermenschen*, Mongols and Jews? To be sure, it was easier to shoot women and children if one designated them as enemy agents, less disturbing to wipe out whole villages if one called them partisan nests, seemingly self-evident to murder commissars if one claimed they were Jews. Yet the historian may employ these same euphemisms only when constructing the soldiers' perspective, and even in that case one assumes that not all soldiers failed to see through them and recognize the humanity of their victims. When reconstructing the event as a whole, one must also include the victims' perspective; without doing so, historians cannot fully grasp the meaning and nature of that which they have set out to explain.

There is nothing remarkable, of course, about empathizing with more than one group of protagonists when writing on a given historical event.[37] And yet, especially when writing one's own national history, this is often a difficult exercise, which calls for both greater detachment and keener sensibilities, let alone more specialized knowledge of peoples and cultures with which one may initially be less familiar.[38] What is called for is not a sense of pity or compassion for victims about whose normal, previctimized existence one is largely ignorant, for both the existence and the disappearance of abstract beings can elicit very little historical understanding. Difficult as it may be, what is needed is to familiarize oneself with the victims as ordinary human beings, not as an exotic and now extinct species, who led lives not markedly dissimilar to one's own. And it is just as important (but also more common in recent German historiography) not merely to condemn the perpetrators for their actions, but also to uncover their pre-perpetrator existence and view them, once more, as people not fundamentally different from oneself. For the historian needs to recognize that only a fine line distinguishes between us and the perpetrators, and between us and the victims; it is precisely this fine line that needs to be identified and explained, rather than any abyss that makes for simple distinctions.

What has distinguished German scholarship on the Holocaust in general, and on the Wehrmacht in particular, is therefore its lack of interest in the victims. Conversely, German scholars of the Third Reich have concentrated on two major interpretive modes, both of which make for pronounced detachment between them and the victims. The first is the grand explanatory models of the Holocaust, and most especially the so-called functionalist school and its more recent revisions and rearticulations.[39] These are works that seek to identify a process whereby certain administrative and bureaucratic, as well as at times political and ideological mechanisms ultimately led to genocide. Reading such scholars as Hans Mommsen, Martin Broszat, Götz Aly and Ulrich Herbert, we rarely encounter victims; when victims are mentioned, they appear only as represented by the perpetrators, as threatening imaginary figures or as dry statistics, as administrative abstractions or as ideological constructs. They rarely make an appearance as normal, ordinary human beings. To be sure, one may argue that the victims are not necessary to explain the process that led to their destruction, but to my mind this contention must be rejected since the destruction cannot be explained without being represented, and it cannot be represented without the testimony of the victims. If we wish to understand the psychology of the perpetrators, we must see both what they saw and how they were seen in turn by their victims; not in separate bodies of literature on victims and perpetrators, but in the very same account of an event that contained both types at the same place and time. We must not allow the distinctions that made for genocide determine our historical reconstruction of it. For ultimately, people's self-perception is derived from the manner in which they and their environment interact with each other. We have no right to eliminate the gaze of the victim.

The other explanatory mode of German scholarship is almost the direct opposite of the first, namely that of *Alltagsgeschichte*, exemplified in such works as Martin Broszat's Bavaria project and an array of studies published in the 1970s and 1980s.[40] This mode is also related to biographical portraits and accounts, ranging from Joachim Fest's *Hitler* (and the subsequent film) and *The Face of the Third Reich* to Ulrich Herbert's intellectual biography of Werner Best.[41] Here we have attempts to understand individuals rather than systems, to see ideology in context rather than as an abstract entity, to unravel the complexities of human psychology rather than of doctrine and structure.[42] Yet all these works suffer from precisely the same absence of the victims. Complexity and ambiguity, identity and personality, are given only to the German perpetrators and bystanders, resisters and collaborators. The other side, those who were in fact either saved or killed due to those attitudes, receive very little attention and hardly any analysis.[43] This is a void noticed not only by outside observers, I believe, but also by the lay German public, and perhaps most of all by the younger generation. Hence, perhaps, one reason for the tremendous public attention given to both Victor Klemperer's recently published diary and, indeed, to Goldhagen's above-mentioned book.[44] For what distinguishes Klemperer's diary from the bulk of German scholarly works on the Holocaust and the Nazi period is that it is an *Alltagsgeschichte* written from the perspective of the victim, who was simultaneously an insider, a patriotic, conservative, well-educated and Christian German, who was declared a Jew by the regime and employed his great powers of observation to analyze the transformation of German society day by day during all twelve years of Hitler's rule. Through his eyes another kind of Germany is seen; that is, through his gaze we gain an understanding of the everyday life of the bystanders and perpetrators, victims and their helpers, that we could not have grasped merely by reference to the testimonies of "ordinary" Germans. And since Klemperer was concerned with understanding the gaze of German society at him, he offers us an unprecedented view of the complex relationship between victim and victimizer, which is always, by definition, reciprocal, since neither can exist without the other.[45]

Similarly, Goldhagen's book, though ostensibly an analysis of the perpetrators, is the only such study that demands and elicits direct and immediate empathy for the victims, by means of its rhetoric, through its obsession and fascination with horror and the resulting kitsch that fills its pages, and by dint of the author's voyeuristic fantasies of the victims' sufferings and the perpetrators' pleasure at causing and observing them.[46] In this sense, this book is related to the spate of quasi-pornographic films on the Holocaust made in the 1970s and 1980s, but it differs from them both by being a scholarly study and by its unrelenting accusatory tone which instills a certain sense of moral comfort in the reader not offered by those earlier cinematic works of fiction on Nazi depravity.[47] Hence, Goldhagen's detailed (and only partially documented) descriptions of the killings evoke in readers emotions and thoughts that the conventional historical literature fails to stimulate, including, for instance, Christopher Browning's earlier study of the very same perpetrators, not least because of the latter's conscious detachment and intentional separation between victims and perpetrators.[48]

This is also true regarding studies of the victims, which are always in danger of representing the perpetrators as not quite belonging to the human race and tend to portray them as evil shadows all cast in the same shape and form. By and large, however, this tendency is more present in survivors' memoirs than in recent scholarship on the victims and is of course part and parcel of more popular forms of representation, dependent as they are on stark polarities between good and evil.[49] Both in the case of memoirs and in that of popular representation, this is a way of coming to terms with disaster, since only by a sharp distinction between humanity and its murderers can one acquit both civilization and "Man" of the responsibility for murder and thereby continue to exist in the world as a member of the human race; but it is an exercise in self-delusion that leads away from understanding. The victim too can ultimately be understood only through the relationship with the perpetrator. This is an insight we owe to some of the most remarkable memoirs of survivors, but one that is sorely lacking in German scholarship on the Nazi period.[50]

Returning from this vantage point to the specific case of the Wehrmacht, we can conclude that in order to gain an understanding of the process whereby "ordinary" German soldiers came to practice genocide we must also know more about the interaction between them and their victims. This can and should be done also by German scholars writing today on the Wehrmacht. To be sure, there are now works in progress on the Holocaust by young German historians, but they seem still to be mainly about the bureaucracy and organization of genocide, not about the manner in which the victims experienced it.[51] There is a crucial difference between writing on the concentration camps' administration and on their inmates, between analyzing the system and trying to comprehend how it translated into reality for those subjected to it. German scholarship has been primarily engaged with the complexity of the emergence of genocide, on the one hand, and with the suffering (or normality) of German soldiers and civilians, on the other. It is time for it to engage no less with the complex mechanism that created widespread complicity in, and even greater indifference to, genocide in German society and the military, as well as with the very real, everyday suffering of the victims. In other words, detachment and empathy could and should be reversed, to the benefit of scholarly understanding of the past and scholarly cooperation in the present.[52]

Hypothetically it is not hard to imagine a work of scholarship written in Germany that would encompass both perspectives, that of victimizers and that of their victims, that would, so to speak, provide both ends of the process.[53] This would eliminate much of the talk about who is to feel more empathy for whom, or who should identify with which group. For the task of the historian is to achieve empathy with the protagonists of the event he or she is writing on; and in the case of genocide, just as in any other historical event, there are always (at least) two sides. True *Verstehen*, as I see it, can be achieved only by empathy with the other, not through mere pity or shame, guilt or rage, but through learning, study and an effort at understanding. This could be the first step toward reconciliation in the true sense of the word, based on seeing the world through the eyes of those whose humanity had been denied them even before they were turned into ashes.

NOTES

1 On formation chronicles and generals' memoirs, see Omer Bartov, *The Eastern Front, 1941–1945: German Troops and the Barbarisation of Warfare* (London, 1985), 1–4, and the literature cited therein. On German film in the 1950s, see Heide Fehrenbach, *Cinema in Democratizing Germany: Reconstructing National Identity after Hitler* (Chapel Hill, NC, 1995). For examples of German magazine covers between 1950 and 1962 relating to this theme, see *Mittelweg 36* 5, no. 1 (1996): 1–9. On the debate over German rearmament and its implications for the image of the Wehrmacht, see David Clay Large, *Germans to the Front: West German Rearmament in the Adenauer Era* (Chapel Hill, NC, 1996); Donald Abenheim, *Reforging the Iron Cross: The Search for Tradition in the West German Armed Forces* (Princeton, 1988).
2 Hermann Graml et al., *The German Resistance to Hitler* (London, 1970). See also

Peter Hoffmann, *The History of the German Resistance, 1933–1945* (Cambridge, MA, 1977); Joachim C. Fest, *Plotting Hitler's Death: The Story of the German Resistance* (New York, 1996); and Inge Scholl, *The White Rose: Munich, 1942–1943*, 2d ed. (Hanover, NH, 1983).

3 See, for example, B. H. Liddell Hart, *The Other Side of the Hill* (London, 1948); Desmond Young, *Rommell: The Desert Fox* (New York, 1950).

4 See, for example, James F. Tent, *Mission on the Rhine: Re-education and Denazification in American-Occupied Germany* (Chicago, 1982); C. Fitzgibbon, *Denazification* (London, 1969).

5 Large, *Germans to the Front*.

6 On the role of philo-Semitism in this process, see also Frank Stern, *The Whitewashing of the Yellow Badge: Antisemitism and Philosemitism in Postwar Germany* (Oxford, 1992).

7 Elazar Barkan is currently completing a book on the role of restitution in normalizing international relations and reducing the potential for conflict between governments and ethnic or cultural minorities. On the debate in Israel over the reparations agreement with Germany, see Tom Segev, *The Seventh Million: The Israelis and the Holocaust* (New York, 1993), 189–252.

8 See further in Omer Bartov, "The Missing Years: German Workers, German Soldiers," in David Crew, ed., *Nazism and German Society 1933–1945* (London, 1994), 41–66.

9 Gerhard Ritter, *The German Problem: Basic Questions of German Political Life, Past and Present* (1948; Columbus, 1965); Friedrich Meinecke, *The German Catastrophe: Reflections and Recollections*, 2d ed. (1946; Boston, 1963); Heinz Guderian, *Panzer Leader*, 3d ed. (1952; London, 1977); Erich von Manstein, *Verlorene Siege*, 2d ed. (Frankfurt/Main, 1964); B. H. Liddell Hart, *History of the Second World War, 1939–45* (London, 1947); Gordon A. Craig, *The Politics of the Prussian Army, 1640–1945*, 3d ed. (1955; London, 1978); John Wheeler-Bennett, *The Nemesis of Power: The German Army in Politics, 1918–1945*, 2d ed. (1953; London, 1980).

10 *Das Deutsche Reich und der Zweite Weltkrieg*, ed. Militärgeschichtliches Forschungsamt (Stuttgart, 1979–). Until now 6 volumes have been published out of at least 10, but more likely 12, planned.

11 Hans-Adolf Jacobsen, "Kommissarbefehl und Massenexekutionen sowjetische Kriegsgefangener," in Hans Buchheim et al., eds., *Anatomie des SS-Staates* (Olten, 1965). This essay is not included in the abridged paperback English translation, Helmut Krausnick and Martin Broszat, *Anatomy of the SS State* (London, 1970).

12 Manfred Messerschmidt, *Die Wehrmacht im NS-Staat: Zeit der Indoktrination* (Hamburg, 1969); Christian Streit, *Keine Kameraden: Die Wehrmacht und die sowjetischen Kriegsgefangenen, 1941–1945* (Stuttgart, 1978); see also Alfred Streim, *Die Behandlung sowjetischer Kriegsgefangener im "Fall Barbarossa." Ein Dokumentation* (Heidelberg, 1981); Helmut Krausnick and Hans-Heinrich Wilhelm, *Die Truppe des Weltanschauungskrieges: Die Einsatzgruppen der Sicherheitspolizei und des SD, 1938–1942* (Stuttgart, 1981).

13 Volker R. Berghahn, "NSDAP und 'Geistige Führung' der Wehrmacht," *Vierteljahrshefte für Zeitgeschichte* (hereafter *VfZ*) 17 (1969): 17–71; Klaus-Jürgen Müller, *Das Heer und Hitler: Armee und nationalsozialistisches Regime, 1933–1940* (Stuttgart, 1969).

14 Horst Boog et al., *Der Angriff auf die Sowjetunion* (Stuttgart, 1983), vol. 4 of *Das Deutsche Reich und der Zweite Weltkrieg*.

15 Alexander Dallin, *German Rule in Russia 1941–45: A Study of Occupation Policies* (London, 1957); Robert J. O'Neill, *The German Army and the Nazi Party 1933–39* (London, 1966).

16 See, for example, Martin Broszat and Elke Fröhlich, *Alltag und Widerstand: Bayern im Nationalsozialismus* (Munich, 1987). At the back of this volume is a list of all 32 studies published in 6 volumes in 1977–1983 in the series edited by Broszat, *Bayern in der NS-Zeit*. See also Klaus Bergmann and Rolf Schörcken, eds., *Geschichte im Alltag—Alltag in der Geschichte* (Düsseldorf, 1982); Harald Focke and Monika Strocka, *Alltag der Gleichgeschalteten: Wie die Nazis Kirche, Kultur, Justiz und Presse braun färbten* (Reinbeck bei Hamburg, 1985), vol. 3 of Rowohlt Verlag's series *Alltag unterm Hakenkreuz*; Ian Kershaw, *Popular Opinion and Political Dissent in the Third Reich: Bavaria 1933–1945* (Oxford, 1983), a much expanded version of an essay originally published in Broszat's above-mentioned series. More generally on *Alltagsgeschichte*, see Alf Lüdtke, ed., *The History of Everyday Life: Reconstructing Historical Experience and Ways of Life* (Princeton, 1965).

17 See, for example, William Sheridan Allan, *The Nazi Seizure of Power: The Experience of a Single German Town, 1930–1935* (New York, 1965); Rudy Koshar, " 'Two Nazisms': The Social Context of Nazi Mobilization in Marburg and Tübingen," *Social History* 7 (1982); Herbert Schwarzwälder, *Die Machtergreifung der NSDAP in Bremen 1933* (Bremen, 1966).

18 Apart from the literature cited above, see also the comments in Hans Mommsen, "Kriegserfahrungen," in Ulrich Borsdorf and Mathilde Jamin, eds., *Über Leben im Krieg: Kriegserfahrungen in eine Industrieregion, 1939–1945* (Reinbeck bei Hamburg, 1989), esp. 13.

19 Bartov, *Eastern Front*; idem, *Hitler's Army: Soldiers, Nazis, and War in the Third Reich* (New York, 1991); Theo Schulte, *The German Army and Nazi Policies in Occupied Russia* (Oxford, 1989); Stephen Fritz, *Frontsoldaten: The German Soldier in World War II* (Kentucky, 1995); Thomas Kühne, "Kameradschaft—'Das Beste im Leben des Mannes': Die deutsche Soldaten des II. Weltkrieges in erfahrungs- und geschlechtergeschichtlicher perspektive" (unpublished manuscript); idem, " '. . . aus diesem Krieg werden nicht nur harte Männer heimkehren': Kriegskameradschaft und Männlichkeit im 20. Jahrhundert," in idem, ed., *Männergeschichte—Geschlechtergeschichte: Männlichkeit im Wandel der Moderne* (Frankfurt/Main, 1996). More generally, recent important work in this genre includes Stéphane Audoin-Rouzeau, *Men at War, 1914–1918: National Sentiment and Trench Journalism in France during the First World War* (Providence, 1992); Leonard V. Smith, *Between Mutiny and Obedience: The Case of the French Fifth Infantry Division during World War I* (Princeton, 1994); Gerhard Hirschfeld et al., eds., *Keiner fühlt sich hier mehr als Mensch . . . Erlebnis und Wirkung des Ersten Weltkriegs* (Essen, 1993); Detlev Vogel and Wofram Wette, eds., *Andere Helme—Andere Menschen? Heimaterfahrung und Frontalltag im Zweiten Weltkrieg. Ein Internationaler Vergleich* (Essen, 1995).

20 Most of the important contributions to the debate are now available in *Forever in the Shadow of Hitler? Original Documents of the* Historikerstreit, *the Controversy Concerning the Singularity of the Holocaust*, ed. and trans. James Knowlton and Truett Cates (Atlantic Highlands, NJ, 1993).

21 Andreas Hillgruber, *Zweierlei Untergang: Die Zerschlagung des deutschen Reiches und das Ende des europäischen Judentums* (Berlin, 1986). See also Omer Bartov, "Historians on the Eastern Front: Andreas Hillgruber and Germany's Tragedy," in idem, *Murder in Our Midst: The Holocaust, Industrial Killing, and Representation* (New York, 1996), 71–88.

22 Richard Evans, *In Hitler's Shadow: West German Historians and the Attempt to Escape from the Nazi Past* (New York, 1989); Hans-Ulrich Wehler, *Entsorgung der deutschen Vergangenheit? Bin polemischer Essay zum "Historikerstreit"*

(Munich, 1988); Charles S. Maier, *The Unmasterable Past: History, Holocaust, and German National Identity* (Cambridge, MA, 1988).

23 For a report on the exhibition, relevant publications and media reactions to it in Germany, see Klaus Naumann, "Wenn ein Tabu bricht: Die Wehrmachts-Ausstellung in der Bundesrepublik"; and in Austria, Walter Manoschek, "Die Wehrmachtsausstellung in Österreich: Ein Bericht," both in *Mittelweg 36* 5, no. 1 (1996): 11–24 and 25–32, respectively. The essay collection is Hannes Heer and Klaus Naumann, eds., *Vernichtungskrieg: Verbrechen der Wehrmacht, 1941–1944* (Hamburg, 1995).

24 *Zeit-Punkte: Gerhorsam bis zum Mord? Der verschwiegene Krieg der deutschen Wehrmacht—Fakten, Analysen, Debatte* (Hamburg, nd.).

25 Hannes Heer, "Killing Fields: Die Wehrmacht und der Holocaust," in *Vernichtungskrieg*, 57–77.

26 Daniel Jonah Goldhagen, *Hitler's Willing Executioners: Ordinary Germans and the Holocaust* (New York, 1996). For a critique of the book, see Omer Bartov, "Ordinary Monsters," *New Republic*, 29 Apr. 1996, 32–38; Christopher R. Browning, "Daniel Goldhagen's Willing Executioners," *History & Memory* 8, no. 1 (Spring/Summer 1996): 88–108.

27 Many of the contributions to the debate have now been published in Julius Schoeps, ed., *Ein Volk von Mördern? Die Dokumentation zur Goldhagen-Kontroverse um die Rolle der Deutschen im Holocaust* (Hamburg, 1996).

28 Mommsen, "Kriegserfahrungen." Note, for example, the concluding remarks in the introduction to the chronicle of the 18th Panzer Division, whose involvement in the implementation of Nazi policies and the ideological indoctrination of its soldiers were documented in my book *The Eastern Front*. The author and former officer of that division writes: "None of those who did not return home wanted to go to that land [the USSR]; none of them wanted to occupy it. The records of the 18th Panzer Division . . . are free of any ideological propaganda on our side. They are records of soldiers." Wolfgang Paul, *Geschichte der 18. Panzer-Division, 1940–1943* (Freiburg, nd.), xx.

29 The debate over the Wehrmachtsausstellung has recently been revived following the arrival of the exhibition in Munich. See Theo Sommer, "Münchner Lektionen: Die Rolle der Wehrmacht läßt sich nicht beschönigen," *Die Zeit*, 28 Feb. 1997; Rudolf Augstein, "Anschlag auf die 'Ehre' des deutschen Soldaten?" *Der Spiegel*, no. 11 (1997); Alan Cowell, "The Past Erupts in Munich as War Guilt Is Put on Display," *New York Times*, 3 Mar. 1997. See further Ruth Beckermann's recent documentary film, *Jenseits des Krieges*, on the reception of the Wehrmacht exhibition in Vienna.

30 See, for example, Édouard Husson, "Le phénomène Goldhagen," and Philippe Burrin, "Il n'y a pas de peuple assassin!" both in *L'Histoire* 206 (Jan. 1997): 80–85.

31 David Hoffman, "U.S. Holocaust Museum Gets KGB Files," *Washington Post Foreign Service*, 29 Oct. 1996, A12; Michael Dobbs, "Decoded Cables Revise History of Holocaust: German Police Implicated; British Knew," *Washington Post*, 10 Nov. 1996, A1; Bronwen Maddox, "British Knew Jews Were Being Killed 'before Auschwitz'," *Times*, 11 Nov. 1996; Alan Cowel, "Files Suggest British Knew Early of Nazi Atrocities Against Jews," *New York Times*, 19 Nov. 1996, A1, A6; transcript (from WWW) of interview on the PBS television *Newshour with Jim Lehrer*, "What the Allies Knew: Charles Krause Speaks with Richard Breitman," 20 Nov. 1996.

32 Manfred Messerschmidt, "Einleitung," in *Ursachen und Voraussetzung der deutschen Kriegspolitik* (Stuttgart, 1979), vol. 1 of *Das Deutsche Reich und der Zweite Weltkrieg*, 15–22.

33 The best recent study on degrees of complicity with the regime, however, is by a Canadian historian: Robert Gellately, *The Gestapo and German Society: Enforcing Racial Policy, 1933–1945* (Oxford, 1990). See also Gisela Diewald-Kerkmann, *Politische Denunziation im NS-Regime oder Die kleine Macht der "Volksgenossen"* (Bonn, 1995).

34 This point was raised by Martin Broszat, "A Plea for the Historicization of National Socialism," in Peter Baldwin, ed., *Reworking the Past: Hitler, the Holocaust, and the Historians' Debate* (Boston, 1990), 77–87.

35 See further on this issue in Omer Bartov, "'. . . seit die Juden weg sind': Germany, History, and Representations of Absence," in Scott Denham et al., eds., *A User's Guide to German Cultural Studies* (Ann Arbor, 1997).

36 Bartov, *Eastern Front*, 119–29. See also C. Berning, *Vom "Abstammungsnachweis" zum "Zuchtwart": Vokabular des Nationalsozialismus* (Berlin, 1964); Victor Klemperer, *LTI: Notizbuch eines Philologen*, 3d ed. (Frankfurt/Main, 1985).

37 As is often the case, for instance, when writing on such events as the Thirty Years' War or the Great War. See Geoffrey Parker, *The Thirty Years' War* (London, 1984); Modris Eksteins, *The Rites of Spring: The Great War and the Birth of the Modern Age* (Boston, 1989).

38 One interesting case in point is the ongoing attempt by young Israeli scholars to rewrite their national history with the Palestinians in mind. See *Israeli Historiography Revisited*, special issue of *History & Memory* 7, no. 1 (Spring/Summer 1995); Benny Morris, *The Birth of the Palestinian Refugee Problem, 1947–1949* (Cambridge, 1987); Baruch Kimmerling and Joel S. Migdal, *Palestinians: The Making of a People* (Cambridge, MA, 1994). A balanced history of *that* conflict is Mark Tessler, *A History of the Israeli–Palestinian Conflict* (Bloomington, 1994).

39 The best summaries of the debates between the "functionalists" and the "intentionalists" are in Christopher R. Browning, *Fateful Months: Essays on the Emergence of the Final Solution* (New York, 1985), 8–38; idem, *The Path to Genocide: Essays on Launching the Final Solution* (Cambridge, 1992), 86–121. On new historiographical trends in reunified Germany, see Ian Kershaw, *The Nazi Dictatorship: Problems and Perspectives of Interpretation*, 3d ed. (London, 1993). Two of the most recent interpretations are Götz Aly, *"Endlosung": Völkerverschiebung und der Mord an den europäischen Juden* (Frankfurt/Main, 1995); Ulrich Herbert, "Den Gegner vernichten, ohne ihn zu hassen: Loathing the Jews in the World View of the Intellectual Leadership of the SS in the 1920s and 1930s" (unpublished paper, 1996); idem, "Knappe Formeln erklären den Mord an den Juden nicht: Über die aufklärerische Herausforderung der Geschichte des Holocausts," *Frankfurter Rundschau*, 25 Jan. 1997. Examples of the paradigmatic works of the older scholars include Hans Mommsen, "The Realization of the Unthinkable: The 'Final Solution of the Jewish Problem' in the Third Reich," in idem, *From Weimar to Auschwitz: Essays in German History* (Princeton, 1991), 224–53; Martin Broszat, "Hitler and the Genesis of the 'Final Solution': An Assessment of David Irving's Theses," *Yad Vashem Studies* 13 (1979): 61–98.

40 See n. 16 above.

41 Joachim C. Fest, *Hitler*, 3d ed. (Harmondsworth, 1982); idem, *The Face of the Third Reich* (Harmondsworth, 1979); Ulrich Herbert, *Best: Biographische Studien über Radikalismus, Weltanschauung und Vernunft, 1903–1989* (Bonn, 1996).

42 Earlier grand explanatory schemes include Hannah Arendt, *The Origins of Totalitarianism*, 6th ed. (1951; London, 1986), and Ernst Nolte, *Three Faces of Fascism: Action Française, Italian Fascism, National Socialism* (1963; New York, 1969), whereas the early functionalist approach in Martin Broszat, *The Hitler*

OMER BARTOV

State: The Foundation and Development of the Internal Structure of the Third Reich (1969; London, 1981), itself related to Franz Neumann's *Behemoth: The Structure and Practice of National Socialism* (London 1942), was opposed by Eberhard Jäckel, *Hitler's World View: A Blueprint for Power*, 2d ed. (1969; Cambridge, MA, 1981).

43 In recent decades some German studies of the everyday life of various Jewish communities were in fact written, but they have by and large not entered the mainstream of German scholarship on the Third Reich, not least because they were rarely perceived as scholarly works. See, for example, the Fischer-Verlag's *Jüdische Lebensbilder* series, now being issued in English by Northwestern University Press.

44 See, for example, Evelyn Roll, "Goldhagens Diskussionreise: Der schwierige Streit um die Deutschen und den Holocaust: Eine These und drei gebrochene Tabus," *Süddeutsche Zeitung*, 9 Sept. 1996; Volker Ullrich, "Daniel J. Goldhagen in Deutschland: Die Buchtournee wurde zum Triumphzug," *Die Zeit*, 13 Sept. 1996; Josef Joffe, "Goldhagen in Germany," *New York Review of Books*, 28 Nov. 1996, 18–21.

45 Victor Klemperer, *Ich will Zeugnis ablegen bis zum letzten* (Berlin, 1995).

46 See, for example, Goldhagen, *Hitler's Willing Executioners*, 218. For a more elaborate analysis of this issue, see Omer Bartov, "Kitsch and Sadism in Ka-Tzetnik's Other Planet: Israeli Youth Imagine the Holocaust," *Jewish Social Studies* (Spring 1997): 42–76.

47 See esp. Saul Friedländer, *Reflections of Nazism: An Essay on Kitsch and Death*, 2d ed. (Bloomington, 1993). See also Susan Sontag, "Fascinating Fascism," in idem, *Under the Sign of Saturn*, 7th ed. (New York, 1981), 73–105.

48 Christopher R. Browning, *Ordinary Men: Reserve Police Battalion 101 and the Final Solution in Poland* (New York, 1992). For two important critiques of Goldhagen's use of documents and manner of argumentation, see Ruth Bettina Birn, "Revising the Holocaust," *The Historical Journal* 40, no. 1 (1997): 195–215; and Dieter Pohl, "Die Holocaust Forschung und Goldhagens Thesen," *VfZ*, no. 1 (1997): 1–48. However, for a positive evaluation of Goldhagen's contribution to the German public debate on Nazism and the Holocaust, see Jürgen Habermas, "Geschichte ist ein Teil von uns: Warum ein 'Demokratiepreis' für Daniel J. Goldhagen? Eine Laudatio," *Die Zeit*, 14 Mar. 1997.

49 See further on this in Omer Bartov, "Spielberg's Oskar: Hollywood Tries Evil," in Yosefa Loshitzky, ed. *Spielberg's Holocaust: Critical Perspectives on Schindler's List* (Bloomington, 1997), 41–60.

50 The most important such memoirs, to my mind, are Primo Levi, *The Drowned and the Saved* (New York, 1988), esp. the chapter "The Gray Zone," 36–69; and Ka-Tzetnik, *Ha-Tzofen: Masa ha-Gar'in shel Auschwitz* (The code: The burden of the nucleus of Auschwitz) (1987; Tel Aviv, 1994) (in Hebrew); translated into English as *Shivitti: A Vision* (San Francisco, 1989).

51 I would like to thank Ulrich Herbert and Norbert Frei for this information.

52 The most instructive and often troubling discussion of this issue is Martin Broszat and Saul Friedländer, "A Controversy about the Historicization of National Socialism," in Baldwin, ed., *Reworking the Past*, 102–34.

53 One work by a Jewish historian that begins this process is Saul Friedländer, *Nazi Germany and the Jews*, vol. 1, *The Years of Persecution, 1933–1939* (New York, 1997).

8

"ONCE AGAIN I'VE GOT TO PLAY GENERAL TO THE JEWS"

From the war diary of Blutordensträger Felix Landau[1]

Ernst Klee, Willi Dressen and Volker Riess (eds)

In selecting an appropriate passage from diaries, letters, or testimonies of the perpetrators, one faces a dilemma not unlike that confronted by filmmakers. Claude Lanzmann, for instance, chose not to use any original footage from the Holocaust in making his film Shoah, *since that type of material would obviously be contaminated by the Nazi perception of their victims and their will to reduce them to the status of subhumans. Yet by avoiding such documentation altogether one also eschews any attempt to understand the psychology of the killers. This, in turn, leads to a dehumanization of the perpetrators which facilitates avoiding any sense of common human responsibility for their crimes; they become wholly alien and therefore relevant to us only in so far as they may pose a threat to our existence. If we do choose to use filmic or written material by the Nazis, however, the very familiarity with the manner in which they perceived the reality they created can lead viewers or readers to identify with the makers of these images and empathize with their viewpoint. Moreover, these distorted portrayals of the victims may contain the kind of sadistic, pornographic imagery that would turn their audience into voyeurs, thereby making them complicit in the obscenity of mass murder (which is of course their very purpose). We have been exposed to a multitude of dehumanizing, brutalizing images of the victims of Nazism, reprinted over and over again whenever the Holocaust is mentioned, until we think we know what it was like, we almost "remember" it, when in fact all we remember are photographs taken by the killers or scraps of Nazi speeches and propaganda leaflets. They teach us very little either about the killers or about their victims.*

It is for this reason that I did not choose one of numerous horrifying accounts of the killing process. Reading such accounts arouses in us empathy neither for those doing the killing nor for the dying; we are too close to the atrocity to feel anything but horror, perhaps shame, possibly curiosity, but hardly any sense of the humanity of either side. Rather, I chose a far less directly horrifying account, yet one whose ultimate effect appears to me to be far more chilling and more conducive to some understanding of the mind of the perpetrators. For what we see here is the humanity, potential for true affection for another human being, curiosity about different peoples and cultures, devotion to work and duty, capacity for hard work and pleasure at a job well done, along with a deep ideological conviction and powerful prejudices, of a man who is a cog in the mass murder of the Jews. This man is no monster, and his capacity for indifference and compassion is probably not much different from any other average person's. Yet he is one of hundreds of thousands of little people who made the machinery of genocide tick. Had we erased the lines in his diary that mention the brutalization of the Jews, it would not have been very hard to identify with him. What makes his diary so revealing, and so terrifying, is that there is no gradual transition from one to another. It is the very same man who is both just like us, and a mass murderer.

* * *

On 25 July 1934 members of the 89th SS-Standarte forced their way into the Bundeskanzleramt (the Austrian Chancellor's Office) in Vienna. Although they fatally injured the Chancellor, Engelbert Dollfuss, the coup failed.

One of those arrested was cabinetmaker Felix Landau, who held up the staff of the Chancellor's office at gun point with a sub-machine-gun [see 'Appendix: biographical details' for a detailed biography]. Landau was sent to Wöllersdorf detention camp charged with being an accomplice in the crime. He was released in 1937. He became a naturalized German citizen and obtained a post as a Kriminalassistent. When on 12 March 1938 the German troops marched into Austria he was an SS-Hauptscharführer in a Security Police and SD Einsatzkommando.

Landau was then employed at the Gestapo regional headquarters in Vienna with the responsibility for 'securing' Jewish property. He married and moved into a villa that belonged to a Jew who had fled. In April 1940 he was assigned to KdS (Commander of the Security Police and the SD) in Radom (Polish General-Gouvernement). He was first sent to participate in the fight against scattered Polish units. Afterwards he worked in the records office. On 31 August 1940 his role in the attempted coup in Vienna and his time spent in imprisonment in Austria were recognized and he was awarded the Blutorden of the NSDAP.

At the office in Radom he met a twenty-year-old shorthand typist, Gertrude, who was engaged to a soldier from Vienna but wanted to break off the engagement. Landau learnt that Gertrude – despite her promise to him – was still seeing her fiancé. He thus resolved to break off the relationship. On 30 June 1941, just at the start of the Russian campaign, he reported to an Einsatzkommando (EK). At this point the diary begins.

Lemberg, 3 July 1941

On Monday, 30 June 1941, after a sleepless night I volunteered for a number of reasons to join an EK. By 9 o'clock I had heard that I had been accepted. It was not easy for me to leave. Suddenly everything had changed in me. I almost thought that I would not be able to tear myself from a certain person. I felt acutely how attached one can become to another human being.

As usual our departure was delayed several times but at 17.00 hours we finally left. We stopped one more time and once again I saw the person who has become so dear to me. Then we set off again. At 22.30 we finally reached Cracow. The accommodation was good. No creature comforts whatsoever. You can actually become a soldier in just a few hours if you want to. We then passed through Przemyśl. The town was still burning, on the street we saw shot-up German and Russian tanks. It was the first time I had seen two-tier Russian tanks.

After a short time we set off again towards Millnicze. It was becoming increasingly clear that the troops had recently been through. . . . At 21.30 on 1 July 1941 we arrived in M. We stood around aimlessly without any plan.

We quartered ourselves in a Russian military school. It was still burning here too. At 23.00 hours we finally went to bed. I set up my bed and kipped down. Naturally I inquired whether it was possible to send letters but unfortunately it wasn't. On 2 July 1941 we were woken at 6.00 as at the front. There were women and children standing by burning houses and rummaging around in the rubble. During the journey we came across more Ukrainian soldiers. As we got closer and closer to the Russians the smell of decaying corpses got stronger and stronger.

At 4.00 pm on 2 July 1941 we arrived in Lemberg. First impression: Warsaw harmless in comparison. Shortly after our arrival the first Jews were shot by us. As usual a few of the new officers became megalomaniacs, they really enter into the role wholeheartedly. We took over another military school in the Bolshevik quarter. Here the Russians must have been caught in their sleep.

We quickly gathered together the bare essentials. At midnight after the Jews had cleaned the building, we went to bed.

3 July 1941. This morning I found out that we can write and it looks as though the post will actually be dispatched.

So while listening to wildly sensual music I wrote my first letter to my Trude. While I was writing the letter we were ordered to get ready. EK with steel helmets, carbines, thirty rounds of ammunition. We have just come back. Five hundred Jews were lined up ready to be shot. Beforehand we paid our respects to the murdered German airmen and Ukrainians. Eight hundred people were murdered here in Lemberg. The scum did not even draw the line at children. In the children's home they were nailed to the walls. Some of the occupants of a prison nailed to the wall.

Today a rumour went round that we are going to return to Radom. In all honesty I would be happy to see my loved ones again. They mean more to me than I was ever prepared to admit to myself. So far there hasn't been an execution. Today we were on alert all day. It should be happening tonight.

Things are pretty tense. In this confusion I have only written notes. I have little inclination to shoot defenceless people – even if they are only Jews. I would far rather good honest open combat. Now good night, my dear Hasi [bunny].

5 July 1941

It's 11.00 am. Wonderful music, 'Do You Hear My Secret Call' ('Hörst Du mein heimliches Rufen'). How weak can a heart become! My thoughts are so much with the person who caused me to come here. What I wouldn't give to see her even for just ten minutes. I was up all of last night on guard duty, in other words kept watch.

A small incident demonstrated to me the complete fanaticism of these people. One of the Poles tried to put up some resistance. He tried to snatch the carbine out of the hands of one of the men but did not succeed. A few seconds later there was a crack of gunfire and it was all over. A few minutes later after a short interrogation a second one was finished off. I was just taking over the watch when a Kommando reported that just a few streets away from us a guard from the Wehrmacht had been discovered shot dead.

One hour later, at 5 in the morning, a further thirty-two Poles, members of the intelligentsia and Resistance, were shot about two hundred metres from our quarters after they had dug their own grave. One of them simply would not die. The first layer of sand had already been thrown on the first group when a hand emerged from out of the sand, waved and pointed to a place, presumably his heart. A couple more shots rang out, then someone shouted – in fact the Pole himself— 'Shoot faster!' What is a human being?

It looks like we'll be getting our first warm meal today. We've all been given 10 RM so that we can buy ourselves a few small necessities. I bought myself a whip costing 2 RM. The stench of corpses is all-pervasive when you pass the burnt-out houses. We pass the time by sleeping.

During the afternoon some three hundred more Jews and Poles were finished off. In the evening we went into town just for an hour. There we saw things that are almost impossible to describe. We drove past a prison. You could already tell from a few streets away that a lot of killing had taken place here. We wanted to go in and visit it but did not have any gas masks with us so it was impossible to enter the rooms in the cellar or the cells. Then we set off back to our quarters. At a street corner we saw some Jews covered in sand from head to foot. We looked at one another. We were all thinking the same thing. These Jews must have crawled out of the grave where the executed are buried. We stopped a Jew who was unsteady on his feet. We were wrong. The Ukrainians had taken some Jews up to the former GPU citadel. These Jews had apparently helped the GPU persecute the Ukrainians and the Germans. They had rounded up 800 Jews there, who were also supposed to be shot by us tomorrow. They had now released them.

We continued going along the road. There were hundreds of Jews walking along the street with blood pouring down their faces, holes in their heads, their hands broken and their eyes hanging out of their sockets. They were covered in blood. Some of them were carrying others who had collapsed. We went to the citadel; there we saw things that few people have ever seen. At the entrance of the citadel there were soldiers standing guard. They were holding clubs as thick as a man's wrist and were lashing out and hitting anyone who crossed their path. The Jews were pouring out of the entrance. There were rows of Jews lying one on top of the other like pigs whimpering horribly. The Jews kept streaming out of the citadel completely covered in blood. We stopped and tried to see who was in charge of the

Kommando. 'Nobody.' Someone had let the Jews go. They were just being hit out of rage and hatred.

Nothing against that – only they should not let the Jews walk about in such a state. Finally we learned from the soldiers standing there that they had just visited some comrades of theirs, airmen in fact, in hospital here in Lemberg who had been brutally injured. They'd had their fingernails torn out, ears cut off and also their eyes gouged out. This explained their actions: perfectly understandable.

Our work is over for today. Camaraderie is still good for the time being. Crazy, beautiful, sensuous music playing on the radio again and my longing for you, the person who has hurt me so much, is growing and growing. Our only hope is to get away from here – most would prefer to be back in Radom. I for one – like many of the other men – have been disillusioned with this Einsatz. Too little combat in my view, hence this lousy atmosphere.

Lemberg, 6 July 1941

I had a terrible night last night. How true to life and intense a dream can be! The whole Warsaw affair, the reason why I am here, passed before my eyes so clearly there was nothing more I could wish for.

Once again I am psychologically shattered, just as I was then. I feel as if I won't be able to do it – to see beyond it and forget what I have gone through. If I don't meet T. again very soon I will go and do what I planned to do. No one will stop me. My mood is ghastly. I must get to Radom come what may.

Today I managed to send another letter to my Trude. It wasn't a very lovely letter, it expressed my despair to the full. I couldn't help it. I am now more hopeful that we will see each other again. This afternoon we learned that the Kommando will be going to Radom on Monday, 8 July 1941, after it has been to Drohobycz, an industrial town. We all breathed a sigh of relief. If we'd had to go on indefinitely it would have become impossible for us to continue working together. Four lorries have been taken from our EK. We have found some new telephones and gas masks of Russian origin which we took with us.

Things should start moving at our new post, thank God. Today I am reporting for a dangerous special mission [Sonderaufträge]. If we do have to stay there I will arrange things so that Trude can come.

The reveillé came at 8 o'clock. We sleep a long time so that the days are shorter. Once again work to do. Today I went into town for the nth time to look for a stationery shop. I actually managed to find one. Stationery shops have become my great passion. Naturally I rummaged through everything there and even found something usable. Writing paper, as we know it at home, does not exist here. But I finally have envelopes and now don't have to go round scrounging anymore. I also bought myself a lovely big travelling-bag for 32 roubles/3.80 RM.

So we are finally moving on to Drohobycz tomorrow morning at 8.00. We've been told that the area is partly occupied by the Russians. I am glad we are finally moving on a little. Tomorrow there's another post going to Cracow and Lublin from where it will be forwarded. I can write a quick letter to my little Trude. My feelings for all other women have been dead for a long time. I don't actually know myself how it happened.

This morning there was a special announcement that a further 52,000 Russians had capitulated. I should think there'll be a revolution in Russia in under two weeks. By then Moscow will certainly have fallen. Tonight we are having a social evening with our 'Kameraden' from Cracow.

Drohobycz, 7 July 1941

The social evening ended at 6.30 in the morning. There were no incidents. I picked up my two companions at about half past midnight and then we went together to our room to spend the rest of the night there. Our luggage has grown visibly. Oberführer Schönrad is the head of the EK. Sturmbannführer Röck works at the command post. We should have set off at 8.00. We finally left at 10.00 after a lot of quarrelling.

The people of Cracow are almost without exception complete arse-lickers. We had to go back along quite a stretch of the way we had come. We could already smell the prison where hundreds of people were murdered several streets away. There were hundreds of people standing in front of the shops trying to get hold of food of some kind. On our way two Jews were stopped. They said that they had fled from the Russian army. Their story was fairly unbelievable. Six of our men got out, loaded up and the next minute both were dead. When the order to take aim was given, one of the Jews, an engineer, was still shouting, 'Long live Germany.' Strange, I thought. What on earth had this Jew been hoping for?

At 16.00 we reached our destination. We were divided into several teams, in order to look for quarters for all the men. We found three houses which had been barely lived in. Baths everywhere, former Communist Party functionaries' homes. We were also able to establish that the Ukrainians had done a pretty good job plundering. They had really thought they were the masters for a while. There's going to be an almighty clash here – it's inevitable. Another interesting discovery: although there are very few radio sets here, almost every flat has its own speaker. The speakers can be switched on and off and have an adjustable volume so that means there won't be any need to forbid the men to listen to foreign broadcasts. In this case it won't be necessary.

I have a strong feeling that we will not be going back to Radom. My little Trudchen will thus have to come out here instead. We have occupied a Jewish hotel for a few days. I was ravenously hungry, so I have just 'inspected' the kitchen and managed to find a little something to eat. The quarters are very basic. The place is teeming with bugs. Now I must close because I have to report for guard duty. I'll be relieved at 1.00 tomorrow. My darling Trudchen, good night.

8 July 1941

Today more crazy toing and froing. The Ortskommandant has said that we should not have been here in the first place, since there's no work for us. Marvellous! In the afternoon our Hauptsturmführer went to the General-kommando to clarify the situation. The explanation: a misunderstanding on the part of the Ortskommandant. Everything now in order. My explanation: no communication and no cooperation with the Wehrmacht. No further comment necessary.

Around midday we moved into new quarters, a former Communist Party military school. I am to work in the financial running of the place and with the horses. In the stable I discovered three small ponies. Actually a whole family: a male, a female and a foal. A small pony cart and also a saddle, and complete harness. People are strange. When I reported for guard duty there were three ugly dirty women, former chambermaids, standing in the lobby gawping at me. An interpreter came up to us and talked to them. One of these women was asking whether I wanted to go to bed with her. These goddamned people are unbelievable. Of course that had the others clamouring round all the more. I thought she'd end up in bed with someone but she didn't, thank God. Otherwise all hell would have been let loose during room inspection.

In the evening we had another comrades' get-together. During supper a couple of the men wanted to take me to the flat with some women – waitresses from the hotel. I refused point blank. They were both very disappointed. I don't want to and can't. My Trude is far too much on my mind. At the social evening I just could not get her out of my thoughts. I am so worried about her. Who knows whether she is still thinking of me. Still not a word from her and I don't even know if she's been receiving my letters.

9 July 1941

Today there were more surprises. In the morning a letter arrived from the Ortskommandantur. In an unfriendly tone we were informed that our work is to be limited merely to checking papers. In addition the letter declared that we were to ask nothing of the Referent for Jewish Affairs. As predicted, an impossible relationship. There was a tremendous amount of work. Once again I have got to play general to the Jews. Today I organized a carriage and harness despite the ban. Today there was beer from the barrel, we could also buy a bottle of Sekt for 1 RM. If only I had post from my Trude. During the day when I am buried in work it is all right but during the night the loneliness and inactivity simply make me despair. Good night Trudchen. Think a little of your Lexi.

10 July 1941

I left the social evening at 2 o'clock in the morning. I poured as much drink down me as I could to lighten my spirits and forget for a short while. Unfortunately to no avail. Ten litres of beer and a few schnapps as well as a litre of red wine still did not have the desired effect. The next day I felt as if I had been hit around the head with a sledgehammer. Today I was called to attend the allocation of assignments. I was working with a colleague from the SD [name illegible – Ed.] Department II Economics, in addition I was officially assigned as 'Judengeneral' ('General to the Jews'). I requisitioned two military vehicles for the department. Others have already done so for their own use. I have no time for that. The only thing I wanted was a decent apartment. The arguments with the Wehrmacht continue. The Major in charge must be the worst kind of state enemy. I remarked today that I would apply to Berlin for this M. to be put into preventive detention immediately; his actions are a danger to the state. Take his remark that the Jews fall under the protection of the German Wehrmacht. Who could have thought such a thing possible? That's no National Socialist.

14 July 1941[2]

I haven't managed to get round to writing any more in my diary till today. A great many things have happened. New experiences and new impressions.

On 11 July 1941 a vehicle finally left for Radom carrying Dolte, Binder, Gürth and Mireck. Regrettably I could not go with them. At least I was able to give them a letter which I can be sure will arrive. I also have the prospect of hearing from my little Trude to look forward to. Unfortunately I'll be getting other letters as well. Of course, as was to have been expected, our KK [Kriminalkommissar – Ed.] . . . immediately took advantage of Dolte's absence to quench his thirst for action. Barely an hour later his wonderful orders such as 'Get a move on, gentlemen, get that whole pile over here to me' and the like were ringing out. He had arrests and shootings to his heart's desire. The prisoners, mostly Jews but also some Ukrainians, keep on coming. . . . We 'work' right through the night. In the evening a comrade, Urban, and I managed to snatch some time to go and see a cook from whom we can get *Mischlanka*, sour milk and new potatoes. Although the rooms are very small, everything is clean and pleasant. The people were friendly and obliging. There was also a very pretty young Ukrainian girl there. Communication – try as she might – was impossible. The only thing I managed to gather was that she was very interested in me. But my thoughts as ever are still with my Trude. I am not tempted nor do I want to be.

At 11 in the evening we got back to base. A flurry of activity down in the cellar, which I had just cleared up that morning. There were fifty prisoners, two of whom were women. I immediately volunteered to relieve the person who was on guard duty. Almost all of them will be shot tomorrow. Most of the Jews amongst them were from Vienna. Still dreaming of Vienna. I was on duty until three in the morning the next day. Finally went to bed dog tired at 3.30.

12 July 1941

At 6.00 in the morning I was suddenly awoken from a deep sleep. Report for an execution. Fine, so I'll just play executioner and then grave-digger, why not? Isn't it strange, you love battle and then have to shoot defenceless people. Twenty-three had to be shot, amongst them the two above-mentioned women. They are unbelievable. They even refused to accept a glass of water from us. I was detailed as marksman and had to shoot any runaways. We drove one kilometre along the road out of town and then turned right into a wood. There were only six of us at that point and we had to find a suitable spot to shoot and bury them. After a few minutes we found a place. The death candidates assembled with shovels to dig their own graves. Two of them were weeping. The others certainly have incredible courage. What on earth is running through their minds during those moments? I think that each of them harbours a small hope that somehow he won't be shot. The death candidates are organized into three shifts as there are not many shovels. Strange, *I am completely unmoved. No pity, nothing.* That's the way it is and then it's all over. My heart beats just a little faster when involuntarily I recall the feelings and thoughts I had when I was in a similar situation. On 24 July 1934 in the Bundeskanzleramt [Chancellery] when I was confronted with the machine-gun barrels of the Heimwehr [Austrian militia, 1919–38]. Then there were moments when I came close to weakening. I would not have allowed it to show, no, that would have been out of the question with my character. 'So young and now it's all over.' Those were my thoughts, then I pushed these feelings aside and in their place came a sense of defiance and the realization that my death would not have been in vain.

And here I am today, a survivor standing in front of others in order to shoot them. Slowly the hole gets bigger and bigger; two of them are crying continuously. I keep them digging longer and longer; they don't think so much when they're digging. While they're working they are in fact calmer. Valuables, watches and money, are put into a pile. When all of them have been brought to stand next to one another on a stretch of open ground, the two women are lined up at one end of the grave ready to be shot first. Two men had already been shot in the bushes by our KK [Kriminalkommissar] . . . I did not see this as I had to keep my eyes on the others. As the women walked to the grave they were completely composed. They turned round. Six of us had to shoot them. The job was assigned thus: three at the heart, three at the head. I took the heart. The shots were fired and the brains whizzed through the air. Two in the head is too much. They almost tear it off. Almost all of them fell to the ground without a sound. Only with two

194

of them it didn't work. They screamed and whimpered for a long time. Revolvers were no use. The two of us who were shooting together had no failures. The penultimate group had to throw those who had already been shot into the mass grave then line up and fall in themselves. *The last two had to place themselves at the front edge of the grave so that they would fall in at just the right spot.* Then a few bodies were rearranged with a pickaxe and after that then we began the gravedigging work.

I came back dog tired but the work went on. Everything in the building had to be straightened up. And so it went on without respite. In the afternoon the car came back from Radom unexpectedly. Like a small child I couldn't wait to get my post. That was my first question. Unfortunately I didn't get a chance to read all my post, there was so much; no sooner had I begun than the Hauptsturmführer came up to me and asked me to get started on the move to the new offices and set things up there as well.

So I worked until 11 o'clock and had to make myself a plan like a proper little architect. Everyone admired my work.

On Sunday, 13 July 1941, the work started again straight away. I hardly got any sleep. My feet and my head hurt as though I had just been on two pack marches. We also learned that Communists had taken control in the mountainous area behind us. Yet more work. Finally I managed to read all my post. It's strange, my mood completely changed. A lot of what I read gave me great cause for worry. Apart from anything else Trude wrote that she doesn't know whether she can keep her promise and whether she will be strong enough. Why does this have to happen to me with a person I love so much? I have to see her and talk to her, then my little Trude will be strong again. She must come here.

14 July 1941

Attended various meetings. Council of the Jews. Otherwise mostly organized and moved. In the evening found a sheepdog bitch.

20 July 1941

Today is Sunday. Once again I worked until 8 o'clock. It is now 10.00 and I have finally managed to find the time to record in my diary the few events which, in the larger context of what is happening in the world, are so insignificant.

[On] 15 July 1941 I went together with a comrade to the aforementioned Ukrainian family. It was very cosy and also very interesting for someone who is interested in the ways of another people. We talked over just about everything. The only subject I thought it better not to touch upon was religion, as it would be easy for misunderstandings to arise when communication was somewhat limited. We were still talking at 11.00. On the way there – we had gone there in our pony and trap – something very funny happened to us. First we were caught in a downpour, although that did not last long. Then when we turned into a real Russian track we were confronted by potholes over a metre deep. Naturally we were jolted out of our seats on quite a number of occasions. Then we got to a particularly fine spot and my cart bounced backwards slightly while the pony kept on going. All of a sudden I heard a splash and when I turned round I saw my comrade in a pretty deep puddle, with his legs sticking up in the air. Despite the unpleasantness of the situation I couldn't help roaring with laughter. The trip back looked like becoming even more tragic; had the farmer not taken us to the main road we would have certainly ended up, pony, trap and all, in a ditch.

Because of this delightful track we didn't get back until midnight. As we rode through the gate a car was just starting up. Soon I realized that things were pretty lively for this time of night. My first thought was that something was up. Obviously people were worried on our account and thought that something had happened to us. . . . The next morning we were informed that all social intercourse with the Ukrainians was forbidden. He, that is the Hauptsturmführer, had no objections if any of us spent the odd night with an *U-Mädel* [Ukrainian girl] but all other contact was forbidden. Odd attitude. Well as far as I am concerned that is out of the question, since all I wanted was to get to know the people. My small young dog is coming along fine. As each day passes she is becoming more and more devoted but she's still as nervous as ever.

On 16 July 1941 more moving again. My role here is more one of architect than of official. I am now, in addition, responsible for overseeing and conducting the training of 150 Ukrainians. I'm quite happy to play at being master builder and architect, the only thing I wish is that I had workmen and not Jews to carry out the work. Still, that's the way it has to be.

On 17 July 1941 nothing much happened. I messed around with the Jews some more – and that's my work.

18 July 1941. The question of the day is who will travel to Radom. All of a sudden everybody has got to go there. They've all left things they can't do without there. Nobody has a suitcase, nobody has clean laundry. Usually in the military, failure to carry out orders is punished harshly; here, however, it's rewarded with a Sunday excursion to Radom. At midday there was a meeting and yes, as expected, once again I was not amongst those who were to go. I was bursting with rage. Here I am slaving away day and night so that everyone has a nice apartment and is assured every comfort, and then when I make the smallest request others are given preferential treatment.

19 July 1941. The entire day I could not get the thought out of my head that at that very moment I could have been with Trudchen in R. Try as I might to push these thoughts to one side I still imagine my little Trudl there waiting and hoping to see me. What use is my fine apartment fitted out with every comfort if that very thing is missing? Everything is dead in my flat.

19 July 1941. So I was not able to travel to Radom. The way I feel I could kill everyone. I of all people was not permitted to go. I am not very optimistic about my chances next time. Spent the whole day working solidly. How disappointed my little Trude will be when instead of me only a letter arrives. In the evening we had another visit, only a day after the Oberführer arrived without any prior warning. He was very pleased with the rooms and the buildings. As usual others took all the credit. That's the way it will always be given human nature. In the evening as I was lying in bed I was filled with a tremendous yearning, yearning for quiet, peace and love.

21 July 1941

After waiting in vain yesterday for the men to return from Radom, all I could do again today was wait. Every five minutes I asked whether the vehicles had returned from Radom. Again and again my question was in vain. Finally towards midday the car arrived. By that time I no longer needed to ask for they all shouted to me in unison, 'Felix there's a packet for you.' I breathed a sigh of relief. When I read the letter I locked myself in my room. It was short and sketchy. I began to worry and think dark thoughts. Could Trude have been unfaithful after such a short time? I am uneasy. What I would give for Trudchen to be with me. Well, this is how I wanted it, only I thought it would turn out differently. Oh well, ordinary life is far too tame for me. I don't understand Trudchen. She sent me the pictures of my children and my wife. I could understand why she'd send the former, but the latter is beyond me. The men had the day off today, some of them went hunting. I had to work here. Thanks and praise is sure to come my way. The above-mentioned Sturmbannführer went off hunting once again with his five men. The work is going ahead well. I have just been informed by the Hauptsturmführer that I am to take over the training of the militia. Apparently I have the right attitude. Today I answered my wife's letters and sent her 180 RM. Trudchen got a short letter from me.

Another eventful day. In the morning the workers I had ordered failed to appear. Just as I was about to go to the Jewish Committee one of my colleagues from the council came and asked me for my support as the Jews were refusing to work here. I went over. When those arseholes saw me they ran in all directions. Pity I did not have a pistol on me or else I would have shot some of them down. I then went to the Council of Jews and informed them that if 100 Jews did not report for work within an hour I would select 100 of them *not for work but for the firing-squad*. Barely half an hour later 100 Jews arrived together with a further seventeen for those who had run away. I reported the incident and at the same time gave orders for the fugitives to be shot for refusing to work, *which happened precisely twelve hours later. Twenty Jews were finished off*.

Another incident. I sent one of the men off with two Jews to get hold of some material we needed. He took the keys from the usual place and went off. While we were clearing up one of the Ukrainians started pestering the Jews, who were carrying out our orders, naturally with the full agreement of the Germans. Amongst other things he asked the Jews who they thought they were, letting on to the Germans what was in the storeroom. He said he would come and find them in the evening and beat them to death. Well, that really got my blood up. Such people in my opinion are the real enemies of the state, so I had the lad brought in. In my room he received by way of introduction a little bit of my special treatment. After the first beating, blood was spurting. First he tried to deny he had done anything. After the fourth beating however he gave up this tactic. I gave orders for him to be arrested for having an anti-German attitude.

In a village near Drohobycz four released convicts were shot on the spot. This time the Slovaks dug the graves and did the burying.

I am very curious to know how the Council of Jews will take it. They'll all be wailing and gnashing their teeth tomorrow. We also found that No. 13 barracks had been broken into again, and an attempt had been made to steal the rubber tyres from our vehicles. One of the tyres had been sliced right through with a sharp knife. So in the evening I made yet another arrest.

Tomorrow I am going to make a concerted effort to ask about my Trudchen coming here. As a final resort, if I get a refusal I am going to ask for a transfer or obtain one somehow. At the same time I'm also going to sort out the Radom trip. Then tomorrow I'll write a long letter to Trudchen. Good night my dear little rascal, please still love me, think of me and stay true to me. Now I am going to bed, to look at your picture and read your book. When my eyes begin to get tired I shall put the book aside and look at your picture again, give you a big kiss, switch off the light and go to sleep.

23 July 1941

Well, I was not able to put yesterday's plans into action. The reason is simply the unbelievable amount of work. I sometimes wonder how much more I can take of this. At 8 o'clock this morning I should have detailed the Jews for various tasks and drilled the Ukrainian militia at the same time as well. In the afternoon I was given a lot more jobs but I am determined to write the letter to Trudchen. I must see her, speak to her come what may. Today I found quite a few Communist Party banners and weapons. Work is progressing quickly on all the buildings. The new militiamen certainly seem to be finding it difficult to adjust to my tempo and tone. Today ten out of forty men failed to report.

Our chief once again threatened some of the comrades with execution and again for no reason whatsoever. He said to Urban, 'If you don't change your tone with me you will be included in the next execution.' There have already been complaints about him. He has been nicknamed 'Revolver-kommissar' and 'Sonnensoldat' ('Sunshine Soldier'). He is the only one who goes about with a white battle tunic and long trousers. It's now already 23.00 but I must write the letter without fail.

28 July 1941

All of my good intentions – come what may – to write my diary every evening have come to naught. It's midnight and I have finally got round to writing a few lines. I was quite amazed when I discovered on Saturday morning what day it was. I had intended to approach Dolte again on Friday about going to Radom. I was devastated and spent the rest of the day in a frightful frame of mind. I worked until 11 at night. What else can I do? Some of the other men went out at midday and returned towards 7.00 in the evening with some Ukrainian girls whom they took up to their quarters. I was still clearing the place and having carpets laid. On Sunday I worked until 3.00 and then for the first time since my Einsatz I am having a break.

On Friday and Saturday there was an interesting development on the work front. Some Ukrainians brought a report from a neighbouring village which went more or less as follows: Someone had discovered the bodies of twenty-four Ukrainians who had been murdered by the Russians in the woods. The bodies were almost unrecognizable. As this was a murder case the criminal police took it up immediately and went to the place in question. There they were solemnly received by a cleric who told them how pleased he was to see them. The cleric said that it was extremely kind of the Germans to take such an interest in the murder and fate of the Ukrainians. The bodies were solemnly buried and our officials had no choice but to take part. On the way the cleric said to me, 'Do you know, the vilest thing about it is that Jewish passes and papers were put in their pockets.' Now this is unbelievable! These supposed Ukrainians were in fact the very twenty-three Jews plus, I think, two Ukrainians we ourselves had shot! Cheers, bon appetit. The papers on the bodies stank terribly. I had petroleum poured over them, then ordered them to be burnt and buried in the grave. . . .

30 July 1941

I had a wonderful surprise. Post from Trude. I had been waiting for so long! Her post arrived just as I was writing a letter. My mood shot up 100%. What a funny girl my Trude is. In her letter she wrote a philosophical treatise about my love life and marriage, utterly serious as though her life depended on it. Full of intellectual utterances like a wise and experienced woman. There was not a thought or a word about herself. She had excluded herself entirely from the letter. Sometimes there is a slight sense that she wants to convince me of something so that she can be rid of me more easily. But then when I read the letters from the day before and the day after I cannot help smiling at these thoughts, for out of these lines emerges a hot and passionate love, like the one I feel for her. Sometimes I begin to feel afraid, as though in a dream. She has no idea what she has come to mean to me. Also she

does not realize what has happened inside me recently. If she, who has come to mean so much to me, disappointed me I would be completely devastated. I think that I would lose my belief in humanity right up to the day I died. Yesterday evening, despite the ridiculous amount of work,
I wrote Trudchen another six-page letter. Today I was summoned in confidence to D. who informed me that the GG [General-Gouverneur] will be coming on Saturday. So no trip once again. I am not giving up hope. I sent Trudchen a letter and a small miniature – a baroque love scene.

Today, 31 July 1941, there was a crazy amount of work again. The letter left today with the vehicle for Radom.

1 August 1941

Yesterday I managed to have my much requested conversation with Dolte. This time I refused to let myself be fobbed off. At 8.00 in the evening I went to Dolte's apartment, which is above mine, and asked him whether he had time to see me. He did and asked me to come in and sit down at the table. He had Briese with him. He was just in the middle of reading out a ten-page letter from his girlfriend in Radom to Briese. I was initially slightly embarrassed but in this respect Dolte is as open as I am and does not have any secrets. So much the better for me and my affair. I could not have hit on a better moment. He told me he has not got any further with his divorce and that he has now engaged four lawyers. Then good old Briese left. Dolte offered me some wine and cigarettes and we sat together like old chums. Then I fired away. I no longer had any need to mention what I wanted because it is so widely known and has already been referred to. His position was the following: Every support . . . of course. First of all Trudchen must come here and only then will we take it further. As far as going to Radom was concerned I received a promise that I could travel on Saturday, 9 August 1941. So something is fixed. I was very satisfied with the outcome. My spirits were finally restored after so long. My Ukrainian militia got a 'honeymoon period'. The Jews were 'more considerately' treated. I gave away more cigarettes than usual. You could tell by my whole behaviour that something pleasant had happened to me. However during supper I couldn't avoid getting angry.

A certain Herr Gabriel, a man with an inferiority complex and bulging eyes, became angry because I had dismissed for incompetence a Jewess who was working for me. The gentleman forgets that we have introduced the race law into the National Socialist state. I'd already caught him once tenderly stroking the chin of a Jewess and given him a thorough talking-to. At the time he was pretty discomfited. The gentleman must have already forgotten this.

Once again plenty of work, until 22.00. The General-Gouverneur is due to arrive tomorrow, so my militia have to be properly kitted out. At 7.00 in the evening I went to their barracks and established that out of sixty men only twelve are fully kitted out. About forty tailors had been working for almost three days and could not finish the uniforms. I was furious. Of course, most of the blame lay with the leadership of the militia. I immediately summoned the Council of Elders to me and told them that all the remaining uniforms had to be ready by midday the following day or else I would have five tailors executed for sabotage by firing-squad.

A man was brought before me who wanted to report his sixteen-year-old daughter for whoring. According to his own account his daughter has been on the make since she was thirteen. So now it's up to the police to teach the child how to behave! I gave the father who wanted to put his own flesh and blood in prison such a good clip round the ear that he lost his balance five times. . . .

2 August 1941

Work goes on. This morning we started at 6. The GG is not coming. At 12.00 the Council of Elders reported to me that all the uniforms were ready. *Since I had twenty of its men shot for refusing to work*, everything's been running smoothly. This evening four of the men are off to Radom. So that means a quick letter to my Trude. I also have to send the money, 180 RM, to my wife. I've written the letters and given them to Laufmann. Will Trudchen be pleased? I also sent some toys to my wife for the children. The men left for Radom at 22.00 hours. . . .

5 August 1941

Today we took over four buildings for the women and wives who are due to arrive. Dolte is sometimes too weak, not ruthless enough. . . .

6 August 1941

I already know that it is going to take a tough and difficult fight to make her strong enough to get her to assert herself against her parents. She should not simply stumble into a marriage as I did. I will not let her. She is worth more than I am. She is far too good to be thrown away for something which offers her nothing. She will gain far more if she is allowed to love the person who can love her back completely. Today some of the men and I got the Jewish housemaid to roast some chickens for us. We also had new potatoes, cucumber salad and raspberry compote. I contributed the wine. Everything was perfect except for the empty places on my right and left. I looked at both chairs and said to my companions that all that was missing was our sweethearts. Then one of the men talked about his wife and their happy life together. Whether I like it or not I always become dejected and sad during such conversations. There is nothing I can do about it. For the time being there is no happy family life for me. Perhaps somebody will help me to become happy. Good night, Trudchen. Please remain true to me. . . .

Despite the extreme stress, which every single SS and police member had to contend with during these actions, the mood and morale of the men from the first to the last day was exceptionally good and praiseworthy. It was only by a personal sense of duty that every officer and man was able to overcome this pestilence in the shortest space of time.

SS- und Polizeiführer of Galicia, SS-Gruppenführer Friedrich Katzmann, in a report dated 30th June 1943

8 August 1941

... My first thought when I awoke and dawn was breaking: tomorrow at this time we could already be leaving for Radom and if all goes well we could be there at 11 or 12 in the morning. Once I had begun to think about this subject naturally I could not go back to sleep. I imagined where I'd meet T., whether she would be able to go with me straight away or if I didn't arrive until the afternoon where I would find her. At her apartment, at the hairdresser's, at the sports centre, at German House, or – I hope not – out with one of my dear comrades. Then I thought about where I would actually be sleeping. If [illegible name – Ed.] is not at my apartment, or rather his apartment, then there. If he's at home then I will ask him to let me borrow my former flat for the night. I have so much to tell T. and I want my Hasi [bunny] to tell me everything on her mind. I fear a lot of unpleasantness. If only she had a quarter of my decisiveness and strength of will. I would love to give her everything and transfer [some of] my will to her. I still have more than twenty-two hours to wait. I am already more nervous than I have ever been in my entire life. ...

Appendix: biographical details

Landau, Felix. Born 1910. In 1911 his mother married Landau, a Jew, who gave his name to the child. Following his stepfather's death (1919), Landau attended a boarding-school run by a Catholic lay order. Was expelled from apprentice boarding-school for active recruitment activities for the NS Youth (joined National Socialist Worker Youth in 1925). Apprenticeship as skilled furniture-maker. In 1930 joined Austrian Bundesheer (2. Dragonerschwadron). Joined NSDAP March 1931. May 1931 political leader of a NS-Heeressprengels (army district). June 1933 expulsion from Bundesheer for NS activities. Member of SA from June 1933 to April 1934, after that in SS. Participated in Dollfuss affair 1934. Imprisoned until 1937. Renewed propaganda activities. Because of threat of arrest fled to Germany, where he became a naturalized citizen. Found employment as a police official (Kriminalassistent). In 1938 posted to Vienna Gestapo regional headquarters and married first wife. In 1940 transferred to KdS/SD in Radom (General-Gouvernement) where he met shorthand-typist Gertrude. Reported to an Einsatzkommando in June 1941. From July 1941 in Drohobycz, Lvov district (30,000 inhabitants, half of whom were Jews), where the Einsatzkommando was reorganized into an outpost of the Sicherheitspolizei and SD. Until May 1943 Landau was in charge of organizing Jewish labour. At the end of 1941 he lived with his mistress in an aristocratic villa. After his divorce from his wife in 1942 (his wife was judged the guilty party) married Gertrude in 1943 (divorced 1946). Last rank SS-Hauptscharführer. In 1946 recognized in Linz by a former 'worker Jew' and arrested by the Americans. In August 1947 escaped from Glasenbach prison camp. Lived under the name Rudolf Jaschke, ('design, planning, consultancy, interior decoration, refrigeration equipment') in the Nördlingen district. Was sentenced to life imprisonment by Stuttgart Landesgericht in 1963.

NOTES

1 Blutordensträger means Bearer of the Order of the Blood.
2 The first 14 July entry should almost certainly read 11 July, but even then, there are some problems, since that entry mentions 11 July, and ends by saying that he went to bed at 3.30, that is, already on 12 July. Similarly, the 12 July entry includes descriptions of activities on 13 July. Hence one would assume that Landau continued filling in information that went beyond the date he wrote at the top of each entry.

9

PLACES FAR AWAY, PLACES VERY NEAR

Mauthausen, the camps of the Shoah, and the bystanders

Gordon J. Horwitz

The majority of the estimated 300 million people under German rule during the Holocaust were neither victims of the camps nor perpetrators. They were bystanders of various degrees and types. Some belonged to Greater Germany, and their kin were either fighting for Hitler or running his camps. Others belonged to Germany's allies, and more likely than not were more supportive of the partnership with the Third Reich in the early phases of the war than toward the end. Others still belonged to the occupied nations, and stood a good chance of becoming victims themselves, especially if they resisted Nazi policies or tried to protect those slated for exter-mination. But by and large, those who did not carry out genocide and related atrocities, and those who were not subjected to these policies, namely, the vast majority of German-occupied Europe's population, mostly watched in silence or did their best not to see at all. If, as Mao Tse-tung claimed, the guerrilla fighter must feel like a fish in the sea, so too, the perpetrators of genocide must feel that their environment, if not supportive of their actions, is either indifferent or sufficiently terrorized not to dare to act against them. Genocide cannot take place without a majority of passive bystanders.

The great merit of this chapter by Gordon J. Horwitz is that he provides us with a detailed picture not merely of the existence of bystanders within earshot of the camps, but also of their crucial role in the functioning of such institutions. The case that he examines, one of the worst camps the Nazis ever built, is an excellent example of how empty the claim of ignorance of Nazi crimes, so often repeated after the war, really was. For the camp was not built in isolation from the population, but right next to it. Nor was Mauthausen the only such camp. Auschwitz was right next to the town of Oswiecim, Majdanek on the outskirts of Lublin, Buchenwald close to Weimar, Dachau next to Munich, and so forth. These camps depended to a large extent on the towns next to which they were built for supplies, housing and entertainment, while the towns benefited from the presence of the camps' personnel for their own economy. The bystanders in these cases were not an anonymous mass of indifferent people, but an active part of the camps' operation. The only difference being that the often amicable relationship between bystanders and camp guards (especially but not exclusively in Germany and Austria) did not extend to the inmates, who were at the same time dying in their thousands, normally after being reduced to a state barely recognizable as human. It is this necessary, indeed essential, link between atrocity and normality that Horwitz's chapter portrays so powerfully.

* * *

We turn to the world of the ghettos and concentration camps and we imagine we are on a journey to a world apart, a world far away. You and I are not the first to think in these terms. Images of a distant and forbidding realm occupied the thoughts of those who first set foot in these places. One thinks of Jan Karski, envoy of the Polish government-in-exile, on a clandestine journey into the Warsaw ghetto in October 1942. His story, repeated decades later before the camera for Claude Lanzmann's film *Shoah*, was told in print as early as 1944. To enter the ghetto he was led through a doorway and then, by way of a cellar passage, he emerged on the other side, inside the Jewish zone. "Indeed, at that time, the building had become like a modern version of the River Styx which connected the world of the living with the world of the dead."[1] He described the terrifying sight of the persons he encountered inside the ghetto. He found people, "the shadows of what had once been men or women," who "flitted by" crazed with starvation, "enveloped in a haze of disease and death through which their bodies appeared to be throbbing in disintegration." He came upon bodies left unattended, unclothed in the streets because, he was told, their families could not afford to bury them. His guides, a pair of Jewish leaders—"two dejected shadows" who "seemed like apparitions," he had earlier described them—told him not to worry, as the ghetto dwellers, just barely alive, passed before him. "They are dying, that's all," they said, "they are dying." Yet they urged him, above all, to "remember, remember."[2]

Overwhelmed, after a brief stay, he said he had to leave. He described running through the streets of the ghetto, not because he was being pursued, but because he wished to get away; he could stand no more. He returned to the secret passage and entryway and departed. He was on a trip to the land of the dead, and from that realm of the shades he reemerged on the other side of the wall. "It was not a world," Karski said, groping for words to describe this fantastic city within a city that was beyond his imagination. "It was not a part of humanity. I was not part of it. I did not belong there."[3]

Karski was not alone in being initially unprepared to fit the ghettos and the camps into a picture of the world of common experience. When the concentration camps were liberated and open to view, the soldier-liberators and those who came in their wake could hardly believe their eyes.[4] This realm was unlike any known to humankind. Few could enter without experiencing something akin to Karski's reaction to the Warsaw ghetto, seeking as soon as possible to flee. In May 1945 a priest from the Austrian town of Ebensee entered the camp of this name, a subsidiary of Mauthausen, in order to minister to the sick; he confessed he was appalled at the assault upon his senses, the smell of the bodies stacked in or near the crematorium, the wretched odors emanating from bodies still alive, the sight of human wrecks dragging themselves forward, begging for some food, for a warm gesture. Following a stay inside the camp, the priest describes how, once at home, fearing infection, he washed his hands in a strong disinfectant. He could hardly believe that this lovely town of Ebensee where he had been raised, nestled picturesquely amid the hills and lakes of the scenic Salzkammmergut, home to forests and luxurious grazing land, had been simultaneously the setting of this horrific institution, the concentration camp of Ebensee. "This screaming contradiction," as he termed it, had altered the world as he knew it. Prompting the priest's despair was the displacement of long-cherished images of this setting so close to his heart, so evocative of nature and family, by the things he witnessed in the aftermath of the liberation.[5] He was being forced to admit that that place, the concentration camp of Ebensee, was not far away, not distant, but very near.

In the opening sequence of his film, Claude Lanzmann presents his viewers with an image of Simon Srebnik, survivor of Chełmno, seated in a boat. An oarsman, standing, silently ferries him past the Polish village of Chełmno along the placid River Ner, river of ashes, river of time, back to the land of the dead he had miraculously escaped as a child. We are meant to sense, at least at first, the remoteness of this place to which one journeys by water, and whose silence is the absent voice of the dead. That silence is broken by Srebnik's song, a soldier's tune, a song of the executioners, a haunting echo of the killers and a lullaby of death. The last trip by river lies at the heart of one of our oldest and most moving representations of death. But ultimately, the metaphor proves inadequate to describe what happened to people who were forced to journey to these places. For, as we discover, this place far away is not deserted. The villagers of what seems to many of us a place remote in time as well as space are still here, just as they had been when Chełmno was the site of a death camp. We learn that Chełmno was, and that it is still a place on earth, locatable on the map, a place populated by the living as well as by the dead.

Let there be no confusion: these places *were* repellent. They did have about them, quite literally, the sight and stench of death. The camps were a unique synthesis of sordid imaginings and very real exercise of man-made violence and force. They were places into which perfectly whole human beings were driven, held briefly between life and death before being beaten, or hung, or shot, or electrocuted on the wire, or gassed, then burned and blown through a chimney into the sky. The scope of the undertaking alone was enough to create among outsiders a sense of incredulity. That incredulity was one manifestation of a system designed to create a division in society between a normal world, inhabited by the citizenry, and a "phantom world," to borrow Hannah Arendt's phrase, into which the outcasts of society would slip before exiting this world without a trace.[6]

Even so, the project to seal from observation, to isolate the killing from the outside world, to wipe free all traces of lives destroyed and to screen the deeds of the killers, was an imperfect endeavor. In 1938 a concentration camp was built in Mauthausen, a market community on the Danube, fourteen miles east of Linz. For the next seven years the camp spread its shadow over the town and its inhabitants. As the original camp expanded to include a network of more than forty outlying, subsidiary camps, the shadow fell across additional towns and villages that dotted the landscape. The shadow represented torment and death for more than 100,000 individuals swept into the Mauthausen system over seven years. Much of that torment was visible to persons who lived in the vicinity of these camps. They were witness to repeated beatings and shootings. Their eyes saw what few eyes would have wished to see. Assuredly, they were spared the worst of sights: few were given the dubious privilege of witnessing the gassing of inmates. The masters of the camp, the SS, were at pains to keep residents somewhat in the dark concerning the extent and the details of the killing. But it was impossible for them to keep all of their doings a complete mystery to the townsfolk. Rather, they asked of the residents both a discreet silence, a tactful averting of their gaze. Through tacit understanding, though all knew it to be in fact near and present, the camp was to be considered a realm distant and apart.

One of the first notions to be grasped in considering the relationship between a concentration camp and the town and townspeople nearby, is to understand how, in numerous ways, a concentration camp touches upon the affairs of the citizenry. A concentration camp such as Mauthausen can be likened to a new enterprise locating in a given community. The comparison is particularly apt in the case of a camp such as Mauthausen because, quite above and beyond its planned role as a center of torture and death, it was designed as an economic enterprise centering on the extraction of granite from rock quarries, operating for the benefit of an SS-owned and operated corporation, the German Earth and Stone Works. That enterprise profited from the exploitation of slave labor in the form of inmates brought to Mauthausen to be worked to death. The Mauthausen quarry, an impos- ing and frightful pit whose walls ranged some 300 feet in height round about, was at once an enclave of terror and a work site. For these same quarry operations, for example, local stone masons were needed to carry out skilled tasks as well as to serve as foremen on labor details which were simultaneously under SS guard. During Mauthausen's establishment phase, for example, barracks were built and outfitted, and civilian car- penters were called in from the surrounding communities to do some of the work. In operation, the camp needed basic supplies, and for these it turned to area merchants. Regular food purchases were made from nearby farmers and from an agricultural cooperative located near the railway station. Goods had to be trucked in, and here too a local firm was engaged to provide vehicles and drivers. The camp staff also liked to drink and dine out, frequenting local taverns and restaurants. SS families were housed in the community, and local women took on housekeeping duties, tidying SS residences. Local merchants were a ready source of necessities for the SS and their families. In short, there was on one level a routine, everyday quality to the interaction between the camp and the town.[7]

Still, the nature of contacts, for some, evolved beyond the everyday to a level more direct and sinister. In the early phase of the camp's existence, before such facilities were installed on site, inmates who died at Mauthausen were routinely shipped for disposal to a public crematorium in Steyr, a city to the south of Mauthausen. We are also informed of the case of a small businessman from Linz, owner of a commercial extermination firm, who acted as a supplier of deadly Zyklon-B to the camp.[8] Moreover, a number of local persons representing a variety of trades and professions—ranging from simple mechanics, plumbers, and bus drivers, to secretaries and nurses and doctors—served in the so-called euthanasia center at Castle Hartheim, located just west of Linz. Hartheim operated not only as a center for killing, first, by means of carbon monoxide gas, mentally ill and physically infirm patients from Austria and southern Germany, but also, beginning in August 1941, inmates from the concentration camps of Mauthausen and Dachau. Hartheim thus doubled as a killing outpost for Mauthausen, its own gas chamber a forerunner to the gas chamber installed in Mauthausen and operating by the spring of 1942. Local persons, many sharing Nazi party connections, carried out the task of assembling the pipes, the tiles, and the doors of the gas chamber in Castle Hartheim. Custodians kept the physical plant in running order; bus drivers drove the victims to the castle; nurses met the vehicles and escorted the victims inside, readying them for the gas chamber; secretaries carried out correspondence informing loved ones of the death of their relatives in Hartheim, processing false information concerning the cause of death; above all, overseeing these activities, were the doctors. When gassing was completed, local men assigned to the crematory carried out the heavy task of stacking and then disposing of the bodies in the oven they serviced.[9]

Local businessmen not only profitably took on contracts for services rendered to the camp but exploited the availability of cheap labor rented out from the SS slave pool. Beyond this, however, there were opportunities for corruption and enrichment. The adjacent black market included the exchange of rare foodstuffs for valuables seized from the inmates themselves. In particular, items such as watches of silver and gold, skimmed from the treasure house of items taken from the inmates (and in the case of much of the gold, literally routinely wrenched from their teeth), served in Mauthausen and in other camps as items for barter with persons from the local population.[10] Yitzhak Arad recounts extensively instances of this trade at Treblinka. He estimates that easily more than a thousand boxcars of property were loaded and shipped from the camp. But not all of the loot was funneled into the "proper" channels. Rather, some guards had valuables smuggled out of the camp to nearby Malkinia, where they could expropriate it and return with the goods to Germany when on leave. Farmers in the vicinity of Treblinka were said to have been seen with these watches stuffed into their baskets. Guards took advantage of their access to the expanding pile of wealth, providing a windfall for greedy area residents, including "farmers' daughters" near Treblinka who went out with the guards and received these stolen goods.[11] Soon after the war, civilians could be found rooting about the former camp terrain, digging up remains in a frantic search for what was presumed to be buried loot scattered among the human remains. Observing evidence of this treasure hunt, Rachel Auerbach, a Jewish investigator with a team examining Treblinka in November 1945 appropriately described these people as human "jackals and hyenas" who would "drag parts of half-rotted corpses from the earth, bones and scattered refuse in the hope that they may come upon at least a coin or a gold tooth."[12]

The people living round about had to see to it that even should an inmate escape, not only would he be turned away, but turned in by a hostile population. In the event of breakouts, the local citizenry were to be the eyes and ears of the guard corps. In Sobibor, in Treblinka, mass escapes did occur. Nothing is more damning to the reputation of the outside world as is the indifference and, above all, the hostility of persons in the surrounding areas where the escaped prisoners sought assistance. In Poland, Jewish prisoners had to evade denunciations and tip-offs by the local citizenry to the Germans. Few Polish partisans came to their assistance. Some killed escaped Jews on their own.[13]

What is more, just as the German army units were on hand near Auschwitz, in reserve to back up the guard staff in the event of mass escapes,[14] the citizenry living in the vicinity of those camps inside Germany formed a potential auxiliary force to be armed in a similar emergency. In Mauthausen, in fact, on a moonlit night in early February 1945, a group of some four hundred badly weakened Soviet prisoners of war, under sentence of slow death in an isolation barrack in the main camp, miraculously succeeded in scaling one of the walls of the camp. Those who were not immediately cut down by gunfire succeeded in scattering into the countryside. They desperately sought morsels of food and help at the doorways of the local citizenry in Mauthausen and surrounding villages and towns in the area; they begged not to be turned in to the SS. According to the written account of the local police commander, these men, even in their desperate situation, did not do harm to persons or property. They asked only that citizens allow them, for a brief while, to hide in their farm buildings. But a manhunt was immediately called up by the SS and local Nazi party officials. Aged men and teenage boys not yet eligible for army service were assembled and armed to participate. The citizenry had been, in effect, deputized to act as killers. By all accounts, numerous citizens—and not only men, for farm women and women shopkeepers took a hand in this as well—thoughtlessly seized the opportunity to participate in the sport of chasing and killing. In hunting down the inmates—with guns and knives and pitchforks—the local citizenry revealed unmistakably that the surrounding communities were in fact extensions of the camp.[15]

The concentration and extermination camps called forth particular ways of seeing.[16] It is precisely because the camps were in fact constructed so close to populated areas that their designs incorporated elements of disguise and camouflage. Mauthausen was able to take advantage of the natural, semicircular enclosure of its rock quarry, the very center of operations, and to have built for the prisoner compound, assembled on a height overlooking the quarry, thick walls made of stones hauled up from the pit below. In Treblinka, a camp of relatively lighter construction, the SS had to make do with earthen bafflers and with wire, but here care was taken to weave foliage into the mesh to obstruct the vision not only of the victims themselves but of anyone looking in on the camp from surrounding fields. At Sobibor and Treblinka the forest was similarly used as a natural barrier to sight. Enhancing these natural shields were a host of improvised and inexpensive additions whose major purpose was to mislead or to conceal from view what went on inside or near the camps. We are reminded that the killers also experimented at Treblinka with the by now familiar stage-set deception of a Potemkin-like village railway station complete with its "fake clock" and "fake ticket windows."[17] The buses that drove the victims to the gassing center at Castle Hartheim had their windows painted over; passengers were to be prevented from looking out, outsiders from looking in. Also at Hartheim a wooden canopy was placed at the entrance where buses pulled up and unloaded those about to be led to their deaths in the gas chamber inside the castle.[18]

There were, of course, euphemisms for murder built into the linguistic codes enforced in the verbal commands and in the correspondence of the bureaucrats. Radically new techniques of distancing were effected for the perpetrators on the scene, however, with the substitution of mobile and fixed gas killing devices for the previously relied upon killing squads, whose victims had been lined up before their eyes. This was critical, because it helped to remove most of the killers from the line of sight.[19] Shoshana Felman, however, in her salient review of the Lanzmann film, suggests that similar restrictions of visual encounters, above and beyond those ingeniously developed to protect the sensibilities of the killers, played a critical role in safeguarding the bystanders from the act of witnessing, helping them, too, to avoid seeing with their own eyes things that in fact were happening within range of their senses. Combined with ruses aimed at deceiving the victims of their fate, deliberately sparing them until the final instant the site of the pit at the edge of a forest or the interior of the sealed gassing room, perpetrators and bystanders, in narrowing their vision, acceded to a process that was designed to make the killing "invisible" and to make of the Holocaust "*an event without a witness*, an event which historically consists in the scheme of the literal *erasure of its witnesses*."[20]

Primo Levi is one of our best guides to the implications of these strategies of visual and other sensory avoidances. It was he who wrote of the "cordon sanitaire" people may draw up around those things they wish not to see; nothing so effectively protects one against later unpleasant memories of a sight or an experience than does not looking at the moment it presents itself before one's field of vision. By not seeing, by turning away, one is already selecting one's memories, screening those memories, and hence screening oneself from unpleasant and potentially bothersome thoughts in the future.[21]

Still, we have come to recognize that the bystanders, to the extent that they participated in this process of blocking disturbing sensations associated with the activities of the camps, did so against a background of numerous, often unavoidable daily contacts with these institutions. We discover that in negotiating such interactions, residents of the communities bordering on the camps often collaborated in narrowing their vision to a minimum. In 1941 a woman whose farm lay on a height above the rock quarry in Mauthausen filed an anguished request with the police after witnessing bodies of inmates who had been shot and left in the open. Indicating that the sight of inmates lying dead at the rock quarry was burdensome to her nerves, she was compelled to ask that the killing be halted or at least done elsewhere and out of sight.[22] The priest from Ebensee who arrived at the end of the war to enter the liberated camp wrote in 1946 that he had spoken with residents of the town, discovering not only women whose nerves suffered because of the unavoidable sights and sounds of persons being beaten, but also farmers who avoided working certain fields too near to the camp, and mountaineers who went out of their way just in order to avoid coming into contact with such "horrifying events."[23]

People had some control over what they saw, and could try to look away, but what of what they smelled? The stench was simply unavoidable for persons living near camps that had operating crematoria, as in Mauthausen and its main subsidiaries in Melk and Ebensee. Smoke respected no absolute boundaries. The unmistakable, sickly sweet odor of burning human flesh was, as townsfolk readily admit, a part of the atmosphere. Read enough testimonies to this effect and one learns that these people, undoubtedly already experts in the vagaries of the local climate, had become veritable specialists in detecting the interaction between wind and cremation fumes.[24] Approximately thirty kilometers from Nuremberg, in the vicinity of the Hersbruck camp, subsidiary to the Flossenbürg main camp, a crematorium whose "chimney stood clear of obstructing terrain features" was available to the sight of "all who traveled the two valley roads to the market town of Hersbruck from the south." As the wife of a local minister noted, "From our house one had a view down the valley to Happurg and beyond. One could see smoke pouring out the chimney on a low brick building. Often when I opened the door in the morning there would be an awful smell. It was always the same. At different times I said to my husband, 'There's that awful smell again.'" Also established in the area were two open pyres, one of which was located on "a hilltop site" fed by "wood being requisitioned from farmers" in the area. Those working their fields came across the sight of bodies being incinerated. Another woman noted, "One evening one of my sons came running into the house and shouted, 'Mama the woods are on fire.' Sometimes the flames were so high that it looked as if the trees were burning. Whenever they were burning bodies the smell was awful, and when the wind brought the smoke toward Molsberg it was terrible."[25]

Characteristically, the SS attempted to explain away the unmaskable odors. The explanations were designed to permit persons to ignore, rationalize, or cancel these sensations by offering a more palatable interpretation. Immediately after the crematorium in Hartheim went into operation a representative of the castle administration assembled residents in a tavern to try to convince people that in fact the heavy smoke was the result of a war-related "chemical treatment" for processing oil for use in submarines.[26] Similarly, the SS at first attempted to explain away open-air cremation at one of the pyres in the Hersbruck area by first restricting access to the area and stating that "an Allied plane had crashed there."[27] For those who wished to believe so, there existed rationales for the burning of bodies in wartime. A woman from Melk who remembered the smoke recalled, "I said, 'uh huh, someone is being burned again.' One smells that you know. That is, I believe none were shot in Melk. They often simply died of hunger or something. They often died of weakness."[28]

To those who looked away, the towns beside the camps embodied goodness and decency. In Mauthausen the local Nazis and camp staffers mingled at recitals, lectures, youth assemblies, sporting competitions, and hunts. Here the executioners found relaxation in local taverns and with some of the local women at private gatherings held in farmhouses. Here resided the wives and children of SS family men; here were the shop-keepers—hairdressers, druggists, grocery owners—whom they patronized. Above all, here resided the decent folk, as opposed to the outcasts and criminals sealed within the walls of the camp. One is pained to read the words of a wife whose husband, a dentist, oversaw the removal and preparation of gold extracted from the teeth of inmates at Mauthausen before shipment to Berlin. In June 1946, pleading for his life, she stated, "He was always a devoted husband who valued his family above anything else and I love him with all my heart." And she continued, "The children are too small to beg for their father. I enclose a picture of the children in the hope that their innocent eyes will plead with you and save their father from death by hanging. Furthermore, I enclose a picture of my husband showing him as a happy family man. Please look at his eyes. You will see in them how

213

good and unselfish he is and that he does not belong among the criminals of Mauthausen."[29] From this to Heinrich Himmler's SS men of 1943 who, in his words, "apart from exceptions caused by human weakness . . . have remained decent fellows" to the defiant remarks of Austrian presidential candidate Kurt Waldheim, defending in the year 1986 "the reputation of a whole generation" against the attack of those who would "make all these people bad people," the upholding of goodness was essential. "We were not doing anything but our duty as decent soldiers, we were not criminals but decent men who faced a terrible fate."[30]

We confront repeatedly a binary vision permitting alternate versions of the self: the perpetrator who is simultaneously the caring family man; the bystander, the honored citizen of a town that is a town like any other save that it also serves a killing establishment. The two sides of the self, however, cannot be neatly separated. Each person trails, close by, his shadow.[31] So, too, the camp, bounded as it was by stone and by wire, patrolled by guards, cast its presence upon the nearby towns, its inmates at once confined within, yet also routinely led through neighboring communities; killing went on within its walls, but not exclusively, and the remains of the dead, let loose, rode the breeze. Lines were sharply drawn, yet never absolute and impermeable.

Not all townsfolk took up instruments to strike directly at the inmates; some of the former took refuge in a spurious neutrality. It was of no small comfort to know that one did not kill; one was not a murderer, one concluded, so long as one's own hand did not strike down a life. But to allow matters to rest at that overlooked the simple fact that the rulers of the concentration camps asked, at a minimum, but one thing of the residents of these bordering communities: not to interfere, so that the SS could proceed with their tasks. In complying, assuming what amounted to an attitude of noninvolvement, they not only made life easier for the executioners but denied the inmates what they most needed: assistance from the outside world. As we know, one can contribute to evil as easily by thoughtlessness as by deed. That lesson is one not readily acknowledged, as the philosopher Mary Midgley is at pains to point out: "If we ask whether exploiters and oppressors know what they are doing, the right answer seems to be that they do *not* know, because they carefully avoid thinking about it— but that they could know, and therefore their deliberate avoidance is a responsible act."[32]

Throughout the years the bystanders have been reluctant to come forward. Like the perpetrators, they have no reason to speak; what is more, they preferred to forget the past. Have we waited too long to approach them? Claude Lanzmann conducted his interviews in the late 1970s and the early 1980s. It was not too late at that time, but is it too late now? I recall that as a college student I had been influenced greatly by William Sheridan Allen's by now classic history of the rise of the Nazi party in a single German town.[33] But the book I really wanted to read did not exist: a study of a town that was located near a concentration camp. By the time I took the chance on such an undertaking in the succeeding decade, more than thirty-five years had passed since the end of the Second World War. And now the war is half a century behind us, not a great span for most historians; measured against the course of an individual life, however, fifty years is indeed a long time. Many adult witnesses from that era have slipped away, silent in their own lifetimes, and now silent in death. But one of the things my investigation of Mauthausen made me aware of was that there were not only adults but also children who viewed what went on from the periphery of the camps. Indeed, in some instances they were afforded a closer look at things, for the guards were less likely to threaten or chase them away. Born during the years, roughly, 1928–1933, they are only now approaching retirement, or would be just recently retired. In the year 1943, such persons would have been between ten and fifteen years old, certainly old enough, had they lived near one of these places, to have seen the camps. Even someone born as long ago as 1923 would have celebrated in 1993 no more than his or her seventieth year. No, it is not too late. The witnesses are still among us. Or, at the least, they are still in their home towns, many of them. Shall we not ask of them what they saw, what they heard for themselves, and what their parents may have seen and heard and said? And in so doing we can find among them and among later generations valuable allies: local historians, archivists in the Second World War research institutes, Gymnasium teachers who came of age in the 1960s and 1970s. They are a ready resource, often with ties to the towns where the camps were located, helpful in locating contacts in these communities. Peter Sichrovsky's success in interviewing the children of perpetrators and victims underscores the need to speak with the children of the bystanders as well.[34]

In the meantime, we await the development of a new imagination, akin to that "imagination of the heart" which, Karl Jaspers noted, when missing, leaves the individual open to moral "blindness" and "inner indifference toward the witnessed evil."[35] Still, we have before us the example of Jan Karski, a man whose vision was, however painful to him, directed to taking in with his eyes all that he needed to see, that he might bear witness to the crime before the world. He sought out what was human in those he encountered. And in the figure of Szmul Zygielbojm, a Jewish leader with whom Karski spoke when he reached London, we find an example of one who responded to Karski's message with all his heart. With the messenger, Zygielbojm was a man seeking to place himself, a man at a distance, far away in London, with Karski in the ghetto. Zygielbojm pressed his witness for precise descriptions: "He asked me what the houses looked like, what the children looked like."[36] The vision he sought was internal; it was the vision of the mind's eye.

In the year 1944 Arthur Koestler wrote of a man he knew, "a well-known London publisher," who had taken upon himself the task of reporting on the destruction of the Jews:

Before each meeting he used to lock himself up in a room, close his eyes, and imagine in detail, for twenty minutes, that he was one of the people in Poland who were killed. One day he tried to feel what it was like to be suffocated . . . ; the other he had to dig his grave with two hundred others and then face a machine gun, which, of course, is rather imprecise and capricious in its aiming. Then he walked out to the platform and talked. He kept going for a full year before he collapsed with a nervous breakdown. He had a great command of his audiences and perhaps he has done some good,

concluded Koestler.[37]

Agonized that year by a recurring dream in which he found himself left to die as others indifferently walked past, Koestler acknowledged that there are degrees of knowing: "I believe in spiral nebulae, can see them in a telescope and express their distance in figures; but they have a lower degree of reality for me than the inkpot on my table. Distance in space and time degrades intensity of awareness."[38] Günther Anders, in his parable of a woman who, from the height of a tower, witnesses the death of her child, then exclaims, had she but been down below she would have been overwhelmed, expressed, chillingly, a like notion.[39] But not only does distance diminish perception,

So does magnitude. Seventeen is a figure which I know intimately like a friend; fifty billion is just a sound. A dog run over by a car upsets our emotional balance and digestion; three million Jews killed in Poland cause but a moderate uneasiness. Statistics don't bleed; it is the detail which counts. We are unable to embrace the total process with our awareness; we can only focus on little lumps of reality.[40]

Karski was a rare individual, as were at this time Zygielbojm, Koestler, and the London publisher he mentions. Few were willing to suffer the unpleasant sensation of dwelling on such matters. It was not always the case, Koestler noted:

There were periods and moments in history—in Athens, in the early Renaissance, during the first years of the Russian Revolution—when at least certain representative layers of society had attained a relatively high level of mental integration; times when people seemed to rub their eyes and come awake, when their cosmic awareness seemed to expand, when they were 'contemporaries' in a much broader and fuller sense; when the trivial and the cosmic planes seemed on the point of fusing.[41]

We are not there yet; we can only look forward to such a time when sensibilities are more refined, when each of us, in approaching both present and past, learns to have the courage to see, even when, safe within our homes, within ourselves, we "rub [our] eyes and come awake" to sense this world far away close to us, and a part of us.

But in so doing let us acknowledge that we awaken upon this world, not an underworld, and recall that among the rivers that course its landscape are the fabled Danube, which, just east of Linz, bathes the shores of a place called Mauthausen, and lesser ones, among them the River Ner, a body of water as real as the mightiest and proudest of all Europe's riverways, which drinks the ashes of a place called Chełmno.

NOTES

1 Jan Karski, *Story of a Secret State* (Boston: Houghton Mifflin, 1944), p. 329.
2 Karski, *Story of a Secret State*, pp. 325–26, 329–30; Claude Lanzmann, *Shoah: An Oral History of the Holocaust* (New York: Pantheon, 1985), p. 174.
3 Lanzmann, *Shoah*, p. 174.
4 Robert H. Abzug, *Inside the Vicious Heart: Americans and the Liberation of Nazi Concentration Camps* (New York: Oxford University Press, 1985), p. 10.
5 Franz Loidl, *Entweihte Heimat* (Linz, 1946), pp. 15–16.
6 See the discussion entitled "Total Domination" in Hannah Arendt, *The Origins of Totalitarianism*, 2nd enl. ed. (New York: World Publishing, A Meridian Book, 1958; 12th printing 1972), pp. 437–59. The phrase "phantom world" appears on page 445.
7 Gordon J. Horwitz, *In the Shadow of Death: Living Outside the Gates of Mauthausen* (New York: Free Press, 1990), pp. 26–27, 29, 40–41.
8 Ibid., p. 41; Eugen Kogon, Hermann Langbein, Adalbert Ruckerl et al., *Nationalsozialistische Massentötungen durch Giftgas* (Frankfurt/M.: S. Fischer Verlag, 1983), p. 248.
9 See the chapter entitled "The Castle" in Horwitz, *In the Shadow*, pp. 55–82.
10 Ibid., pp. 41, 43–44.
11 Yitzhad Arad, *Belzec, Sobibor, Treblinka: The Operation Reinhard Death Camps* (Bloomington: Indiana University Press, 1987), pp. 158–59, 163.
12 Rachel Auerbach, "In the Fields of Treblinka," in Alexander Donat, ed., *The Death Camp Treblinka: A Documentary* (New York: Holocaust Library, 1979), p. 69. See also Arad, *Belzec, Sobibor, Treblinka*, pp. 371, 379.
13 Arad, *Belzec, Sobibor, Treblinka*, pp. 342–48.
14 Raul Hilberg, "Bitburg as Symbol," in *Bitburg in Moral and Political Perspective*, ed. Geoffrey Hartman (Bloomington: Indiana University Press, 1986), p. 22.
15 Horwitz, *In the Shadow*, pp. 124–27, 131–34.
16 Shoshana Felman speaks of "*three different performances of the act of seeing,*" in which "in effect, the victims, the bystanders, and the perpetrators are here differentiated not so much by what they actually see (what they all see, although discontinuous, does in fact follow a logic of corroboration), as by what and how they *do not see*, by what and how they fail to witness" (emphasis in original) (Shoshana Felman, "In an Era of Testimony: Claude Lanzmann's Shoah," *Yale French Studies* 79 [1991]: p. 42).
17 See diagram and accompanying description of the camp layout in Gitta

Sereny, *Into that Darkness: An Examination of Conscience* (New York: McGraw-Hill, 1974; Random House, Vintage Books edition, 1983), pp. 146–47.

18 Horwitz, *In the Shadow*, p. 72.

19 See Pierre Vidal-Naquet, *Les Juifs, la mémoire et le présent: II.* (Paris: Editions La Découverte, 1991), p. 233.

20 Felman, "In an Era of Testimony," pp. 44–45.

21 Primo Levi, *The Drowned and the Saved*, trans. Raymond Rosenthal (New York: Summit Books, 1988), p. 31 (also in Hartman, *Bitburg*, p. 135).

22 Horwitz, *In the Shadow*, p. 35.

23 Dokumentationsarchiv des österreichischen Widerstandes, *Widerstand und Verfolgung in Oberösterreich 1934–1945* (Vienna: Österreichischer Bundes-verlag, 1982), vol. 2, p. 592.

24 See Claude Lanzmann, "J'ai enquêté en Pologne," in *Au sujet de Shoah: Le film de Claude Lanzmann*, ed. Michel Deguy (Paris: Editions Belin, 1990), p. 214.

25 Elmer Luchterhand, "Knowing and Not Knowing: Involvement in Nazi Genocide," in *Our Common History: The Transformation of Europe*, ed. Paul Thompson with Natasha Burchardt (Atlantic Highlands, NJ: Humanities Press, 1982), pp. 254, 264–65.

26 Horwitz, *In the Shadow*, p. 62.

27 Luchterhand, "Knowing and Not Knowing," p. 255.

28 Horwitz, *In the Shadow*, p. 110.

29 National Archives, RG 153–5–31, vol. 1. Trial record Court Dachau, pt. 5, pp. 1462ff., Case of Walther H., clemency petition dated June 12, 1946.

30 Jeremy Noakes and Geoffrey Pridham, eds., *Documents on Nazism* (New York: Viking Press, 1974), p. 492; James M. Markham, "Waldheim Campaigns to Memories in Borderland," New York Times, May 1, 1986, p. 2.

31 See the discussion of "Selves and Shadows" in Mary Midgley's *Wickedness: A Philosophical Essay* (London: Ark Paperbacks, 1986), pp. 113–31; and "Doubling: The Faustian Bargain," in Robert J. Lifton, *The Nazi Doctors: Medical Killing and the Psychology of Genocide* (New York: Basic Books, 1986), pp. 418–29.

32 Midgley, *Wickedness*, pp. 62–63.

33 William S. Allen, *The Nazi Seizure of Power: The Experience of a Single German Town*, 1942–1945, rev. ed. (New York: Franklin Watts, 1984).

34 Peter Sichrovsky, *Born Guilty: Children of Nazi Families* (New York: Basic Books, 1987).

35 Karl Jaspers, *The Question of German Guilt*, trans. E. B: Ashton (New York: Capricorn Books, 1961), p. 70.

36 Karski, *Story of a Secret State*, p. 337.

37 Arthur Koestler, "On Disbelieving Atrocities," *New York Times Magazine*, January 1944, cited in Arthur Koestler, *The Yogi and the Commissar and Other Essays* (New York: Macmillan, 1967; 1st ed. 1945), p. 93. The publisher, whom Koestler did not identify by name, would be Victor Gollancz. See Ruth Dudley Edwards, *Victor Gollancz: A Biography* (London: Victor Gollancz, 1987), p. 377.

38 Koestler, *The Yogi and the Commissar*, pp. 91–92.

39 Gunther Anders, *Der Blick vom Turm* (Munich: Verlag C. H. Beck, 1968), p. 7.

40 Koestler, *The Yogi and the Commissar*, p. 92.

41 Ibid., p. 93.

10

UNDER A CRUEL STAR

A life in Prague 1941–1968

Heda Margolius Kovály

If it is difficult to choose a suitable text by one of the perpetrators, it is all the more difficult to pick out an appropriate survivor's recollection. The number of survivor memoirs published over the years has grown tremendously. The perpetrators, for obvious reasons, rarely wished to write or talk about their experiences after the war. Only a few left behind testimonies, such as the commandant of Auschwitz, Rudolf Höss, who wrote his memoirs just before he was executed, and Franz Stangl, who spoke at length to Gitta Sereny while he was on trial as former commandant of Treblinka. Conversely, the survivors were often motivated by an urgent need to record the events of the past for the sake of the majority who perished and as a warning to posterity. Some memoirs were published, or at least written, very soon after the liberation. But they rarely received much attention, especially when written by "passive" victims, namely innocent Jewish inmates, rather than heroic resistance fighters. This early period was followed by a relative lull, during which survivors tried to pick up the pieces and resume their previous lives, or, in most cases, build new ones. But as of the 1970s we are witnessing a new wave of publications and a tremendous rise in public interest. Survivors who feel that they will soon no longer be able to tell their stories now find a public far more willing to listen than in the past. Obviously, this influx in publications will have a limited duration, as the survivors are rapidly dying out. But it reflects the extent of memory's reach and potency fifty years after the event, as well as the changing sensibilities of a public, the majority of whom had not even been born at the time.

The reasons I chose Heda Margolius Kovály's memoirs are complex. For one, her account is far less known than those which nowadays (but only since the late 1980s) are read by almost every college student, such as Primo Levi's or Elie Wiesel's. For another, she is a woman, whereas most readers are more familiar with accounts written by men. But there are other reasons as well. Margolius Kovály writes with extraordinary conciseness and precision, insight and sensibility. She packs into a brief account a series of scenes and pictures that the reader will never forget, and which seem to contain a gist of her own experience and of many fellow victims. Moreover, while she is victimized as a Jew by the Nazis, her suffering does not come to an end with the liberation. Indeed, she is never liberated. The false sense that many of us have of a return to normality by those who survived is belied by her story, for she soon finds herself under another brutal dictatorship.

Throughout, Margolius Kovály's tale defies conventional depictions of the Holocaust and its aftermath. As they escape from a death march, she and her fellow inmates burst into a mad laughter, confirming what many other survivors have recounted, namely, that humor was at times crucial to survival. Those critics who attacked Roberto Benigni's Life Is Beautiful for introducing laughter into the camps may well have been more interested in the manner they thought the Holocaust should be represented than in its reality, despite their insistence on realism. But when Margolius Kovály reaches Prague, no one will let her in, for fear of the Nazis. Here the stories of heroic resistance are belied once more, even on the very eve of the liberation and in the case of a camp inmate who had already gone through all chambers of hell. Margolius Kovály experiences the arrival of Communism as a moment of liberation and hope; but soon thereafter her husband, a top Communist official and Czech Jewish survivor of the Nazi camps, falls victim to Stalin's antisemitic campaign. Now she once more experiences fear and rejection by everyone; she is the wife of a victim and anyone who comes close to her may end up the same way.

Margolius Kovály makes no attempt to conflate her experience in the Nazi camps with her life under a Communist dictatorship. She knows the difference, having been subjected to the brutalities of both. The Nazis were out to murder in vast numbers; the Communists raised the hopes of a whole generation and then dashed them in the most cynical, often violent manner. They were out to control and manage, and isolated and crushed physically or mentally anyone who stood up to them. But they were not genocidal, nor did they need to be. What these two systems destroyed in Eastern Europe and Russia will take a long time to revive, and much of it will never return. Which is why Margolius Kovály's memoir is so tragic. And yet, her own survival, not only physically but also as a sensitive, creative, and, in a careful and anything but naive manner, even optimistic human being, fills us with some hope at the end of this bloody century.

* * *

Three forces carved the landscape of my life. Two of them crushed half the world. The third was very small and weak and, actually, invisible. It was a shy little bird hidden in my rib cage an inch or two above my stomach. Sometimes in the most unexpected moments the bird would wake up, lift its head, and flutter its wings in rapture. Then I too would lift my head because, for that short moment, I would know for certain that love and hope are infinitely more powerful than hate and fury, and that somewhere beyond the line of my horizon there was life indestructible, always triumphant.

The first force was Adolf Hitler; the second, Iosif Vissarionovich Stalin. They made my life a microcosm in which the history of a small country in the heart of Europe was condensed. The little bird, the third force, kept me alive to tell the story.

I carry the past inside me folded up like an accordion, like a book of picture postcards that people bring home as souvenirs from foreign cities, small and neat. But all it takes is to lift one corner of the top card for an endless snake to escape, zigzag joined to zigzag, the sign of the viper, and instantly all the pictures line up before my eyes. They linger, sharpen, and a moment of that distant past gets wedged into the works of my inner time clock. It stops, skips a beat, and loses part of the irreplaceable, irretrievable present.

The mass deportation of Jews from Prague began two years after the outbreak of the war, in the fall of 1941. Our transport left in October and we had no idea of our destination. The order was to report to the Exposition Hall, to bring food for several days and essential baggage. No more.

When I got up that morning, my mother turned to me from the window and said, like a child, "Look, it's almost dawn. And I thought the sun would not even want to rise today."

The inside of the Exposition Hall was like a medieval madhouse. All but the steadiest nerves were on the point of snapping. Several people who were seriously ill and had been brought there on stretchers died on the spot. A Mrs. Tausig went completely crazy, tore her false teeth out of her mouth, and threw them at our lord and master, Obersturmbannfuehrer Fiedler. There were babies and small children who cried incessantly and, just beside my parents, a small fat bald man sat on his suitcase playing his violin as if none of the surrounding bedlam were any concern of his. He played Beethoven's Concerto in D Major; practicing the same passages over and over again.

I wandered around among those thousands of people looking for familiar faces. That was how I first happened to see him. To this day, I believe he was the most handsome man I have ever seen. He was sitting, calm and erect, on a black trunk with silver brackets, wearing a black suit, a white shirt, a gray tie, and a black overcoat topped by a black homburg. He had gray eyes and a perfectly trimmed gray moustache. His slim, delicate hands were folded on the handle of an umbrella rolled up as thin as a toothpick. In the middle of that chaos, among all those people dressed in sweaters, heavy boots, and ski jackets, he looked as incongruous as if he were sitting there naked.

Startled, I stopped, and he rose. With a slight bow and a smile, he offered me a seat beside him on his trunk. He was a professor of classical philology from Vienna. After the Nazis had annexed Austria, he had found refuge in Prague, and there the Germans had caught up with him. When I asked why he had not dressed in a more practical way for such a journey into the unknown, he answered that he always dressed in the same way and disliked the idea of changing his habits under the pressure of circumstances. In any event, he said, he considered it most important to maintain equanimity *rebus in arduis*. Then he began talking about classical literature and ancient Rome. I listened with rapt attention. From that time on I sought him out whenever I had the opportunity, and he always welcomed me with his courteous smile and, it seemed, with pleasure.

Two days later, we boarded the train. Even though in the following years I would experience infinitely more grueling transports, this one seemed to be the worst because it was the first. If every beginning is hard, the beginning of hardship is the hardest. We were not yet inured to sounds of gunshots followed by agonizing screams, to unendurable thirst, nor to the suffocating air in the crammed cattle cars.

Upon our arrival in Lodz, we were greeted by a snowstorm. It was only October, but in the three years I spent there I never again saw such a blizzard. We left the railroad station, plodding with difficulty against the wind and, for the first time, saw people who were dying of hunger, little children almost naked and barefoot in the snow.

A few days later, I wandered into a basement. The young people from our transport were sitting on the floor around a kerosene lamp and someone was playing Czech folk songs on a harmonica. There was an arched ceiling on which the lamp cast long strangely shaped shadows, making it look like the vault of a cathedral. I stood in the doorway and thought: now an angel should appear and leave a mark of blood on the forehead of everyone who will die here.

The concentration camp of Lodz, officially called the Litzmannstadt Ghetto, was really part of the outskirts of the city, a dilapidated slum enclosed by a wall that was made of wooden boards and barbed wire. For some time after our arrival, people in our transport stayed together in one of the few undamaged buildings of the ghetto, and I could still see my professor once in a while. Some weeks later, another transport arrived and we received orders to move. We scattered into the decaying tenements already populated by close to one hundred thousand Polish Jews living in unimaginable conditions, and we lost track of one another.

One of the people in our transport was our family doctor, a splendid old gentleman, who had known me since birth. He was now more than seventy years old, but every day he would go out into the streets of the ghetto, walking at an even pace, cane in hand, searching for those who needed his help. Medications were in pitifully short supply, but he would say that often just the appearance of a doctor would make a patient feel a little better. I was glad when he accepted my offer to help him. The two of us wandered together from one hovel to the next, climbing thousands of stairs, often unable to offer the sick more than the comfort of a few kind words. Frequently, I had to bring in a pail of water first and wash and tidy up around the patient before the doctor could examine him.

One day we entered an almost bare but spotlessly scrubbed room where a child lay on a heap of rags, a little boy of four, just a small skeleton with huge eyes. His mother, so thin that she herself looked like a child, was crying quietly in the corner. The doctor took out his stethoscope, listened for a while, patted the little boy's head and sighed; he could do no more. At that moment, the child turned toward his mother and sternly, like an adult, said, "You see Mother? I told you all the time I was hungry but you didn't give me anything to eat. And now I'm going to die."

As we left the house, we were stopped by an elderly woman who asked us to call in at the next building. There was a sick man there, she said, who had not been seen for several days. The building was deserted, split in two from the roof all the way down to the cellar, and looked on the verge of collapse. It took some time before we found the one room which still had a door. We knocked, but there was no answer. Then the doctor opened the door, and we walked in. A torn mattress lay on the narrow strip of floor. There was a pile of dirty rags and refuse in one corner; next to the mattress was a suitcase half-filled with books. Lying on the mattress was a dead man, his body swarming with a myriad of fat white lice. They also crawled over the face of the Venus de Milo, who smiled serenely from a page of the open book on the man's chest. The book had dropped from his hand as he lay dying.

I leaned over him. It was my professor.

The doctor said, "He's only been dead a few hours."

About a year later, at work, I heard the bell of the ghetto's one fire engine. Although this was nearly a daily occurrence at the time, I somehow knew that the fire was at the house where I was living. It was strictly forbidden to leave a place of work, but I sneaked out and ran along the walls toward the half-ruin where we were housed. I arrived breathless to find only my mother, throwing some essentials into a suitcase. My father came running a moment later and, although he had already grown quite weak by that time, began darting back and forth trying to help. My cousin Jindrisek was lying motionless in a heap, nailed to the floor by tuberculosis of almost every organ in his body. His black hopeless eyes followed our every move.

Firemen surrounded the house. There was lots of smoke and screaming. The cold was bitter and the water did not run, but people did not panic. Even then, resignation prevailed. I remember how, with my father, I dragged out two suitcases, sat my mother down on them wrapped in blankets, and how I returned to the house to get Jindrisek.

The firemen would not let me back in. One of them swung at me with his stick and, while my father tried to stop him, I slipped back inside. Jindrisek tried to get up but could not. I started yelling at him, fiercely, desperately. I pulled his arm up around my neck—he was terribly heavy for someone made up only of skin and bones—and I dragged him outside, shouting at him all the while, trying to infuse him with my will, my energy. Over the threshold. Across the yard. Across the street. He sagged with every step but we got there and he fell, exhausted, onto another suitcase. My mother covered him and put his head in her lap. My father and I stood beside them and I hid my face on my father's shoulder.

The fire was finally brought under control, and we dragged the suitcases back into the house. Now people began to help one another, all of us exhausted from the exertion and the excitement. After everything was back in place, I put a big pot of water on to heat. Jindrisek was lying on the floor with his face to the wall, his eyes closed, a slight smile on his face. Slowly I undressed, scrubbed myself clean, combed my hair, dressed, polished my shoes, and then went unhurriedly back to work.

Jindrisek died about three weeks later. When I returned home one evening, my mother told me in a whisper that he had asked her to sing the Czech national anthem, "Where is my home?" and a folk song called "Where have all my young days gone?" I sat down beside him on the floor. He was in a coma. I tried to force spoonfuls of food into his mouth and, although he was unconscious, his craving for food was so strong that he clenched his teeth around the spoon. It required some effort on my part to free it. I slipped my hands under his head and back and held him. He stopped breathing minutes later.

My mother prayed, but I could not see the point of pleading with God for someone who had to die at the age of sixteen after much suffering. There is nothing more senseless, more cruel, than dying before we have become guilty of sins that might justify death. For a long time afterward, I felt as though those black yearning eyes were watching me from Jindrisek's corner of the room.

It seems to me, sometimes, when people say that everything passes, that they don't know what they are saying. The real past is what Jindrisek was thinking as he lay there in his corner on the floor and watched me walk out into the sun and the cold. It is what went through my mother's mind as she sang "Where is my home?" to her dying nephew behind barbed wire in the Lodz Ghetto. The real past is enclosed in itself and leaves no memory behind.

* * *

It seems beyond belief that in Czechoslovakia after the Communist coup in 1948, people were once again beaten and tortured by the police, that prison camps existed and we did not know, and that if anyone had told us the truth we would have refused to believe it. When these facts were discussed on foreign broadcasts, over Radio Free Europe or the BBC, we thought it only more proof of the way the "imperialists" lied about us. It took the full impact of the Stalinist terror of the 1950s to open our eyes.

It is not hard for a totalitarian regime to keep people ignorant. Once you relinquish your freedom for the sake of "understood necessity," for Party discipline, for conformity with the regime, for the greatness and glory of the Fatherland, or for any of the substitutes that are so convincingly offered, you cede your claim to the truth. Slowly, drop by drop, your life begins to ooze away just as surely as if you had slashed your wrists; you have voluntarily condemned yourself to helplessness.

In the last of the concentration camps that held me during the war, we worked in a brickyard, far from the camp. It was late autumn, beautiful but cold. In the mornings when we stood for roll call long before dawn, a thick crust of hoarfrost covered the ground. It would not thaw until afternoon. We wore nothing but short shifts made of burlap, no shoes, no underwear. We used to collect the scraps of paper that were strewn about our work-place, especially the heavy cement bags that were thrown out. Even though it was strictly forbidden, we stuffed them under our shifts so that we would freeze a little less. The morning roll call lasted two hours. Then we marched to a funny little train made up of flatcars, each holding two long benches mounted on a wooden floor. The trip to work took one hour. Then there was a half-hour hike to the factory, twelve hours of passing along bricks, the trip back to camp, another roll call, a little turnip soup, a slice of bread, and a short restless night.

The trip on the train was the worst thing about it all for most of the girls. During that hour we became so chilled that when we finally reached our destination, we fell rather than stepped off the train. It took us half the day to warm up a little. But I loved those trips. The tracks crossed an area under which an entire industrial complex had been built. Clouds of steam issued out from the earth in many places; mysterious iron constructions and fantastic twisted pipes rose from the moss-covered ground of the woods. The sun was already rising and, since there was always a thick fog hugging the ground, the sun's rays broke through it and colored the mist a variety of deep pinks, an orange, gold and blue. Out of this shimmering vapor, dark shapes of trees and bushes emerged, drifted toward us, and vanished again. Several clusters of trees seemed especially beautiful to me, and I always looked out for them. I remember, even now, a small uprooted spruce resting on a mound while another handsome symmetrical one stood above it straight and solemn, as if standing guard over the body of a fallen comrade.

225

Sunday was designated for work in the camp, but most often, we worked without food because our camp kommandant had calculated that even so cheap a thing as a turnip when multiplied by one thousand could bring a nice sum on the black market. We fasted on most Sundays as a result, until the management of the enterprise we worked for complained that the work force was fainting on Mondays and was not cost-efficient.

The owner of the brickyard where about fifty of us worked was an odd fellow. He must have been of Russian or German-Russian origin, skinny, with a shock of white hair, and he always wore a black belted Russian shirt. He would say, over and over again to our great amusement, that if we did not work hard and help the Reich to victory, the Russians would come and murder us all.

One Monday a trainload of coal arrived at the brickyard and the order was given to unload it, on the double. The chunks of coal were huge, mixed with stones, and very few of us had enough strength to lift our shovels. After a few hours, most of the girls were stretched out on the piles of coal, exhausted, nearly unconscious. At that moment, our boss appeared and began to shout: What kind of workers were we that we didn't even know how to handle a shovel? For the money he paid us, all we ever did was loll around!

I don't know what came over me then. The fast must have softened my brain. I threw down my shovel and screamed back at him: How dare he yell at us? Almost all of us were students, educated women. If he expected us to perform hard labor, why didn't he see to it that we were fed properly and treated as laborers? The girl lying on the coal pile nearest me grabbed my ankles and tried to pull me down, but I went right on screaming as if I had lost my senses. The boss stared at me but did not pull his gun or call the guards. To everyone's amazement, he turned around and left. The rest of the day passed in great trepidation as we all waited for the consequences of my madness. But nothing happened.

The next morning he appeared as soon as we had picked up our shovels and asked: *Wo ist die Studentin?* My anger had long since cooled and I was stiff with fear as he led me away into the brickyard. But that strange man only announced to me in a dry and rather polite tone that, from that day on, I would be working at the kiln bringing in the coal from outside in a wheelbarrow and stoking the fire. It was the cherished dream of every inmate of a concentration camp to work under a roof where it was warm. However, this was labor for two strong men and I could not possibly have handled it had it not been for the workers inside, French prisoners-of-war, good fellows who helped me and who, in fact, often did a good deal of my work.

One afternoon, toward evening, the boss appeared with two Frenchmen and ordered them to help me bring in a supply of coal. He returned about an hour later, sent them out, asked me to sit down beside him on a stone ledge in the wall of the kiln and said only: Tell me.

As long as I live I shall not forget that dark cave-like place, the black walls streaked with the reflection of flames, the old man dressed in black who listened and listened and seemed to wither, to shrink before my eyes as if, with each of my sentences, part of him faded. Only once again was I to have a similar experience—my own child, when I finally dared tell him how his father died.

I told the old man in the Russian shirt about the ghetto in Lodz where the cesspool cleaners had whistled Beethoven as they worked and where close to one hundred thousand people had been murdered or had died of starvation. I told him how the trains would arrive from Polish villages bringing men with bloody heads and women wrapped in shawls and how, once the trains were gone, the women undid their wraps and pulled out their babies, some of them dead by suffocation but a few still alive, saved from German bayonets. I told him how, a few months later, the SS would arrive and throw those same babies into trucks and cart them off to the gas chambers. I talked about the public executions, about hangings where the bodies were left on the gallows for weeks while we walked by, about the carloads of bloody clothing that we tore into strips and wove into mats for German tanks so that the soldiers could keep their feet warm. How, when the battlefront had come into earshot of our camp, a German colonel bedecked with gold braid had arrived, assembled all of us, and proclaimed: "We have to evacuate the ghetto now but do not be afraid. I give you my word of honor as a German officer that no harm will come to you. You will be well cared for . . ."and how, one week later, those who had survived the transport in sealed cattle cars walked through the gates of the electrified wire fence, straight into the black smoke of Auschwitz.

By then, I had forgotten where I was and who I was talking to. I saw the Auschwitz block again, the barracks that had been horse stables crowded with a thousand half-crazed girls shaved bald, who howled under the whips like a pack of wolves. The guards, just as demented in their fury as the prisoners in their pain and terror, ran up and down the center aisle of the block, lashing out in blind rage at the girls in the stalls. And above all this, Mrs. Steinova from Prague stood on a platform, shaven bare like the rest of us, singing the aria "The moonlight on my golden hair" from Dvorak's opera *Rusalka* by order of the block Kommandant who had decided the mood on her block should be cheerful.

I saw myself as we knelt for a whole day and night, our knees scraped raw against the sandy ground, propping up the girls who fainted because we knew that whoever collapsed would never get up again. That was the time one of the girls had tried to escape. All of Auschwitz had to kneel until they captured her and when they did, they called a roll call, broke her arms and legs while we watched and only then dragged her off to the gas.

But I did not say much about Auschwitz. Human speech can only express what the mind can hold. You cannot describe hammer blows that crush your brain. Instead, I gave the old man a detailed account of the kind of life we led in the camp from which we arrived every morning in his brickyard. I also told him that there had been girls with us who had arrived directly from home and that a few dozen of them were pregnant. One evening they had all been summoned to the main barracks and we never saw them again. The following morning, a special detail was ordered to clean puddles of blood from the barracks floor.

I do not remember what else I told him. I only know that he did not say a word for as long as I spoke and, when I heard the shouting of orders outside that meant we were returning to camp and got up to leave, he remained sitting, hunched into himself, his head in his palms.

That man lived in Nazi Germany and had daily contact with a concentration camp and its inmates, yet he knew nothing. I am quite sure he did not. He had simply thought that we were convicts, sentenced by a regular court of law for proven crimes.

People often ask me: How did you manage? To survive the camps! To escape! Everyone assumes it is easy to die but that the struggle to live requires a superhuman effort. Mostly, it is the other way around. There is, perhaps, nothing harder than waiting passively for death. Staying alive is simple and natural and does not require any particular resolve.

The idea of escape began, I think, back when our guard Franz shot yet another girl. At the time we had already been marching for a few weeks. The Eastern front had come so close to our camp that we could hear the rumbling of battle. The camp had to be evacuated. Our guard was reinforced; we received civilian coats—taken, we found out later, from people killed in the gas chambers—and an extra allotment of bread. Then we set out on foot, under twice the usual number of bayonets, toward the west, out of Poland into Germany.

Our column plodded along, inching its way across the frozen snow. Only a few of us had the strength left to turn our heads and look back as we heard the occasional shot from behind. Redheaded Franz kept close to little Eva from dawn to dusk, taking fatherly care of her, scrounging up food for her, full of affable concern. He turned around only now and then, mostly whenever the column rounded a convenient curve, and fired his gun into the rear where there were always a few stragglers. Whenever he scored a hit, he ran back along with another of our guards. Then the two of them would dig and scrape for a while in the ditch by the side of the road. Franz would then hurry back to fawn over the terrified Eva, who was only fifteen and would sob whole nights through.

During all these days and weeks of marching, I walked next to Hanka, my head bent, looking at our bare feet sinking into the slush. We talked only a little, softly, and only about one thing: escape. Just as Franz fired the last shot of his that I remember, we passed a crudely-lettered sign which read TO PRAGUE. We slowed down, pressed each other's hands, and exchanged a solemn and somewhat ridiculous promise not to deviate from that direction. Whatever happened, we would reach Prague. From the moment we had left the camp behind and with it the crackling of gunshots as the SS finished off the girls in the hospital barracks, we had thought of nothing else but escape. Many of the others were thinking the same thing; some even made small attempts. Somewhere along the way, they would slip into the bushes and let the whole column pass by. But then they would always rejoin us. It was just too difficult to face the unknown alone.

"You see," Hanka said, "as long as we march like this, all together, there's nothing we can do but walk and walk and wait until Franz guns us down somewhere. We can't reproach ourselves for anything, and nobody can expect us to do more. But once we're free, everything will be up to us. Then we'll have to act."

She was right I thought. As long as we marched together, we had the comfort of belonging. We all shivered and starved and were abused together. We shared a common destiny, a common journey, and at the end of that journey, maybe even the same death. But should we free ourselves. . . . At that moment, I understood—one single act would be enough. All it would take was one decision and I would reach the greatest freedom that anyone at that time and place on earth could possibly have. Once I slipped out from under the bayonets, I would be standing outside the system. I would not belong anywhere or to anything. No one would know of my existence. Perhaps I would only gain a few days or a few hours, but it would be a freedom that millions of people could not even imagine: No prohibitions, no orders would be of concern to me. Should I be caught, I would be like a bird shot in flight, like the wind caught in a sail.

Usually we slept under the open sky but that night we stopped in a village. First we stood on the village green where we were watched by curious eyes peeping out from every window, and then later alongside a wall that ran around a large farm. Finally, we marched through a gate of that wall into a vast yard, then through a smaller gate of a picket fence, and we came into an inner yard enclosing a huge barn. Hanka shrugged her shoulders and said, "Well that's that. Our worries are over for tonight— not even a mouse could get out of here. A barn door, a fence, and a wall!"

We stamped our feet in the mud for a long while, waiting for our dinner. The villagers provided it from their own stockpiles: two warm potatoes for each of us. Then came the rush into the barn and a fight for a sleeping place where it was least likely that someone would, in the pitch dark, step on your face with a wooden clog.

For a moment, I lingered by the gate of the barn. Surely by morning there would be no one awake to watch us. The guards would take naps as they always did whenever we could be locked in somewhere. The lock hanging by two rusty nails on the barn door was an ordinary padlock.

"Listen!" One of the girls grabbed my hand and pulled me into the shadows behind the door. "I heard we're turning north tomorrow. We'll never be as close as today."

So it seemed that everybody knew what was on my mind!

"And look what I found: a pair of shoes! They don't match and the tops are only tied to the soles with wire but they're better than nothing."

I hid the shoes under my coat. Then I took another look at the lock. Since I owned the greatest treasure a prisoner could have—a knife—and had been guarding it all these months for an occasion such as this, I thought I had better pull out one nail right away. Hanka and I whispered together for a while before we fell asleep, but the leap into freedom still seemed too steep. It demanded a clear decision; we had grown unaccustomed to thinking clearly and had almost forgotten how to make decisions. We fell asleep in the middle of a sentence, without a plan.

I woke up with a start, with the feeling that I was going to miss something crucial. I had to do something very important in a hurry—oh yes! There was darkness all around me, and the rustle of straw. From time to time, a slight moan, as though a large tired animal was turning and stretching in the dark. The slits in the barnboards were paling. Soon it would be dawn. I shook the knee that dug into my ribs from the right. "Hanka!" I said. "Let's go!"

Hanka woke up right away and understood what I was saying but she could not get a grip on herself. "I'm just so cold," she said, and started to crawl back under the straw.

"Hanka, I'm going," I whispered. "If you want, follow me. But make it fast."

At the door, I twisted out the second nail and was out. The guard on duty was still snoring somewhere. A premonition of light had already tinged the darkness; daybreak was very near.

I tied a piece of cloth over my stubby head that had been shaved bald as a knee only six months earlier in Auschwitz. Then I started picking blades of straw off my coat, but still no one came. At long last, the door opened and Hanka ran out. I did not leave her any time to change her mind. I climbed over the fence and ran across the yard to where the outer wall was crumbling and could easily be scaled. Before I could get up from my knees on the other side, Hanka landed beside me. We scrambled up and had not yet reached the corner where the wall turned when another head appeared. It was Zuzka, who whispered hoarsely, "Mana and Andula are right behind me."

The three of us squeezed into a recess in the wall of the next farm. Mana came running toward us. As we saw her we heard a gunshot; Andula did not make it.

We cowered in our little nook, trembling so hard it was almost audible, and someone said, "Let's go back."

"Nonsense. Once you're out, you're not going to crawl back, are you? They're in a big mess now. First the old man's going to give them hell for slaughtering a girl in the middle of the village—you know he doesn't like that kind of thing—and then they'll have to have a roll call. Before they count everybody and think of a way to explain why four of us are missing, we have to be miles away."

That sounded logical and we calmed down. The sun was rising. From where we stood, we had a good view of the flat landscape which rose in a slight wave on the horizon. There was not much snow, just earth and bare trees. It was a landscape as open as the palm of a hand, with no forest, no sign of a hiding place. In the distance we could see columns of men flanked by bands of soldiers, probably prisoners-of-war.

Just then, from around the corner of the wall, appeared a skinny little girl of about twelve holding two large slices of bread.

"Don't be afraid of me," she said in Czech. "I know who you are."

When I recovered from shock, I stammered in panic, "Little girl, for God's sake, you must not talk to us. Go home! Run!"

The little girl only smiled and pushed the bread into Mana's hand.

"Take it," she said. "We have plenty. And I'll lead you out of here. I'm sure you want to go home and don't know how."

"Run along! What would your mother say? Run!"

But the child only glanced over to her side where an older woman, her head wrapped in a scarf, was standing nodding.

"That's my mother! She sent me. We're also Czechs, you know."

We stared at her in amazement for a moment, but then set about ripping off the striped squares of cloth from the backs of one another's coats, the squares that marked us as concentration camp inmates. Seconds later, we were on our way, running after the little girl across a field. It was high time.

By then the countryside was wide awake. Fortunately for us, the roads were crowded. Wagons piled high with evacuated families and their household implements lumbered slowly by, alongside detachments of prisoners under guard and local people hurrying to work. Some of them turned to look at us but we walked rapidly, our eyes to the ground. Our temples pulsed with the beat of an almost insane joy. Free at last! No bayonets! No electrified or barbed wire!

Hanka was once again walking beside me, musing, "You know, there's just one thing about this situation that bothers me: the fact that, right now, we exist totally outside of the law."

I looked at her and exploded with laughter. I laughed until I wept. I laughed as I had not laughed in at least five years.

Part III

AFTERMATH
Testimony, justice, and denial

11

REDEFINING HEROIC BEHAVIOR

The impromptu self and the Holocaust experience

Lawrence Langer

In the aftermath of genocide, we are faced with a massive erasure of life and its traces in artifacts and memory. Yet for those who survived the experience, its memory is both an unbearable, unrelenting presence, and a remnant of a ruined past that must be cherished and guarded from oblivion. Conversely, for the perpetrators and their apologists, the incomplete erasure of their deeds must be followed by a redefinition of their meaning, lest the memory of the victims monopolize the narrative of the past. As for us who were not there and for the post-Holocaust societies we inhabit, there is the need to listen to the voices from a universe we cannot penetrate, even if we will never understand; to reject the apologists for murder, even as we recognize that time will make the horror seems less acute and the apologies more reasonable; and to insist on justice and punishment, even as we realize that justice is always relative and punishment often misdirected and disproportionate.

For Heda Margolius Kovály liberation was a fleeting moment between the collapse of Nazism and the fall of the "iron curtain" on her homeland; it was denied her by the movement of vast, invincible, outside forces. For Primo Levi, liberation came with the realization of all that was lost for ever, a profound sense of melancholia that was confronted by feverishly writing on the experience and by a commitment to tell the tale so as to prevent its recurrence. This enabled him to return to a sort of normality, and to argue vehemently against disillusion and despair; but the shadows of the past ultimately caught up with him too. For the men and women whose oral testimonies Lawrence Langer has analyzed in this chapter, liberation is denied from within, by the inability to reconcile one's present existence with the self that had lived through the Holocaust. Such oral testimonies, which have now been videotaped in the tens of thousands, are meant to keep a record of the past as experienced by those who lived through it before they pass away. They are, that is, what we will be left with when the direct witnesses are gone. But as Langer

235

demonstrates, they are also at least as much about the permanent damage caused by the disaster, a horrible wound inflicted on the psyche of the few who survived and then passed on in a variety of forms we may not yet be able to discern to the next generations. For what we find here is not only a realization that one had gone through a metamorphosis in order to survive, a transformation that may be remembered, but scarcely understood or accepted, in retrospect; but also, that this realization, even if kept locked away from one's environment, is always suspect of having seeped through, of having been inherited by or bequeathed to the rest of us. It is a secret knowledge about human nature of which we can no longer claim ignorance: that we all contain an impromptu self whose character and capacities will be revealed to us only if we too are ever faced with imminent destruction.

* * *

"The disaster ruins everything," Maurice Blanchot begins his paradoxical commentary on *The Writing of the Disaster*, "all the while leaving everything intact." This is the contradiction we still wrestle with nearly half a century after the event. The foundations of moral behavior remain in place, as the goal if not the reality of decent societies; meanwhile, victims of the Nazi attempt to annihilate European Jewry tell tales of survival that reduce such moral systems to an irrelevant luxury. The "luxury," to be sure, remains valid for us, as we continue to strive for what is morally right; however, as these tales unfold, in written or oral narrative, the insufficiency of the idea of moral striving as a frame for hearing them, or for understanding victim behavior, becomes ever plainer. When Blanchot says that those whom accounts of the disaster threaten—presumably *us*—remain out of reach, he urges us not to abandon the confrontation but to ask why, and to seek means of narrowing the space that separates us from the event.[1]

Sometimes this seems a futile task, even for surviving victims, who in the process of remembering betray their own difficulty when they use the language of "now" to describe the experience of "then." Consider the opening paragraphs of two narratives by former victims, each in quest of a perspective to illuminate the ordeal of remembering. The first, written in 1973, is from a book called *The Victors and the Vanquished*:

> I do not want to write. I do not want to remember. My memories are not simple recollections. They are a return to the bottom of an abyss; I have to gather up the shattered bones that have lain still for so long, climb back over the crags, and tumble in once more. Only this time I have to do it deliberately, in slow motion, noticing and examining each wound, each bruise on the way, most of all the ones of which I was least conscious in my first headlong fall. But I know I have to do it. My future stands aside, waiting until I find meaning in all that has been. I feel as if I had to overcome some almost physical obstacle, and feel drained, breathless from the effort.[2]

This victim is still consumed by her past, a sealed pain, recaptured only through struggle; her vivid imagery confirms Blanchot's conclusion that "there is no future for the disaster, just as there is no time or space [in the present] for its accomplishment."[3] Her experience seems insulated, not only from us, but from herself, the self that has survived, entered a new life, and now resists sinking back into a charnel house that even she may no longer recognize.

The second passage, written in 1986, opens a survivor narrative called *Under a Cruel Star*. The shift in tone is evident:

> Three forces carved the landscape of my life. Two of them crushed half the world. The third was very small and weak and, actually,

237

invisible. It was a shy little bird hidden in my rib cage an inch or two above my stomach. Sometimes in the most unexpected moments the bird would wake up, lift its head, and flutter its wings in rapture. Then I too would lift my head because, for that short moment, I would know for certain that love and hope are infinitely more powerful than hate and fury, and that somewhere beyond the line of my horizon there was life indestructible, always triumphant.[4]

Both the nature and the direction of the language alter, from falling to rising, from pain and anguish to rapture and hope. Authors, of course, have a right to their own mood, temperament, and vision. The problem here is that both opening paragraphs are by the *same* author, and for the *same* book, the later version, though a different translation, being virtually identical with the former one, except for the initial paragraphs. We might say that the first passage confirms Blanchot's notion that the disaster ruins everything; the second affirms its sequel, that at the same time it leaves everything intact. On the one hand, that particular disaster we call the Holocaust denies a future consistent with its violations of the self; on the other, human need requires a future where love and hope reign as motives for human conduct and aspiration despite the scope of the disaster. We as audience inhabit both worlds; and if we listen carefully to the testimonies of enough former victims, we learn that they do, too. The task before us is to understand and interpret the implications of this situation.

Memory excavates from the ruins of the past fragile shapes to augment our understanding of those ruins. What transforms "shattered bones" into "life indestructible, always triumphant"? The evolution warns us that our encounter with the narratives of former victims demands a wary intimacy with the story far beyond the passive acceptance of details. We cannot know why the author of these two introductory paragraphs decided to change the thrust of her intentions. But we do know that the first version, with its Miltonic plunge into a purely physical abyss, creates tensions for the writer and the reader that the spiritual optimism of the second version avoids. Does a self-conscious literary voice intervene here between the experience and the effect, so that language and imagery obscure even as they seek to clarify? Perhaps; perhaps not. But as we examine definitions and redefinitions of self emerging from victim narratives, we must keep in mind that each one of them represents a combat, more often than not unconscious, between fragment and form, disaster and intactness, birdsong and pandemonium. A hopeful surface story vies with a darker subtext, although—as in this instance—we scarcely recognize that the two voices are the same.

Oral testimonies of former Nazi victims slightly simplify our task, since most of these have neither time nor inclination nor gift to draw on the resources of literary artifice in their narratives. After having watched more than three hundred such testimonies, ranging in length from thirty minutes to seven hours, I've reached the conclusion that the process of recall divorced from literary effort results in a narrative form unlike the written text, equally valuable, rich in spontaneous rather than calculated effects. A member of the Norwegian underground who survived Natzweiler, Dachau, and other camps, and is writing a book about his ordeal, is asked how his oral testimony differs from his written account. "The book is different because you have more time to phrase your words," he replies. "In a book, you're also trying to be poetic—you're trying to write."[5] The equation of "writing" with "poetic," though perhaps a trifle unsophisticated, nonetheless confirms the role of style in the written memoir—that is, having time to face the conscious choice of "phrasing your words." This is a complex issue, and I mention it here only because it affects, in different ways, the sense of character that emerges from written and oral testimonies.

The "headlong fall" in the first passage quoted above unavoidably (and maybe deliberately) conjures up the image of Satan plummeting into Milton's hell, and this in turn influences our response to the experience of the victim. Such analogies rarely intrude on oral testimonies. When they do, they create a disjunctive resonance, attesting to the *in*sufficiency of familiar analogy. I am reminded, for example, of the woman who tells of being transported from Auschwitz to a labor site in Germany, looking out from the tiny window high up in her boxcar as it pauses at a small station during the journey, and exclaims: "I saw Paradise!"[6] What she saw was a group of people standing on the platform, including a mother and her child, and this normal, innocuous view, far from Edenic, nevertheless in the context of her deportation comes to represent for her a vision of Paradise. We witness a metamorphosis of meaning before our eyes, as a commonplace panorama displaces the archetypal idyllic scene, leading in turn to a spontaneous adaptation of familiar formula to an alien situation.

Devotion to orthodox versions of the self, an inability to pry oneself loose from these versions paralyzed the will of many former victims, by their own account. Rarely, however, do we find a simple opposition between paralysis and action. Oral testimonies dramatize for us, often implicitly rather than explicitly, the constantly warring impulses that bewildered the former victims. Such tensions are frequently evident in the narrative manner itself. Schifra Z., for example, born near Vilna (Vilnius), begins her testimony with perfect composure, a model of the integrated self. Slowly, as her narrative unfolds, her facial gestures and head movements, her stretching neck, the licking of her lips, her uncontrollable perspiring, and deep sighs reveal a woman increasingly possessed by rather than possessing her story. For the rest of her narrative, she alternates between control and submission, a clear illustration of the struggle to remain intact despite the disaster at the heart of her testimony.

She was between twelve and thirteen years old when German troops entered Vilna. She reports that some friendly members of the Wehrmacht asked her, "Why don't you just walk west and get out of here?" "I couldn't just walk off by myself," she tells us. "I couldn't beg, steal, I couldn't travel with false papers." It seems she is more in dialogue with herself than with us as she explains: "I couldn't see myself going off alone." Conventional moral terminology ("beg," "steal," "false,") and the sense of an inflexible persona combine to thwart the perception of a self that could respond to the urgency of the situation instead of to an inner vision of possible behavior. But when the abstract "urgency" takes on a more concrete shape, her sense of possible personae shifts dramatically.

She learns from a neighbor of the massacre of Jews in Ponary outside of Vilna, and recalls, "I decided that I wouldn't let them decide how or when I was going to die. I was going to die on my own terms, not theirs. I was not going to let them take me and put me against a wall and be shot." Out of context, statements like these resonate with the splendor of heroic determination. But as she recreates the agony of the slaughter of members of her own family, we learn along with her how provisional was *any* position under those circumstances. Her resolution to choose her own fate dissolves into one more verbal formula as the horror of the situation invades her various defenses. "We were helpless," she continues, unaware of any contradiction, "in finding our way out, and there was no way out." They had no idea, she says, why they were being killed, when they might be killed, what might happen next, or where to go. They didn't know if it was better to hide in the city, in the surrounding villages, in the forest, in a barn, with others, or alone. She admits now that they simply couldn't see their way ahead, and thus were unable to plan the best route to survival.

We encounter in this narrative memories of several versions of the self, from the reluctance to venture into unfamiliar moral terrain through the resolve to resist an imposed death sentence to total uncertainty, a kind of learned helplessness, as Jewish doom imposed by the Nazis replaced the vision of an individual, self-defined fate. Which is authentic? The question confirms the folly of searching for authenticity amidst the moral quicksand of atrocity. Schifra Z. herself unwittingly supports this conclusion when she responds to the interviewer's question at the very end about how she feels today, having gone through all this, with the surprising reply: "I believe in the goodness of man." Is this an attempt to restore the apparent order of the pre-Holocaust era, or a private concept of the self that decomposed slowly through the years of her ordeal? Perhaps as an answer to her own homiletic statement, she then adds, again with no apparent feeling of contradiction: "I believe every person has a right to be alive and to save—has a responsibility to save—his own life if he can."[7] The legacy of multiple voices is part of the heritage of survival; any attempt to resolve these voices would seem to betray or falsify that experience.

The "responsibility" of the victim to "save his [or her] own life if he can" led in unpredictable directions, hardly consistent with pre- or post-disaster ideas of the goodness of man. The "gray zone" that Primo Levi speaks of in the last of his Auschwitz memoirs represents those moments when staying alive could not be practiced as a common pursuit. Neither heroic endeavor nor selfish exploitation satisfactorily defines the options available to the victim. Narrative moments, such as the following, from one of the oral testimonies, help us to refine our appreciation of how an individual reacts when situation rather than character controls response, and what I call the impromptu self replaces the faculty of moral choice.

Having lost her proper shoes, Hanna F. is left with a dilemma: "Without shoes," she reports, "you couldn't go to work. You were dead." One evening she is standing outside her barracks when she notices a woman who is sitting on the ground and delousing her clothes. Her shoes are beside her. "I was very brave," says Hanna F., who was temporarily wearing some totally inadequate wooden clogs. She approaches the woman, surreptitiously steps out of her clogs and into the woman's regular shoes, and then, she concludes, "I walked away."[8] She looks pained while telling this story. She closes her eyes and wipes her lips, but doesn't apologize for the conduct of the impromptu self in the process of staying alive. We, however, would search in vain through familiar dictionaries of moral vocabulary for a definition of "brave" commensurate with the details of this episode.

Subversive or dismaying as it may sound, the impromptu self of the victim spontaneously detached itself from familiar value systems without apparent anguish. After liberation, that self survives in the narrative as a kind of alter ego, often unfamiliar even to the witness. "When you're hungry," admits one former victim from the Lodz ghetto, "nothing else in the world matters. . . . When you're hungry, it gets to the point where you don't mind stealing from your own sister, your own father. . . . I would get up in the middle of the night," he confesses, "and slice a piece of bread off my sister's ration. Now I—you would never picture me, and I can't even imagine myself doing that now. But it happened."[9] He is perfectly sensitive, however, to the implications of his narrative. Far from the image of the inviolable self, still our heritage from the romantic era, the impromptu self appears as a *violated* self, in part—a source of chagrin and humiliation to many witnesses—a seemingly self-violated self. One of the most distressing ironies of these oral testimonies is the ease with which, as in this instance, one is tempted to overlook the concealed persecutors, the creators rather than the inhabitants of the Lodz ghetto, and blame the victim's weakness instead.

Witnesses themselves are bewildered by the disequilibrium between the impromptu self, that followed impulse in order to stay alive, and memories of the morally distinguished life that was the goal of their prewar existence. The chronological sequence on the surface of the survivor narrative, leading through liberation to marriage, family, and/or career, cheers only the naive audience. The subtext of loss exerts its own influence on the narrative. Asked by an interviewer near the end of her testimony, "Tell me, in your life afterwards have you rebuilt some of the things that you have lost?" one former victim sabotages the illusion of continuity by exclaiming:

> No, no, everything that happened destroyed part of me. I was dying slowly. Piece by piece. And I built a new family. I am not what I would have been if I didn't go through these things. . . . Life was one big hell even after the war. So you make believe that you go on. This is not something that you put behind. And people think that they can get away from it, or you don't talk about it, or you forget your fear when you lay in an attic and you know that the Gestapo is a minute away from you. And rifles always against your head. You can't be normal. As a matter of fact, I think that we are not normal because we are so normal.

Like the woman who saw Paradise in the spectacle of a mother and child standing on a railroad platform, this former victim frustrates efforts to see survival as a simple chronology of returning from an abnormal to a normal world. Without denying the reality or the significance of her present life, she insists on the discontinuity between it and her past, an unresolved and for her unresolvable stress that nurtures anxiety. After the war, she insists, they weren't allowed to fall apart because "circumstances didn't let us." Just as situation often became a form of necessity in the camps, dictating response far more than fixed principles of character, so here, according to this testimony, postwar life required an abandonment of the impromptu self with all its painful memories. "We had to educate our children," she says, "and we had to guide our children and be nice parents and make parties. But that was all make-believe [shaking her head in a strong gesture of negation]."[10] One of the surprising revelations of these testimonies is the frequency with which such a dual sense of the self emerges, with what we would have considered a solid layer of resistance, reinforced by time, turning out to be only a thin and vulnerable veneer. "Now I am talking here," another former victim concludes his testimony, "as if this were a normal thing. Inside my heart burns. My brain boils."[11]

Of course, not everyone expresses this duality. But even contrary accounts of apparently successful adaptation betray some contradiction to the careful hearer. Sigmund W., for example, insists that after coming to America in 1948, he put his camp experiences in a time capsule and decided not to think about them. "I recognized that in order to become a part of society I had a choice to make: to stay a survivor or a prisoner and be in prison for the rest of my life, or try to preserve my sanity by putting this away in my mind and integrating myself into society as if nothing had ever happened. And obviously I chose the latter." Yet, he admits, his wife tells him that for the first *ten* years of their life together, he woke up *every night* screaming. "I am fully unaware of this," he confesses, adding: "So integration into everyday life, I believe, was possible by shutting out the indescribable events that have occurred."

Just before saying this, however, he had shown a gouache portrait of himself made in Paris in 1946 by a friend and barrack-mate from the camps, and given to his brother with the observation: "This is how I remember your brother [i.e., the speaker in this testimony]." He holds his "other self" up to the camera, a prisoner in striped uniform and cap, with sallow complexion, an utterly forlorn expression on his face, a blank stare in his eyes. He chooses to present his suppressed self through the portrait, leaving to the viewer the interpretation of the human—or inhuman—condition it represents. And in fact, his strategy is shrewder and less evasive than it appears. He explains his rationale for putting his camp experiences—he was in Blechhammer, Gross Rosen, Buchenwald, Dachau, and several lesser-known labor camps—in a time capsule by arguing: "It can only be told, I think it is important to be told, but it cannot be felt, it cannot be experienced. *I* cannot even experience it." He distinguishes between making a record and letting others *know* what happened, between details and the face in the portrait, or, on the most complex level, we might say, between the concreteness of history and the suggestiveness of art.

The appeal of written narrative is based in part on the recognition of affinities, the premise that style and structure can help the imagination to penetrate strange façades, resulting in a shared intimacy with the depicted persons and events. When witnesses like the one we have just heard insist on the *unshareability* of the experience, of an estrangement even between one's present and past persona, we understand more clearly the crucial role of the impromptu self in oral testimony. That self survived in ways no longer comprehensible even to this witness, who at one point, he tells us, was so weak that he *volunteered* to die (only to be deported to another camp instead).

On the one hand, he speaks of "survival per se" as the "ultimate resistance," of the "will of survival" as the "ultimate feat." On the other, in addition to his own momentary loss of the vaunted will to survival (which led him to volunteer to die), he tells the story of a prisoner who had scooped up some gray powder that had leaked from a split bomb, thinking it was soap, being publicly *strangled* together with his Kapo and a fellow inmate for attempted insurrection.[12] He makes no effort to connect the two moments in his narrative; but an attentive audience will speculate on the implications of a memory that is never "innocent" because of the very juxtaposition that has just emerged. Oral testimony may not always engage us in the inner workings for the former victim of what I call tainted memory; but it offers some valuable insights into its genesis and consequences, and these in turn help to explain the insistence by witnesses like this one that the gulf between their experience and our sense of it is impassable.

Tainted memory, memory of that impromptu self unrecognizable even through the act of mental recovery, is a monument to ruin rather than reconstruction. This is one of the most melancholy legacies in the subtexts of these testimonies. In another example, throughout his narrative Leo G. hints at the degradation that "transpired" between victims during the worst moments of the disaster, but firmly refuses to offer details because "it can't be described." Nonetheless, after more than three hours, the interviewer asks him "What are you left with today," and to this he readily if allusively replies:

> I envy people that can get out of themself for one minute sometimes. . . . They can laugh, enjoy. You know, you see a movie. Anybody in my situation cannot laugh and enjoy, through inside, you know. Only superficially. There's always in the back of your mind everything. How can you, how can you *enjoy* yourself? It's almost a crime against the people that you lost [in his case, mother, father, and six brothers and sisters], that you can live and enjoy yourself.

He acknowledges the joy he receives from his family, his children, their marriages, their accomplishments, but he continues, "Enjoyment is cut to the end of my days. I just can't get out of myself."

"Self" here clearly operates on two levels, separated by an intervening, untranscended loss. The exasperation of this witness at his inability to explain the difference, together with his simultaneous conviction that no one would understand anyway, frames for us but does not clarify the buried dilemma of testifying. Once again, however, the careful hearer may be able to suspect what is troubling him:

> You almost need to educate them for them to understand. If they don't understand it, I don't blame them. They can't. They can't. Talking about it, all this or more, each incident needs so much explaining. It needs explaining to the other person how and why, for them to grasp it, that you could live through it. That you could live through it without doing anything, without converting your own person to a different person than you are right now. All this you lived through, all this you saw, and you go out to work for money, drive a car or whatever. . . . How could you? . . . It should be as, you know, some people that turn away from life. It's sense-less, it doesn't add up. And I and the kind of people that went through it should know that it doesn't add up. Nothing adds up. It doesn't make any sense. Nothing justifies it. To go on and on after you know what the world is like or what it was.[13]

244

He echoes the woman who lamented "I think we are not normal because we are so normal." If a nostalgia for the heroic spirit that enabled him and his fellow victims to endure were available, it would offer him the support he needs to restore continuity to his existence. What gnaws at his memory is the question of *how* one lived through it, and then, of how one lived through it *"without converting your own person to a different person than you are right now"* (italics added). Obviously, he cannot fall back on a heroic tradition to transcend this dilemma, because to do so would violate his sense of nothing adding up. But what else could remove the obstacles impeding his quest for an image of the integrated self?[14]

The logic of character informing his vision now is neither cause nor consequence of the humiliation he experienced through more than three years in Gross Rosen, Dora/Nordhausen, and Bergen-Belsen. "I couldn't in good conscience even tell you privately about the horrors on that train," he says about the seven-day journey in open boxcars to the latter camp.[15] But other accounts of such voyages, which include death by freezing and starvation, and even cannibalism, give us a clue to his reluctance to use the vocabulary of heroic resistance to justify—or rectify—his ordeal. His reluctance betrays not only a disinclination to speak about such things, but the absence of an idiom and a context of values to enable such a discussion.

"Nazism and its effects," writes the historian Richard J. Evans, speaking of the current *Historikerstreit* in West Germany, "cannot be made real to people who . . . were born long after the event, if they are presented in crude terms of heroes and villains." If he had added "to people who were born during the event but did not share any of its experiences," he might have been talking of the audiences of victim testimony too. "The nature of the moral choices people had to make," Evans continues, "can only be accurately judged by taking into account the full complexities of the situations in which they found themselves."[16] But it may be easier for historians, with archives of documents available for research, to reconstruct the moral complexities of Hitler's rise to power and the evolution of the Final Solution, than it is for students of the camp experience, even after a collaborative effort with the victims themselves, to assess the impact on the private (as against the public) self of such an ordeal.

One of the distinctive qualities of oral testimony is its immediacy. Even though witnesses obviously have reflected on their past before their interview, they re-encounter the duality of their experience in the process of retelling it. Oddly enough, they say little of their Nazi oppressors once the deportations have begun. They wrestle instead with the dilemma of their own identity and the impossibility of functioning as a normal self in situations so unprecedented and unpredictable. They struggle further with the incompatibility between the impromptu self that endured atrocity and the self that sought reintegration into society after "liberation." Both the nature of the "villainy" and the range of "heroic" responses during the

245

ordeal elude traditional categories, and this unsettling quandary itself becomes the underground theme of many testimonies. For example, although a concept like "spiritual resistance" has gained increasing popularity among some commentators, including former victims, in their *written* accounts of the disaster, witnesses in the oral testimonies I have seen avoid this expression, or anything resembling it. They demur virtually unanimously when it is raised by an interviewer, as they do when the word "heroic" is introduced. Their response to such language ranges from dismay to disdain, despite the tempting offer of a verbal way out of their dilemma.

The experience apparently separating atrocity from survival, the so-called moment of liberation, provides some of the most dramatic testimony in these narratives. Through the content of their questions, interviewers *invite* witnesses to give detailed accounts of their feelings of joy when they realized that their ordeal was over. We need to understand more about how this psychology of expectation can impose itself on the reality of the situation and gradually forge a myth that would displace the truth. Asked how she felt when liberated, one witness replies: "We were weak. We were starving. We were in a state of apathy. We simply sat and stared into space."[17] Another is more graphic—and more suggestive: "And you know, when I was liberated . . . I was two days on my bed. I not was hungry, I not want dresses, I was [so] sick two days. But at this moment I realize I am alive and I have nobody and I am living." The sudden conjunction of the discontinuous (or impromptu) self that had managed to stay alive, with the continuous self (the family member who no longer had a family) receives eloquent understatement here. Terms like "spiritual resistance" and "heroic behavior" dwindle into irrelevancy.

The following brief exchange between an interviewer and this same witness illustrates the kind of well-intentioned but subtle prodding that often results when the normal world encounters the unfamiliar lineaments of atrocity:

Witness: I sometimes myself not can believe that a person can be so strong. And can lift over so many things.
Interviewer: As you did.
Witness: You know, I think I'm normal, and still be normal, and still have children, raise families, and talk and walk. [But] something *stimmt nicht*. Something is wrong here. In the chemistry something is wrong.
Interviewer: But you must be very strong and you must have had a will to have survived it.
Witness: [Shrugs, looks away.]
Interviewer: And you're here to talk about it, and to tell future generations.
Witness: I'm strong, I'm strong, *aber* [but] when I tell you I never was doing anything *really* to live. . . .

Interviewer: To help yourself. . . .
Witness: My fate push me, you know, I not help myself.

She then explains, in an apparent attempt to define what she means by "fate," that while she was in Auschwitz her parents (already murdered) came to her twice in dreams, and gave her advice that, as she now believes, saved her life. "They came to you when you needed them," the narrator encourages, hopefully. "I need them *now* too," the witness drily replies, ending the dialogue.[18]

"*Keep watch over absent meaning*,"[19] Maurice Blanchot warns in one of the gnomic fragments from *The Writing of the Disaster*. Our belief in heroic will, deeply etched on the modern sensibility by literary and scriptural traditions from ancient times to the present, intrudes on the need to understand what lies behind the troubled avowal by a former victim that despite her contented present life, something still "*stimmt nicht*." I am reminded of the unsettling, paradoxical discovery by a former death camp inmate that one can be alive after Sobibor without having survived Sobibor. When Blanchot distinguishes between "knowledge of the disaster" (*du désastre*) and "knowledge as disaster" (*comme désastre*), he defines the frontiers separating the violated self of the witness from the inviolable self of the audience—of us. It can scarcely be accidental that he begins the passage introducing this distinction by quoting Nietzsche's question, a virtual classical formula, "Have you suffered for knowledge's sake?"[20] The disaster of the Holocaust invalidated forever whatever force that formula once retained, though Blanchot fully appreciates the possibility of "knowledge as disaster" smiting us and nonetheless leaving us untouched. This would estrange us even further from the testimonies of former victims, the burden of whose stories is the *impossibility* for them of such an eventuality.

Blanchot presses language to its limits in his efforts to prod the imagination into original vision. "Knowledge of the disaster" skirts the subversive essence of the event, while "knowledge as disaster" affirms its disruptive impact. But formulation in words is one thing, conversion to insight another matter entirely, as Blanchot himself confesses when he admits that knowledge *as* disaster (like knowledge *via* disaster) often shields us from its implications and "carries (*porte*) us off, deports (*déporte*) us [surely a scrupulously chosen term] . . . straight to ignorance, and puts us face to face with ignorance of the unknown, so that we forget, endlessly."[21] Oral testimony is a form of endless remembering, a direct challenge to us to convert our ignorance of the unknown into some appreciation of the disparate, half-articulated tensions that inhabit the former victims' narratives. We gain this appreciation not by transforming words into meaning, but by observing the process by which one meaning cancels or neutralizes another as the narratives unfold. Because so many witnesses themselves have a vivid sense of the division resulting from having survived disaster, their testimonies invite us to participate in the painful difficulties they experience reorganizing disorder. The absence of a complex verbal texture like Blanchot's in their narratives highlights the value of his commentary, which stretches language to meet the demanding requirements of atrocity; but it also reminds us of a preliminary and perhaps more urgent need—to abandon the preconceptions that our "unstretched" language offers to protect our comfortable ignorance. Blanchot follows a bold and innovative verbal path, conjuring the reader's imagination to do the same in its pursuit of this disaster's impact on the self.

Because they do *not* provide us with the kind of constant verbal stimulus that Blanchot or authors of written survivor narratives do, oral testimonies initiate us into thinking about the disaster with fewer guidelines than a reader is usually provided with. Interviewers' attempts to provoke such frames invariably fail, so we are left with unassimilated texts that demand of us what we might call interpretive remembering. Most written texts flow continuously, compelling us to follow their sinuous turns if we wish to stay mentally afloat. Oral testimonies pause in a variety of ways, one of them being moments when witnesses display visual icons, like the gouache portrait mentioned earlier, that challenge our capacity for construing silence. Many witnesses, for example, begin or end their testimonies by holding up family photographs, some of them containing a dozen persons or more. Conventional thinking responds to the dignity of the faces before us. But we are prompted to ask by the subtext of the narrative whether the point is to remind us that they once *were*, or no longer *are*, alive. Is it an effort at rescue, or an avowal of loss? Are we gazing at presence—or absence? In fact, oral testimonies offer us both, although the "un-story," as Blanchot calls it, raises the issue of how to establish a connection between consequential living, and inconsequential dying.

This is the essential dilemma for surviving victims in these testimonies. It may be the insoluble riddle of the Holocaust itself. An underlying discontinuity assaults the integrity of the self and threatens the very continuity of the oral narrative. Perceiving the imbalance is more than just a passive critical reaction to a text. As we listen to the shifting idioms of the multiple voices emerging from the same person, we are present at the birth of a self made permanently provisional as a result of fragmentary excavations that never coalesce into a single, recognizable monument to the past. A last example of multiple voices issuing from the same individual will have to illustrate this idea. They belong to Leo L., who began his encounter with Nazi oppression in a little-known labor camp called Rachotsky Mlin—the first and the worst, he calls it—followed by Auschwitz, Dachau, Sachsenhausen, Buchenwald, and Ohrdruf. Asked what effect this has had on his life, he replies almost automatically with the language of heroic enterprise: "It makes you a stronger human being to fight for the right of humanity." But other voices possess him too, since less than a minute later he adds that anyone who went through this kind of atrocity ends up "not being the way you should be." No doubt he means both; can one also *be* both? Earlier in his testimony, he had helped to define the impromptu self by deploring his inability to relate to his own tragedy. The heroic self, by definition, helps to *create* its own tragedy, and to live or die by the consequences. Leo L. crystallizes the difference by his last words, the abrupt and forlorn questions that end his two hours of testimony, and that will seem non sequiturs only to those who have not been hearing him and his fellow witnesses: "How did my mother look? When did they take her away?"[22] Unanswered and unanswerable, they remain permanent obstacles to the rebirth of the heroic self in the oral narratives of former Holocaust victims.

NOTES

1 Maurice Blanchot, *The Writing of the Disaster* (*L'Écriture du désastre*), trans. Ann Smock (Lincoln: University of Nebraska Press, 1986), p. 1.
2 Heda Kovály and Erazim Kohák, *The Victors and the Vanquished* (New York: Horizon Press, 1973), p. 1. The citation is from Part One, "The Victors: Memoirs of Heda Margolius Kovály," trans. and ed. Erazim Kohák. Part Two comprises "The Vanquished: Perspective of Erazim Kohák."
3 Blanchot, *The Writing of the Disaster*, p. 2.
4 Heda Margolius Kovály, *Under a Cruel Star: A Life in Prague, 1941–1968*, trans. Franci Epstein and Helen Epstein with the author (Cambridge, Mass.: Plunkett Lake Press, 1986), p. 5.
5 Fortunoff Video Archive for Holocaust Testimonies at Yale, tape T-1123. Testimony of Arne L.
6 Tape T-107. Testimony of Edith P.
7 Tape T-11. Testimony of Schifra Z.
8 Tape T-18. Testimony of Hanna F.
9 Tape T-2. Testimony of Leon W.
10 Tape T-285. Testimony of Hanna H.
11 Tape T-192. Testimony of Viktor K.
12 Tape T-55. Testimony of Sigmund W.
13 Tape T-158. Testimony of Leo G.
14 Here and elsewhere, I use "integrated" as a contrasting rather than a descriptive term. The idea of an integrated self is probably mostly mythical to begin with, though under normal circumstances—the reverse of the Holocaust universe—the armor preserving its external appearance seems more secure. The "integrated" self of the former victim adapts to society's conventions by re-embracing goals like marriage, family, career. Oral testimonies reveal the existence of multiple selves that usually function in more-or-less satisfactory versions of equilibrium. Some may see this merely as a reflection of the general human condition, though I believe that the exceptional nature of the former victims' experience is a crucial differentiating factor.
15 Tape T-158. Testimony of Leo G.
16 Richard J. Evans, *In Hitler's Shadow: West German Historians and the Attempt to Escape from the Nazi Past* (New York: Pantheon Books, 1989), p. 120.

17 Tape T-65. Testimony of Irene W.
18 Tape T-845. Testimony of Eva K.
19 Blanchot, *The Writing of the Disaster*, p. 42.
20 Ibid., p. 3. Blanchot also speaks of knowledge "via disaster" (*par désastre*), fusing consciousness even more keenly with the event. Apparently trying to convey Blanchot's unorthodox sense of verbal and mental intimacy, his translator renders *par désastre* as "knowledge disastrously," suggesting in English what is less obvious in the original French—literally, a new grammar of thought.
21 Ibid., p. 3.
22 Tape T-729. Testimony of Leo L.

12

THE GRAY ZONE

Primo Levi

In this chapter, one of the most sincere, painful and searching essays ever written by a survivor of the Holocaust, Primo Levi poses the fundamental question of testimony and representation: how can the survivors make sense of their experience, how can they help others understand it? From this central quandary of writing on the Holocaust emanate all other moral, psychological, and aesthetic dilemmas. Upon his liberation, Levi, along with many other survivors, felt charged with a mission to recount the events he had barely survived as truthfully and accurately as humanly possible, so as to save from oblivion at least some fragments of all that the Nazis had tried totally to erase. By telling the tale, he might preserve the memory of those who perished; by reading his account, future generations would perhaps learn to put a stop to evil before it spreads out and devours them too. And yet, forty years after he told his story of Auschwitz for the first time, Levi concedes that the only way to recount the horror to those who were not there is by simplifying it, and that the first rule of simplification is always to divide the protagonists as neatly as possible into "they" and "us," the "bad" and the "good."

Such simplifications may indeed facilitate understanding; but is it an understanding of the past's reality that is thereby achieved, or merely of its pale reflection in a story carefully constructed and selectively told by those who will transmit the past to us? And, if it is the latter, are we not bound to draw false conclusions, to distort our own reality by reacting inappropriately to what we wrongly perceive as identical situations in the present? Speaking at a school about his experience in Auschwitz, Levi was scolded by one of the children for having failed to escape; the child went so far as to show him precisely how this feat could have been accomplished, basing his assertion on Levi's own description of the camp. The despair Levi increasingly felt toward the end of his life had much to do with his perceived inability to explain the past to later generations, and with the nagging sense of guilt toward those who perished, whose tale he had, to his mind, inadvertently yet inevitably distorted, not only because it had to be simplified, but also because only they, the "drowned," would have been able to tell the story of the millions who were murdered, but they had all perished. Yet Levi's despair was also projected into the future of the Holocaust, as he realized that recounting the horrors of the Nazi camps had not even served the purpose of preventing humanity from perpetrating ever more massacres and atrocities; whether because of the manner in which it inevitably had to be told, or because it simply reflected an inherent human predilection, his tale appeared to him to become merely a chapter in a longer narrative of devastation and inhumanity, rather than its closing episode.

This is why Levi chose to write on the "gray zone," the region of ambiguity and perplexity, where none of our conventional categories and norms, models of conduct and conceptions of morality seem to apply. This chapter warns us that ultimately, we understand nothing, that therefore we may not presume to judge, that once we step into the Lager we can expect no clarity, no neat division of good and evil, beauty and hideousness, courage and cowardice. Once inside, there is no telling who will take up which role, which qualities will make for survival and which will spell extinction. Our notions of solidarity and comradeship are shattered by the animosity between the inmates that swiftly destroys the newcomer's powers of resistance; our desire to empathize with the victims is undermined by the prisoner "functionaries" who survive by lording it over the rest of the camp population. But just as we accept these truths about human conduct in extreme situations, and think that we have finally understood, Levi blocks our path toward complacent cynicism and clichés about the nature of man. If some collaborated with the SS for personal survival, he insists, others used this role to organize heroic resistance; if the Kapos were a repulsive outgrowth of camp existence, they should never be confused with the true perpetrators who had created the system that made for the emergence of such types, indeed, whose most vile accomplishment was to make some of the victims emulate the conduct of their executioners.

Levi thus examines some of the most notorious examples of such "gray, ambiguous persons," only to demonstrate the limits on our judgment from the relative safety of our perspective. He writes on the Sonderkommandos of Auschwitz, those teams of inmates charged with the actual operation of the killing process in the gas chambers and crematoria, and reminds us that they also staged the only rebellion in the history of the camp. He cites the case of an SS man who momentarily relented from killing a girl who had survived a gassing, and while he has no doubt about this man's guilt and the justice of his punishment, he perceives this moment of hesitation as an indication of humanity even in the heart of a mass murderer. And he tells the story of Chaim Rumkowski, the "king" of the Lodz ghetto, who ruled the Jews as a dictator, surrounded himself with flatterers and regal pomp, and yet managed to negotiate the survival of the ghetto with the Germans until the very last moment, only to be sent to the gas chambers with the remainders of his "flock" shortly before the Red Army appeared in the gate. It is such episodes that we must keep in mind when we speak about the conduct of the victims, when we relegate the perpetrators to a lower species, when we insist on the kind of realism in representations of the Holocaust that merely reflects our contemporary conventions, and when we hasten to draw lessons from an event we can never fully comprehend. It is also such episodes that should always remind us of Levi's closing words, that "we are all in the ghetto, that the ghetto is walled in, that outside the ghetto reign the lords of death, and that close by the train is waiting."

* * *

Have we—we who have returned—been able to understand and make others understand our experience? What we commonly mean by "understand" coincides with "simplify": without a profound simplification the world around us would be an infinite, undefined tangle that would defy our ability to orient ourselves and decide upon our actions. In short, we are compelled to reduce the knowable to a schema: with this purpose in view we have built for ourselves admirable tools in the course of evolution, tools which are the specific property of the human species—language and conceptual thought.

We also tend to simplify history; but the pattern within which events are ordered is not always identifiable in a single, unequivocal fashion, and therefore different historians may understand and construe history in ways that are incompatible with one another. Nevertheless, perhaps for reasons that go back to our origins as social animals, the need to divide the field into "we" and "they" is so strong that this pattern, this bipartition—friend/enemy—prevails over all others. Popular history, and also the history taught in schools, is influenced by this Manichaean tendency, which shuns half-tints and complexities: it is prone to reduce the river of human occurrences to conflicts, and the conflicts to duels—we and they, Athenians and Spartans, Romans and Carthaginians. This is certainly the reason for the enormous popularity of spectator sports, such as soccer, baseball, and boxing: the contenders are two teams or two individuals, clearly distinct and identifiable, and at the end of the match there are vanquished and victors. If the result is a draw, the spectator feels defrauded and disappointed. At the more or less unconscious level, he wanted winners and losers, which he identified with the good guys and the bad guys, respectively, because the good must prevail, otherwise the world would be subverted.

This *desire* for simplification is justified, but the same does not always apply to simplification itself, which is a working hypothesis, useful as long as it is recognized as such and not mistaken for reality. The greater part of historical and natural phenomena are not simple, or not simple in the way that we would like. Now, the network of human relationships inside the Lagers was not simple: it could not be reduced to the two blocs of victims and persecutors. Anyone who today reads (or writes) the history of the Lager reveals the tendency, indeed the need, to separate evil from good, to be able to take sides, to emulate Christ's gesture on Judgment Day: here, the righteous, over there the reprobates. The young above all demand clarity, a sharp cut; their experience of the world being meager, they do not like ambiguity. In any case, their expectation reproduces exactly that of the newcomers to the Lagers, whether young or not; all of them, with the exception of those who had already gone through an analogous experience, expected to find a terrible but decipherable world, in conformity with that simple model which we atavistically carry within us—"we" inside and the enemy outside, separated by a sharply defined geographic frontier.

Instead, the arrival in the Lager was indeed a shock because of the surprise it entailed. The world into which one was precipitated was terrible, yes, but also indecipherable: it did not conform to any model; the enemy was all around but also inside, the "we" lost its limits, the contenders were not two, one could not discern a single frontier but rather many confused, perhaps innumerable frontiers, which stretched between each of us. One entered hoping at least for the solidarity of one's companions in misfortune, but the hoped for allies, except in special cases, were not there; there were instead a thousand sealed off monads, and between them a desperate covert and continuous struggle. This brusque revelation, which became manifest from the very first hours of imprisonments, often in the instant form of a concentric aggression on the part of those in whom one hoped to find future allies, was so harsh as to cause the immediate collapse of one's capacity to resist. For many it was lethal, indirectly or even directly: it is difficult to defend oneself against a blow for which one is not prepared.

Various aspects can be identified in this aggression. Remember that the concentration camp system even from its origins (which coincide with the rise to power of Nazism in Germany) had as its primary purpose shattering the adversaries' capacity to resist: for the camp management the new arrival was by definition an adversary, whatever the label attached to him might be, and he must immediately be demolished to make sure that he did not become an example or a germ of organized resistance. On this point the SS had very clear ideas, and it is from this viewpoint that the entire sinister ritual must be interpreted—varying from Lager to Lager, but basically similar—which accompanied the arrival: kicks and punches right away, often in the face; an orgy of orders screamed with true or simulated rage; complete nakedness after being stripped; the shaving off of all one's hair; the outfitting in rags. It is difficult to say whether all these details were devised by some expert or methodically perfected on the basis of experience, but they certainly were willed and not casual: it was all staged, as was quite obvious.

Nevertheless, the entry ritual, and the moral collapse it promoted, was abetted more or less consciously by the other components of the concentration camp world: the simple prisoners and the privileged ones. Rarely was a newcomer received, I won't say as a friend but at least as a companion-in-misfortune; in the majority of cases, those with seniority (and seniority was acquired in three or four months; the changeover was swift!) showed irritation or even hostility. The "newcomer" (*Zugang*: one should note that in German this is an abstract, administrative term, meaning "access," "entry") was envied because he still seemed to have on him the smell of home, and it was an absurd envy, because in fact one suffered much more during the first days of imprisonment than later on, when habituation on one hand and experience on the other made it possible to construct oneself a shelter. He was derided and subjected to cruel pranks, as happens in all communities with "conscripts" and "rookies," as well as in the initiation ceremonies of primitive peoples: and there is no doubt that life in the Lager involved a regression, leading back precisely to primitive behavior.

It is probable that the hostility toward the *Zugang* was in substance motivated like all other forms of intolerance, that is, it consisted in an unconscious attempt to consolidate the "we" at the expense of the "they," to create, in short, that solidarity among the oppressed whose absence was the source of additional suffering, even though not perceived openly. Vying for prestige also came into play, a seemingly irrepressible need in our civilization: the despised crowd of seniors was prone to recognize in the new arrival a target on which to vent its humiliation, to find compensation at his expense, to build for itself and at his expense a figure of a lower rank on whom to discharge the burden of the offenses received from above.

As for the privileged prisoners, the situation was more complex, and also more important: in my opinion, it is in fact fundamental. It is naive, absurd, and historically false to believe that an infernal system such as National Socialism sanctifies its victims: on the contrary, it degrades them, it makes them resemble itself, and this all the more when they are available, blank, and lacking a political or moral armature. From many signs it would seem the time has come to explore the space which separates (and not only in Nazi Lagers) the victims from the persecutors, and to do so with a lighter hand, and with a less turbid spirit than has been done, for instance, in a number of films. Only a schematic rhetoric can claim that that space is empty: it never is, it is studded with obscene or pathetic figures (sometimes they possess both qualities simultaneously) whom it is indispensable to know if we want to know the human species, if we want to know how to defend our souls when a similar test should once more loom before us, or even if we only want to understand what takes place in a big industrial factory.

Privileged prisoners were a minority within the Lager population, nevertheless they represent a potent majority among survivors. In fact, even apart from the hard labor, the beatings, the cold, and the illnesses, the food ration was decisively insufficient for even the most frugal prisoner: the physiological reserves of the organism were consumed in two or three months, and death by hunger, or by diseases induced by hunger, was the prisoner's normal destiny, avoidable only with additional food. Obtaining that extra nourishment required a privilege—large or small, granted or conquered, astute or violent, licit or illicit—whatever it took to lift oneself above the norm.

Now, one mustn't forget that the greater part of the memories, spoken or written, of those who came back begin with the collision with the concentrationary reality and, simultaneously, the unforeseen and uncomprehended aggression on the part of a new and strange enemy, the

255

functionary-prisoner, who instead of taking you by the hand, reassuring you, teaching you the way, throws himself at you, screaming in a language you do not understand, and strikes you in the face. He wants to tame you, extinguish any spark of dignity that he has lost and you perhaps still preserve. But trouble is in store for you if this dignity drives you to react. There is an unwritten but iron law, *Zurüchschlagen*: answering blows with blows is an intolerable transgression that can only occur to the mind of a "newcomer," and anyone who commits it must be made an example. Other functionaries rush to the defense of the threatened order, and the culprit is beaten with rage and method until he's tamed or dead. Privilege, by definition, defends and protects privilege.

I remember now that the local Yiddish and Polish term to indicate privilege was *protekcja*, pronounced "protektsia," and is of obvious Italian and Latin origin. I was told the story of an Italian "newcomer," a Partisan, flung into a work Lager with the label "political prisoner" when he still had his full strength. He had been beaten when the soup was being distributed and he had dared to shove the distributor-functionary: the latter's colleagues rushed to his aid, and the culprit was made an example of by being drowned, his head held down in the soup tub.

The ascent of the privileged, not only in the Lager but in all human coexistence, is an anguishing but unfailing phenomenon: only in utopias is it absent. It is the duty of righteous men to make war on all undeserved privilege, but one must not forget that this is a war without end. Where power is exercised by few or only one against the many, privilege is born and proliferates, even against the will of the power itself. On the other hand, it is normal for power to tolerate and encourage privilege. Let us confine ourselves to the Lager, which (even in its Soviet version) can be considered an excellent "laboratory": the hybrid class of the prisoner-functionary constitutes its armature and at the same time its most disquieting feature. It is a gray zone, poorly defined, where the two camps of masters and servants both diverge and converge. This gray zone possesses an incredibly complicated internal structure and contains within itself enough to confuse our need to judge.

The gray zone of *protekcja* and collaboration springs from multiple roots. In the first place, the more the sphere of power is restricted, the more it needs external auxiliaries. The Nazism of the final years could not do without these external auxiliaries, determined as it was to maintain its order within subjugated Europe and feed the front lines of the war, bled white by their opponents' growing military resistance. The occupied countries had to provide not only labor but also forces of order, delegates and adminis-trators of the German power, which was by now committed elsewhere to the point of exhaustion. Within this category fall, albeit to varying degrees, Quisling in Norway, the Vichy government in France, the Judenrat in Warsaw, the Saló Republic in Italy, right down to the Ukrainian and Baltic mercenaries employed elsewhere for the filthiest tasks (never in combat) and the *Sonderkommandos*, about which we will have more to say.

But collaborators who originate in the adversary camp, ex-enemies, are untrustworthy by definition: they betrayed once and they can betray again. It is not enough to relegate them to marginal tasks; the best way to bind them is to burden them with guilt, cover them with blood, compromise them as much as possible, thus establishing a bond of complicity so that they can no longer turn back. This way of proceeding has been well known to criminal associations of all times and places. The Mafia has always practiced it. It is also the only way to explain the otherwise indecipherable excesses of Italian terrorism in the 1970s.

In the second place, and in contrast to a certain hagiographic and rhetorical stylization, the harsher the oppression, the more widespread among the oppressed is the willingness, with all its infinite nuances and motivations, to collaborate: terror, ideological seduction, servile imitation of the victor, myopic desire for any power whatsoever, even though ridiculously circumscribed in space and time, cowardice, and, finally, lucid calculation aimed at eluding the imposed orders and order. All these motives, singly or combined, have come into play in the creation of this gray zone, whose components are bonded together by the wish to preserve and consolidate established privilege *vis-à-vis* those without privilege.

Before discussing separately the motives that impelled some prisoners to collaborate to some extent with the Lager authorities, however, it is necessary to declare the imprudence of issuing hasty moral judgment on such human cases. Certainly, the greatest responsibility lies with the system, the very structure of the totalitarian state; the concurrent guilt on the part of individual big and small collaborators (never likable, never transparent!) is always difficult to evaluate. It is a judgment that we would like to entrust only to those who found themselves in similar circumstances and had the opportunity to test for themselves what it means to act in a state of coercion. Alessandro Manzoni, the nineteenth-century novelist and poet knew this quite well: "Provocateurs, oppressors, all those who in some way injure others, are guilty, not only of the evil they commit, but also of the perversion into which they lead the spirit of the offended." The condition of the offended does not exclude culpability, which is often objectively serious, but I know of no human tribunal to which one could delegate the judgment.

If it were up to me, if I were forced to judge, I would lightheartedly absolve all those whose concurrence in the guilt was minimal and for whom coercion was of the highest degree. Around us, prisoners without rank, swarmed low-ranking functionaries, a picturesque fauna: sweepers, kettle washers, night watchmen, bed smoothers (who exploited to their minuscule advantage the German fixation about bunks made up flat and square), checkers of lice and scabies, messengers, interpreters, assistants' assistants. In general, they were poor devils like ourselves, who worked full time like everyone else but who for an extra half-liter of soup were willing to carry out these and other "tertiary" functions: innocuous, sometimes useful, often invented out of the whole cloth. They were rarely violent, but they tended to develop a typically corporate mentality and energetically defended their "job" against anyone from below or above who might covet it. Their privilege, which at any rate entailed supplementary hardships and efforts, gained them very little and did not spare them from the discipline and suffering of everyone else; their hope for life was substantially the same as that of the unprivileged. They were coarse and arrogant, but they were not regarded as enemies.

Judgment becomes more tentative and varied for those who occupied commanding positions: the chiefs (*Kapos*: the German term derives directly from the Italian *capo*, and the truncated pronunciation, introduced by the French prisoners, spread only many years later, popularized by Pontecorvo's movie of the same name and preferred in Italy precisely because of its differentiating value) of the labor squads, the barracks chiefs, the clerks, all the way to the world (whose existence at that time I did not even suspect) of the prisoners who performed diverse, at times most delicate duties in the camps' administrative offices, the Political Section (actually a section of the Gestapo), the Labor Service, and the punishment cells. Some of these, thanks to skill or luck, had access to the most secret information of the respective Lagers and, like Herman Langbein in Auschwitz, Eugen Kogon in Buchenwald, and Hans Marsalek in Mauthausen, later became their historians. One does not know whether to admire more their personal courage or their cunning, which enabled them to help their companions in many concrete ways, by attentively studying the individual SS officers with whom they had contact and sensing who among them might be corrupted, who dissuaded from the crueler decisions, who blackmailed, who deceived, who frightened by the prospect of a *redde rationem* at the war's end. Some of them, the three mentioned, for example, were also members of secret defense organizations, and therefore the power they wielded thanks to their positions was counterbalanced by the extreme risk they ran, inasmuch as they were both "resistors" and the repositories of secrets.

The functionaries described were not at all, or were only apparently, collaborators, but on the contrary camouflaged opponents. Not so the greater part of the other persons with positions of command, human specimens who ranged from the mediocre to the execrable. Rather than wearing one down, power corrupts; all the more intensely did their power corrupt, since it had a peculiar nature.

Power exists in all the varieties of the human social organization, more or less controlled, usurped, conferred from above or recognized from below, assigned by merit, corporate solidarity, blood, or position. Probably a certain degree of man's domination over man is inscribed in our genetic patrimony as gregarious animals. There is no proof that power is intrinsically harmful to the collectivity. But the power of which the functionaries of whom we are speaking disposed, even if they were low-ranking, such as the *Kapos* of the work squads, was, in substance, unlimited; or, more accurately put, a lower limit was imposed on their violence, in the sense that they were punished or deposed if they did not prove to be sufficiently harsh, but there was no upper limit. In other words, they were free to commit the worst atrocities on their subjects as punishment for any transgressions, or even without any motive whatsoever: until the end of 1943 it was not unusual for a prisoner to be beaten to death by a *Kapo* without the latter having to fear any sanctions. Only later on, when the need for labor became more acute, were a number of limitations introduced: the mistreatment the *Kapos* were allowed to inflict on the prisoners could not permanently diminish their working ability. But by then the malpractice was established and the regulation was not always respected.

Thus the Lager, on a smaller scale but with amplified characteristics, reproduced the hierarchical structure of the totalitarian state, in which all power is invested from above and control from below is almost impossible. But this "almost" is important: never has there existed a state that was really "totalitarian" from this point of view. Never has some form of reaction, a corrective of the total tyranny, been lacking, not even in the Third Reich or Stalin's Soviet Union: in both cases public opinion, the magistrature, the foreign press, the churches, the feeling for justice and humanity that ten or twenty years of tyranny were not enough to eradicate, have to a greater or lesser extent acted as a brake. Only in the Lager was the restraint from below nonexistent and the power of these small satraps absolute. It is understandable that power of such magnitude overwhelmingly attracted the human type who is greedy for power, that even individuals with moderate instincts aspired to it, seduced by the many material advantages of the position, and that the latter became fatally intoxicated by the power at their disposal.

Who became a *Kapo*? It is once again necessary to distinguish. The first to be offered this possibility, that is, those individuals in whom the Lager commander or his delegates (who were often good psychologists) discerned a potential collaborator, were the common criminals, taken from prisons, to whom a career as a torturer offered an excellent alternative to detention. Then came political prisoners broken by five or ten years of sufferings, or in any case morally debilitated. Later on it was Jews who saw in the particle of authority being offered them the only possible escape from the "final solution." But many, as we mentioned, spontaneously aspired to power, sadists, for example, certainly not numerous but very much feared, because for them the position of privilege coincided with the possibility of inflicting suffering and humiliation on those below them. The frustrated sought power as well, and this too is a feature in which the microcosm of the Lager reproduced the macrocosm of totalitarian society: in both, without regard to ability and merit, power was generously granted to those willing to pay homage to hierarchic authority, thus attaining an otherwise unattainable social elevation. Finally, power was sought by the many among the oppressed who had been contaminated by their oppressors and unconsciously strove to identify with them.

This mimesis, this identification or imitation, or exchange of roles between oppressor and victim, has provoked much discussion. True and invented, disturbing and banal, acute and stupid things have been said: it is not virgin terrain; on the contrary it is a badly plowed field, trampled and torn up. The film director Liliana Cavani, who was asked to express briefly the meaning of a beautiful and false film of hers, declared: "We are all victims or murderers, and we accept these roles voluntarily. Only Sade and Dostoevsky have really understood this." She also said she believed "that in every environment, in every relationship, there is a victim–executioner dynamism more or less clearly expressed and generally lived on an unconscious level."

I am not an expert on the unconscious and the mind's depths, but I do know that few people are experts in this sphere and that these few are the most cautious. I do not know, and it does not much interest me to know, whether in my depths there lurks a murderer, but I do know that I was a guiltless victim and I was not a murderer. I know that the murderers existed, not only in Germany, and still exist, retired or on active duty, and that to confuse them with their victims is a moral disease or an aesthetic affectation or a sinister sign of complicity; above all, it is precious service rendered (intentionally or not) to the negators of truth. I know that in the Lager, and more generally on the human stage, everything happens, and that therefore the single example proves little. Having said all this quite clearly, and reaffirmed that confusing the two roles means wanting to becloud our need for justice at its foundation, I should make a few more remarks.

It remains true that in the Lager, and outside, there exist gray, ambiguous persons, ready to compromise. The extreme pressure of the Lager tends to increase their ranks; they are the rightful owners of a quota of guilt (which grows apace with their freedom of choice), and besides this they are the vectors and instruments of the system's guilt. It remains true that the majority of the oppressors, during or (more often) after their deeds, realized that what they were doing or had done was iniquitous, or perhaps experienced doubts or discomfort, or were even punished, but this suffering is not enough to enroll them among the victims. By the same token, the prisoners' errors and weaknesses are not enough to rank them with their custodians: the prisoners of the Lagers, hundreds of thousands of persons of all social classes, from almost all the countries of Europe, represented an average, unselected sample of humanity. Even if one did not want to take into account the infernal environment into which they had been abruptly flung, it is illogical to demand—and rhetorical and false to maintain—that they all and always followed the behavior expected of saints and stoic philosophers. In reality, in the vast majority of cases, their behavior was rigidly preordained. In the space of a few weeks or months the deprivations to which they were subjected led them to a condition of pure survival, a daily struggle against hunger, cold, fatigue, and blows in which the room for choices (especially moral choices) was reduced to zero. Among these, very few survived the test, and this thanks to the conjunction of many improbable events. In short, they were saved by luck, and there is not much sense in trying to find something common to all their destinies, beyond perhaps their initial good health.

An extreme case of collaboration is represented by the *Sonderkommandos* of Auschwitz and the other extermination camps. Here one hesitates to speak of privilege: whoever belonged to this group was privileged only to the extent that—but at what cost!—he had enough to eat for a few months, certainly not because he could be envied. With this duly vague definition, "Special Squad," the SS referred to the group of prisoners entrusted with running the crematoria. It was their task to maintain order among the new arrivals (often completely unaware of the destiny awaiting them) who were to be sent into the gas chambers, to extract the corpses from the chambers, to pull gold teeth from jaws, to cut women's hair, to sort and classify clothes, shoes, and the contents of the luggage, to transport the bodies to the crematoria and oversee the operation of the ovens, to extract and eliminate the ashes. The Special Squad in Auschwitz numbered, depending on the moment, from seven hundred to one thousand active members.

These Special Squads did not escape everyone else's fate. On the contrary, the SS exerted the greatest diligence to prevent any man who had been part of it from surviving and telling. Twelve squads succeeded each other in Auschwitz, each remaining operative for a few months, whereupon it was suppressed, each time with a different trick to head off possible resistance. As its initiation, the next squad burnt the corpses of its predecessors. In October 1944 the last squad rebelled against the SS, blew up one of the crematoria, and was exterminated in an unequal battle that I will discuss later on. The survivors of the Special Squad were therefore very few, having escaped death because of some unforeseeable whim of fate. None of them, after the Liberation, has spoken willingly, and no one speaks willingly about their frightful condition. The information we have about these squads comes from the meager depositions of survivors, from the admissions of their "instigators" tried in various courts, from hints contained in the depositions of German or Polish "civilians" who by chance came into contact with the squads, and lastly, from diary pages written feverishly for future memory and buried with extreme care near the crematoria in Auschwitz by some of the squads' members. All these sources are in agreement, and yet we have found it difficult, almost impossible, to form an image for ourselves of how these men lived day by day, saw themselves, accepted their condition.

At first, the SS chose them from among the prisoners already registered in the Lager, and it has been testified that the choice was made not only on the basis of physical strength but also by a deep study of physiognomies. In a few rare cases enrollment took place as a punishment. Later on it was considered preferable to pick out the candidates directly at the railroad platform, on the arrival of each convoy: the SS "psychologists" noticed that recruitment was easier if one drew them from among those desperate, disoriented people, exhausted from the journey, bereft of resistance, at the crucial moment of stepping off the train, when every new arrival truly felt on the threshold of the darkness and terror of an unearthly space.

The Special Squads were made up largely of Jews. In a certain sense this is not surprising since the Lager's main purpose was to destroy Jews, and, beginning in 1943, the Auschwitz population was 90–95 percent Jews. From another point of view, one is stunned by this paroxysm of perfidy and hatred: it must be the Jews who put the Jews into the ovens; it must be shown that the Jews, the subrace, the submen, bow to any and all humiliation, even to destroying themselves. On the other hand, we know that not all the SS gladly accepted massacre as a daily task; delegating part of the work—and indeed the filthiest part—to the victims themselves was meant to (and probably did) ease a few consciences here and there.

Obviously it would be iniquitous to attribute such acquiescence to some specifically Jewish peculiarity: members of the Special Squads were also non-Jewish, German and Polish prisoners, although with the "more dignified" duties of *Kapos*, and also Russian prisoners of war, whom the Nazis considered only one degree superior to the Jews. They were few, because the Russians in Auschwitz were few (for the greater part having been exterminated before, immediately after capture, machine-gunned at the edge of enormous common graves): but they did not behave any differently from the Jews.

The Special Squads, being bearers of a horrendous secret, were kept rigorously apart from the other prisoners and the outside world. Nevertheless, as anyone who has gone through similar experiences knows, no barrier is ever without a flaw: information, possibly incomplete or distorted, has a tremendous power of penetration, and some of it always does filter through. Concerning these squads, vague and mangled rumors already circulated among us during our imprisonment and were confirmed afterward by the other sources mentioned before. But the intrinsic horror of this human condition has imposed a sort of reserve on all the testimony, so that even today it is difficult to conjure up an image of "what it meant" to be forced to exercise this trade for months. It has been testified that a large amount of alcohol was put at the disposal of those wretches and that they were in a permanent state of complete debasement and prostration.

One of them declared: "Doing this work, one either goes crazy the first day or gets accustomed to it." Another, though: "Certainly, I could have killed myself or got myself killed; but I wanted to survive, to avenge myself and bear witness. You mustn't think that we are monsters; we are the same as you, only much more unhappy."

Clearly what we know they said, and the innumerable other things they probably said but did not reach us, cannot be taken literally. One cannot expect from men who have known such extreme destitution a deposition in the juridical sense, but something that is at once a lament, a curse, an expiation, an attempt to justify and rehabilitate oneself: a liberating outburst rather than a Medusa-faced truth.

Conceiving and organizing the squads was National Socialism's most demonic crime. Behind the pragmatic aspect (to economize on able men, to impose on others the most atrocious tasks) other more subtle aspects can be perceived. This institution represented an attempt to shift onto others—specifically, the victims—the burden of guilt, so that they were deprived of even the solace of innocence. It is neither easy nor agreeable to dredge this abyss of viciousness, and yet I think it must be done, because what could be perpetrated yesterday could be attempted again tomorrow, could overwhelm us and our children. One is tempted to turn away with a grimace and close one's mind: this is a temptation one must resist. In fact, the existence of the squads had a meaning, a message: "We, the master race, are your destroyers, but you are no better than we are; if we so wish, and we do so wish, we can destroy not only your bodies but also your souls, just as we have destroyed ours."

Miklos Nyiszli, a Hungarian physician, was one of the very few survivors of the last Special Squad in Auschwitz. He was a renowned anatomical pathologist, expert in autopsies and the chief doctor of the Birkenau SS whose services Mengele—who died a few years ago, escaping justice—had secured; he had given him special treatment and considered him almost a colleague. Nyiszli was supposed to devote himself in particular to the study of twins: in fact, Birkenau was the only place in the world where it was possible to study the corpses of twins killed at the same moment. Alongside this particular task of his, to which, it should be said in passing, it does not appear he strenuously objected, Nyiszli was also the attending physician of the squad, with which he lived in close contact. Well, he recounts an episode that seems significant to me.

The SS, as I already said, carefully chose, from the Lagers or the arriving convoys, the candidates for the squads, and did not hesitate to eliminate on the spot anyone who refused or seemed unsuitable for those duties. The SS treated the newly engaged members with the same contempt and detachment that they were accustomed to show toward all prisoners and Jews in particular. It had been inculcated in them that these were despicable beings, enemies of Germany, and therefore not entitled to life; in the most favorable instance, they should be compelled to work until they died of exhaustion. But this is not how they behaved with the veterans of the squad: in them, they recognized to some extent colleagues, by now as inhuman as themselves, hitched to the same cart, bound together by the foul link of imposed complicity. So, Nyiszli tells how during a "work" pause he attended a soccer game between the SS and the SK (*Sonderkommando*), that is to say, between a group representing the SS on guard at the crematorium and a group representing the Special Squad. Other men of the SS and the rest of the squad are present at the game; they take sides, bet, applaud, urge the players on as if, rather than at the gates of hell, the game were taking place on the village green.

Nothing of this kind ever took place, nor would it have been conceivable, with other categories of prisoners; but with them, with the "crematorium ravens," the SS could enter the field on an equal footing, or almost. Behind this armistice one hears satanic laughter: it is consummated, we have succeeded, you no longer are the other race, the anti-race, the prime enemy of the millennial Reich; you are no longer the people who reject idols. We have embraced you, corrupted you, dragged you to the bottom with us. You are like us, you proud people: dirtied with your own blood, as we are. You too, like us and like Cain, have killed the brother. Come, we can play together.

Nyiszli describes another episode that deserves consideration. In the gas chamber have been jammed together and murdered the components of a recently arrived convoy, and the squad is performing its horrendous everyday work, sorting out the tangle of corpses, washing them with hoses, and transporting them to the crematorium, but on the floor they find a young woman who is still alive. The event is exceptional, unique; perhaps the human bodies formed a barrier around her, sequestered a pocket of air that remained breathable. The men are perplexed. Death is their trade at all hours, death is a habit because, precisely, "one either goes mad on the first day or becomes accustomed to it," but this woman is alive. They hide her, warm her, bring her beef broth, question her: the girl is sixteen years old, she cannot orient herself in space or time, does not know where she is, has gone through without understanding it the sequence of the sealed train, the brutal preliminary selection, the stripping, the entry into the chamber from which no one had ever come out alive. She has not understood, but she has seen; therefore she must die, and the men of the squad know it just as they know that they too must die for the same reason. But these slaves debased by alcohol and the daily slaughter are transformed; they no longer have before them the anonymous mass, the flood of frightened, stunned people coming off the boxcars: they have a person.

Can one help but think of the "unusual respect" and the hesitation of the "foul Monatto"[1] when faced by the individual case, faced by the child Cecilia killed by the plague whom, in Manzoni's novel *The Betrothed*, the mother refused to let be flung on the cart together with the heaped up corpses? Occurrences like this astonish because they conflict with the image we have of man in harmony with himself, coherent, monolithic; and they should not astonish because that is not how man is. Compassion and brutality can coexist in the same individual and in the same moment, despite all logic; and for all that, compassion itself eludes logic. There is no proportion between the pity we feel and the extent of the pain by which the pity is aroused: a single Anne Frank excites more emotion than the myriads who suffered as she did but whose image has remained in the shadows. Perhaps it is necessary that it can be so. If we had to and were able to suffer the sufferings of everyone, we could not live. Perhaps the dreadful gift of pity for the many is granted only to saints; to the Monatti, to the members of the Special Squad, and to all of us there remains in the best of cases only the sporadic pity addressed to the single individual, the *Mitmensch*, the co-man: the human being of flesh and blood standing before us, within the reach of our providentially myopic senses.

A doctor is called, and he revives the girl with an injection: yes, the gas has not had its effect, she will survive, but where and how? Just then Muhsfeld, one of the SS men attached to the death installations, arrives. The doctor calls him to one side and presents the case to him. Muhsfeld hesitates, then he decides: No, the girl must die. If she were older, it would be a different matter, she would have more sense, perhaps she could be convinced to keep quiet about what has happened to her. But she's only sixteen: she can't be trusted. And yet, he does not kill her with his own hands. He calls one of his underlings to eliminate her with a blow to the nape of the neck. Now, this man Muhsfeld was not a compassionate person; his daily ration of slaughter was studded with arbitrary and capricious acts, marked by his inventions of refined cruelty. He was tried in 1947, sentenced to death and hung in Krakow and this was right, but not even he was a monolith. Had he lived in a different environment and epoch, he probably would have behaved like any other common man.

In *The Brothers Karamazov* Grushenka tells the fable of the little onion. A vicious old woman dies and goes to hell, but her guardian angel, straining his memory, recalls that she once, only once, gave a beggar the gift of a little onion she had dug up from her garden. He holds the little onion out to her, and the old woman grasps it and is lifted out of the flames of hell. This fable has always struck me as revolting: what human monster did not throughout his life make the gift of a little onion; if not to others, to his children, his wife, his dog? That single, immediately erased instant of pity is certainly not enough to absolve Muhsfeld. It is enough, however, to place him too, although at its extreme boundary, within the gray band, that zone of ambiguity which radiates out from regimes based on terror and obsequiousness.

It is not difficult to judge Muhsfeld, and I do not believe that the tribunal which sentenced him had any doubts. On the other hand, in contrast to this, our need and our ability to judge falters when confronted by the Special

Squad. Questions immediately arise, convulsed questions for which one would be hard pressed to find an answer that reassures us about man's nature. Why did they accept that task? Why didn't they rebel? Why didn't they prefer death?

To a certain extent, the facts available to us permit us to attempt an answer. Not all did accept; some did rebel, knowing they would die. Concerning at least one case we have precise information: a group of four hundred Jews from Corfu, who in July 1944 had been included in the squad, refused without exception to do the work and were immediately gassed to death. We have learned of various individual mutinies, all immediately punished by an atrocious death (Filip Müller, one of the squads' very few survivors, tells of a companion whom the SS pushed into the oven alive), and many cases of suicide at the moment of recruitment, or immediately after. Finally, it must be remembered that it was the Special Squad which in October 1944 organized the only desperate attempt at revolt in the history of the Auschwitz Lager.

The information about this exploit that has come down to us is neither complete nor without contradictions. It is known that the insurgents (the personnel of two of the five Auschwitz-Birkenau crematoria), poorly armed and without contacts with the Polish Partisans outside the Lager or the clandestine defense organization inside the Lager, blew up Crematorium no. 3 and engaged the SS in battle. The battle was soon over, and a number of the insurgents managed to cut the barbed wire and escape to the outside but were captured soon afterward. Not one of them survived: approximately four hundred and fifty were immediately killed by the SS; among the latter [i.e. the SS], three were killed and twelve wounded.

Those whom we know about, the miserable manual laborers of the slaughter, are therefore the others, those who from one shift to the next preferred a few more weeks of life (what a life) to immediate death, but who in no instance induced themselves, or were induced, to kill with their own hands. I repeat: I believe that no one is authorized to judge them, not those who lived through the experience of the Lager and even less those who did not. I would invite anyone who dares pass judgment to carry out upon himself, with sincerity, a conceptual experiment: Let him imagine, if he can, that he has lived for months or years in a ghetto, tormented by chronic hunger, fatigue, promiscuity, and humiliation; that he has seen die around him, one by one, his beloved; that he is cut off from the world, unable to receive or transmit news; that, finally, he is loaded onto a train, eighty or a hundred persons to a boxcar; that he travels into the unknown, blindly, for sleepless days and nights; and that he is at last flung inside the walls of an indecipherable inferno. This, it seems to me, is the true *Befehlnotstand*, the "state of compulsion following an order": not the one systematically and impudently invoked by the Nazis dragged to judgment and, later on (but in their footsteps), by the war criminals of many other countries. The former is a rigid either/or, immediate obedience or death; the latter is an internal fact at the center of power and could have been resolved (actually often was resolved) by some maneuver, some slowdown in career, moderate punishment, or, in the worst of cases, the objector's transfer to the front.

The experiment I have proposed is not pleasant. Vercors tried to describe it in his story *Les Armes de la nuit* (Albin Michel, Paris, 1953), in which he speaks of "the death of the soul," and which reread today seems to me intolerably infected by aestheticism and literary lechery. Undoubtedly, however, it deals with the death of the soul. Now nobody can know for how long and under what trials his soul can resist before yielding or breaking. Every human being possesses a reserve of strength whose extent is unknown to him, be it large, small, or nonexistent, and only through extreme adversity can we evaluate it. Even apart from the extreme case of the Special Squads, often those of us who have returned, when we describe our vicissitudes, hear in response: "In your place I would not have lasted for a single day." This statement does not have a precise meaning: one is never in another's place. Each individual is so complex that there is no point in trying to foresee his behavior, all the more so in extreme situations; nor is it possible to foresee one's own behavior. Therefore I ask that we meditate on the story of "the crematorium ravens" with pity and rigor, but that judgment of them be suspended.

The same *impotentia judicandi* paralyzes us when confronted by the Rumkowski case. The story of Chaim Rumkowski is not exactly a Lager story, although it reaches its conclusion in the Lager. It is a ghetto story, but so eloquent on the fundamental theme of human ambiguity fatally provoked by oppression that I would say it fits our discourse only too well. I repeat it here, even though I have already told it elsewhere.[2] On my return from Auschwitz I found in my pocket a curious coin of light alloy, which I have saved to this day. Scratched and corroded, on one side it has the Hebrew star (the "shield of David"), the date 1943, and the word *getto*; on the other side is the inscription *QUITTUNG ÜBER 10 MARK* and *DER ÄLTESTE DER JUDEN IN LITZMANNSTADT*, that is, respectively, *Receipt for ten marks* and *The elder of the Jews in Litzmannstadt*. In short, it was a coin for internal ghetto use. For many years I forgot about its existence, and then, around 1974, I was able to reconstruct its story, which is fascinating and sinister.

In honor of a certain General Litzmann, who had defeated the Russians during World War I, the Nazis had rechristened the Polish city of Lodz "Litzmannstadt." During the final months of 1944 the last survivors of the Lodz ghetto were deported to Auschwitz, and I probably found that now useless coin on the ground in the Lager.

In 1939 Lodz had seven hundred and fifty thousand inhabitants and was the most industrialized Polish city, the most "modern" and the ugliest: it made its living from the textile industry, like Manchester and Biella, and it was conditioned by the presence of a myriad of small and large factories, which were mostly antiquated even then. As in all cities of a certain importance in occupied Eastern Europe, the Nazis hastened to set up a ghetto in it, reinstating, aggravated by their modern ferocity, the regime of the medieval and Counter-Reformation ghettos. The Lodz ghetto, begun as early as February 1940, was first chronologically and, after Warsaw's, second in number: it grew to more than one hundred and sixty thousand Jews and was disbanded only in the autumn of 1944. So it was the longest lived of the Nazi ghettos, and this must be attributed to two reasons: its economic importance and the perplexing personality of its president.

His name was Chaim Rumkowski. A failed minor industrialist, after varied travels and uneven fortunes he had settled in Lodz in 1917. In 1940 he was almost sixty and a widower without children. He enjoyed a certain esteem and was known as the director of Jewish charities and as an energetic, uncultivated, and authoritarian man. The position of president (or elder) of a ghetto was intrinsically frightful, but it was a position. It constituted social recognition, raised one a step up the ladder, and conferred rights and privileges, that is, authority—and Rumkowski passionately loved authority. How he happened to obtain the investiture is not known. Perhaps it was simply a hoax in the sinister Nazi style (Rumkowski was, or seemed to be, a fool with an air of respectability—in short, the ideal dupe); perhaps he himself had intrigued to be chosen, so strong in him must have been the will to power. The four years of his presidency, or, more, precisely, his dictatorship, were an astonishing tangle of megalomaniac dream, barbaric vitality, and real diplomatic and organizational skill. He soon came to see himself in the role of absolute but enlightened monarch, and he was certainly encouraged along this path by his German masters, who, true enough, toyed with him, but appreciated his talents as a good administrator and man of order. He obtained from them the authorization to mint currency—both in metal (that coin of mine) and on watermarked paper that was officially supplied him—which was used to pay the exhausted workers in the ghetto. They could spend it in the ghetto stores to acquire their food rations, which on the average amounted to eight hundred calories a day (although at least two thousand are needed to survive in a condition of total repose).

From these famished citizens of his, Rumkowski aspired to obtain not only obedience and respect but also love: in this respect modern dictatorships differ from the ancient ones. Since he disposed of an army of excellent artists and craftsmen ready to perform at his slightest hint in exchange for a quarter loaf of bread, he gave orders to design and print stamps bearing his effigy, with his snow-white hair and beard haloed by the light of Hope and Faith. He had a carriage drawn by a skeleton nag in which he rode through the streets of his minuscule kingdom, streets crowded with beggars and postulants. He had a regal mantle and surrounded himself with a court of flatterers and henchmen; he had his courtier-poets compose hymns in which "his firm and powerful hands" were celebrated, as well as the peace and order which thanks to him reigned in the ghetto. He ordered that the children in the nefarious schools, devastated daily by epidemics, malnutrition, and German raids, should be assigned essays in praise "of our beloved and providential president." Like all autocrats, he hastened to organize an efficient police force, ostensibly to maintain order, but in fact to protect his own person and impose his discipline: six hundred guards armed with clubs, and an unspecified number of spies. He delivered many speeches, some of which have been preserved for us and whose style is unmistakable: he had adopted the oratorical technique of Mussolini and Hitler, the style of inspired recitation, the pseudo-colloquy with the crowd, the creation of consent through subjugation and plaudit. Perhaps this imitation of his was deliberate; perhaps instead it was unconscious identification with the model of the "necessary hero" who at the time dominated Europe and was sung by D'Annunzio. More likely, however, his attitude sprang from his condition as a small tyrant, impotent with those above him and omnipotent with those below him. He spoke like a man who has throne and scepter, who is not afraid of being contradicted or derided.

And yet his figure was more complex than it may appear thus far. Rumkowski was not only a renegade and an accomplice; to some extent, besides convincing others, he must have progressively convinced himself that he *was* a messiah, a savior of his people, whose welfare, at least at intervals, he must certainly have desired. One must benefit in order to feel beneficent, and feeling beneficent is gratifying even for a corrupt satrap. Paradoxically, his identification with the oppressor alternates, or goes hand in hand, with an identification with the oppressed, because, as Thomas Mann says, man is a mixed up creature. He becomes all the more confused, we might add, the more he is subjected to tensions: at that point he evades our judgment, just as a compass goes wild at the magnetic pole.

Even though he was constantly despised and derided by the Germans, Rumkowski probably thought of himself not as a servant but as a lord. He must have taken his own authority seriously: when the Gestapo, without warning, seized *his* councilmen, he came courageously to their rescue, exposing himself to jeers and slaps which he knew how to endure with dignity. On other occasions he tried to bargain with the Germans, who kept exacting more and more cloth from Lodz and from him ever more numerous contingents of useless mouths (children, old and sick people) to send to the gas chamber in Treblinka and, later on, Auschwitz. The very harshness with which he hastened to repress signs of insubordination on the part of his subjects (there existed in Lodz, as in other ghettos, nuclei of bold political resistance, with Zionist, Bundist, or Communist roots) did not originate so much in servility toward the Germans, as in lese-majesty, indignation over the outrage inflicted on his regal person.

In September 1944, as the Russian front approached, the Nazis initiated the liquidation of the Lodz ghetto. Men and women by the tens of thousands were deported to Auschwitz, *anus mundi*, ultimate drainage site of the German universe. Worn out as they were, they were all eliminated almost immediately. About a thousand men remained in the ghetto, to dismantle the machinery of the factories and cancel the traces of the slaughter. They were liberated by the Red Army shortly afterward, and it is to them that we owe the information recorded here.

About Chaim Rumkowski's final fate two versions exist, as though the ambiguity under whose sign he lived was protracted to envelop his death. According to the first version, in the course of the ghetto's liquidation he supposedly tried to oppose the deportation of his brother, from whom he did not want to be separated, whereupon a German officer, it is said, proposed he should leave voluntarily with his brother, and he is supposed to have accepted. Another version claims instead that Rumkowski's rescue was attempted by Hans Biebow, another figure drenched in duplicity. This shady German industrialist was the functionary responsible for the ghetto's administration and at the same time its exclusive contractor. Hence, his was a delicate position, because the textile factories in Lodz worked for the armed forces. Biebow was not a ferocious beast. He was not interested in creating useless suffering or punishing the Jews for the sin of being Jewish, but he was interested in profiting from his contracts, in both legitimate and other ways. The torment in the ghetto touched him, but only indirectly. He wanted the slave-workers to work, and therefore he did not want them to die of hunger: his moral sense ended there. In reality, he was the true master of the ghetto, and he was linked to Rumkowski by that buyer–supplier relationship which often becomes a crude friendship. Biebow, a small jackal too cynical to take race demonology seriously, would have liked to put off forever the dismantling of the ghetto, which, for him, was an excellent business deal, and to preserve Rumkowski, on whose complicity he relied, from deportation. Here one sees how often a realist is objectively better than a theoretician. But the theoreticians of the SS thought otherwise, and they were the stronger. They were *grundlich* radicals: get rid of the ghetto and get rid of Rumkowski.

Unable to deal with the matter otherwise, Biebow, who had good connections, handed Rumkowski a letter addressed to the Lager of his destination and guaranteed that it would protect him and assure him special treatment. Rumkowski supposedly asked for and obtained from Biebow the right to travel to Auschwitz—he and his family—with the decorum becoming his rank, that is, in a special car, attached to the end of a convoy of freight cars packed with deportees without privileges. But there was only one fate for Jews in German hands, whether they were cowards or heroes, humble or proud. Neither the letter nor the special carriage were able to save Chaim Rumkowski, the king of the Jews, from the gas chamber.

* * *

A story like this is not self-contained. It is pregnant, full of significance, asks more questions than it answers, sums up in itself the entire theme of the gray zone and leaves one dangling. It shouts and clamors to be understood, because in it one perceives a symbol, as in dreams and the signs of heaven.

Who was Rumkowski? Not a monster, nor a common man; yet many around us are like him. The failures that preceded his "career" are significant: few are the men who draw moral strength from failure. It seems to me that in his story it is possible to recognize in an exemplary form the almost physical necessity with which political coercion gives birth to that ill-defined sphere of ambiguity and compromise. At the foot of every absolute throne, men such as Rumkowski crowd in order to grab their small portion of power. It is a recurrent spectacle: we remember the deadly struggles during the last months of World War II in Hitler's court and among the ministers of Mussolini's Republic of Saló; there too gray men, blind first and criminal later, frenziedly dividing among themselves the shreds of an iniquitous and moribund authority. Power is like a drug: the need for either is unknown to anyone who has not tried them, but after the initiation, which (as for Rumkowski) can be fortuitous, the dependency and need for ever larger doses is born, as are the denial of reality and the return to childish dreams of omnipotence. If the interpretation of a Rumkowski intoxicated with power is valid, then the intoxication occurred not because of but rather despite the ghetto environment. In other words, the intoxication with power is so powerful as to prevail even under conditions seemingly designed to extinguish all individual will. In fact, in him as in his more famous models, the syndrome produced by protracted and undisputed power is clearly visible: a distorted view of the world, dogmatic arrogance, the need for adulation, convulsive clinging to the levers of command, and contempt for the law.

All this does note exonerate Rumkowski from his responsibilities. That a Rumkowski should have emerged from Lodz's affliction is painful and distressing. Had he survived his own tragedy, and the tragedy of the ghetto he contaminated, superimposing on it his histrionic image, no tribunal would have absolved him, nor, certainly, can we absolve him on the moral plane. But there are extenuating circumstances: an infernal order such as National Socialism exercises a frightful power of corruption, against which it is difficult to guard oneself. It degrades its victims and makes them similar to itself, because it needs both great and small complicities. To resist it requires a truly solid moral armature, and the one available to Chaim Rumkowski, the Lodz merchant, together with his entire generation, was fragile. But how strong is ours, the Europeans of today? How would each of us behave if driven by necessity and at the same time lured by seduction?

Rumkowski's story is the sorry, disquieting story of the *Kapos* and Lager functionaries, the small hierarchs who serve a regime to whose misdeeds they are willingly blind, the subordinates who sign everything because a signature costs little, those who shake their heads but acquiesce, those who say, "If I did not do it, someone else worse than I would."

Rumkowski, a symbolic and compendiary figure, must be placed in this band of half-consciences. Whether high or low it is difficult to say: only he could clarify this if he could speak before us, even lying, as he perhaps always lied, also to himself. He would in any case help us understand him, as every defendant helps his judge, even though he does not want to, even if he lies, because man's capacity to play a role is not unlimited.

But all this is not enough to explain the sense of urgency and threat that emanates from this story. Perhaps its meaning is vaster: we are all mirrored in Rumkowski, his ambiguity is ours, it is our second nature, we hybrids molded from clay and spirit. His fever is ours, the fever of our Western civilization that "descends into hell with trumpets and drums," and its miserable adornments are the distorting image of our symbols of social prestige. His folly is that of presumptuous and mortal Man as he is described by Isabella in *Measure for Measure*, the Man who,

Dressed in a little brief authority,
Most ignorant of what he's most assured,
His glassy essence, like an angry ape
Plays such fantastic tricks before high heaven
As makes the angels weep.

Like Rumkowski, we too are so dazzled by power and prestige as to forget our essential fragility. Willingly or not we come to terms with power, forgetting that we are all in the ghetto, that the ghetto is walled in, that outside the ghetto reign the lords of death, and that close by the train is waiting.

NOTES

1 The men employed to bury the dead during a plague.
2 In *Moments of Reprieve* (New York: Summit Books, 1986).

272

13

REMEMBERING IN VAIN

The Klaus Barbie trial and crimes against humanity

Alain Finkielkraut

In the last few years, the term "crimes against humanity," coined first during the Nuremberg Trials, has increasingly come into both media and legal use. The reasons for this are unfortunately all too clear. In part, as in the case analyzed by Alain Finkielkraut, this has had to do with the belated trials of Nazi war criminals. In part—and ultimately more relevant because of its long-term prospects—the term has been applied to a variety of mass murders and atrocities committed since 1945. Particularly the genocide in Rwanda, "ethnic cleansing" and mass rape in Bosnia, and, most recently, the employment of similar policies in Kosovo, have featured widely in the media and have brought charges of "crimes against humanity" against the instigators of these actions by the International Tribunal in The Hague.

One can hardly describe this development as positive. It reflects the ability of Nazi mass murderers to escape justice for most of the remainder of their lives—while most perpetrators and their collaborators avoided punishment altogether; similarly, it demonstrates the ubiquity of genocide and atrocity in the second part of the twentieth century—of which only a few cases have aroused more than fleeting media attention and even fewer were followed by legal action. And yet, the very public and legal recognition of such a phenomenon as "crimes against humanity," an act or a series of acts which transcend, while also encompassing, the definition of conventional crime, and which can neither be allowed ever to expire nor may ever be forgotten or integrated into the ordinary chronicles of the past, but must stand out as a warning and a threat to all future generations, this very realization and its consequent institutionalization in law and practice, is of immense importance. To be sure, the need for this term reflects the prevalence of the phenomenon it is intended to recognize, define, and prosecute. But the phenomenon predates the term, and the option we now have of identifying it and going after the perpetrators with the concerted energy of the international community, even if it is often not employed, must be seen as a step forward within the context of a global community whose destructive capacities and often willingness to employ them are greater than ever before.

It is this crucial importance of the term "crimes against humanity" that Finkielkraut points out in his brilliant essay, only an excerpt from which can be included here. But Finkielkraut draws our attention to another troubling development that has accompanied the increasing recognition of genocide as a central event of our time. This is the argument that the preoccupation with certain types of crimes against humanity, indeed, the very notion that there is such an entity as "humanity" against which crimes can be committed, is not only false but also an excuse for the perpetuation of mass crimes against specific populations and categories of human beings. This is the argument that was used by the defense in the trial of Klaus Barbie, the Gestapo officer known by the population during the German Occupation of France as the "butcher of Lyons." Finkielkraut will not allow for this argument to pass, since for him the abandonment of "humanity" as a concept will destroy all the accomplishments of Western civilization since the Enlightenment and lead in the direction sought by fascism and Nazism, namely, that there indeed is such a thing as "life unworthy of life," or, even worse, such forms of human life as "the Jew," "Gypsies," "degenerates," and so forth, who threaten "noble humanity" and must therefore be eradicated. Conversely, for Barbie's defense the West's sanctimonious preoccupation with the Holocaust is precisely what allows it to go on subjugating, exploiting, or murdering the rest of the world while feeling that it has moved far beyond the abyss of Nazism into a "brave new world."

Since the publication of Finkielkraut's essay in 1989, many more crimes against humanity have been committed, and an international tribunal has, for the first time since Nuremberg, been set up to judge and sentence those charged with such crimes. It is a problematic institution since international law can be applied only if the international community recognizes it, and no state will readily submit to international law if it threatens to infringe on its own sovereignty. But the mechanism is there and will hopefully expand the scope of its activities in the future. Since Barbie's trial, however, charges about the abuse of the Holocaust as a means to justify criminal policies by other nations have also greatly increased, not least in France and Germany. This, of course, is one of the most tragic legacies of the Shoah. Such survivors as Primo Levi, along with many others, hoped that the Holocaust would serve to teach humanity a lesson about its own fragility and the need to preserve it as an idea, an aspiration, a vision. They never would have predicted that their insistence on preserving the memory of the Nazi camps would be presented as an instrumentalization of the past for the purpose of legitimizing new crimes (in the Third World) or conspiring against a normalization of the present (as argued recently in Germany). We can only hope that such clear and penetrating voices as that of Finkielkraut will continue to be heard above the din of apologetics, obfuscation, political rhetoric and faddish self-righteousness.

* * *

White prisoners, white executioners

A few dissenting voices thus reopened in court the debate the lawyers had wanted to close before the beginning of the trial. But to what avail? Of what use, what impact could these testimonies and the contradictions they brought to the official version of crimes against humanity be, since material humanity—flesh-and-blood humanity—let the judges and the prosecution down, undermined those who spoke in its name, and even carried sarcasm to the point of ostensibly choosing its designated assassins against its own spokesmen? If what Durkheim wrote is true—that "an act is criminal when it offends strong and definite states of the collective consciousness"—the presence on the bench of Jacques Vergès, Nabil Bouaïta, and Jean-Martin M'Bemba for the defense said in itself that the extermination of the Jews was a crime of local interest, a drop of European blood in the ocean of human suffering, and thus offended only the consciousness of white people.

Try to imagine for a moment at Nuremberg the Nazis' lawyers pleading the case of their clients (among others, Goering, Bormann, Frank, Rosenberg, Kaltenbrunner, Julius Streicher) by quoting from André Gide's *Voyage to the Congo* and by passionately invoking their own experience of racism or of European colonialism. Such a grotesque scene is unimaginable. It took place forty years later, however, and without making too many waves, in the Palais de Justice at Lyons. The Barbie trial was therefore not, as most commentators claimed, an exemplary continuation of the Nuremberg Trials. Through the spectacular collusion of the representatives of the Third World with a Nazi torturer, it was, on the contrary, a mockery of the Nuremberg Trials, and it nullified the official finding established by the international community following the victory over the Nazis—that humanity *itself* is mortal.

Before Hitler, confidence reigned; no one believed that humanity could die. Of course, said the current metaphysics, individuals die—alone or en masse, violently or naturally, from disease or accident—but the human race renews itself, like other living species: "In every era, plants grow green and flower, insects hum, animals and men subsist in their indestructible youth, and every summer we rediscover the cherries already tasted a thousand times."[1] Moreover, human history advances. Men were aware of their finiteness, they knew themselves to be mortal; they also knew, from the beginning, that life never stopped. And since with the advent of the modern era they had reversed their relationship to the ancients—no longer considering them as patriarchs but as children "truly new in all things"[2]— they thought that humanity had broken away from its eternal rebirth, in order to grow from century to century and thereby to arrive, according to a dialectical or rectilinear trajectory, at a total mastery of its own destiny.

In a sense, death had its own double standard. It severed without pity individual lives ("The last act is bloody, no matter how good the show is up until then—in the end they cover your head with dirt and that's it"),[3] but it spared humanity. ("The long procession of men over the course of the centuries must be considered as one same man who always survives and continues to learn.")[4] Thus everyone died, and nothing died. Everyone—a people, a person—left a heritage that others coming afterwards gathered up and brought to fruition. The wisdom of dead civilizations was carried over into those that superseded them; if man succumbed at the individual level, at the group level he made continual progress. Fleeting and perishable, he simultaneously belonged to a forward-moving totality, perfectible and immortal. His humanity, in the sense of human nature (as opposed to divine nature), or in the sense of the humane virtue of gentleness (as opposed to inhumanity) was absorbed by humanity, in the sense of a generic and universal being. His acts, his undertakings, his inventions—despite what he might do—contributed to the collective product. His separate individuality was taken in hand by a transcendental and unifying subject, a kind of all-encompassing "ego" whose Promethean march ardently spanned the generations.

Within this evolutionary or revolutionary perspective, people's rights could very well be flouted here and there; such deplorable infringements never called into question the positive movement of civilization. Even if, legally and morally, humanity happened to come unhinged, historically it never ceased to move forward, to progress in the accomplishment of its vocation—to pursue, with indefatigable energy, its march toward exhaustive knowledge and betterment. An event that, from the point of view of sensibility, was an unjustifiable scandal, appeared—as soon as one took the point of view of evolution—as a minor accident, if not a ploy, of the reason underlying the order of things. Beneath the appalling guises of violence or barbarity, human passions conveyed the destiny of superior ends, and attested to the role played by human unsociability within the very career of humanity. "It's not true that a straight line is always the shortest distance," Lessing had warned in *The Education of the Human Race*. In other words, history progressed also by its bad side, and it contradicted the universal conditions defining humanity only in order to subsequently give birth to a humanity truly and universally humane. The triumphal procession of history thus marched over those bodies strewn on the ground;[5] the blood (*le sang*) of the victims was drained into the meaning (*le sens*) of the future; individual tragedies were compensated by the universal epic; as they say in French, broken eggs make a fine omelette. In short, the idea of humanity remained untouched by harsh realities and was a more efficient consolation for evil than all the ancient theodicies.

At Nuremberg, this consolation stopped working. Historical realism was denounced there along with political realism. If the floor was given over to the lawyers and magistrates, it is because it was no more possible to "write off the death camps as work-related accidents in the victorious advancement of civilization,"[6] than it was to resign oneself to the fact that the relations between countries are governed by force and not by law. Furthermore, how was it possible to persist in converting suffering into reason, to forget the men who die in favor of the Man who marches forward, when it was this forward march that had made possible this industrialized death? There is nothing more regimented, more methodical, more modern than the Final Solution. This "criminal enterprise against the human condition"[7] did not burst forth from the depths of time to convulsively undo the patient work of civilization. In this unleashing of a cruelty without limits, progress was implicated in its technological form (the sophistication of the death machine) as well as in its moral form (domestication of urges, submission of will to the law).

In the aftermath of the First World War, Valéry wrote:

> We have seen, seen with our own eyes conscientious work, the most solid teaching, the most serious discipline and assiduity adapted to unspeakable projects. . . . So many horrors would not have been possible without so many virtues. A lot of science was needed, no doubt, in order to kill so many people, to waste so many assets, to obliterate so many cities in such a short time—but moral qualities were no less needed. Knowledge and Duty, are you then suspect?[8]

In 1945, this suspicion became a certainty. Life had surely resumed its busy course, but *its victims could no longer be chalked up to progress*, and history ceased to be that cartoon in which the hero—battered, mutilated, robbed of speech, crushed—always rises up again intact (if not strengthened) to continue his throbbing adventure. It was clear that this time the blow was mortal. From whatever angle one looked at it, *the crime was murder*. The human race had been forever impoverished by the destruction of the world of European Jews. A catastrophe had taken place that no logic could possibly efface; no amount of reason could attenuate its irrevocable nature. That is why, instead of letting mankind continue on its way without dwelling on the wounds inflicted on individuals, men themselves decided to dwell at length on the wound that Nazism had inflicted on humanity.[9]

And the dogma of humanity's self-fulfilling destiny through history was refuted not only by the scope and meticulousness of the crime; it was also compromised by the statements of the torturers. As Jankélévitch has rightly noted, the extermination of the Jews "was doctrinally founded, philosophically explained, methodically prepared by the most pedantic doctrinarians ever to have existed."[10] The Nazis were not, in effect, brutes, but theorists. It was not because of blood-thirsty instincts, economic or political interests, or even because of prejudice that they sacrificed all scruples. On the contrary, it could be said that the objections and scruples of interest, of instinctive pity, and of prejudice were sacrificed on the altar of their philosophy of history. "It is thus an erroneous and stupid conception," Theodore Fritsch commented as early as 1910 in his *Anti-Semite's Catechism*, "to explain the opposition to Judaism as an outgrowth of a stupid racial and religious hatred, whereas in fact it is a disinterested battle animated by the most noble ideals, against an enemy of humanity, morality and culture."[11] As faithful disciples of this benevolent anti-Semitism, the Nazis felt that they were accomplishing a spiritual mission by taking what Himmler called "the grave decision to make the Jewish people disappear from the face of the earth," and in refusing, up to the end, to be deterred from this objective, even by the efforts of war. In the service of mankind, these metaphysical killers broke all the bonds of humanity, from morality to calculated self-interest.

Here is Primo Levi's account:

> Panwitz is tall, thin, blond; he has eyes, hair, and nose as all Germans ought to have them, and sits formidably behind a complicated writing-table. I, Häftling 174517, stand in his office, which is a real office, shining, clean and ordered, and I feel that I would leave a dirty stain on whatever I touched.
>
> When he finished writing, he raised his eyes and looked at me.
>
> From that day I have thought about Doktor Panwitz many times and in many ways. I have asked myself how he really functioned as a man; how he filled his time, outside of the Polymerization and the Indo-Germanic conscience; above all when I was once more a free man, I wanted to meet him again, not from a spirit of revenge, but merely from a personal curiosity about the human soul.
>
> Because that look was not one between two men; and if I had known how completely to explain the nature of that look, which came as if across the glass window of an aquarium between two beings who live in different worlds, I would also have explained the essence of the great insanity of the third Germany.[12]

Impossible, after such an experience, to continue to believe the grandeur of a collective destiny that contains and surpasses the existence of individuals. For what gives Doctor Panwitz's gaze its coldness (without pity but also without hate) is the absolute certainty of contributing, through the elimination of parasites, to the accomplishment of the human race.

Thus civilization discovered (or rediscovered) in 1945 that men are not the *means*, the instruments, or the representatives of a superior subject—humanity—that is fulfilled through them, but that humanity is their responsibility, that they are its *guardians*. Since this responsibility is revocable, since this tie can be broken, humanity found itself suddenly stripped of the divine privilege that had been conferred on it by the various theories of progress. Exposed and vulnerable, humanity itself can die. It is at the mercy of men, and most especially of those who consider themselves as its emissaries or as the executors of its great designs. The notion of crimes against humanity is the legal evidence of this realization.

Speaking as delegates of nonwhite humanity and displaying their colors like banners, the three lawyers for Klaus Barbie (the Congolese M'Bemba, the Algerian Bouaïta, and the French-Vietnamese Vergès) wanted to wipe out the lesson of Nuremberg. They could have sought attenuating circumstances for their client, could have emphasized the difference in the scope of the atrocities committed by the Nazis and the marginal role of the head of the Lyons Gestapo in the extermination process. They could have portrayed Barbie as a formidable police officer, exclusively charged with dismantling the Resistance. They could thereby have used the crimes whose statute of limitations had expired, and of which he was in fact guilty, to counter the crimes without limitations for which he was arraigned. They could have, finally, invoked the bureaucratic excuse of obedience to orders, the sociological excuse of indoctrination, and the psychological excuse of a difficult coming-of-age in a ravaged Germany. Without completely disdaining this classical argument, they preferred to set themselves up as accusers, and to transfer the racism of the crime itself onto the memory of the crime. Or, one might say, to transfer the racism of the crime from Doctor Panwitz—whose gaze upon Primo Levi clearly said, "This something in front of me belongs to a species which it is obviously opportune to suppress. In this particular case, one has to first make sure that it does not contain some utilizable element"[13]—onto all those who today persist in honoring the victims of that madness, or who bring to trial the surviving agents of that madness.

"You ask us to suffer with you, but your memories are not ours, and your narcissistic lamentations do not bring tears to our eyes," was the message to the Western world from Mr. Vergès and his satellites. They said, in effect,

> It is you who refuse to share the earth with other races; it is you who, mistaking yourself for the center of the universe, seek to fill with your single existence, with your single race, the concept of humanity and the archives of history. It is you who, not content with having the wealth and the power, demand in addition, sympathy—and who try to make yourselves pitied by the very people whom you continue to exploit, after years of treating them as subhuman. Whites, you have pity for the fate of whites. Europeans, you inflate a family quarrel into a world war and crime without limitation. As infatuated with yourselves as you are indifferent to the sufferings of the truly oppressed, you only attend to your own scrapes and bruises, and you elevate the Jews—that is, your own—to the dignity of a condemned race or of chosen

martyrs, in order to make people forget, by your one-time ordeal, the cruelties that you have never ceased to inflict upon the races of the south. But point your finger as you may at Barbie and his ilk for the world's condemnation; go ahead and drench the Nazi crimes with your long, tearful sobs—echoed and amplified by the huge force of the media at your disposal; we are there, face-to-face with you in this place, and our multicolored presence proves that, in spite of all your efforts, the manipulation has failed. Through our intervention, in fact, it is humanity itself that bursts out laughing, and which says that *your* disaster is not *its* business.

What is striking in such reasoning is not the fact of men acting as devil's advocates, using all of their talents' resources to render Barbie innocent of the horrible acts he was accused of (this mission was imperatively conferred upon them by state law, which would repudiate itself if it withdrew its guarantees to certain categories of criminals); rather, it is striking to see resurfacing, on the occasion of the trial of an SS officer, a tradition that might not have been expected to survive the attempted extermination of the Jews by the Nazis: left-wing anti-Dreyfusism.

In the same way the most rigid spokesmen of the proletariat refused to take Dreyfus's part because they did not want to be side-tracked from the revolutionary struggle by a fratricidal battle between two rival factions of the *bourgeoisie*, similarly, for Messrs. Vergès, M'Bemba, and Bouaïta the six million Jews killed under Hitler had no right to universal commiseration, since in the Final Solution it was white prisoners and white executioners; when a massacre took place in the camp of the enemies of Man, one could not ask the other camp—that is, those in charge of humanity's progress—to sink into eternal mourning.

These militant lawyers were thus not content to merely plead their client's case as best they could—by treating the *victims* of Hitler's racism as *symptoms* of Western racism and imperialism, they reintroduced the metaphysics shattered by the catastrophe in its most radical version; they recast humanity once again as a "forward-moving totality," and made men themselves the instruments or adversaries of its achievement.

It is true that Soviet propaganda had for a long time paved the way for them. Stalinist Russia, present at Nuremberg, had easily adopted the penal category of "crimes against humanity" but without abandoning its Promethean faith in the march of history. Far from seeing Auschwitz as a refutation of progress, they saw Hitler as the paradigm and the paroxysm of all the reactionary forces allied against progress. Protean enemy, thousand-headed hydra, the Führer had been destroyed only to imme- diately reappear in other places and under other guises. As Ilya Ehrenbourg wrote in the volume of his memoirs entitled *Russia at War*, "What is called into question here, is the fact that of the fifty million victims of World War

II, there is one missing: Fascism. It survived 1945. To be sure, it had a period of *malaise* and decline, but it did not die."[14] A handy principle, which until recently allowed the Soviet government to "Nazify" all adversaries that came along, from unempowered dissidents to American nuclear might.

But this propaganda, which is today (for the time being?) more moderate, retained through the power of things a memory link with the event from which it had sprung. The same can no longer be said (as the Barbie trial demonstrated) about the religious or secular ideologies now competing with Soviet Communism for humanity's torch. Nor can it be said of history's new subjects, who, outside the West, want to take up where the European proletariat or socialist homeland left off. Frenchmen at Sétif, Americans at My Lai, Jews of the UGIF (Union Générale des Israélites de France, created by the Vichy regime in 1941 as a replacement for all existing Jewish organizations), or Zionists at Deir Yassin—everyone, in effect, according to Mr. Vergès, is a Nazi, everyone except the Nazis themselves. Because they are the losers. Crushed by the Allies, having served as a guarantee or an excuse for the creation and expansion of the racist State of Israel, how could they be totally bad—that is, Nazi? Faced with two aspects of the West, with two modalities of horror, it was thus choosing the lesser of two evils to defend one who had been *vanquished*. And furthermore, at the very moment when the offspring of the deportees were—in good conscience—hounding Palestinians in Libya or the West Bank, didn't Klaus Barbie shake his black lawyer's two hands without the slightest hint of racist hesitation, as the lawyer movingly revealed to us during his closing speech for the defense?[15]

At Nuremberg, the world judged history, instead of submitting to its verdicts or seeking the truth in its unfolding. Defining the human race by its *diversity* and no longer by its *forward march*, realizing that it is not Man who inhabits the earth, but men in their infinite plurality,[16] the judges spoke in the name of all of international society, because, as they thought, it was society as a whole that had suffered an irreparable wrong "by the fact of the disappearance of one of its racial, national, or cultural elements."[17]

This new perception of humanity no doubt accelerated the struggle against racial segregation in the United States and contributed to the downfall of colonialism in Europe. It was under the effects of the Nazis' shocking destruction of the Jews that the movement for the integration of American blacks received its momentum[18] and public opinion in the West was able to consider and oppose as *attacks on humanity* the violations committed by its own imperialism—from the former slave trade to the contemporary wars in Algeria and Vietnam. As Paul Ricoeur writes, profoundly, "The victims of Auschwitz are, par excellence, delegates to our memory for all the victims of history."[19]

Now, in Lyons in 1987, in the first trial conducted in France for crimes against humanity, the defense lined up the martyrs of colonialism and the black slave trade in the camp of the accused; it did this by reducing the diversity of the human race to the history of Man, and by pitting this Man (for whom it claimed to be the only true representative in the courtroom) against the Nazism of white-Jewish Europe.

Sheer delirium? Except for two former leaders of the Algerian National Liberation Front,[20] no one withdrew their symbolic mandate from this defense that boasted "all the colors of the human rainbow";[21] no intellectual, no poet, no journalist, no African, Asian, or Arab leader spoke up to say that one could neither accuse Jewish pain of obstructing the world's memory nor present former slaves or former victims of colonialism as victims of "the conspiracy of the remnants of Zion."

This tacit (and sometimes noisy)[22] approval suggests that if France had decided to present its prisoner to the United Nations, in keeping with the wish expressed by Hannah Arendt at the time of the Eichmann trial, numerous countries would have followed Vergès and voted for an acquittal. For a large segment of international opinion, Hitler has nothing to do with Hitler, nor does the Third Reich have anything to do with the catastrophe of humanity. For this majority inhabiting the planet, what remains from World War II is a word: Nazi. A word henceforth without referent, anchored to nothing, a word that is no longer a fact but simply a label, a floating word—available, completely adaptable—that regroups under one infamous heading every form of opposition the self-proclaimed representatives of forward-marching Man encounter in their path. A word, to put it differently, that denies the adversary the very quality of being human, degrades him into a monster against whom all means are justified, and, failing that, can consecrate as anti-Nazism the two practices that were judged and solemnly condemned at Nuremberg: total war and extermination.

The night of the idyll

What is Ideology? According to Hannah Arendt, it is "the logic of an idea," the claim to explain history as "one consistent process"[23] whose conclusion is the accomplishment, the production of humanity itself. Ideology thus refuses all relevance to the distinction made at Nuremberg between massacres committed in the name of the law by a "criminal public service" and violations by certain countries, in certain circumstances, of their own internal law. For what Ideology calls law is the formal expression of evolution and nothing else. Whether it speaks of the "law of history" or the "law of life," whether it refers to Marx or Darwin, Ideology places humanity in submission to the same rule as nature—that is, to an order that is not a commandment. The ends that men propose for themselves and the imperatives they impose on themselves dissimulate, in the eyes of Ideology, the causes that make them act. In short, Ideology substitutes necessity for duty and the scientific law of "becoming" for the transcendence of judicial or moral law. While using legal terminology, it excludes the law from its vision of the world. In Ideology, Hannah Arendt describes how "the term *law* itself changed its meaning: from expressing the framework of stability within which human actions and motions can take place, it became the expression of the motion itself."[24]

For Mr. Vergès, the north/south conflict being the law of history, France in Algeria and the United States in Vietnam showed their true face as predators, torturers, antihumanitarians. And if it is true that internal public opinion against the war carried weight in these two countries, this did not spring from the contradiction between the *values* of the West and its crimes—it only means that the West at that moment revealed its criminal essence to a significant number of Westerners.

And in the same way that the truth about the West comes down to its imperialistic violence, so crimes committed by non-western nations do not exist by virtue of their positive evolutionary role. Armed with this line of argument, Barbie's lawyers achieved the marvel of relentlessly demanding the broadening of crimes against humanity by systematically pushing aside all the recognized cases of "criminal public service," and even by reintroducing in the courtroom the kind of logic that could lead to their emergence.

The extermination of three million Cambodians was not, in fact, the result of a passing fury or an outburst of bestiality. The youthful cadres of Angkar (this genocide was carried out by adolescents) had the same gaze as Doctor Panwitz; with an implacable calm they executed the sentence pronounced by history against those who carried the mark of Western influence, and they thus pushed Ideology to its ultimate consequences. It was in the name of the law that they overcame the moral imperative "Thou shalt not kill." It was the "science" in them, and not nature, that smothered the voice of conscience. It was *idea* that dominated *instinct*, and not, as in the pogroms, instinct that unleashed all its force. As Hannah Arendt has written, "Terror is the realization of the law of movement; its chief aim is to make it possible for the force of nature or of history to race freely through mankind, unhindered by any spontaneous human action."[25]

Thus, in this trial, which became for the defense the trial of all genocides, and in which the deputy director of public prosecution himself descried a deepening of judicial thought, the Khmer Rouge revolution was scarcely considered. Analysis of that event, however, could not have failed to bring to light the true deficiencies of Nuremberg. With its methodical elimination of the bourgeoisie and the intelligentsia (recognizable by the fact that they wore glasses and spoke several languages) and of all the enemies of the New Man, the Pol Pot regime directly inscribed itself in the murderous lineage of the Hitler regime. Whereas formerly crimes took place "counter to a moral law, which was simultaneously in effect," in this case, as in the case of the Nazis, "it was the crime that was transformed into doctrine and moral law."[26] But since that crime was not perpetrated within the framework or advancement of a war, the judgment at Nuremberg does not allow for its punishment. In fact, after some hesitation, the allied military court finally decided to restrict the notion of the crime against humanity to those crimes committed *in time of war*:

> It is beyond all doubt [one reads in the judgment], that even before the war political opponents of Nazism were being killed or interned in concentration camps. The regime in these camps was odious. Terror often reigned—it was organized and systematic. A politics of harassment, repression, and murder was pursued without scruple toward civilians presumed hostile to the government; the persecution of Jews was already rampant. But in order to be considered crimes against humanity, acts of this sort committed before the war must be part of a plot or a concerted plan executed with the design of unleashing and furthering a war of aggression. They must at least be related to this. Now, the Tribunal does not find that the proof of this relationship has been established, however revolting and atrocious the acts in question may some-times have been. It cannot therefore declare that these acts imputed to Nazism and taking place before September 1, 1939, constitute, in the sense of the statute, crimes against humanity.[27]

The judgment at Nuremberg was thus made in two stages: having clearly foreseen a distinct category of crimes, having affirmed—through the American delegate to the United Nations Judicial Committee on War Crimes—that "the crimes perpetrated against stateless persons or against any other people by reason of their race or religion must be considered crimes against humanity" because they attacked the very foundations of civilization, independent of their place or date, and independent of whether or not they constituted infractions of the laws and customs of war,[28] the Allies then limited, *in fine*, their legal jurisdiction to crimes committed *after* the outbreak of hostilities. They originally rejected the arguments of realism, as we have seen, only to rally around them in the end, sacrificing on the altar of noninterference the universal principles they had just affirmed. Fearful of endangering all international order, they engaged in a difficult compromise between reference to a law of all mankind and the idea that a government has the right to do at home what it does not have the right to do outside its borders. As the American justice Robert Jackson, responsible for preparing the case, explained at the Charter Conference in London:

> It has been a general principle from time immemorial that the internal affairs of another government are not ordinarily our

business; that is to say, the way Germany treats its inhabitants, or any other country treats its inhabitants, is not our affair any more than it is the affair of some other government to interpose itself in our problems. . . . We have some regrettable circumstances at times in our own country in which minorities are unfairly treated. We think that it is justifiable that we interfere or attempt to bring retribution to individuals or to states only because the concentration camps and the deportations were in pursuance of a common plan or enterprise of making an unjust war in which we became involved. We see no other basis on which we are justified in reaching the atrocities which were committed inside Germany, under German law, or even in violation of German law, by authorities of the German state.[29]

As a result, the anti-Jewish decrees made before the war were excluded from the case for the prosecution, even though they constituted the first stage of the Final Solution.

It is true that the United Nations General Assembly broke this artificial link between war and crimes against humanity by taking up, on its own account, the term *genocide* (coined by Raphaël Lemkin during the last months of the Nazi occupation to designate the liquidation of an ethnic group), and by adopting, on December 9, 1948, a treaty whose first article read as follows: "The contracting parties confirm that genocide, whether committed in time of peace or war, is a crime against human rights, and they pledge themselves to prevent and punish it." The problem is that in the absence of an international criminal court, the agreement foresees entrusting the state on whose territory the said genocide occurred with the task of bringing the guilty parties before their own tribunals. Which comes down to having the repression of crimes against humanity guaranteed by either the criminal (an absurd hypothesis) or the few survivors (a hypothesis that contradicts the idea of a *law* or *destiny* common to all humanity). Genocide becomes an internal affair, its punishment reduced (when it takes place) to a purge, and one is thus left with the very situation that one sought to correct: the breaking up of the human race into a multitude of states.

Perhaps there is no way to remedy these gaps in international law. At least something might have happened in Lyons if they had been recognized. Instead, French justice took refuge behind the ambiguities of the judgment at Nuremberg and blurred even further the definition of crimes against humanity. Emotional thought surrendered to totalitarian thought, reintroduced under the guise of antiracism by Barbie's defenders.

We must admire the paradox: it was in reaction to Ideology that the West became so *feeling*. It is because the concern with upsetting Billancourt has lost its power of intimidation, that today we feel free enough to denounce all crimes, without drawing distinctions about their origin or finality. It is from history and its dubious sources of prestige that we have reconquered—in high combat—the gift of tears. It is the defeat of the idea of the Revolution that has enabled us to mobilize ourselves, without preliminary selection, for all the victims of inhumanity. Now, where does all this lead us, this moral liberation and this pity at last freed from restraint? To consecrate, totally unconsciously, the grand return of Ideology in the first trial to take place in France for crimes against humanity.

The problem is that, despite its vehemence and its radicalism, our critique missed the main point: Ideology is paved with good feelings. With the promise of the advent of a united and happy humanity tomorrow, relegating the diversity of opinions, interests, and conflicts born of life in society to a single Manichaean confrontation today, Ideology speaks the language of science but appeals first of all to the emotions. It flatters that part of us that cannot be resigned to the idea that plurality is the law of the earth, that part of us wishing stubbornly for a marvelously simple world where politics never strays from morality or thought from feeling, where the Other always has either the tender face of a brother or the frightening face of a killer. To be sure, excluding from the human species all those who do not belong to the family, the race, or the nation is not the same as wishing to generalize the sense of family to all humanity. But in either case—whether it is withdrawing into elementary tribalism or seeing the planet as a single and immense brotherhood—it is the law of the heart that rules, and any discord is seen as "spitting in the smiling face of brotherhood."[30]

Beyond their actual differences, either kind of totalitarian propaganda plunges us again into the idyllic and barbarous era situated by Goethe at the beginning of humanity's cultural history: everything there has "a domestic and family-oriented air about it";[31] no social relation departs from the model of intimacy; an identical, unfailing camaraderie glows on identical youthful and radiant faces.

We must, therefore, ascribe to ideology in general the definition Thomas Mann gave to National Socialism in 1940:

> National Socialism means: "I don't care about social consequences. What I want is a simple folktale." This formulation is no doubt the mildest and the most abstract. That in reality National Socialism is also a repugnant barbarism stems from the fact that in the world of politics, fairytales turn into lies.[32]

The catastrophe of fairy tales is this: the worst kind of violence does not spring from the antagonism between men, but from the certainty of delivering them from it forever. "*Polemos*," said Heraclitus, "is the father of all things." As Patočka powerfully demonstrates, it was to stop this reign that Ideology plunged humanity into unprecedented distress.[33] Its absolute immorality springs not from its cynicism or from its Machiavelianism but from the exclusively moral nature of its categories. Its inhumane character, brought out by the prosecutor, comes from its impatient desire for fraternity. For if one admits, with Eluard, the great poet of Ideology, that "you don't need everything to make a world; you need happiness and nothing more," then is it not criminal to permit—without reacting—the militant proclaimers of unhappiness, the implacable enemies of a society that has no enemies to live and prosper?

One can conclude that humanity ceases to be humane as soon as there is no longer a place for an "enemy" in the idea it holds of itself and its destiny. Which means, *a contrario*, that *angelism is not humanism*, that discord, far from being a failure or an anachronism of society, is our most precious political good, and that the excellence of democracy, its superiority over all other forms of human coexistence, springs precisely from the fact that it institutionalized conflict by inscribing it in its guiding principles.

Now, try as we may to be henceforth—and so ardently!—democratic anti-Nazis, antitotalitarians, antifascists, antiracists and antiapartheid—we have not yet learned to be wary of the beatific smile of fraternity. In spite of Patočka, Kundera, Hannah Arendt, or Thomas Mann, the lesson of this century has not been heard: we continue to consider life in unison as the very apotheosis of being. Great legal proceedings carried out in planetary concert—this is the enchanted picture of universal sympathy that we hold up in opposition to xenophobes, to the partisans of withdrawal and the sowers of hatred. When confronted with the racist, our current object of weekly execration, we are all brothers, next-of-kin, buddies; we are all uplifted by the same feelings, our bodies move to the same rhythm of a "great Euro-world dance,"[34] our "ten billion ears"[35] are enchanted by the same harmonies, our pulses accelerate simultaneously, a like energy electrifies us, and rejecting the "old authority of verbal order"[36] in favor of a culture of sound, we sing, by the glimmer of cigarette lighters, the same hymn of hope and love across the entire face of the earth. The certainty thus spreads that if it were not for the Nazis and their epigones, all the diverse elements of humanity would melt together in an immense musical embrace.

So we cannot really blame the successive postwar generations for a general lack of memory or vigilance. Hitler, we know, but it is, alas, a kind of knowing that invests anti-Nazism with the totalitarian fantasy of transparent hearts and group happiness. To the dream of a community homogeneous in its blood and in its land, we respond by "the excessive closeness of a brotherliness that obliterate[s] all distinctions."[37] As though, in fact, nothing had happened—as though no catastrophe had cast a deathly pall over the era—the night of the idyll descends once again over humanity. Love dethrones *Polemos*, emotion invades the space of disputation and replaces the agonistic expression of opinions with the lyrical communion of persons.

Far from defending the legitimacy of *conflict* against those who seek to abolish it, we gradually lose the capacity, thus, to conceive of any other division than the exclusively moral one that separates "them" and "us"—that is, Cain and Abel. Antiracism takes the place of politics where it should only be the prerequisite for it. And it is at the moment when we congratulate ourselves on being—once and for all—rid of the blunt language of simplistic categories, that, reducing all antagonism to the cosmic and schematized combat of Light vs. Darkness, we speak that language the most ardently.

Under the guise of a great reconciliation with democratic ideals the political disappears; the moral vision of the world triumphs once again. Formerly, (that is, during the CRS-SS years), this moral vision drew its examples and slogans from the epic story of the Resistance. Today, inspired more by the martyrdom of the yellow star than by the example of the underground partisans, this vision builds on the Jewish genocide in order to impose its childishly terrible seriousness on public life as well as on culture. By virtue of Auschwitz and the call of "Never again!" ("*Plus jamais ça!*"), the value of a work now resides not in its power to reveal but in the intensity of its opposition to all discriminatory practices; not in its richness in the world but in its aptitude for purging the world of all profundity and all indeterminacy; not in its opening up to what is relative, paradoxical, ambiguous, chiaroscuro, but in the dizzying simplicity of its good sentiments. According to this point of view, from the beginning of time, poets, thinkers and writers, film-makers, great composers and singing stars have been charged with a single and magnificent mandate: to denounce the still and forever fertile womb of racism. On television, the director of a great entertainment company confides that Baudelaire taught him tolerance. According to an anti-Heideggerian philosopher, Homer was the first to speak out against the practice of genocide. Kafka's *Metamorphosis*, we are told in countless student essays, is essentially a deeply moving parable of intolerance and exclusion, like *The Boy with Green Hair*, that very lovely film by Joseph Losey. With the best of intentions, this businessman, this philosopher, and these students rob the authors they admire (and literature in general) of everything except an edifying discourse that is pronounced, from generation to generation in ever newer guises, by some sort of perpetual Victor Hugo.

Contemporary sentiment thus makes antiracism play the same role that the Stalinist vulgate assigned to class struggle. And it is by invoking the *shoah* with indecent smugness that the aspiration to the simple folktale has today depoliticized political debate, has transformed culture into pious images, and, with no concern for the truth, has reduced the unmasterable multiplicity of mankind to an exultant face-to-face confrontation between Innocence and the Unspeakable Beast.

NOTES

1 Arthur Schopenhauer, *Le Monde comme volonté et comme représentation* (Paris: Presses Universitaires de France, 1966), p. 1222; E. F. J. Payne, tr., *The World as Will and Representation* (Indian Hills, CO: Falcon's Wing, 1958).

2 Pascal, "Préface au Traité du vide," in *De l'esprit géométrique, Ecrits sur la Grâce et autres textes* (Paris: GF-Flammarion, 1985), p. 62.

3 Pascal, *Pensées*, no. 210, ed. Brunschvicg (Paris: Garnier, 1964), p. 131.

4 Pascal, "Préface au Traité du vide," p. 62.

5 I borrow this expression from Walter Benjamin's *Thèses sur la philosophie de l'histoire*.

6 Theodor Adorno, *Minima Moralia* (Paris: Payot, 1980), p. 218; E. F. N. Jephcott, tr., *Minima Moralia* (London: NLB, 1974).

7 Edgar Faure, Introduction to *La Persécution des Juifs en France et dans les autres pays de l'Ouest* (Paris: Center of Contemporary Jewish Documentation, 1947), p. 24.

8 Paul Valery, "La crise de l'esprit," in *Variété I* (Paris: Gallimard, 1978), p. 15.

9 "Reason can't linger over the wounds inflicted on individuals, for individual destinies are swallowed up in the universal destiny." Hegel, *La Raison dans l'Histoire* (Paris: Union Generale D'Editions, 1965), p. 68; Robert S. Hartman, tr., *Reason in History* (Indianapolis: Bobbs-Merrill, 1953).

10 V. Jankélévitch, *L'Impréscriptible* (Paris: Seuil, 1986), p. 43.

11 Quoted by Shulamit Volkov, in *L'Allemagne nazie et le génocide juif*, Colloquium at the Ecole des Hautes Etudes en Sciences Sociales (Paris: Gallimard-Seuil, 1985), p. 83.

12 Primo Levi, *Survival in Auschwitz*, tr. Stuart Woolf (New York: Collier-Macmillan, 1961), p. 96. First published as *If This is a Man* (New York: Orion, 1959).

13 Levi, *Survival in Auschwitz*, p. 96.

14 Ilya Ehrenbourg, *La Russie en guerre* (Paris: Gallimard, 1968), pp. 45–46; Gerard Shelley, tr., *Russia at War* (London: H. Hamilton, 1943).

15 Hearing of July 1, 1987.

16 I borrow this expression from Hannah Arendt, who uses it in several of her works, notably in *Men in Dark Times* (New York: Harcourt, Brace, World, 1968).

17 Marcel Merle, *Le Procès de Nuremberg et le châtiment des criminels de guerre* (Paris: Pedonc, 1949), p. 158.

18 Of course we had to wait until the sixties to see this struggle culminate and result in equal rights. But it was in November 1945—that is, scarcely six months after the unconditional surrender of the German army—that the American Jewish Congress created a Commission on Law and Social Action with a view toward helping all those who suffered from discrimination. Thus, President Truman rightly noted in his *Memoirs*: "Hitler's persecution of the Jews did much to awaken Americans to the dangerous extremes to which prejudice can be carried if allowed to control government actions." Quoted in Raul Hilberg, *The Destruction of the European Jews* (Chicago: Quadrangle Books, 1961), p. 761.

19 Paul Ricoeur, *Le Temps raconté, Temps et Récit III* (Paris: Seuil, 1985), p. 273.

20 "If we Algerians are to have any place whatsoever in this trial, it is not as witnesses for the defense, on behalf of Barbie, but as witnesses for the prosecution, in the name of the rights of Man that legitimize our own struggle." Hocine Ait Ahmed and Mohammed Harbi, in *Le Nouvel Observateur*, no. 1183, July 10, 1987.

21 Jacques Vergès, *Je défends Barbie* (Paris: Jean Piccolec, 1988), p. 13.
22 For example, here is what one could read in the section devoted to the Barbie trial in the weekly newspaper *Algérie-Actualité* (no. 1127, week of May 21–27, 1987) entitled, bluntly. "What do Jews Want?"

> More than forty years later, the Holocaust is causing a furor. As soon as a Jew starts to cry somewhere in this vast world, humanity is accused of being basically anti-Semitic, and, one after the other, History and the men who made it are dragged in.
>
> The Holocaust is the Jewish flame of Olympus. maintained by a world-wide financial power, with the aid of the media.
>
> How can you tell Palestinians to commit to memory the dramas of the past, when they are living through far more unbearable ones? What difference is there between a gas chamber and a cluster bomb that falls on an Arab house on a night of Ramadan?
>
> What can you say to Palestinian children about the common foundations of humanity if one day the men who deprived them of memories don't suffer the infamy of being in the dock of the accused? While awaiting brotherly love, which has been sublimated like death, there exists this truth. The truth of Mr. Jacques Vergès, "anti-Semite" in spite of himself, surrounded by the insulting slogans of these fanatics of persecution: "The Zionists go so far back in time that they assume the aspect of Teutonic knights."

23 Hannah Arendt, *The Origins of Totalitarianism*, 2d ed. (Cleveland: World Publishing, 1958), p. 469.
24 Ibid., p. 464.
25 Ibid., p. 465.
26 Max Picard, *L'Homme du néant* [*Hitler in uns selbst*], tr. Jean Rousset (Paris: La Balconnière, 1947), p. 191.
27 *Le Procès de Nuremberg, Le verdict* (Paris: Office français d'édition, 1947).
28 Quoted and discussed in Henri Meyrowitz, *La Répression par les tribunaux allemands des crimes contre l'humanité et de l'appartenance à une organisation criminelle* (Paris: LGDJ, 1960), p. 18.
29 Quoted in Raul Hilberg, *The Destruction of the European Jews* (Chicago: Quadrangle Books, 1961), pp. 686–687.
30 Milan Kundera, *L'Insoutenable légèreté de l'être* (Paris: Gallimard, 1983), p. 316; Michael Henry Heim, tr., *The Unbearable Lightness of Being* (New York: Harper and Row), 1984.
31 Goethe, "Les époques de la culture sociale" [1832], in *Ecrits sur l'Art,*. tr. and ed. by Jean-Marie Schaeffer (Klincksieck, 1983); Ellen von Nordroff and Ernest H. von Nordroff, tr., John Gearey, ed., *Essays on Art and Literature* (New York: Suhrkamp, 1986).
32 Thomas Mann, "Défense de Wagner," in *Wagner et notre temps* (Paris: Pluriel, 1978), p. 178.
33 Jan Patočka, *Essais hérétiques* (Paris: Verdier, 1981).
34 Jean-François Bizot, *Libération*, June 18–19, 1989 (speaking about the triple concert Paris–New York–Dakar organized by SOS Racism to mark the anniversary of June 18, 1988).
35 I borrow this expression from the advertising campaign of Megastore, the large record store opened by Virgin Records in October 1988 on the Champs-Elysées in Paris.

36 George Steiner, *In Bluebeard's Castle: Some Notes Toward the Redefinition of Culture* (New Haven: Yale University Press, 1971), p. 118.

37 Hannah Arendt, *Men in Dark Times* (New York: Harcourt, Brace, World, 1968), p. 30.

INDEX

administration 26–9, 30
Adorno, T.W. 82
Ahlwardt, Deputy 32–4, 36
Alexandria 38
Algeria 281, 283
Algerian National Liberation Front 282
Allen, W.S. 214
alleviation 37, 38–9, 40
Alltagsgeschichte (history of everyday life) 8, 168–9, 177–8
Aly, G. 87–8, 177
Améry, J. 9
Anatomie des SS-Staates 167
Anders, G. 216
annihilation 25; campaign in the East as war of 169
anticipatory compliance 39
anti-Dreyfusism 280
antisemitism 1, 2–3, 65, 81, 82; Christian Europe and Nazism 3, 21–42; redemptive 79, 83–4, 87–8; as spiritual mission 277–8
Apion 38
Arad, Y. 209–10
Arctic Ocean labour/penal colonies 131
Arendt, H. 1, 7, 94, 104, 207, 282; ideology 282–3
armaments industry 103–4, 116
army, German *see* German soldiers
Army Group Centre 112
Aryanisation 95, 96–8
asylums 46–9; euthanasia programme 54–6, 57, 96
Auerbach, R. 210
Auschwitz 56, 210, 225–8, 270; 'gray zone' 11, 252, 261–7; revolt in 1944 266

Austria 97; *see also* Vienna
authorization for killings 68–9, 94
avoidance, sensory 211–13
awareness (perception) 215–17

Bankier, D. 86
barbarization of warfare 169–70, 171
Barbarossa, Operation 173
Barbie, K., trial 12–13, 273–91
Bartov, O. 169
Bauer, E. 56
Bauer, Y. 69
Becker, A. 70, 150
Belzec extermination camp 109–10, 121, 127, 136
Benigni, R. 11, 220
Berger, G. 126
Berghahn, V. 167
Bernotat, F. 48, 49
Bethel Sarepta 55
Bettauer, H., *Die Stadt ohne Juden* 41
Biebow, H. 270
Binding, K. 46, 51–2
biologically determined groups 3, 63–76
Birkenau 263
black market 209–10
Blanchot, M. 237, 247–8
Blobel, P. 130
Boeckh, R. 55
bolshevism 88, 171
Bormann, M. 69, 116, 123, 134–5
Bosnia 273
Bouaïta, N. 275, 279–80
Bouhler, P. 52, 56, 67, 121, 123
Boy with Green Hair, The 288
Bracht, F. 123
Brack, V. 56, 67, 96, 120–1
Brandt, K. 52, 67

Lösener, B. 115, 118, 129, 132
Losey, J. 288
loss 242
love 221, 238
Lowenstein, K. 114–15
Lublin 134
Luther, Martin (founder of
  Protestantism) 24, 31–2, 36
Luther, Martin (of Reich foreign
  ministry) 128, 130, 134

Madagascar project 25
Maelicke, A. 102–3
Mafia 257
Main Trustees for the East 102
Mainz 37
Mandelstam, N. 9
Mann, T. 269, 286
Manstein, E. von 166
Manzoni, A. 257, 264
Marsalek, H. 258
Mauthausen 8, 204–18
Mayer (chief of genealogy office) 133
M'Bemba, J.-M. 275, 279–80
medical profession: murder of
  biologically determined groups 3,
  63–76; psychiatry and the euthanasia
  programme 3, 43–62
Meinecke, F. 166
Meltzer, E. 51–2
memory 10–11; see also survivors'
  memoirs
Mengele, J. 43, 263
Mennecke, F. 57
'mercy killing' see euthanasia
  programme
Messerschmidt, M. 167, 174
Meyer, A. 114, 115, 123, 129, 131, 132
Midgley, M. 214
migration 37, 39–40
Militärgeschichtliches Forschungsamt
  (Institute of Military History) 166,
  167, 174
Millnicze 187–8
Ministry for the East (Ostministerium)
  113, 114, 117
Minsk 112, 114, 133–4
mixed marriages 114, 115, 119, 129,
  132–3
'modernisation' plans for psychiatry
  58
modernity 81–2; and myth 82–4
Mogilev 136

Mombert, P. 98–9
Mommsen, H. 84, 85, 96, 177
moral vision 288
Morante, E. 9
Moscow, Battle of 127
Muhsfeld (SS man) 265
Müller, F. 266
Müller, H. 115
Müller, K.-J. 167
Müller, R.-D. 167
munitions production 103–4, 116
murderers: and victims 260
Mutschmann, M. 124
myth 82–4

National Security Agency 173
National Socialist Party functionaries
  122–5, 134–5
Naumann, K. 171–2
Nazism (National Socialism):
  antisemitism compared with that in
  Christian Europe 2–3, 21–42;
  approaches to nature of 1–2, 81–2;
  Mann's definition 286
'necessary hero' 269
negationism 11–12
negative demographic policy 98–100,
  101
Ner, River 207, 217
Netherlands 38, 133; hostages from
  117, 147
Neumann, E. 98, 115, 116
neutrality 214
'new' interpretation 81–2
newcomers, in concentration camps
  254–5
Nitsche, P. 53, 58
Nolte, E. 88
noninterference 214, 284–5
Nuremberg 38
Nuremberg Trials 165, 172, 273, 275,
  276–7, 281; crimes against humanity
  limited to time of war 284
nurses 49, 54
Nyiszli, M. 263–4

Oberhauser, J. 56
Oberländer, T. 98, 99
occupational redistribution 39
occupational therapy, in asylums 47
O'Neill, R. 167
optimum population 98–9
oral testimonies 10, 235–50

3.1 *Reform in the UK*

Reform is never finished. While the UK Higher Education Act 2004 largely coheres with the arguments in this book, issues remain.

As far as fees are concerned, as discussed in Chapters 13 and 15, there are good arguments for imposing a maximum. However, some participants in the UK debate argue that the fees cap of £3,000 per year is too low and/or that it will be kept at its initial level for too long. This is very much an issue where policy design and politics must flow together. If the cap is too high, it risks destabilising the system politically; but if it is too low for too long, most universities will charge the maximum, approximating a system of flat fees, thus restoring central planning by the back door. Thus the task for politicians is to ensure sufficient political support for a fees cap high enough to ensure a competitive regime.

On the loans front, the interest subsidy is expensive and regressive. In addition, the 2004 reforms raised the threshold at which graduates start to make repayments. As a result, all graduates make lower monthly repayments, increasing the average duration of the loan and hence increasing the leakage caused by the interest subsidy. To make matters worse, UK student loans are off-budget. Thus eliminating the blanket interest subsidy yields savings only off-budget. Redirecting those savings towards larger grants would involve on-budget spending, that is, would increase measured public spending.

Thus twofold reform is necessary: replacing the blanket interest subsidy by a targeted subsidy; and bringing loans on-budget for reasons of rational public accounting. These reforms would make it possible to offer larger loans, and to offer all students a full loan; they would also free considerable resources for policies to promote access.

On access measures, more could be done to protect low-earning graduates in some of the ways described in Chapter 13, for example targeted interest subsidies, loan write-off for some public-sector workers and loan remission for people involved in caring activities.

3.2 *The unfinished agenda: technical*

Policy makers continue to grapple with a range of technical puzzles: designing loans with income-contingent repayments but which are privately financed; cooperating in collecting student loan repayments across countries; and devising effective loan repayments in developing countries with limited institutional capacity.

Private finance

A loan scheme, by definition, lends out money first and collects repayments later. Most OECD countries can afford to meet these upfront costs from public funds. Poorer countries, however, face tighter fiscal constraints, and new members of the EU are particularly constrained by the Stability and Growth Pact and the Convergence Criteria. Thus a scheme in which students borrow from private sources, with income-contingent repayments collected by the tax authorities has considerable attractions.

Such a scheme, however, is more difficult than it sounds. To illustrate the problem, suppose that a student takes out a loan from a bank, but the government gives the bank a full guarantee. Under international statistical guidelines, the *entire* loan counts as public spending. Though on the face of it paradoxical, the logic is straightforward: since the government guarantees repayment, no risk is transferred to the private lender: thus the loans are really the government's loans, but with private administration. Though the student nominally borrows from a private bank, all such lending is classified as public.

Though these are complex matters, the critical element is risk transfer. The fact that a student borrows from private sources is not on its own sufficient to ensure that the loan is private; it is private only if the lender faces a significant fraction of the risk. This creates a serious dilemma for policy makers. If there is a significant government guarantee, the loan will be classified as public; but if there is little or no guarantee, the lender will charge students a risk premium which will be large because there is no security for the loan.

There are two broad strategies for bringing in private resources. With debt sales, students borrow public money. Having lent the money, the loans administrator retrospectively sells student debt to a private buyer. Debt sales are a well-known technique – for example, sales of credit card debt – which has been extensively discussed (Barr and Falkingham 1993, 1996). Two tranches of student debt were sold by the UK government in the late 1990s. A second approach is front-end funding, whereby students borrow more directly from private sources. The role of the loans administrator in this case is to hold the ring and to administer any subsidies and guarantees. There has been less exploration of this approach; there has been some headway, but no country yet has a large-scale system of privately financed income-contingent loans.

The country that has perhaps come closest is Hungary, based on collaboration in the late 1990s/early 2000s between UK and Hungarian teams.[5] In important respects, the collaboration was successful. Since 2001, Hungary has had a system of student loans run by a free-standing student loans administration; loans have income-contingent repayments; the

---

5 The UK team comprised Nicholas Barr, Iain Crawford, and, with the agreement of the UK government, Colin Ward and Hugh Macadie from the UK Student Loans Company. The Hungarian team included Dr Gyula Gilly, the first Chief Executive of the Hungarian Student Loans Company, and Erika Papp, the Deputy Chief Executive. The driving political force was the Education Minister, Zoltán Pokorni.

scheme incorporates a positive real interest rate, thus avoiding one of the strategic problems of UK arrangements; and the sale of two tranches of student loan bonds alongside conventional government bonds attracted strong interest in financial markets. The scheme gives Hungary what is arguably the most advanced student loan scheme in the new member states of the EU, and more advanced than many in Western Europe. The outcome – a loan scheme from scratch to a very tight deadline – stemmed from a process with three central elements: sparkling teamwork, the presence of all three legs of the tripod on both the UK and the Hungarian sides, and strong commitment by the Education Minister.

The outcome, however, was only a partial success, not least because of political pressures connected with the electoral cycle. The scheme implemented in 2001 differed in two important ways from the original design: loan repayments are not collected by the tax authorities; and, notwithstanding the market's appetite for the student loan bonds, the scheme does not achieve the genuine private finance of the original design.[6] Thus large-scale privately funded income-contingent loans with repayments collected by the tax authorities – complex but feasible – have yet to be implemented.

International cooperation in collecting loan repayments

How should loan repayments be collected when workers are internationally mobile? This issue, though always important, is all the more salient given EU enlargement.

In the simplest arrangement, income-contingent repayments are collected by the tax authorities. If a person is outside the tax net – for example, working abroad or emigrated – his or her loan reverts to mortgage-type repayments as, for example, with student loans in New Zealand, Sweden and the UK. The UK experience suggests that the task is well within the scope of an efficient loans administration. Enforcement is not a huge task where the borrower has a known address and job, and is easier given the speed of communication, the international integration of private finance and the ability of loans administrations to put a black mark on a person's credit rating.

The main enforcement problem arises where a borrower's address is not known. Progress is possible with relatively minor cooperation between tax authorities. If someone moves from the UK to Germany, the German tax authorities could routinely notify their UK counterpart that Joe Bloggs, date of birth X, is working in Germany, tax file number Y, and living at the following address. The only task of the German tax administration is to

---

6 The issues of student loan bonds in 2003 and 2004 involved only limited risk transfer to private buyers. What is needed is not *some* risk transfer, but *enough* transfer, the definition of 'enough' being a matter for national statistical agencies and, in the EU context, ultimately for Eurostat.

provide information to the UK authorities; it makes no attempt to collect repayment, which remains a matter for the UK loans administration.

Various factors make the task easier than it appears. Cooperation within the EU already exists, with more in prospect. Some countries, both within the EU and elsewhere, are already in bilateral discussions; and the US authorities already record the home-country social insurance number of would-be immigrants. Furthermore, migration tends to be mainly from poorer to richer countries. Thus cooperation by tax authorities in OECD countries would deal with the great bulk of loan repayments.

The great advantage of this approach is that it does not require tax systems to be integrated – merely the capacity for one tax administration to send emails to another. Fuller integration would, of course, have advantages, making it possible for loan repayments to be collected wherever a graduate works, for example, the Irish authorities could collect the loan repayments of UK graduates and transfer them to the UK loans administration. The same could happen when Hungarians emigrate to Germany, or Jamaicans to Canada. Thus loan repayments would be transparent with respect to international boundaries, with benefits both for labour mobility and individual freedom. Such an approach, however, is very much for the future.

Collecting loan repayments in less-developed countries

Poorer countries need highly skilled people. But they are fiscally constrained; and tax funding of universities is highly regressive. A good loan scheme helps to resolve both problems; but a good loan scheme requires the capacity to collect repayments, something that has not been entirely solved in the West, and which remains a major problem in countries with a large informal sector and limited public-sector capacity. Designing a scheme which mimics income-contingent repayments in such countries is a challenge that continues to haunt commentators.[7]

3.3 The unfinished agenda: political

In mainland Europe, in contrast, the major unfinished business is not so much technical as political. In many Western and Northern European countries fees are an anathema, though this is less the case in the former communist countries; and in many countries loan schemes are patchy.

Clearly these countries have the technical capacity to implement the strategy in section 2.1. What is needed is political activity which creates an environment in which such schemes can be contemplated. It is

---

7 It is a mistake to think that it is possible to get round the problem through a system of loans with private collection – see Barr (2001a, Ch. 12).

important that governments fight such campaigns on the front foot; if they lose control of the agenda, there is an opening for opposition politicians to present the proposals as 'high fees, high debt' – exactly what happened in the UK. Though such a political campaign is essential, it is not the task of this chapter to map it out, not least because it needs to be rooted in the specifics of each country.

But politicians should be clear that there is little choice. The logic is clear:

- Technological advance requires diverse, mass higher education.
- But mass higher education collides with fiscal constraints; thus graduate contributions are essential for reasons of macroeconomic efficiency.
- Equally, diverse higher education implies that competition plus consumer and producer choice should replace central planning for reasons of microeconomic efficiency; it also implies that price signals (i.e. variable fees) are useful.
- Equity considerations support these efficiency arguments: without graduate contributions the system is regressive.

This is not a comfortable agenda. But nor is it one that can be avoided. This book offers solutions.

4 Conclusion

The model in section 2 has three elements: variable fees, income-contingent loans and active measures to promote access, in particular financial measures, information measures and improved quality of schools. It is a strategic whole, designed to improve quality and to promote access.

In an era of mass higher education, moreover, it is a dominant strategy. The model is universal in two ways.

- Each of the three elements is essential but each can – and should – be tailored to each country's objectives and constraints.
- The model can be implemented in any country with the capacity to collect income tax – and hence loan repayments – and is thus applicable to all advanced countries and to many middle-income developing countries.

Moreover, the model can be implemented quickly if the conditions are right, specifically if the institutional capacity is in place, there is strong political leadership and broadly-based political support, the civil service understand and support the policy, and the media understand the policy and support it. In the UK the first of these applied, but the rest developed only partially and later, hence the long time span covered by this book.

Why, in conclusion, is any of this important? It is important because higher education matters. In today's world it is an essential element in national economic performance. And it has a major bearing on a person's life chances. Thus the model takes as its starting point the imperative of access for all who have the ability and desire. It frees resources, allows competition between universities and – centrally – harnesses rather than wastes the talent of the people. Many policies require painful choices between efficiency and social justice. This one enhances both.

References

Barr, Nicholas (1990), 'MacGregor's Loan Doubts Are Old Hat', *Guardian*, 30 January, p. 23.

Barr, Nicholas (2001a), *The Welfare State as Piggy Bank: Information, Risk, Uncertainty and the Role of the State*, Oxford and New York: Oxford University Press.

Barr, Nicholas (ed.) (2001b), *Economic Theory and the Welfare State, Vol. I: Theory, Vol. II: Income Transfers, and Vol. III: Benefits in Kind*, Edward Elgar Library in Critical Writings in Economics, Cheltenham and Northampton, Mass.: Edward Elgar.

Barr, Nicholas (2003), 'Financing Higher Education in the UK: The 2003 White Paper', House of Commons Education and Skills Committee, *The Future of Higher Education, Fifth Report of Session 2002–03, Volume II, Oral and Written Evidence*, HC 425-II, (TSO, 2003), pp. Ev 292–309. Available at: http://econ.lse.ac.uk/staff/nb.

Barr, Nicholas and Falkingham, Jane (1993), *Paying for Learning*, Welfare State Programme, Discussion Paper WSP/94, London: London School of Economics.

Barr, Nicholas and Falkingham, Jane (1996), *Repayment Rates for Student Loans: Some Sensitivity Tests*, Welfare State Programme, Discussion Paper WSP/127, London: London School of Economics.

Chapman, Bruce (1997), 'Conceptual Issues and the Australian Experience with Income Contingent Charges for Higher Education', *Economic Journal*, Vol. 107, No. 442 (May), pp. 738–51, reprinted in Barr (2001b, Vol. III, pp. 610–23).

Chapman, Bruce and Ryan, Chris (2003), 'The Access Implications of Income Contingent Charges for Higher Education: Lessons from Australia', Australian National University, Centre for Economic Policy Research, Discussion Paper No. 463, April.

Corak, Miles, Lipps, Garth and Zhao, John (2003), *Family Income and Participation in Post-secondary Education*, Statistics Canada, Family and Labour Studies Division, Analytical Studies Branch, Research Paper No. 210, Ottawa: Canada.

Education and Skills Committee (2003), *The Future of Higher Education, Volumes I, Report and Formal Minutes, and Volume II, Oral and Written Evidence*, Fifth Report of Session 2002–3, HC425-I and II, London: TSO. Available at: http://www.parliament.uk.

Feinstein, Leon (2003), 'Inequality in the Early Cognitive Development of British Children in the 1970 Cohort', *Economica*, Vol. 70, No. 277, pp. 73–98.

Kornai, János (1992), *The Socialist System: The Political Economy of Communism*, Princeton, NJ: Princeton University Press.

New Zealand Ministry of Education (2002), *Annual Report: Student Loan Scheme*, Wellington: Ministry of Education.

Palacios Lleras, Miguel (2004), *Investing in Human Capital: A Capital Markets Approach to Student Funding*, Cambridge: Cambridge University Press.

Index